Don't Stop Thinking about the Music

The Politics of Songs and Musicians in Presidential Campaigns

Benjamin S. Schoening and Eric T. Kasper

LEXINGTON BOOKS
Lanham • Boulder • New York • Toronto • Plymouth, UK

Published by Lexington Books
A wholly owned subsidiary of The Rowman & Littlefield Publishing Group, Inc.
4501 Forbes Boulevard, Suite 200, Lanham, Maryland 20706
http://www.lexingtonbooks.com

Estover Road, Plymouth PL6 7PY, United Kingdom

British Library Cataloguing in Publication Information Available

Library of Congress Cataloging-in-Publication Data
Schoening, Benjamin S., 1978-
  Don't stop thinking about the music : the politics of songs and musicians in Presidential campaigns / Benjamin S. Schoening and Eric T. Kasper.
      p. cm.
  Includes bibliographical references and index.
  ISBN 978-0-7391-6546-1 (cloth : alk. paper) -- ISBN 978-0-7391-6547-8 (pbk. : alk. paper) -- ISBN 978-0-7391-7299-5 (electronic)
  1. Campaign songs--United States--History and criticism. 2. Political ballads and songs--United States--History and criticism. I. Kasper, Eric T. II. Title.
  ML3551.S33 2012
  781.5'990973--dc23
                                                    2011041143

™ The paper used in this publication meets the minimum requirements of American National Standard for Information Sciences—Permanence of Paper for Printed Library Materials, ANSI/NISO Z39.48-1992.

Printed in the United States of America

Don't Stop Thinking about the Music

To my wife, Melissa, and daughter, Liljaana,
who have allowed me to pursue my musical dreams
and supported their every step

B. Schoening

To my daughter, Madison, who has a passion for music

E.T.K.

Contents

Acknowledgments

Researching for and writing this book became a labor of love for the two of us. Thus, we are very happy to acknowledge the great support that was given to us by our family, friends, colleagues, and others.

The idea for this book arose out of discussions the two of us had when preparing for an interdisciplinary course that we team-teach together at the University of Wisconsin-Barron County, titled "Political Science 104: American Government, Politics, and Music." Among the many topics discussed in the class was the use of music in U.S. presidential campaigns. Thinking that we had something profound to say about this topic, we wrote a paper for presentation at the 67th Midwest Political Science Association (MPSA) Annual National Conference in April 2009. When preparing that paper, we received helpful feedback from two colleagues at UW-Barron County, Anthony van Groningen and Jayant Anand. After presenting the paper at our MPSA panel (Various Methods of Communicating with the Electorate), we received additional advice from the panel's discussants, Elizabeth Bergman and Stephen C. Brooks.

Of course, we are quite indebted to Lexington Books and Rowman & Littlefield for agreeing to publish this work. First and foremost in need of thanks is our editors, Joseph C. Parry and Melissa Wilks. Joseph and Melissa have been a pleasure to work with, and they have done an excellent job in helping us through the publishing process. Also of note from Lexington Books was the work done by Julie E. Kirsch, Jason Aronson, Erin E. Walpole, and Alison Northridge.

Once the first draft of the manuscript was written, two reviewers also provided us with a plethora of ways to improve the book. Brett S. Sharp, professor of political science at the University of Central Oklahoma, and Patricia Peknik, professor of liberal arts at the Berklee College of Music, gave us invaluable and detailed tips that have made the book a substantially stronger work of scholarship. In addition, we would like to thank our colleague Anthony Millevolte for his scientific expertise regarding the development of the television in chapter four and Raquel Oxford for her information regarding the compact disc issued by the Obama campaign we make reference to in chapter seven.

We have attempted to include as many examples of lyrics as possible within this book to help demonstrate the concepts we are exploring. However, due to the cost of reprinting lyrics and the fact that some publishers denied us permission to use their works, among other factors, it was not possible for us to include lyrics to every song that we discuss. However, we would like to acknowledge the following groups for permissions kindly granted to us to reproduce excerpts from song lyrics or illustrations: Alfred Music Publishing, barleypolitical.com (Ben Relles), Belmont Mall Publishing, BMG, Irving Berlin Music Company, Bocephus Music, Inc., Elvis Presley Music, EMI April Music, Getty Images, Gone Gator Music, Hal Leonard Corporation, JibJab Media, Inc. (Evan and Gregg Spiridellis), Judd Kessler, Maraville Music Corp., Mercury Radio Arts, Inc., MPL Music Publishing, Mugambi Publishing, Nash Notes, Neeb Music, Peer Music, Primary Wave Lamm, Premiere Radio Networks, Inc., Schwonson Music, Songs of Peer Ltd., Sony/ATV, Spirit Two Music, Bruce Springsteen, Bill Tong, United Artists Corporation (EMI), Universal Music, Warner Bros. Music Corporation. We were kindly given permission to use the lyrics from the following copyrighted songs within our book:

"Better Times With AL" by Irving Berlin
© Copyright 1928 by Irving Berlin
© Copyright Renewed
International Copyright Secured   All Rights Reserved   Reprinted by Permission

"I Like Ike" by Irving Berlin
© Copyright 1950, 1952 by Irving Berlin
© Copyright Renewed
International Copyright Secured   All Rights Reserved   Reprinted by Permission

High Hopes (Campaign Version)
Words by Sammy Cahn
Music by James Van Heusen
Copyright © 1959 (Renewed) Maraville Music Corp.
All Rights Reserved   Used by Permission
Reprinted by permission of Hal Leonard Corporation

Click With Dick
Music by George Stork and Clarence Fuhrman, words by Olivia Hoffman
Copyright © 1960 by Elkan-Vogel, Inc.
International copyright secured   All rights reserved
Used with permission

Hello Lyndon
A parody of "Hello Dolly"
From HELLO, DOLLY!
Music and Lyric by Jerry Herman
© 1963 (Renewed) JERRY HERMAN
All Rights Controlled by EDWIN H. MORRIS & COMPANY,
A Division of MPL Music Publishing, Inc.
All Rights Reserved
Reprinted by permission of Hal Leonard Corporation

High Hopes
Words by Sammy Cahn
Music by James Van Heusen
Copyright © 1959 (Renewed) Maraville Music Corp.
All Rights Reserved   Used by Permission
Reprinted by Permission of Hal Leonard Corporation

TEACH YOUR CHILDREN
© 1970 Nash Notes. All rights administered by Sony/ATV Music Publishing LLC,
8 Music Square West, Nashville, TN 37203
All Rights Reserved   Used by Permission

God Bless the U.S.A.
Words and Music by Lee Greenwood
Copyright © 1984 SONGS OF UNIVERSAL, INC. and Universal – SONGS OF POLYGRAM
    INTERNATIONAL, INC.
All Rights Controlled and Administered by SONGS OF UNIVERSAL, INC.
All Rights Reserved   Used by Permission
Reprinted by permission of Hal Leonard Corporation

"Born in the U.S.A." by Bruce Springsteen
Copyright © 1984 Bruce Springsteen (ASCAP)
Reprinted by permission   International copyright secured   All rights reserved

Don't Stop
Words and Music by Christine McVie
Copyright © 1976 by Universal Music – Careers
Copyright Renewed
International Copyright Secured   All Rights Reserved
Reprinted by permission of Hal Leonard Corporation

"Dole Man"
To be sung to the tune of "Soul Man"
Copyright © 1996 by W. Tong
All Rights Reserved   Reprinted with the permission of William Tong

Most importantly, we would like to thank the love and support given to us by our families: Benjamin's wife, Melissa, his daughter, Liljaana, his parents, Stephen and Susan, his grandmother, Ruth, as well as Scott, Jack, and Dan and their families; Eric's wife, Julie, his daughter, Madison, his son, Jackson, his parents, Clint and Sharon, his grandmother, Valeria, as well as Dick, Carol, Andy, Amy, Marshall, and Cole.

Finally, if we have neglected to thank anyone, we sincerely apologize. The oversight was not intentional.

Preface

At approximately 4:00 p.m. on Tuesday, September 16, 2008, Senator John McCain's presidential campaign jet landed at the Youngstown-Warren Regional Airport in Vienna, Ohio. There, he met his running mate, Alaska Governor Sarah Palin, to speak at a campaign rally in a hangar at the airport. As his plane landed, McCain greeted the crowd of approximately 7,000 people with the AC/DC song "Thunderstruck."[1]

At first glance, "Thunderstruck" appears to be a very logical choice to pump up a crowd at a political rally. Lead guitarist Angus Young begins with a fast-paced guitar solo and hard, driving riffs. A high hat and bass drum give the beat. Chanting looms in the background. Then, the lyrics begin. The title of the song, or part of it, is repeated numerous times. Lead singer Brian Johnson describes in the first and second stanzas about being caught in a situation where it is not possible to back down. Referring back to the song's title, he also sings about being struck by thunder.[2]

At first glance, this appears to be an appropriate choice for a presidential campaign rally. Perhaps McCain used this song because he wanted to begin his rally with powerful music and convey the message that he was a candidate who could strike thunder into the hearts of others. Based on his speech at the rally, in which McCain talked about "changing the way Washington does business" and making a "fight" for the "working men and women of Ohio,"[3] McCain also may have been communicating the notion that as president he could strike some thunder into Congress, Washington lobbyists, and even the U.S. economy.

However, upon closer inspection, "Thunderstruck" conveys some very different ideas than the ones that McCain likely wanted to project that day. The lyrics of the song (which are available at AC/DC's official website: http://www.acdc.com/us/music/razors-edge/thunderstruck) continue in the third and fourth stanzas to describe situations quite different that those in the first two stanzas. Indeed, Brian Johnson goes on to state that he, and presumably others, drove over the speed limit while traveling through Texas before meeting some strippers.[4] The lyrics then suggest promiscuous sex as well as illegal activity. As one continues through the song, one can clearly see that AC/DC, a hard rock band famous for songs about sex, drugs, and rock 'n' roll,[5] may have had a different intent when writing this song than John McCain did when he used it in his presidential campaign. These other references in latter stanzas are not exactly the images that a presidential candidate normally wants to express to voters. Still, the McCain campaign saw fit to use this song at its rally. The underlying question is, why use this popular music to warm up the crowd, especially given the underlying message of the song?

"Thunderstruck" was only used by McCain as warm-up music during one stop in his 2008 presidential campaign. He used many other popular tunes, and every major party candidate in 2008 did the same thing at his or her respective rallies. In addition to music used to get a crowd excited for a candidate appearance, presidential candidates will often settle on official campaign songs. These songs tend to be played at the end of rallies, but they also could be played during a candidate's campaign advertisements, or they may be played by supporters at other events.

Why do presidential campaigns use music like this? As we thoroughly discuss in the introduction, music and politics are greatly intertwined. The two authors team-teach a course together entitled "American Government, Politics, and Music." We have taught the course five times. Frequently, when we initially tell people about our course, the common response is that these are two topics that people never thought about together. However, once we explain the extensive use of music in politics, people quickly begin to see how we can build an entire course around the topic. As we demonstrate in the introduction, music has been used quite a bit in politics. This is done because of music's great power, especially emotional power, over human beings. Musicians have used written music with political themes for centuries, and governments have tried to harness the power of music for at least as long. Thus, we have national anthems that promote nationhood and unity, we have pro-war and antiwar protest music, and we have governments trying to censor music that they find threatening. Given this extensive intertwining of music and politics, it should come as no surprise that presidential campaigns have used music too.

Indeed, American presidential campaigns rely on much more than the official candidate statements and speeches to get their messages across to the public. Traditional stump speeches are necessary in a campaign, but they are an insufficient way for a candidate to reach the voters. In addition to trying to convince the electorate with logical reasoning, successful candidates are often very effective at appealing to the electorate's emotions, and this is especially the case when candidates are trying to allure politically unengaged voters.[6] In modern presidential campaigns, candidates have tried to "humanize" themselves by going on late-night talk shows, MTV, and *Oprah*.[7] However, as chapter one will demonstrate, the use of music by presidential candidates is nothing new. What has changed over time is the way in which presidential campaigns have used music to attract voters. There has been great development over time in how presidential campaigns have used music to make their respective cases to the voters. This changing use of music over the last two centuries has been due to a host of factors, ranging from advancements in technology to developments in American political parties to the expansion of the right to vote to the success of music in other American political movements.

If one revisits the earliest American presidential campaigns, there is no record that music was even used. This is not to say that there was no music associated with the presidency in those early years, however. Instead, over the first few presidential campaigns, music was written and used *after*, not during, the campaign. For example, as we explain in chapter one, after George Washington's successful run for office, the song "Follow Washington" was played in support of the nation's first president. This was the early trend for presidential music—it was written for the inauguration and subsequent events, not for the campaign. It was not until the election of 1800 that music really began to be part of presidential campaigns. Even then, the use of music was relatively simplistic. Early campaign songs tended to be patriotic tunes that, in general, only briefly mentioned a candidate's name. While the presidency was in its infancy, the use of presidential campaign music was as well.

During the campaign of 1840, music reached a point where it served a much more integral function in presidential campaigns. During this "traditional" era, music moved out of the shadows and into the forefront of presidential campaigns. This occurred largely because of changes in the American electoral system that developed in the 1820s and 1830s. As the American two-party system became more institutionalized, as the King Caucus ended, and as the franchise was expanding, "the people" were becoming more involved in presidential campaigns. As such, there was more of a need for campaigns to communicate and appeal to the voter who was the "common man." Music became a useful vehicle to serve this purpose. Thus, the 1840 campaign saw widespread use of "Tippecanoe and Tyler Too," a tune that sang the praises of the Whig Party presidential candidate William Henry Harrison and his running mate John Tyler. These types of songs, where existing music was appropriated and candidate-specific lyrics were written, were the norm for official campaign songs for most of U.S. history.

Chapter two explains how presidential campaign theme music became more complex throughout the remainder of the nineteenth century. Candidates' names were mentioned more frequently, and lyrics began to discuss more and more of candidates' platforms. Songs during this era also increased in their range. Instead of just having songs that primarily promoted the good qualities of a candidate, more song lyrics were written that denigrated the opponent. In addition, when African Americans were extended the right to vote, and this right was relatively well protected during Reconstruction, the mid-nineteenth-century trend of using racial epithets in official campaign songs came to an end. By the close of the nineteenth century, songwriters working on behalf of campaigns or writing songs for their preferred candidates began penning both new lyrics and new music in their campaign songs. Music and the composers of music (especially those from the Tin Pan Alley district in New York City) were having more and more power over presidential campaigns at the dawn of the twentieth century. Illustrative examples from various nineteenth-century and early twentieth-century elections make these trends apparent.

Chapter three chronicles the changing campaign music scene during the early and middle twentieth century, one which can be characterized as the "media era." Tin Pan Alley continued to exert a powerful presence, but the advent of radio began to transform the nature of campaign songs. Beginning in the 1920s campaigns were using the radio as a medium to deliver campaign speeches and develop their candidate's platforms. As part of these radio addresses, campaigns began to use Vaudeville stars, who sang campaign songs and popular songs of the day as part of their radio addresses. At the same time, the radio shifted campaigning from retail politics (where politicians campaign to individual voters in person, at meetings or rallies) to wholesale politics (where politicians use advertising and the mass media to speak to the voters). This change created a greater need than ever before to have songs that repeatedly stated a candidate's name. Campaign songs began to market candidates to voters much like businesses would advertise products to consumers. Furthermore, as this gap between candidates and voters increased, music needed to be integrated more into the campaign, so that there was a unifying theme that presented one image to the voters. Thus, by the 1920s campaigns began, on a scale not seen previously, to integrate campaign slogans into campaign music. Also during this decade, as women were guaranteed the right to vote by a constitutional amendment, language in campaign songs began to change to reflect the new electoral realities. Then, just as campaigns were learning how to integrate the old campaign tactics (the singing campaigns) with the new medium of the radio, the economic woes of the 1930s began. At this time music partially receded into the background of campaigns, most likely due to the Great Depression, World War II, and the immense popularity of Franklin Roosevelt. That did not mean the end of campaign music though, as popular artists would write and sing songs in favor of Roosevelt in each of the subsequent elections.

In chapter four we explain how, following World War II, music returned to prominence in elections with such memorable tunes as "I Like Ike," just as the new medium of television was becoming a staple in the American home. We examine how TV had an influence on the music that campaigns were using during the mid to late twentieth century.

Beginning in the 1970s, campaigns started to use more and more theme songs that were simply popular culture songs adopted, lyric for lyric, for the purposes of the campaign. Thus, the period from 1972 to 1984 served as a "transition era" of presidential campaign theme music, one that bridged the gap from the "media era" to what eventually developed by the 1980s—the "pop era." We will detail this evolution in chapter five. The use of popular songs by presidential campaigns first began in the 1930s, but its use was sporadic, and almost nonexistent, until the 1970s. This development of using popular music was partially due to the influence of 1960s popular culture and the use of music during that decade to protest the Vietnam War and to support the Civil Rights Movement. It was also likely a reaction to the lowering of the voting age from 21 to 18, as a way to appeal to younger voters. Furthermore, it was during this time that popular musicians began to travel with candidates they supported on a regular basis. Musicians would "stump" for candidates on the campaign trail, giving way to the candidates at events; the candidates would eventually use popular tunes as part of their campaign strategy.[8] Given the wide use of music for these purposes, by the early 1970s candidates for the presidency began seeing how such pop culture songs could also be co-opted by presidential campaigns to serve the same purpose. For instance, during at the 1984 Republican National Convention, the organizers for Ronald Reagan's campaign chose to play "God Bless the U.S.A." This song, written and recorded by Lee Greenwood in 1984, stated in part that "I'm proud to be an American, where at least I know I'm free, and I won't forget the men who died, who gave that right to me."[9]

This trend continued through the "pop culture era" of the 1980s, the 1990s, and into the first decade of the twenty-first century, something we explore in chapter six. Perhaps most famously of all candidate use of popular music, in 1992 Bill Clinton extensively played "Don't Stop" by Fleetwood Mac.[10] The employment of pop songs allows candidates to latch onto something already proven to be popular; it also gives candidates the opportunity to target the music they use on the campaign trail to something that may be popular in a given geographical area. For instance, John McCain frequently used the Bill Conti song "Gonna Fly Now" when campaigning in and around the Philadelphia area in 2008. Given the use of the song in the movie *Rocky* and its association with the city, this makes perfect sense. However, when McCain visited Tennessee, the music he used was of a different variety. In this state he invoked not Rocky Balboa, but the song "Rocky Top Tennessee." These pop songs allow candidates to pump up a local crowd by using different songs in different places. This gives candidates the freedom to make local changes to a part of their campaign in ways that would be unforgivable if done in a stump speech.

By 2008, popular music was in full use by presidential candidates, as exemplified by the use of John Mellencamp's "Our Country" (John Edwards),[11] Boston's "More Than a Feeling" (Mike Huckabee),[12] Celine Dion's "You and I" (Hillary Clinton),[13] Stevie Wonder's "Signed, Sealed, Delivered I'm Yours"

(Barack Obama), Elvis Presley's "A Little Less Conversation" (Mitt Romney), and Chuck Berry's "Johnny be Goode" (John McCain).[14] As this sampling demonstrates, there is quite a bit of popular music now used by presidential candidates. However, as we will describe in chapter seven, candidates sometimes neglect to look at the song as a whole and understand what message they may be sending to the general public outside of this phrase. This may lead them to choose songs that, on the whole, might sound inappropriate, such as AC/DC's "Thunderstruck," or Elvis' "A Little Less Conversation," which is a song about promiscuous sex. Thus, the commercial marketing trends that began with campaign music in the 1920s have come to fruition.

The most recent presidential election in 2008 begins the "Internet era," where websites such as Facebook and YouTube have democratized the use of songs in presidential campaigns; this is also explored in chapter seven. This democratization has taken many forms. For instance, it gave supporters of Hillary Clinton the opportunity to choose her campaign theme song. It also allowed those outside of the campaigns to post music about the candidates, such as "Obama Girl's" "I Got a Crush on Obama." This trend also included an anti-Obama song, "Oh Hail the Messiah, Lord Obama," in which Glenn Beck used the Russian National Anthem set to anti-Obama text. Although there have always been independent songwriters with respect to presidential elections, the Internet opened up new avenues for the general public to get involved in politics generally, and political music is no exception to this development. In time, this new trend may fundamentally change the nature of campaign music, reorienting it away from the model of commercial advertising.

Finally, we offer several conclusions in chapter eight, including where we think campaign music is headed in the coming decades. Furthermore, we explain how we think music could most effectively be used in future presidential elections.

Ours is fundamentally a qualitative endeavor, as we are exploring the use of music to affect emotions. To demonstrate the validity of our theoretical model above, we proceed below with case studies of this phenomenon. We also engage in explaining how and why these songs are chosen and used. Since our inquiries are primarily questions of "how" and "why," the case study method is the most appropriate form of analysis.[15] Throughout our endeavor, we engage in building an explanation and analyzing changes over time.

Whether a song is chosen from the vast, established popular music repertoire or is written specifically for a candidate, nearly all candidates have tried to use the power of music to convey messages about themselves and their campaigns. Candidates do this because they believe that music is a powerful force that can reach a wide populace with just a few notes and a few words. The use of music in political campaigns is just one small piece of American political development over more than two centuries. However, as we explain in the introduction below, music is a very important piece to the puzzle of political influence.

Notes

1.   Ron Selak Jr. and Amanda Smith-Teutsch, "Thousands Rally for McCain," *Tribune Chronicle*, September 17, 2008.

2.   Angus Young and Malcolm Young, "Thunderstruck," in *The Definitive AC/DC Songbook*, ed. Angus Young (New York: Amsco, 2003), 750-752.

3.   Selak and Smith-Teutsch, "Thousands Rally."

4.   "Thunderstruck," ed. Angus Young, 750-752.

5.   A sampling of their song titles includes "Back Seat Confidential," "Big Balls," "Caught with Your Pants Down," "Dirty Deeds Done Dirt Cheap," "For Those About to Rock (We Salute You)," "Have a Drink on Me," "It's a Long Way to the Top (If You Wanna Rock n' Roll)," "Let There Be Rock," "Love at First Feel," "Overdose," "Rock n' Roll Ain't Noise Pollution," and "You Shook Me All Night Long," *The Definitive AC/DC Songbook*, ed. Angus Young (New York: Amsco, 2003).

6.   Matthew A. Baum, "Talking the Vote: Why Presidential Candidates Hit the Talk Show Circuit," *American Journal of Political Science* 49, no. 2 (April 2005): 213-234.

7.   Baum, "Talking the Vote," 213-234.

8.   Jerry Rodnitzky, "Popular Music," in *The American President in Popular Culture*, ed. John W. Matviko (Westport, CT: Greenwood Press, 2005), 42.

9.   Joanne Morreale, *A New Beginning: A Textual Frame Analysis of the Political Campaign Film* (Albany, NY: SUNY Press, 1991): 121.

10.   Benjamin R. Barber, *The Truth of Power: Intellectual Affairs in the Clinton White House* (New York: Norton, 2001), 45.

11.   Charles Babington, "Edwards Fires Anti-Corporate Bombast," *The Boston Globe,* January 3, 2008, http://www.boston.com/news/nation/articles/2008/01/03/Edwa rds_fires_anti_corporate_bombast/ (accessed February 10, 2009).

12.   "Boston Guitarist Wants to Pull the Plug on Huckabee for Using Hit Song," *Fox News*, February 14, 2008, http://www.foxnews.com/politics/elections/2008/02/14/ boston-guitarist-wants-to-pullthe-plug-on-huckabee-for-using-hit-song/ (accessed February 10, 2009).

13.   "Hillary Clinton Picks Campaign Song She Hopes Is Pleasing to 'You and I,'" *Fox News*, June 19, 2007, http://www.foxnews.com/story/0,2933,284432,00.html (accessed June 3, 2010).

14.   Isaac Mass, "Raisin' McCain: Music to My Ears," *The Boston Globe*, September 5, 2008, http://www.boston.com/news/politics/massvoices/2008/09/raisin_mccain_ music_to_my_ears.html (accessed February 15, 2009).

15.   Robert K. Yin, *Case Study Research: Design and Methods* (Thousand Oaks, CA: Sage Publications, 1994): 1.

Introduction: Why Music Matters

The Power of Music

Before going into great detail and explaining how and why music has been a part of American presidential elections for centuries, it is important for us to justify why we are discussing music at all. Indeed, in a presidential election today, there are many variables that can affect the outcome. These factors range from the candidates themselves to their staffs to media coverage to paid advertisements to volunteers to campaign donations to innumerable other people and things. With all of these potential causal factors, one might ask why focus on music. We contend, however, that music does matter, and it is a topic that should be studied more with respect to its impact on presidential elections. Below we briefly describe the power of music, its history, its political uses, and attempts by governments to silence music that they do not like. Our aim is to prove that music *should* matter because in many cases throughout human history there is evidence that it *has* mattered.

Music has, for whatever reason, an innate power over us. As one scholar put it more than a century ago, "[w]hen we speak of the power of music, we mean that it has a way of forcing itself upon our attention as no other art has. It impresses itself upon our minds, so that we must give it audience and listen to its message."[1] Music is something that we are all born with an inherent desire to listen to and even create on some level. It creates emotional states in us, and it can even serve as a mnemonic device to aid our memories, as the following example demonstrates.

One of the authors of this book vividly remembers watching the popular NBC television show *Cheers* when growing up. To this day, one episode sticks out among all the others, a show from early 1985 entitled "Teacher's Pet." The episode involved the main star of the show, Sam Malone (played by Ted Danson), attending night school to earn a high school diploma that he had never completed. Sam found difficulty when studying for some of his exams, includ-

1

ing one on geometry, so he turned to Ernie "Coach" Pantusso (played by Nicholas Colasanto) for help. Coach recommends to Sam that "you can learn about anything in this world if you'll just follow my little trick. . . . [W]e learn our facts by associating countries with music."[2] Coach then proceeds to teach Sam about Albania by making up a song about the country, set to the tune "When the Saints Go Marching In":

> Albania, Albania,
> You border on the Adriatic,
> Your land is mostly mountainous,
> And your chief export is chrome.
>
> You're a communist republic,
> You're a red regime. . .[3]

This song was written for a sitcom, it is silly, and it was meant to elicit laughter from those watching the program. Still, more than a quarter of a century later, the author who heard that song as a child still recalls that Albania has coastline along the Adriatic Sea, probably for no other reason than that the fact was put to song on this episode. If there was ever evidence of the mnemonic power of music, this is it. As we will demonstrate in later chapters, presidential campaigns throughout American history have used music in an attempt to get potential voters to remember a candidate's name, his or her valuable qualities, and the unfavorable qualities of his or her opponents.

For centuries many people have tried to exploit the power of music for their own purposes in ways that extend well beyond provoking laughter. For instance, the driving force of most military marches has been to motivate soldiers to fight in battle. National anthems are played for both teams before World Cup soccer matches, in part, as a way to inspire both teams. National anthems are also played at Olympic medal ceremonies, often leading the winning athletes to shed tears. These practices occur because music has a powerful effect on us. Oliver Sacks refers to the human propensity toward music as "musicophilia."[4] Some of the more powerful things about our propensity toward music are "earworms," or catchy songs that are designed to get into our ears; these are typically jingles that "infect" us to the point that we cannot get the songs out of our heads.[5] Each of us is familiar with the situation where we hear a certain song before leaving home or just as we are parking our car, and that song is so infectious that we "can't get it out of our head" and are humming it all day.

Music's effect on us is apparent from a very young age. Six-month-old infants show a greater psychological response to their mother's singing than to their speech.[6] Studies of mothers of newborns show all mothers singing to their babies; when asked why they sing, the mothers noted that they did so "to soothe, to entertain, to make the infants laugh, smile, gurgle and make sounds themselves."[7] Babies as young as four months of age show preferences for consonant musical intervals (major and minor thirds and sixths) over dissonant musical intervals (minor seconds, sevenths and tritones).[8] Babies also discriminate two melodies apart more easily if both have a consonant interval structure rather than a dissonant structure.[9] Rhythm itself, manifested in actions as simple as rocking back and forth, has a calming effect on newborns and children.[10] In their totality, these studies are evidence of the influence that music has on us and on our ability when very young to understand what song is and respond to it.

Music is also employed by religion quite frequently. Churches, synagogues, temples, and mosques make use of music to inspire their parishioners and help them seek enlightenment. For instance, many traditional African societies regard music as a bridge between ideas and religious phenomena.[11] African American gospel music has been found to form an important part of the community's aesthetic expression and represent a strong link to African roots.[12] Throughout the southern United States, religious music is seen as an important activity that binds communities together.[13] Religious use of music may also take the form of meditation or prayer using a combination of rhythmic chanting, rocking, and repetition of key phrases.[14] Music has a perceived ability to draw people together, represent their sense of collectivity, and even add symbolic significance to events such as wedding ceremonies and religious festivals.[15]

We would be remiss without noting the important role that music plays as entertainment. *American Idol* is one of the top-rated programs on television, and millions more people watch similar singing programs. Every year, countless people shell out their hard-earned money to purchase compact discs, download music files, and attend concerts. Many musical artists have become millionaires and celebrities because they wrote a few songs that the general public feels compelled to listen to repeatedly. This is more strong evidence that music fulfills some sort of biological need. In this vein, Steven Mithen has made an interesting comparison:

> [T]he human mind evolved to enjoy melody and rhythm, which were critical features of communication before becoming usurped by language. In this regard, music is very similar to food and sex. Those of us living in the affluent West eat more food and have more sex than we biologically require. We have evolved to enjoy both types of behavior and often engage in them for entertainment value alone, although their roles in social bonding continue. Music is the same; in certain circumstances it still provides [its] adaptive value . . . but we also enjoy making music and pursue it as well.[16]

Again, there is something about music that compels us to it. This includes listening to it or singing it just for its own sake, not for some greater religious or mnemonic end.

Music can also have peculiar effects on the human body—and one's personal reaction to music can be fundamentally altered by events in one's life. There are isolated examples of individuals who have a craving for music after being struck by lightning.[17] There are people whose epileptic seizures are triggered by listening to music.[18] These anomalies aside, music has been shown to also have enormous healing capacity. Music therapy has existed in Western medicine since at least the middle of the eighteenth century,[19] and its Middle Eastern roots extend back to at least the tenth century.[20] Music therapy has wide-ranging applications, but the unifying theme is the use of music to help patients maintain their health and to recuperate. It has been used to assist heart attack and stroke victims recover from their conditions. Studies on premature infants have shown that singing improves heart rate and oxygen saturation, and it improves weight gain among preemies.[21] All of these examples demonstrate music's power.

One of the most interesting things about music, and perhaps the most powerful thing about it, is its perceived ability to affect our emotions. As one scholar put it, "music has emotional significance, not merely because it causally arouses feelings (which we may nevertheless admit that it does), but by virtue of its intrinsic emotional character."[22] Furthermore, music is one of the key connections we have to the emotional center of our brain. Scientific studies by Carol Krumhansl indicate that music with a quick tempo in a major key can bring about all of the physical changes associated with happiness in listeners, including an increased breathing rate; slow music in a minor key, however, will lead to sadness, as demonstrated by a slowed pulse, a rise in blood pressure, a drop in the skin's conductivity, and a rise in body temperature.[23] Psychologists conducting research have used this fact to manipulate subjects within their experiments by playing Vivaldi and Mozart to induce happiness in subjects, and by playing Mahler and Rachmaninov when they needed subjects to be sad.[24] The music of Vivaldi and, especially that of Mozart, is a reflection of the classical style of music. This style is typified by "noble simplicity, balance, formal perfection, diversity within unity, seriousness or wit as appropriate, and freedom from excesses of ornamentation and frills."[25] Works during this time tended to be written in major keys more often than not. The tempos of the opening and final movements of large works tend to be brisk and upbeat in nature and written in precise formal structures. The music also was apt to be "lighter" in context. Both Vivaldi and Mozart were very formulaic in their approach to composition and the forms they used. While they did use non-chord tones (notes that make dissonant harmonies), they used them somewhat conservatively.

In contrast, Mahler and Rachmaninov tended to use an advanced Romantic style in their compositions. Romanticism focused on melody, emotion, novelty, and individuality within music.[26] The Romantic style was typified by the "search for the original, interesting, evocative, individual, expressive, or extreme" within music composition.[27] The music of Mahler and Rachmaninov contained harmonies with many non-chord tones used to create sharp dissonances that were designed to stretch the ear and emotions of the listener. Both of these composers used minor keys more often than their Baroque and Classical contemporaries of Vivaldi and Mozart, perhaps making their music more brooding at times, thus bringing out more emotions associated with sadness and pain. Additionally, Romantic composers used whatever musical form was necessary to express their messages. Consequently, Romantic composers did not adhere to the strict forms for their classical contemporaries, but rather expanded to truncated forms as necessary to communicate their music's meaning to the listener. Both styles of music stimulate the brain, but in different ways that cause varied effects on the listener. PET scan imaging research conducted by Robert Zatorre and Anne Blood confirms these effects by music: dissonance causes parts of the brain linked to unpleasant emotions to light up in the PET scans, while consonant melodies excite parts of the brain associated with pleasure.[28]

These scientific studies aside, the idea that music affects mood is well known. As described by one scholar:

> We all know that specific types of music can induce specific types of mood; we play soft, romantic music on a date to induce sexual love, uplifting, optimistic music at weddings, and dirges at funerals. Enlightened factory managers play music to improve employee morale when they have to undertake simple repetitive jobs, while dentists and surgeons use music to soothe and relax their patients, sometimes with such astonishing results that anesthetics become redundant.[29]

Without a doubt, music is often used at various events of emotional significance, and music's emotional appeal has long been used to sell products.[30] The emotional appeal of music was recognized for political purposes long ago, in part because music has been with us since at least the dawn of time.

Political Meaning in Music

Given music's profound effect upon us and the strong evidence it has had this effect on us for so long, it should come as no surprise that music makers have long understood music as a way to express political messages. Composers and musical artists long ago realized that they could have political impact through their songs. Evidence of this phenomenon exists back to at least the Classical period,[31] and it probably extends much farther back into history.

For example, Ludwig van Beethoven had political themes running throughout his music. Beethoven dedicated his Symphony No. 3 to Napoleon Bonaparte, although after Napoleon became emperor, Beethoven changed his dedication to Prince Franz Joseph von Lobkowitz. Beethoven would eventually write numerous musical pieces that supported non-republican German politics and Austrian military battles against Napoleon.[32] In addition, he would write a politically themed opera in *Fidelio*.

In the modern era, there are numerous genres of music that openly espouse political themes. Labor songs, which before 1900 were largely work tunes in America, became more and more activist at the turn of the century due to dissatisfaction with working conditions and pay. Most notable in this regard was the Industrial Workers of the World, also known as the IWW or the Wobblies. The IWW was the first labor organization that used music in an expressly political way in the United States.[33] In 1909 the IWW published its *Little Red Songbook*, which included 32 pro-labor songs.[34] Labor activist Joe Hill wrote many of the Wobbly songs, including "There Is Power in a Union" and "Casey Jones-The Union Scab."[35] Later, during the Great Depression, the new medium of radio helped build a new collective labor identity and movement solidarity through the playing of union songs.[36]

There are many examples of liberal and leftist folk music during the mid-twentieth century. Woody Guthrie was foremost among them. One of Guthrie's most famous songs was "This Land Is Your Land," the words of which are well known to most Americans. This song was very political. For most Americans, this song, written by Guthrie in 1940 but not recorded until 1944, is the unofficial national anthem, since the song's opening lines speak of a land that belongs to all the people, from coast to coast. Unbeknownst to most Americans, however, Guthrie wrote the song in reaction to Irving Berlin's "God Bless America."[37] In fact, later verses of "This Land Is Your Land" are socialist and worker-oriented, opposing the ownership of private property and the posting of "no trespassing" signs.[38] However, since these later verses are rarely sung, most people are not aware of their content. The far leftist position espoused by these verses is perhaps the best explanation for why they are rarely sung. This is an excellent example of music with a political purpose having a negative effect on the distribution of the song, and of the song being interpreted in ways unthinkable to the composer. Overall though, it is again evidence of music written with a political purpose.

Protest music of the 1950s to the 1970s also had a distinctively political element to it. The Civil Rights Movement's most notable song, "We Shall Overcome," gave marchers hope and resolve in their cause to end segregation and racial oppression:[39] Similarly, civil rights protest songs such as "Oh Freedom," "We Shall Not Be Moved," and "Ain't Gonna Let Nobody Turn Me Round" emphasized the need for those already participating in the movement to remain determined to their struggle and strive toward their goals.[40] What is more, these songs were designed to draw attention to the injustice of segregation and the righteousness of the cause.

At approximately the same time, music protesting America's involvement in the Vietnam War was gaining popularity throughout the United States. In some cases, musical artists wrote songs that advocated for civil rights and argued against involvement in Vietnam. Bob Dylan is perhaps the best example of this. Dylan's folk music was reminiscent of, and influenced by, Woody Guthrie,[41] and he is reported to have moved to New York while Guthrie was hospitalized there to learn from the folk music giant.[42] Dylan's "Blowin' in the Wind" made political statements about both war and civil rights, as his lyrics expressed a desire that artillery shells would no longer be necessary and that people would not turn a blind eye to human injustices.[43] Dylan's antiwar sentiment was even more apparent in another 1963 song, "Masters of War." The lyrics blame the military industrial complex for the horrors of war and the human carnage that always results from it, including the building of armaments and the killing of young soldiers. Dylan wrote the song before U.S. escalation had begun in Vietnam, as it was released during Buddhist-led demonstrations in South Vietnam, which were stirring antiwar sentiment among the American public.[44] Over the next few years, there would be much more antiwar protest music in the United States, both of the folk and rock genres. These included the "I-Feel-Like-I'm-Fixin'-to-Die Rag" by Country Joe and the Fish, "Eve of Destruction" by Barry McGuire, "Give Peace a Chance" by John Lennon, and "War" by Norman Whitfield and Barrett Strong.

In the mid-1970s, the Sex Pistols arrived on the punk scene in the United Kingdom and instantly created controversy wherever they played. Led by singer Johnny Rotten and bassist Sid Vicious, political themes were almost always a part of their repertoire. Rotten's vocals in "Anarchy in the U.K." made this political message clear, advocating the political solution suggested by the song's title.[45] Perhaps most notable was their 1977 single "God Save the Queen," which they released for Queen Elizabeth II's Silver Jubilee.[46] The song had the same name as the United Kingdom's national anthem, but it lyrics were much different, referring to the English monarchy as fascist and suggesting that the country had no future. Given the high regard with which the country holds the monarchy, it is no surprise that these incendiary lyrics created an instant firestorm, and that the band was often censored and banned in Britain.[47]

Another U.K. punk band that made a large political splash was the Clash. They espoused just as much of a radical leftist position as the Sex Pistols; their lyrics made this quite obvious. The title track to their 1979 album *London Calling* began by emphasizing the political nature of punk music and the death of old pop. The song goes on to warn about the dangers of nuclear war while also condemning police brutality.[48] Even more overtly political was the Clash's 1982 single "Know Your Rights:" which is chock full of references to police brutality, lack of political and economic equality, and government suppression of ideas.[49]

Punk was not the only genre of music that expressed political themes in the 1970s and 1980s. Bob Marley's reggae also had plenty of political imagery. One of the most notable of these songs was "Get Up, Stand Up," which clearly told the listeners that they needed to fight for their rights.[50]

Progressing through the 1980s, political music remained in America and elsewhere, particularly in rock music. Sting wrote many songs with political messages during the Cold War. His 1985 song "Russians" asks for a hopeful end to the nuclear standoff between the West and the Soviet Union.[51] In 1987, Sting wrote another protest song, "They Dance Alone (Cueca Solo)." This time, his target was the right-wing Pinochet regime in Chile and its systematic use of torture, imprisonment, and execution without trial against its own people. The song was written about the women left behind when their husbands, sons, and fathers were taken by the government.[52]

The Irish band U2 was no stranger to political themes either, especially in the band's early years. Their 1983 song "Sunday Bloody Sunday," referring to the 1922 massacre of over 30 people in Dublin's Croke Park and the 1972 massacre of 14 people in Derry, Northern Ireland, is a call to use pacifism to achieve political goals instead of intensifying an endless cycle of violence.[53] Their 1987 single "Bullet the Blue Sky" was written as an antiwar track, arguing that the United States was partly responsible for carnage in the El Salvador Civil War through its aid and military support for the Salvadoran military government.[54] U2's lead singer, Bono, has also practiced what he preached in his lyrics, involving himself in numerous humanitarian efforts around the globe.[55]

The 1970s and 1980s also saw the emergence of charity rock, whereby musicians, primarily pop/rock artists, sang songs to help raise money and awareness for political causes. A couple of early cases of this include George Harrison's 1971 "Concert for Bangladesh,"[56] and the "Music for UNICEF Concert: A Gift of Song," which was organized in 1970 by popular artists, including the Bee Gees.[57] An even better known example of charity rock is the 1985 song "We Are the World." The song was written by Michael Jackson and Lionel Richie, and performed by a super group of musical artists. The song, a commercial success, raised money to help famine victims in Ethiopia. After the success of "We Are the World," charity rock's focus on Ethiopian famine manifested itself in the Live Aid concert in the summer of 1985. A few months later, artists led by Willie Nelson, John Mellencamp, and Neil Young organized Farm Aid, a benefit concert in support of the American family farm.[58] Overall, the 1980s saw no dearth of concerts supporting political causes.

The entire musical catalogue of the rap-rock fusion band Rage Against the Machine is littered with politics. The band has had no problem displaying its socialist, anti-U.S. government standpoint on its sleeve, as well as its call for revolution. Song titles alone provide ample evidence of this. Their 1992 self-titled debut album contains such songs as "Killing in the Name" and "Wake Up." A song off of the same album, "Take the Power Back," is an illustrative example of the band's political position, as it claims that the American educational system teaches many young people ignorance of true power structures, including institutional racism and classism.[59] Later albums contained songs such as "Revolver," "Guerrilla Radio," and "Calm Like a Bomb."[60] That these men turned to music to express their political message was described by guitarist Tom Morello in the following way: "I believe that culture and politics are inextricably linked and that there is no such thing as apolitical music. Like it or not. Artists don't necessarily realize that and some choose not to look at it that way. Some are naïve. . . But escapist music is very political in upholding the status quo."[61] Morello's statement easily conveys the idea that music has power. He and his fellow band members were not the first, nor were they the last, musicians to understand this point and use their songs as a political weapon.

Moving from rock-rap into pure hip-hop, one finds many songs since the 1980s that have explicitly political themes. In many instances, these songs describe the plight of African Americans and institutional racism in the United States. One the first hip-hop groups to rap about politics was the Furious Five. Their 1982 song, "The Message," described the squalor of the New York City ghettos in the early 1980s and the lack of opportunities that existed for those living there.[62] Even more politically charged was N.W.A. (Niggaz Wit Attitudes) and their 1988 album, *Straight Outta Compton*. The album discussed life in the 1980s in the inner city of Compton, California, the hometown of the band's members. The most notable song on the album for political purposes is "Fuck tha Police," which was set as a mock courtroom scene where the police are put on trial.[63] This indictment of southern California law enforcement described life on the street for African Americans, particularly young African American men. However, its tone toward law enforcement and its incendiary lyrics caused the band's label, Priority Records, to receive a letter from Milt Ahlerich, the Assistant Director of Public Affairs for the Federal Bureau of Investigation.[64] According to Ahlerich, "Seventy-eight law enforcement officers were feloniously slain in the line of duty during 1988, four more than in 1987. Law enforcement officers dedicate their lives to the protection of our citizens, and recordings such as the one from N.W.A. are both discouraging and degrading to these brave, dedicated officers."[65] That the song caught the attention of the FBI demonstrates its political power and far-reaching impact.

The 1980s lyrics of the Furious Five and N.W.A. were only the beginning of politically driven hip-hop. Public Enemy's 1990 song "911 Is a Joke" criticized ineffective public assistance programs in African American neighborhoods.[66] Rapper Ice-T, while performing with the hard rock band Body Count, wrote "Cop Killer" in 1992. "Cop Killer" took aim at police brutality against the African American community and was written as a lethal warning to law enforcement after the Rodney King beating.[67] Not surprisingly, police organizations across the United States called for a boycott of all products by the parent company of the label that signed Body Count, Time-Warner; President George H.W. Bush and Vice President Dan Quayle publicly criticized the song.[68]

Finally, the music of many country artists has a political bent to it, albeit one that tends to be more conservative than any of the music described above (more liberal country artists such as the Dixie Chicks notwithstanding). For example, Merle Haggard released "The Fightin' Side of Me" in 1970. The song was a conservative response to liberal anti-Vietnam War protestors, as Haggard expressed his discontent with people who spoke ill of the United States.[69] "The Fightin' Side of Me" was a commercial success for Haggard, as the song spent three weeks at the number one position on *Billboard*'s country singles chart. The song's position on the U.S. war effort was no doubt part of this success, as the pro-war, "love it or leave it attitude" was prominent among conservatives in the early 1970s as a reaction to years of antiwar protests.[70] More contemporary examples of country's conservatism abound. Perhaps the best example was a release in reaction to the events of September 11, 2001. After the 9/11 attacks, singer Toby Keith advocated a military response. His song "Courtesy of the Red, White, and Blue (The Angry American)," off of his 2002 album *Unleashed*, discussed this position in detail, threatening terrorists with serious repercussions for attacking the United States.[71] Although this tune generated controversy, it was one that Keith embraced: "Most people think I'm a redneck patriot. I'm OK with that."[72] A final example of the political lyrics in country music comes from "Have You Forgotten?" by Darryl Worley. Released shortly before the U.S.-led invasion of Iraq in 2003, Worley wrote the song after he visited U.S. troops in Afghanistan.[73] The song was misinterpreted by many as a defense of the buildup for the war in Iraq.[74] Given the song's reference to 9/11 and its release shortly before the Iraq War, critics mistakenly charged that Worley made faulty connections between Osama bin Laden and Saddam Hussein, even though Hussein was never mentioned in the song's lyrics.[75]

Truly, there are many musicians throughout history who have expressed political messages in their songs. There are many examples of this over the last century, especially in relation to war. There is no doubt that at least some, if not all, of these artists have placed these meanings in their lyrics because they believe that music has the power to persuade. If musicians and composers have come to this realization, it should be no surprise that governments have as well. . . and history is replete with governments using music to their political advantage.

A Brief History of Governments Using Music

The great Greek philosopher Plato wrote his famous dialogue *The Republic* nearly 2400 years ago. The work, still read by many today, is Plato's description of the ideal city-state. At one point in the work, Plato, speaking through the character Socrates, notes the need for government to take interest in music:

> [I]sn't this why the rearing in music is most sovereign? Because rhythm and harmony most of all insinuate themselves into the inmost part of the soul and most vigorously lay hold of it in bringing grade with them; and they make a man graceful if he is correctly reared, if not, the opposite. Furthermore, it is sovereign because the man properly reared on rhythm and harmony would have the sharpest sense for what's been left out and what isn't a fine product of craft or what isn't a fine product of nature. And, due to his having the right kind of dislikes, he would praise the fine things; and, taking pleasure in them and receiving them into his soul, he would be reared on them and become a gentleman.[76]

In this passage, Plato begins by confirming the point made earlier in this chapter—music has a powerful influence on us, as it "insinuate[s]" itself into the "inmost part of the soul." Plato goes even further, however, by claiming that if one is properly taught music when one is young, one will have a better sense of judgment in other areas of life. For this reason, Plato believed it paramount that government take an interest in music and properly teach it to its citizens. In fact, the saying "let me write the laws of the land and I care not who makes its laws" has been erroneously attributed to Plato on numerous occasions in an attempt to adequately express this maxim.[77] Many governments throughout history have taken Plato's advice, whether for his reason of making people better citizens or for more selfish motives. In fact, during the New Deal, the federal government created the Federal Music Project, which was designed, in part, "to educate the public in the appreciation of musical opportunities."[78]

The story of the modern nation-state largely begins in the seventeenth century in what is now Germany at the conclusion of the Thirty Years War, a struggle between two fundamentally different views of how Europe should be politically organized. On one side were the "universalist" Holy Roman Emperor and the Spanish king, who were loyal to the Roman Catholic Church, and who asserted their right, and that of the Pope, to control Christendom in its entirety. On the other side were the "particularist" actors of Denmark, the Dutch Republic, France, Sweden, and German princes; these parties rejected the notion of an imperial overlordship born out of papal authority, and instead advocated the right of all states to full independence.[79]

Upon the signing of peace treaties to end the Thirty Years War at Westphalia in 1648, a diplomatic congress was created in Europe, which fostered the growth of national power and the modern concept of sovereignty—leading to the "particularist" position to eventually dominate international politics. The Peace of Westphalia thus signaled a move away from a religious to a modern, secular, state-centric world. This was the case because it began a shift away from the goal of a united Christendom under the Holy Roman Empire to a system of independent states.[80] The modern nation-state did not magically emerge overnight, however. The growth of nations and nationalism was a phenomenon that did not truly take off until the eighteenth and nineteenth centuries.[81] When that trend toward nationalism was coalescing, music played an important part across Europe. During the Romantic Era of 1820 to 1900, composers began to take a greater interest in the music and history of their home nations. This could be seen in the use of folk and traditional songs and in song styles within the compositions. In addition, composers would use nationalistic topics or folklore as the themes of their compositions and operas. Giuseppe Verdi composed nationalistic operas in Italy. The "Chorus of the Hebrew Slaves," from Verdi's opera *Nabucco*, was considered by contemporary scholars to be a call for nineteenth-century Italian unification. Modest Mussorgsky wrote nationalistic opera and compositions in Russia; his *Pictures at an Exhibition* depicts the wonders of Russia, including the "Great Gate of Kiev". Bedřich Smetana penned music in support of Czech nationalism. For example, Smetana's *Má vlast*, or *My Country* portrays several places in what is now the Czech Republic and Slovakia, including Vyšehrad Castle in Prague and the Moldau River. Finally, Jean Sibelius wrote numerous songs supporting Finnish independence.[82] This "nationalist" trend in music would be one of the dominant features of the Romantic period and would take root in other places, including Spain, England, and the United States.[83]

Nationalistic compositions such as these also caught the ears of those in government, who turned them into national anthems. The earliest national anthems even predated the nineteenth century's nationalistic trend in music, although there is some debate as to which national anthem was truly the first one. Japan's "Kamigayo" draws its lyrics from a poem written in the tenth century,[84] although the words of "Kamigayo" were not put to music until 1869, and it was not officially adopted by the Japanese government as the national anthem until 1888.[85] The Dutch song "Het Wilhelmus," originally written as a protest song in 1568, quickly gained popularity and became the unofficial national anthem of the Netherlands.[86] The song, however, was not officially adopted as the Dutch national anthem until 1932.[87] The U.K.'s "God Save the King" (or "God Save the Queen," depending on who is monarch) first gained popularity during the Jacobite rebellion of 1745-46. The song has been recognized as the country's unofficial national anthem since the early nineteenth century, but it has never been officially adopted by the British Parliament.[88] Set to the same melody as "My Country, 'Tis of Thee," the song asks British citizens to essentially pray for the well-being of the ruler:

> God save our gracious King,
> Long live our noble King,
> God save the King.
>
> Send him victorious,
> Happy and glorious,
> Long to reign over us,
> God save the King.[89]

Regardless of which national anthem was first, the fact remains that virtually every country adopted them, either officially or unofficially, by the end of the nineteenth century and early twentieth century, as a symbol of nationhood.[90] These national anthems harness the power of music. One could argue that this is done, as Plato suggests, to help make people better citizens. In this sense, national anthems can foster a love of nation in citizens, bond them together, and inspire them to do good deeds in the name of the homeland. On the other hand, one could take a more cynical view, and view national anthems as instruments of social control that are orchestrated by those in power. According to Karen Cerulo, "[i]t is political elites who manufacture and distribute national anthems. They 'make over' these symbols with reference to the social conditions they face and the goals they wish to project to their constituents and observers."[91] There is probably a bit of truth to each position, although the degree to which each of these views is embodied in any particular national anthem likely varies quite substantially from country to country.

Those with political power have recognized the strong influence of music in contexts other than national anthems. The most obvious example is in the military and during war. As described by Chang-Tai Hung, there is no question that war music is a common way that governments use song to achieve a political end:

> The power of such music is based on the assumption that songs are written to be sung aloud, which makes their circulation among the illiterate possible. Songs appeal to emotions; they have little need for reason or argument.

Through them—through rhythm and rhyme rather than reasoning and understanding—the patriotic message can be implanted more easily in the memory.
Moreover, singing is a collective exercise in which one feels a sense of belonging, providing a cohesive force that blends individuals into a community. . . .
singing can provide a tremendous boost to troop morale. It is invaluable in uplifting the spirits of the soldiers or in providing temporary relief from the con-
fusion of. . . war.[92]

The use of music to aid in the war effort is not surprising. Indeed, if there is any
place where government may need to emotionally uplift its soldiers, it is when a
country is preparing to send troops off into the horrors and uncertainties of war.
Music can assist in preparing a country's citizenry for war as well. More broadly, music can help create a mood of support for the military during both wartime
and peacetime.

For instance, Congress formally created the United States Marine Corps
Band in 1798.[93] When the band's most famous director, John Phillip Sousa, assumed that post in 1880, he took the band on its first concert tour.[94] Today, Marine Corps bands perform at several hundred concerts and ceremonies every
year.[95] The spreading of this message by military bands such as the Marine
Corps bands fosters support for the military and U.S. incursions overseas. There
is a plethora of examples of music, written to glorify military achievements,
which was later adopted or acknowledged by the government. Francis Scott Key
wrote "The Star-Spangled Banner" after viewing the British bombardment of
Fort McHenry during the War of 1812. Originally titled "Defense of Fort
McHenry," the song famously describes how Key witnessed the battle during
the night, unsure who controlled the fort; when morning came, he was reassured
that American forces held the fort, as the American flag still flew atop it.[96] Key
thus wrote the first verse as follows:

> Oh, say, can you see by the dawn's early light,
> What so proudly we hailed at the twilight's last gleaming,
> Whose broad stripes and bright stars, through the perilous fight,
> O'er the ramparts we watched, were so gallantly streaming?
> And the rockets' red glare, the bombs bursting in air,
> Gave proof through the night that our flag was still there.
> Oh, say, does that star-spangled banner yet wave
> O'er the land of the free and the home of the brave?[97]

Set to the popular drinking song, "To Anacreon in Heaven," "The Star-Spangled
Banner" quickly gained a popularity of its own; the unofficial national anthem
for a century, Congress formally made it the U.S. national anthem in 1931.[98]
Both before and after it became the official national anthem, "The Star-Spangled
Banner" tells a rousing story about a grand military achievement, one that was
secured against the largest military power of the nineteenth century. Today,
there is no question that the song stirs immense emotion among a great many
Americans, serving to promote love of country and its ideals. Thus, it functions

as another example of music being used to exercise political power. Yet, the song's connection to a military battle has led some to call for an alternative, more peaceful national anthem, such as "My Country, 'Tis of Thee," "America the Beautiful," or "God Bless America."

In the American Civil War, music was used to drum up support for the cause on both sides of the Mason Dixon Line. Daniel Emmett's song "Dixie" became an anthem for the South and was played at Jefferson Davis' inauguration as president of the Confederacy.[99] Julia Ward Howe, an ardent abolitionist, wrote "The Battle Hymn of the Republic" in 1861; the song was used to inspire Union troops during the war.[100] George F. Root's "The Battle Cry of Freedom" was so inspirational to Union soldiers that President Abraham Lincoln told Root, "You have done more than a hundred generals and a thousand orators."[101] Apparently Lincoln understood the political power of music too.

The U.S. government's recognition of the power of music continued through World War I. Journalist George Creel was tapped to head the official propaganda agency, the Committee on Public Information (CPI). Creel found singing to be essential to a successful war effort, and he actively sought out composers to write pro-war music. Furthermore, the CPI handed out songbooks and sent song leaders to theaters across the country to lead people in group singing of war songs.[102] Following his successful pro-World War I song "Over There," composer George M. Cohan was the first artist to be awarded the Congressional Gold Medal.[103]

During World War II, there were many examples around the globe of music being used to help the war effort for various countries. Chinese drama propaganda troupes were organized by the government to use choral singing to rally the country's populace behind the war cause in 1937, Russian musicians wrote many nationalistic songs after Hitler's attack in 1941, and American composers helped the war effort from 1941-45 by writing pro-American emotional songs.[104] More specifically in America, the federal government's Office of War Information (OWI) created the National Wartime Music Committee (NWMC) to find a song to boost and maintain morale during the worldwide conflict.[105] Although the NWMC was ultimately unsuccessful in engineering a war anthem, the creation of the committee is certainly evidence of the importance that U.S. policy makers saw for music. After popular band leader Glenn Miller enlisted in the army in 1942, he was given the post of director of army bands. After the War Department transferred Miller to the air force in 1943, he and a 45-piece group did a weekly radio program entitled *I Sustain the Wings*, which was designed not only to play music, but also to recruit men into the armed forces and sell war bonds.[106]

Most countries' use of song for political purposes during World War II pales in comparison to the Nazis' employment of music during that era. The Nazis engaged in a significant amount of propaganda production. Led by Minister of Public Enlightenment and Propaganda Joseph Goebbels, the Nazi regime tried to destroy history and dissent by burning books,[107] and it tried to rewrite history or distort the truth through the use of posters, newspapers, magazines, newsreels, films, novels, histories, and rallies, among other means.[108] Thus, it should come as no surprise that the Nazis also tried to bend music to their twisted political views.

Nazi use of music took various forms. After Adolf Hitler took power in 1933, the Nazis commissioned musicologists to rewrite the history of German music to match Nazi principles. This included purging non-Nazi music journals, awarding prizes to musicians who produced songs about Nazi ideals, and writing books that claimed composer Richard Wagner had suggested the creation of a German Reich.[109] Wagner was of particular interest to the Nazis. Hitler personally idolized Wagner, believing the anti-Semitic composer to be a genius and a prophet.[110] According to Hitler, "[w]hoever wants to understand National Socialist Germany must know Wagner."[111] Hitler's draw to Wagner might have stemmed in part from the composer's 1850 essay, "Judaism in Music," where he claimed that German music was a "worm-infested corpse" that had been taken over by the Jewish community.[112] Whatever the reason for Hitler's obsession with Wagner, the Third Reich made extensive use of the composer's works. Goebbels publicly praised Wagner's writings and music.[113] Wagner's music was excerpted and used as background music for propaganda films, newsreels, and radio announcements.[114] His works were played at Nazi assemblies, in concentration camps, and perhaps even while prisoners were being marched to the gas chambers.[115]

Wagner was not the only composer to be commandeered by the Nazis. For instance, Beethoven was alleged to have embodied National Socialist ideals. Nazis used his works, which they saw as "pure" German music, at party sponsored concerts, festivals, films, and radio programs.[116] Nazi propagandists, in order to ensure Beethoven's music was "pure," eliminated from historical works any doubts as to his German birth.[117] With this convenient rewriting of history, the Nazi Party could use works already beloved by the German people as a way to increase citizens' pride for the regime. The Nazis also used and abused living composers during their reign of terror. After Goebbels set up the Reich Music Chamber in 1933, he persuaded Richard Strauss to become the Chamber's president. Two years later, Strauss was fired from that post, in part, because he did not support the regime's policies.[118]

Finally, the Nazis' attempt at manipulating songs extended to using popular music to their advantage. One example of this involved jazz, and in particular, swing music.[119] The Germans viewed jazz and swing music as a form of "foreign corruption." The demand for this music from the German public was so great, that the government's initial attempts to ban the music eventually gave way to allowing the music over the public airwaves instead of risking people finding it via foreign radio stations:[120]

> For Germans who insisted on listening to swing, they could have it but with German propaganda as its content. The Nazis actually set up a committee of experts, under Goebbels's cultural oversight, to discriminate between *Negerjazz* and acceptable German music. . . . The attack went too far as to encompass an

all-out propaganda campaign via German radio aimed, specifically, to be air-waved back to British and American troops to undermine their morale. . . . [T]he German radio station broadcast parodies of popular British and American songs. The first verse would be sung straight, followed by anti-British or anti-semitic inserts.[121]

The same music was brought by German jazz groups to the front for the purposes of boosting their morale.[122]

Music was also used to encourage patriotic support for the United States during the Cold War. Public schools incorporated patriotic songs such as "America" (better known as "My Country Tis of Thee"). It was also at this time that the words "one nation, under God" were added to the "Pledge of Allegiance" as a way to distinguish the United States and its Judeo-Christian traditions from the Communists who were said to be "Godless."[123]

Whether it is for something like the more laudable purpose of uniting and inspiring America by penning "The Star-Spangled Banner," or for the more destructive intention of using music to promote anti-Semitism in Nazi Germany, there is no question that governments have frequently used, and abused, music for political purposes. If this is not evidence enough of the political power of music, one last example should make the case—censorship.

Censorship

When governments attempt to censor music, it is ever more evidence of music's power over humanity and our emotions. At the very least, censorship is evidence that those who run many governments in human history have *thought* that music has a profound power over human beings. Again, much as was the case with government's using music, the story of music censorship dates back until at least the time of Plato. In *The Republic* Plato noted the following:

> [T]he overseers of the city must cleave to this, not letting it be corrupted unawares, but guarding it against all comers: there must be no innovation in gymnastic and music contrary to the established order; but they will guard against it as much as they can, fearing that when someone says
>
> > Human beings esteem most that song
> > Which floats newest from the singer
>
> someone might perchance suppose the poet means not new songs, but a new way of song, and praises that. Such a saying shouldn't be praised, nor should one be taken in that sense. For they must beware of change to a strange form of music, taking it to be a danger to the whole. For never are the ways of music moved without the greatest political laws being moved.[124]

Plato says quite a bit in this quote. First, it demonstrates his position that government must establish which music will be allowed and which will not. Second, he claims that we must guard against new music being introduced; indeed, he argues that we must make sure that we are not taken in by new songs or new ways of song. Third, he explains why we should take his advice—strange new music will be a danger to society as a whole. Finally, Plato tells us that a change in music will lead to a change in the laws. Thus, in order to protect his carefully constructed republic, Plato advocates a strict form of music censorship.

There are many governments throughout history which have heeded Plato's counsel. During the Middle Ages, when the Roman Catholic Church wielded great power over governments in Europe, church clerics were openly critical of secular music, something which would have been a death knell at that time. More recently, by the turn of the twentieth century, while Finland was seeking its independence, Russian police barred performances of Sibelius' pro-independence piece "Finlandia."

During the Nazi reign, they prohibited performances of Bedrich Smetana's pro-Czech "Moldau in Prague and Frederic Chopin's pro-Polish Polonaises in Warsaw.[125] The Nazis also rejected jazz music, especially after America entered World War II,[126] although their attempts to ban it were later aborted due to the music's infectious popularity. Starting in 1937, the Nazi Music Chamber issued an Order Concerning Undesirable and Dangerous Music that required pre-publican screening of all foreign sheet music, although it was primarily aimed at stamping out jazz in Germany. Within two years, the Reich Music Examination Office had gained the power to review and prohibit any music distributed in Germany.[127]

There are many other examples of music censorship around the world. Soviet censorship dates back until at least 1922 when the Communist Party banned the old national anthem, "God Save the Tsar,"[128] and the Soviet government continued to employ music censors until Mikhail Gorbachev's reforms in the late 1980s.[129] Also during the 1980s, the government of Zaire had a Music Censorship Commission to guard against forbidden thoughts being placed in song.[130] In the twenty-first century, the Chinese government has used its power as the owner of all broadcast media to determine which songs will be played on radio in that country.[131]

In North Korea, perhaps the most repressive regime on earth today, music censorship is the norm. Concerts in the communist country are typically limited to performances that Supreme Leader Kim Jong-il is falsely credited with having written. Listening to radio broadcasts from other nations is enough to subject one to imprisonment. In a particularly egregious example during a party on Christmas in 1992, one of the regime's former propaganda officers, Ji Hae-nam, sang a South Korean song. For this infraction she was imprisoned for three years, and she was beaten so severely she could not get up for a month.[132]

All of the preceding repression is evidence of the power that governments have seen in music, and they have used this as justification for restricting what could be played or sung. Luckily, in the United Sates we have been blessed with the First Amendment to the Constitution, ratified in 1791: "Congress shall make no law. . . abridging the freedom of speech." According to the United States Supreme Court, "[m]usic, as a form of expression and communication, is protected under the First Amendment."[133] For many years the First Amendment has served as a shielding blanket, ensuring that musical performances may not be censored by the government.

Yet, there have been isolated pockets of government officials who have over the years resisted the Constitution's decree. These individual policy makers have tried to exercise power over music and prevent the public from hearing things that would threaten the power or the cherished beliefs of those in power. For instance, in the Antebellum South many in the slave-owning establishment were fearful of slaves communicating with each other during slave revolts, spreading new ideas through song, and playing music that was deemed "uncivilized." Thus, it was common for state and local governments to ban traditional African instruments, prohibit the playing of drums by slaves, and proscribe dancing or playing "worldly" music.[134] After the Civil War, the tables turned for a time, and Southerners were forbidden during Reconstruction from publicly singing pro-Confederate songs such as "I'm a Good Ol' Rebel" and "Bonnie Blue Flag." Northern occupying forces put the ban in place out of fear that the music would fuel another Southern rebellion.[135]

Rare forms of American censorship surfaced from time to time in the twentieth century as well. During a wave of anti-communist hysteria in 1947, the House Un-American Activities Committee [HUAC] called composer Hanns Eisler to testify about whether his music had aided the communist infiltration of the motion picture industry. Although Eisler tried to defend himself by claiming he was "only a musician" and thus not responsible for any communist conspiracy, HUAC eventually had him deported.[136]

From the 1950s on, there are numerous examples of state and local governments attempting to censor rock music. In 1953, several South Carolina counties put restrictions on the use of juke boxes; in 1955, the Juvenile Delinquency and Crime Commission of Houston banned local radio stations from playing 30 songs it deemed obscene; in 1965, Cleveland temporarily banned all rock concerts in the city; in 1970, Country Joe McDonald was fined $500 for using profanities in public and singing anti-Vietnam protest songs in Massachusetts (he led the crowd in a chant of "Gimmie an F-*-*-*" chant as an introduction to the band's performance of the "I Feel Like I'm Fixin' to Die Rag").[137]

By the 1980s, rock music became a national issue, evidenced by the formation of the Parents Music Resource Center (PMRC) in 1985. The PMRC claimed that its purpose was to educate and inform parents about music lyrics that are sexually explicit and music that glorified violence, drug use, other criminal activities, and suicide.[138] The PMRC was able in 1985 to convince the Senate Commerce Committee to hold public hearings on these music trends, although the hearings generated substantial controversy because the PMRC leadership was comprised of several of the senators' wives.[139] The hearings did not result in any government action, but they did lead to the recording industry voluntarily agreeing to place the now infamous warning label, "Explicit Lyrics: Parental Advisory," on albums that made overt references to sex, violence, or substance abuse.[140]

Within a few years of the formation of the PMRC, however, there were some high-profile instances where members of 2 Live Crew and purveyors of their album, *As Nasty as They Wanna Be*, were prosecuted in the United States. Music store owners and employees in Florida and Alabama had been arrested for selling earlier albums of 2 Live Crew, but the *Nasty* album stirred up quite a bit more trouble. In 1990, a trial court judge in Florida declared that the album was obscene, prompting the Broward County sheriff to arrest music store owner Charles Freeman for stocking the work (his fine for $1,000 represents the only instance in American history where a person has been successfully prosecuted for selling obscene music). Luther Campbell and two other members of 2 Live Crew were also arrested in 1990 on obscenity charges while performing at an adults-only show in Florida. Unlike Freeman, however, Campbell and his band mates eventually prevailed when a federal court of appeals overturned the obscenity ruling against them in 1993.[141]

Sporadic instances of censorship like this aside, the United States has an impressive track record of adhering to the promise of the First Amendment. However, when those in power, either here or abroad, try to silence singers and players of music, they do so because they see the music as a threat to their sense of social order or because they think the songs will encroach on their power. Each one of the instances of censorship cited here is more proof of the power of music and its political relevance.

Presidential Campaign Music

Music has a profound effect on the human brain and on human emotions. This has been the case since our distant ancestors walked the earth. Countless composers and musicians throughout history have written political pieces over the centuries. There is a long history of governments attempting to harness the power of music for their own purposes and trying to stifle the use of music against them. Thus, it is no surprise that campaign consultants, who intuitively know that emotional appeals are important in political campaigns,[142] also have tried to harness the power of music and have tried to use music for a similar effect. It makes sense then that politicians often make extensive use of music in their campaigns. Music can be used as an effective tool as a way to have the public recognize who they are and possibly even sway one's vote. In essence, music can help foster a connection between a candidate and a desired emotion. Music may even create a "bond" between a candidate and the electorate. Over the course of American history, there has been a development in the types of songs used, the types of messages used, and finally a push by members of the general public to make their voice known through music. Candidates are always looking for that one line and that one chord that will have us walking away humming and thinking to ourselves, "I'm voting for that candidate." Indeed, music meant to produce enthusiasm among a candidate's supporters has been a part of American politics for over two centuries, and it has been a part of political rallies for well over a century.[143]

Music is also frequently used in television and radio advertisements. There is a plethora of research on the use of music in political campaign ads.[144] Much like product advertisements, political advertisements are carefully tested, with text, image, and music designed to complement and reinforce each other.[145] Studies have found that music in political advertising is used in an attempt to affect voters' choices, often through positive or negative emotional appeals.[146] However, except for works cataloging the music used in presidential campaigns over the last two centuries plus, virtually no major research has been done on the use of campaign theme songs or of music at political rallies. Our goal is to not simply describe which songs were used every four years; instead, we set out to explain why these songs developed and how candidates' musical strategies changed over the years.

Notes

1.   Halbert Hains Britan, "The Power of Music," *The Journal of Philosophy, Psychology, and Scientific Methods* 5, No. 13 (June 1908): 352-57, 353.

2.   *Cheers*, "Teacher's Pet," original air date January 31, 1985.

3.   *Cheers*, "Teacher's Pet."

4.   Oliver Sacks, *Musicophilia: Tales of Music and the Brain* (New York: Vintage Books, 2007), ix.

5.   Sacks, *Musicophelia*, 45-47.

6.   Steven Mithen, *The Singing Neanderthals: The Origins of Music, Language, Mind, and Body* (Cambridge, MA: Harvard University Press, 2006), 79.

7.   Mithen, *The Singing Neanderthals*, 80.

8.   Mark Jude Tramo, "Music of the Hemispheres," *Science*, January 5, 2001, 54.

9.   Gene Wallenstein, *The Pleasure Instinct: Why We Crave Adventure, Chocolate, Pheromones, and Music* (Hoboken, NJ: Wiley), 102.

10.   Wallenstein, *The Pleasure Instinct*, 171.

11.   Ademola Adegbite, "The Concept of Sound in Traditional African Religious Music," *Journal of Black Studies* 22, No. 1 (September 1991): 45-54, 45.

12.   Joyce Marie Jackson, "The Changing Nature of Gospel Music: A Southern Case Study," *African American Review* 29, No. 2 (Summer 1995): 185-200, 185.

13.   Peter V. Marsden et al., "American Regional Cultures and Differences in Leisure Time Activities," *Social Forces*, 60, No. 4 (June 1982): 1023-1049, 1034.

14.   Wallenstein, *The Pleasure Instinct*, 171.

15.   Sara Cohen, "Sounding Out the City: Music and the Sensuous Production of Place," *Transactions of the Institute of British Geographers* 20, no. 4 (1995): 434-446, 436; Ruth Finnegan, *The Hidden Musicians: Music-Making in an English Town*, reprint edition (Middletown, CT: Wesleyan University Press, 2007).

16.   Mithen, *The Singing Neanderthals*, 273.

17. Sacks, *Musicophelia*, 5

18. Sacks, *Musicophelia*, 24.

19. Aris Sarafianos, "Pain, Labor, and the Sublime: Medical Gymnastics and Burke's Aesthetics," *Representations*, no. 91 (Summer 2005): 58-83, 71.

20. Amber Haque, "Psychology from Islamic Perspective: Contributions of Early Muslim Scholars and Challenges to Contemporary Muslim Psychologists," *Journal of Religion and Health* 43, no. 4 (2004): 357-377, 363.

21. Jacquelyn Michele Coleman, "The Effects of the Male and Female Singing and Speaking Voices on Selected Physiological and Behavioral Measures of Premature Infants in the Intensive Care Unit," *International Journal of Arts Medicine* 5 no. 2 (1997): 4-11, 10.

22. David Carr, "Music, Meaning, and Emotion," *The Journal of Aesthetics and Art Criticism* 62, no. 3 (Summer 2004), 225-234, 226.

23. Kristin Leutwyler, "Exploring the Musical Brain," *Scientific American*, January 22, 2001, accessed June 16, 2010, http://www.scientificamerican.com/article.cfm?id=exploring-the-musical-bra.

24. Paula M. Niedenthal and Marc B. Setterlund, "Emotion Congruence in Perception," *Personality and Social Psychology Bulletin* 20, no. 4 (1994): 401-411.

25. J. Peter Burkholder, Donald Jay Grout, and Clause V. Palisca, *A History of Western Music*, (New York: W.W. Norton & Company, 2006), 481.

26. Burkholder, Grout, and Palisca, *A History of Western Music*, 602.

27. Burkholder, Grout, and Palisca, *A History of Western Music*, 602.

28. Leutwyler, "Exploring the Musical Brain."

29. Mithen, *The Singing Neanderthals*, 90.

30. Jon Goss, "The 'Magic of the Mall': An Analysis of Form, Function, and Meaning in the Contemporary Retail Built Environment," *Annals of the Association of American Geographers*, 83, no. 1 (March 1993): 18-47, 32.

31. Courtney Brown, *Politics in Music: Music and Political Transformation from Beethoven to Hip-Hop* (Atlanta: Farsight Press, 2008), 12.

32. Brown, *Politics in Music*, 12-13.

33. Jerome L. Rodnitzky, "Popular Music in American Studies," *The History Teacher* 7, no. 4 (August 1974): 503-10, 506.

34. Todd DePastino, *Citizen Hobo: How a Century of Homelessness Shaped America* (Chicago: University of Chicago Press, 2003), 96-97.

35. Rodnitzky, "Popular Music in American Studies," 506.

36. Vincent J. Roscigno and William F. Danaher, "Media and Mobilization: The Case of Radio and Southern Textile Worker Insurgency, 1929 to 1934," *American Sociological Review* 66, no. 1 (February 2001): 21-48, 42.

37. Woody Guthrie, "This Land Is Your Land," in *The American Reader: Words that Moved a Nation*, ed. Diane Ravitch (New York, HarperCollins, 2000), 478.

38. David R. Shumway, "Your Land: The Lost Legacy of Woody Guthrie," in *Hard Travelin': The Life and Legacy of Woody Guthrie*, ed. Robert Santelli and Emily Davidson (Hanover, NH: University Press of New England, 1999), 129.

39. Kathy Sammis, *The Era of World War II Through Contemporary Times: 1939-Present* (Portland, ME: J. Weston Walch, 2000), 72.

40. R. Serge Denisoff, "Protest Songs: Those on the Top Forty and Those of the Streets," *American Quarterly* 22, no. 4 (Winter 1970): 807-823, 819.

41. Robert Santelli, "Preface," in *Hard Travelin': The Life and Legacy of Woody Guthrie*, ed. Robert Santelli and Emily Davidson (Hanover, NH: University Press of New England, 1999), xi.

42.   Katherine Charleton, *Rock Music Styles: A History* (New York: McGraw-Hill, 2011), 131.

43.   Anthony Varesi, *The Bob Dylan Albums: A Critical Study* (Toronto: Guernica Editions, 2002), 24-25.

44.   Varesi, *The Bob Dylan Albums*, 26.

45.   Noel E. Monk and Jimmy Guterman, *12 Days on the Road: The Sex Pistols and America* (New York: Harper Entertainment, 1990), 20.

46.   Charleton, *Rock Music Styles*, 237-38.

47.   Lars Elleström, *Divine Madness: On Interpreting Literature, Music, and the Visual Arts Ironically* (Cranbury, NJ: Associated University Presses, 2002), 160.

48.   David Machin, *Analyzing Popular Music: Image, Sound and Text* (Thousand Oaks, CA: Sage Publications, 2010), 199.

49.   The Clash, vocal performance of "Know Your Rights," by John Mellor and Michael Jones, original release April 23, 1982, on *The Clash: The Singles*, Sony Music Entertainment 63886, CD.

50.   Bob Marley, *Bob Marley: Songs of Freedom* (Milwaukee: Hal Leonard Corporation, 1992), 65-71.

51.   Sting, *Lyrics* (New York: The Dial Press, 2007), 104-05.

52.   Sting, *Lyrics*, 126-28.

53.   David Kootnikoff, *U2: A Musical Biography* (Santa Barbara, CA: Glenwood Press, 2010), 31.

54.   Kootnikoff, *U2*, 60.

55.   Bono and Michka Assayas, *Bono: In Conversation with Michka Assayas* (New York: Penguin Group, 2006).

56.   Elliot J. Huntley, *Mystical One: George Harrison After the Break-Up of the Beatles* (Toronto: Guernica Editions, 2004), 71.

57.   Fred Bronson, *The Billboard Book of Number 1 Hits: The Inside Story Behind Every Number One Single, on Billboard's Hot 100 from 1955 to the Present* (New York: Billboard Books, 2003), 496.

58.   Reebee Garofalo, *Rockin' Out: Popular Music in the USA* (Upper Saddle River, NJ: Prentice-Hall, 2002), 312-16.

59.   Zack de la Rocha, "Take the Power Back," *Rage Against the Machine* (New York: Sony Music Entertainment, 1992).

60.   Martin C. Strong, *The Great Rock Discography* (Edinburgh: Canongate Books, 2004), 1251.

61.   Colin Devenish, *Rage Against the Machine* (New York: St. Martin's Press, 2001), 43.

62.   Brown, *Politics in Music*, 190.

63.   Phyllis R. Klotman and Janet K. Cutler, *Struggles for Representation: African American Documentary Film and Video* (Bloomington: Indiana University Press, 1999), 241.

64.   John Borgmeyer and Holly Lang, *Dr. Dre: A Biography* (Westport, CT: Greenwood Press, 2007), 38.

65.   Borgmeyer and Lang, *Dr. Dre*, 39.

66.   Charlton, *Rock Music Styles*, 272.

67.   Marcyliena Morgan, *Language, Discourse and Power in African American Culture* (New York: Cambridge University Press, 2002), 51.

68.   Bill Osgerby, *Youth Media* (New York: Routledge, 2004), 68-70.

69.   Merle Haggard, *Merle Haggard: Poet of the Common Man: The Lyrics*, ed. Don Cusic (Milwaukee: Hal Leonard), 51.

70.   James Perone, *Songs of the Vietnam Conflict* (Westport, CT: Greenwood Press, 2001), 99.

71.   Martin Cloonan, "Musical Responses to September 11th: From Conservative Patriotism to Radicalism," in *9-11—The World's All out of Tune*, ed. Dietrich Helms and Thomas Phelps (Bielefeld: Transcript Verlag, 2004), 23.

72.   Dominic J. Pulera, *Sharing the Dream: White Males in Multicultural America* (New York: Continuum International, 2004), 252.

73.   Randy Rudder, "In Whose Name: Country Artists Speak Out on Gulf War II," in *Country Music Goes to War*, ed. Charles K. Wolfe and James E. Akenson (Lexington: University Press of Kentucky, 2005), 219.

74.   Pulera, *Sharing the Dream*, 253.

75.   Rudder, "In Whose Name," 219.

76.   Plato, *The Republic*, trans. Alan Bloom (New York: Basic Books, 1968), 80.

77.   Donald J. Grout and Bertil Wikman, *A History of Western Music (Revised Edition)*, (New York: W.W. Norton & Co. Ltd.), 8.

78.   Library of Congress, "The U.S. Works Projects Administration Federal Music Project (Washington, D.C.: Library of Congress, 1999), iv.

79.   Andreas Osiander, "Sovereignty, International Relations, and the Westphalian Myth," *International Organization* 55, no. 2 (Spring 2001): 251-287, 252.

80.   David L. Blaney and Naeem Inayatullah, "The Westphalian Deferral," *International Studies Review* 2, no. 2 (Summer 2000): 29-64, 33.

81.   James A. Caporaso, "Changes in the Westphalian Order: Territory, Public Authority, and Sovereignty," *International Studies Review* 2, no. 2 (Summer 2000): 1-28, 3.

82.   Brown, *Politics in Music*, 67-91.

83.   Brown, *Politics in Music*, 91-95.

84.   Samuel Hideo Yamashita, *Leaves from an Autumn of Emergencies: Selections from the Wartime Diaries of Ordinary Japanese* (Honolulu: University of Hawaii Press, 2005), 275.

85.   Mark Ravina, "Japanese State Making in Global Context," in *State Making in Asia*, ed. Richard Boyd, Tak-Wing Ngo (New York: Routledge, 2006), 40-41.

86.   Andrew Pettegree, *Reformation and the Culture of Persuasion* (New York: Cambridge University Press, 2005), 71.

87.   Jakob Seibert, *National Anthems* (Mainz, Germany: Schott, 2006), 51.

88.   Andrew Barker, "Setting the Tone: Austria's National Anthems from Haydn to Haider," *Austrian Studies* 17 (2009): 12-28, 13.

89.   Ronald Herder, ed., *500 Best-Loved Song Lyrics* (Mineola, NY: Dover Publications, 1998), 114.

90.   Karen A. Cerulo, "Sociopolitical Control and the Structure of National Symbols: An Empirical Analysis of National Anthems," *Social Forces* 68, no. 1 (September 1989): 76-99, 77.

91.   Cerulo, "Sociopolitical Control," 80.

92.   Chang-Tai Hung, "The Politics of Songs: Myths and Symbols in the Chinese Communist War Music, 1937-1949," *Modern Asian Studies* 30, no. 4 (October 1996): 901-29, 904.

93.   Robert A. Simonsen, ed., *Marines Dodging Death: Sixty-Two Accounts of Close Calls in World War II, Korea, Vietnam, Lebanon, Iraq and Afghanistan* (Jefferson, NC: McFarland, 2009), 19.

94.   Simonsen, *Marines Dodging Death*, 19.

95.   Scott Keller, *Marine Pride: A Salute to America's Elite Fighting Force* (New York: Citadel Press, 2004), 35.

96.   Leslie M. Pockell, ed., *100 Essential American Poems* (New York: St. Martin's Press, 2009), 13.

97.   Francis Scott Key, "The Star-Spangled Banner," *Our Nation's Archive: The History of the United States in Documents*, ed. Erik Bruun and Jay Crosby (New York: Black Dog and Leventhal Publishers, 1999), 211.

98.   Pockell, *100 Essential American Poems*, 13.

99.   Ravitch, "Japanese State Making in Global Context," 243.

100.   Leslie Pockell, ed., *The 100 Best Poems of All Time* (New York: Warner Books, 2001), 90.

101.   Paul D. Sanders, ed., *Lyrics and Borrowed Tunes of the American Temperance Movement* (Columbia: University of Missouri Press, 2006), 190.

102.   Kathleen E. R. Smith, *God Bless America: Tin Pan Alley Goes to War* (Lexington: University Press of Kentucky, 2003), 71.

103.   Stephen W. Stathis, *Congressional Gold Medals, 1776-2002* (Hauppauge, NY: Novinka Books, 2003), 13.

104.   Hung, "The Politics of Songs," 905-06.

105.   William H. Young and Nancy K. Young, *Music of the World War II Era* (Westport, CT: Greenwood Press, 2008), 11.

106.   Young and Young, *Music of the World War II Era*, 17.

107.   Haig Bosmajian, *Burning Books* (Jefferson, NC: McFarland, 2006), 4-5.

108.   Richard J. Evans, *The Third Reich in Power* (New York: Penguin, 2005), 124-25, 162.

109.   Michael Meyer, "The Nazi Musicologist as Myth Maker in the Third Reich," *Journal of Contemporary History* 10, no. 4 (October 1975):649-665, 649-53.

110.   Joachim Fest, *Hitler* (Orlando: Harcourt, 1974), 49-50.

111.   William L. Shirer, *The Rise and Fall of the Third Reich: A History of Nazi Germany* (New York: Fawcett Crest, 1960), 147.

112.   Alan E. Steinweis, "Anti-Semitism and the Arts in Nazi Ideology and Policy," in *The Arts in Nazi Germany: Continuity, Conformity, Change*, ed. Jonathan Huener and Francis R. Nicosia (New York: Berghahn Books, 2006), 19.

113.   Joachim Köhler, *Wagner's Hitler: The Prophet and His Disciple* (Cambridge, UK: Polity Press, 2000), 252.

114.   Pamela M. Potter, "Music in the Third Reich: The Complex Task of Germanization," in *The Arts in Nazi Germany: Continuity, Conformity, Change*, ed. Jonathan Huener and Francis R. Nicosia (New York: Berghahn Books, 2006), 87.

115.   Raphael Cohen-Almagor, *The Scope of Tolerance: Studies on the Costs of Free Expression and Freedom of the Press* (New York: Routledge, 2006), 119.

116.   Mary-Elizabeth O'Brien, *Nazi Cinema as Enchantment: The Politics of Entertainment in the Third Reich* (Rochester, NY: Camden House, 2004), 131.

117.   David B. Dennis, *Beethoven in German Politics, 1870-1989* (New Haven, CT: Yale University Press, 1996), 146.

118.   Evans, *The Third Reich in Power*, 187-89.

119.   Huener and Nicosia, *The Arts in Nazi Germany*, 95.

120.   Huener and Nicosia, *The Arts in Nazi Germany*, 95.

121.   Brenda Dixon Gottschild, *Waltzing in the Dark: African American Vaudeville and Race Politics in the Swing Era* (New York: Palgrave, 2000), 226.

122.   Gottschild, *Waltzing in the Dark*, 227.

123.   David Domke and Kevin Coe, *The God Strategy: How Religion Became a Political Weapon in America* (New York: Oxford University Press, 2010), 14.

124.   Plato, *The Republic* (Placeholder1), 101-02.

125.   Jeffrey B. Kahan, "Bach, Beethoven, and the (Home)Boys: Censoring Violent Rap Music in America," *Southern California Law Review* 66 (September 1993): 2583-2610, 2585.

126.   Meyer, The Nazi Musicologist," 654-55.

127.   Alan E. Steinweis, *Art, Ideology, and Economics in Nazi Germany: The Reich Chambers of Music, Theater, and the Visual Arts* (Chapel Hill: University of North Carolina Press, 1993), 141.

128.   Barbara Makanowitsky, "Music to Serve the State," *Russian Review* 24, no. 3 (July 1965): 266-77, 267.

129.   Judy Dempsey, "Return of a Soviet-Era Genre Lost to Perestroika," *New York Times*, October 21, 2009, accessed June 22, 2010, http://www.nytimes.com/2009/10/22/arts/22iht-realism.html?_r=2&sq=music censorship soviet union&st=cse&adxnnl=1&scp=11&adxnnlx=1277809553YINwrBMCN7Boqg+j1MV9BQ.

130.   A.M. Rosenthal, "On My Mind: This Censored World," *New York Times*, May 27, 1988, accessed June 22, 2010, http://www.nytimes.com/1988/05/27/opinion/on-my-mind-this-censored-world.html?scp=2&sq=music%20censorship%20north%20korea&st=cse.

131. Howard W. French, "The Sound, Not of Music, But of Control," *New York Times*, October 25, 2007, accessed June 22, 2010, http://www.nytimes.com/2007/10/25/world/asia/25shanghai.html?scp=5&sq=music%20censorship%20china&st=cse.

132.   Richard V. Allen and Chuck Downs, "Concert without Strings," *New York Times*, October 28, 2007, accessed June 22, 2010, http://www.nytimes.com/2007/10/28/opinion/28allen.html?scp=14&sq=music%20censorship%20north%20korea&st=cse.

133.   *Ward v. Rock against Racism*, 491 U.S. 781, 790 (1989).

134.   Wilma A. Dunaway, *Slavery in the American Mountain South* (New York: Cambridge University Press, 2003), 221; James Walvin, *Black Ivory: Slavery in the British Empire* (Malden, MA: Blackwell Publishers, 2001), 143.

135.   Eric Nuzum, *Parental Advisory: Music Censorship in America* (New York: HarperCollins, 2001), 211.

136.   Lydia Goehr, "Political Music and the Politics of Music," *The Journal of Aesthetics and Art Criticism* 52, no. 1 (Winter 1994): 99-112, 99.

137.   Nuzum, 214, 217-18, 224, 234.

138.   Thomas E. Larson, *History of Rock and Roll* (Dubuque, IA: Kendall-Hunt, 2004), 246.

139.   Roger L. Sadler, *Electronic Media Law* (Thousand Oaks, CA: Sage Publications, 2005), 286.

140.   John E. Semonche, *Censoring Sex: A Historical Journey through American Media* (Lanham, MD: Roman & Littlefield, 2007), 166-67.

141.   Peter Blecha, *Taboo Tunes: A History of Banned Bands and Censored Songs* (San Francisco: Backbeat Books, 2004), 116-18; Kimberle Williams Crenshaw, "Beyond Racism and Misogyny: Black Feminism and 2 Live Crew," in *Words that Wound: Critical Race Theory, Assaultive Speech, and the First Amendment*, ed. Mari J. Matsuda et al. (Boulder, CO: Westview Press, 1993), 120-22; Garofalo, 359-60.

142.   Christopher F. Arterton, "The Persuasive Art of Politics," in *Under the Watchful Eye*, ed. Mathew D. McCubbins (Washington, DC: CQ Press, 1992), 83-126.

143.   Richard Jensen, "Armies, Admen, and Crusaders: Types of Presidential Election Campaigns," *The History Teacher* 2, no. 2 (January 1969): 33-50, 36.

144.   See David F. Damore, "Candidate Strategy and the Decision to Go Negative," *Political Research Quarterly* 55, no. 3 (September 2002): 669-685, 682.

145.   Paul Freedman, Michael Franz, and Kenneth Goldstein, "Campaign Advertising and Democratic Citizenship," *American Journal of Political Science* 48, no. 4 (October 2004): 723-741, 725.

146.   See Freedman, Franz, and Goldstein; Ted Brader, "Striking a Responsive Chord: How Political Ads Motivate and Persuade Voters by Appealing to Emotions," *American Journal of Political Science* 49, no. 2 (April 2005): 388-405; Ken Goldstein and Paul Freedman, "Campaign Advertising and Voter Turnout: New Evidence for a Stimulation Effect," *The Journal of Politics* 64, no. 3 (August 2002): 721-740, 729; D. Sunshine Hillygus and Todd G. Shields, "Moral Issues and Voter Decision Making in the 2004 Presidential Election," *PS: Political Science and Politics* 38, no. 2 (April 2005): 201-209, 202; Kathleen Hall Jamieson, Erika Falk, and Susan Sherr, "The Enthymeme Gap in the 1996 Presidential Campaign," *PS: Political Science and Politics* 32, no. 1 (March 1999): 12-16, 15.

Part One

The Traditional Era of Campaign Music

~ 1 ~

The Early Use of "Campaign" Music (1789-1840)

As demonstrated in the introduction, there is no shortage of examples of music being used for political purposes. Indeed, music's emotional appeal has made it an enduring fixture in politics.

Nothing is more political than an election. Therefore, one should not be shocked to find music used in presidential elections from very early on in United States history through the present. The use of music has varied quite significantly over the course of America's quadrennial presidential contests. It has developed and evolved to be employed in far more complex ways in these elections over time. As we will explain throughout this book, many of these changes were dependent upon the evolution of technology and voting rights.

The road to the presidency was a long one that did not end with the American Revolution. When the war ended in 1783, the country was still living under the Articles of Confederation, which did not have a separate executive branch. For various reasons, including a lack of executive power, key members of the founding generation met in 1787 to create what would eventually become the U.S. Constitution. Although there were initially no political parties in America after the ratification of the U.S. Constitution in 1788, the divisions between Federalists, who supported the Constitution, and Anti-Federalists, who opposed the Constitution, soon began to harden into partisan conflicts. As parties came to pass, the need for music to differentiate between presidential contenders became ever more important. This importance continued to climb until it reached fruition in 1840.

First in War, First in Peace, and Elected Unanimously

Although music has been used in presidential campaigns from the country's earliest days, in truth some of the very earliest "campaign" songs were not campaign songs at all. This was due, in part, to the fact that political parties did not exist in America until the mid-1790s. Thus, when George Washington won the elections of 1789 and 1792, he faced no opposition, and he was elected by the Electoral College on unanimous ballots each time, a feat that no other presidential candidate has accomplished.[1] This amazing accomplishment was possible because Washington was generally seen as a national hero. There is no question that he was very popular during that era.

With no one actively opposing Washington for the presidency, no new campaign music was composed for his "campaign." However, leading up to his presidency, there were any number of musical tributes that were written about the man who had led the country through the Revolution and who presided over the Constitutional Convention. One of the earliest of these songs was "God Save Great Washington" which was published in the *Philadelphia Continental Journal* on April 7, 1786.[2]

> God save great Washington,
> His worth from ev'ry tongue,
> Demands applause;
> Ye tuneful pow'rs combine,
> And each true Whig now join
> Whose heart did ne'r resign
> The glorious cause.
>
> As found in the *Philadelphia Continental Journal*
> Published April 7, 1786

In a few simple lines, the author spoke of the admiration that the country had (or should have had) for the man who was one of the young country's greatest idols. Like many of the campaign songs that would follow in the coming decades, the tune was taken from a popular and/or common song tune of the day. In this case, the author of the text chose the tune of "God Save the King."[3] This song choice was fitting, in a way, because Washington was the country's first president under the new Constitution, making him the first American to serve as a full executive. The song also functioned as perhaps a political slap in the face to the British Empire from which the United States had just won its independence.

Another tribute to Washington at the time of his 1789 and 1792 presidential elections was "Follow Washington."[4] The song, written in December 1776, was meant to rally Americans to the revolutionary cause and celebrate Washington's victory at the Battle of Trenton.[5] Years later, it also served as a fitting tribute to Washington:

The day is broke; my boys, push on,
And follow, follow Washington
    'Tis he that leads the way,
    'Tis he that leads the way;

When he commands, we will obey,
Through rain or snow, by night or day,
    Determined to be free,
    Determined to be free.

Kind Providence our troops inspires
With more than Greek or Roman fires,
    Until our cause prevails,
    Until our cause prevails.

Heaven has favor'd a virtuous few
The tyrant's legions to subdue;
    For justice never fails,
    For justice never fails.

With heart and hand, and God our trust,
We'll freely fight—our cause is just.
    Push on, my boys, push on,
    Push on, my boys, push on!

Till Freedom reigns, our hearty bands
Will fight like true Americans,
    And follow, follow Washington,
    And follow, follow Washington.

As recalled by Mr. Jesse Moore (former revolutionary soldier), and found in *Songs,
Odes and Other Poems on National Subjects: Military*
Published by William McCarthy (Philadelphia, PA), 1842

Although the song clearly was originally written to unite people around the revolutionary cause and around Washington as a military leader, most of the lyrics also very easily double as a tribute to Washington as a political leader. Since his 1789 election was only 13 years after "Follow Washington" was written, and it was only six years after the Revolutionary War ended, this would have been an easy song to resurrect, as many people would have still remembered singing it during the war.

During the early years of the presidency, the country focused on uniting. Washington had even warned Americans about the potential perils of putting "party before unity" in his farewell address, which was printed in the *American Daily Advertiser* in September of 1796, shortly before he officially declined to run for a third term:

Your Union ought to be considered as a main prop of your liberty, and that the love of the one ought to endear to you the preservation of the other. . . . In contemplating the causes, which may disturb our Union, it occurs as matter of serious concern, that any ground should have been furnished for characterizing parties by Geographical discriminations. . . One of the expedients of party to acquire influence, within particular districts, is to misrepresent the opinions and aims of other districts. You cannot shield yourselves too much against the jealousies and heart-burnings, which spring from these misrepresentations; they tend to render alien to each other those, who ought to be bound together by fraternal affection.[6]

This focus on keeping the new union together made the use of politically charged campaign songs seem rather inappropriate during Washington's two campaigns. All of that would soon change once the country needed to choose Washington's successors.

Indeed, it appears that Washington's words decrying political parties fell on many deaf ears. By the early 1790s the Federalists, who advocated the ratification of the Constitution, soon became a more broadly based political party that was supportive of national power, industry, a national bank, and closer ties to Great Britain. This party was led by Alexander Hamilton and John Adams. Soon after, an opposition party, which came to be known as the Democratic-Republicans, formed. This second party, led by Thomas Jefferson and James Madison, favored more powers at the state level than the Federalists did, and they also supported an agrarian lifestyle and closer ties to the newly democratic France; furthermore, they opposed a national bank. This split resulted in congressional elections being contested along partisan lines in the early 1790s. During Washington's second term, these divisions hardened. Then, in 1796, Adams and Jefferson ran for the presidency against each other. Although America had its first contested partisan election, there is no record of campaign music used. Adams narrowly beat Jefferson, but under the rules of the Electoral College at the time (where the candidate receiving the most votes became president and the candidate finishing second was elected vice president), Jefferson took office as the vice president in the Adams administration. This result almost assured that the two men would vie for the presidency again in 1800.[7]

Party Like It's 1799

The divisions between the Federalist Party and the Democratic-Republican Party were growing ever stronger at the turn of the eighteenth century to the nineteenth century. Consequently, it was in the early 1800s that the political parties began to have more strictly partisan agendas. With this partisanship came campaigns that were more heavily fought and the need for propaganda to stir the electorate toward a particular candidate. By 1800, party divisions were so strong that this propaganda grew beyond the print and spoken word; it would now be disseminated by music. William Miles says of these songs:

> Written by party faithful, aspiring but uninspired and largely untalented lyricists, as well as by composers employed by commercial music publishers, these songs. . . review in verse the qualifications and strong points of the candidates, the popular issues of the particular campaign, and the foibles and weaknesses of the opposition. . . . [That] they often relied more on simplistic jingles and crude humor than on substance was of no real concern, for their purpose was to arouse mass enthusiasm at the expense of reason, 'warm up' the crowds at rallies, political meetings, and parades, and remind the faithful of the virtues of party and candidate."[8]

The election of 1800 thus marked the first time campaign songs were used in an American presidential election. The election was highly contested, with candidates Thomas Jefferson, John Adams, and Aaron Burr all vying for the presidency. With a country divided along the lines of political ideologies, the supporters of each candidate wrote songs in an attempt to propel their respective candidate into the White House. With words written by Robert Treat Paine Jr., John Adams' campaign song was "Adams and Liberty," set to the tune of "To Anacreon in Heaven,"[9] which would later serve as the tune for Francis Scott Key's poem "The Defense of Fort McHenry" or, as we know it today, "The Star Spangled Banner." "Adams and Liberty" was "written for, and sung at the fourth Anniversary of the Massachusetts Charitable Fire Society [in] 1789,"[10] but subsequently became associated with Adams' campaign. The nine verses run as follows:

Verse 1:
Ye sons of Columbia, who bravely have fought,
For those rights, which unstained from your Sires had descended,
May you long taste the blessings your valour has brought,
And your sons reap the soil which their fathers defended.
'Mid the reign of mild Peace,
 May your nation increase,
With the glory of Rome, and the wisdom of Greece;
And ne'er shall the sons of Columbia be slaves,
While the earth bears a plant, or the sea rolls its waves.

Verse 2:
In a clime, whose rich vales feed the marts of the world,
Whose shores are unshaken by Europe's commotion,
The trident of Commerce should never be hurled,
To incense the legitimate powers of the ocean.
But should pirates invade,

Though in thunder arrayed,
For ne'er shall the sons, &c.

Verse 3:
The fame of our arms, of our laws the mild sway,
Had justly ennobled our nation in story,
'Till the dark clouds of faction obscured our young day,
And enveloped the sun of American glory.
But let traitors be told,
Who their country have sold,
And bartered their God for his image in gold,
That ne'er will the sons, &c.

Verse 4:
While France her huge limbs bathes recumbent in blood,
And Society's base threats with wide dissolution;
May Peace like the dove, who returned from the flood,
Find an ark of abode in our mild constitution
But though Peace is our aim,
Yet the boon we disclaim,
If bought by our Sov'reignty, Justice or Fame.
For ne'er shall the sons, &c.

Verse 5:
'Tis the fire of the flint, each American warms;
Let Rome's haughty victors beware of collision,
Let them bring all the vassals of Europe in arms,
We're a world by ourselves, and disdain a division.
While with patriot pride,
To our laws we're allied,
No foe can subdue us, no faction divide.
For ne'er shall the sons, &c.

Verse 6:
Our mountains are crowned with imperial oak;
Whose roots, like our liberties, ages have nourished;
But lone e'er our nation submits to the yoke,
Not a tree shall be left on the field where it flourished.
Should invasion impend,
Every grove would descend,
From the hill-tops, they shaded, our shores to defend.
For ne'er shall the sons, &c.

Verse 7:
Let our patriots destroy Anarch's pestilent worm;
Lest our Liberty's growth should be checked by corrosion;
Then let clouds thicken round us; we heed not the storm;
Our realm fears no shock, but the earth's own explosion.

Foes assail us in vain,
Though their fleets bridge the main,
For our altars and laws with our lives we'll maintain.
For ne'er shall the sons, &c.

Verse 8:
Should the Tempest of War overshadow our land,
Its bolts could ne'er rend Freedom's temple asunder;
For, unmoved, at its portal, would Washington stand,
And repulse, with his Breast, the assaults of the thunder!
His sword, from the sleep
Of its scabbard would leap,
And conduct, with its point, ev'ry flash to the deep!
For ne'er shall the sons, &c.

Verse 9:
Let Fame to the world sound America's voice;
No intrigues can her sons from their government sever;
Her pride is her Adams; Her laws are his choice,
And shall flourish, till Liberty slumbers forever.
Then unite heart and hand,
Like Leonidas' band,
And swear to the God of the ocean and land;
That ne'er shall the sons of Columbia be slaves,
While the earth bears a plant, or the sea rolls its waves.

From the original sheet music "Adams and Liberty"
Printed and Sold by P.A. von Hagen Jr. & Cos. (Boston, MA), 1799 - 1800

"Adams and Liberty" fails to mention Adams by name in any other capacity than the title and briefly in the final verse. The song does, however, mention the country's liberties and, through the title, associates John Adams with the country's progress and the freedom it has acquired. Furthermore, the song offers a warning to those who would collude against the nation—the country will come to arms to protect itself and the liberty it had so bravely fought for in its recent past. On the surface, these are all great ideals to have associated with a candidate, but they are not in reference to anything in particular Adams had done for the country, making this song less effective than it potentially could have been on the campaign trail.

Conversely, the songs that were provided by Jefferson's supporters discussed the candidate and the achievements that were directly associated with him. One of Jefferson's songs, "The Son of Liberty," was set to the tune of "Variety"[11] and discussed Jefferson's exploits in significant depth:

Verse 1:
Music lend thy pleasing aid,
Freedom's will must be obeyed,
Sing, she cries with life and glee,
To the son of liberty.

Verse 2:
He the Declaration framed,
Independence, that proclaimed,
Columbia owes that great decree,
To the son of liberty.

Verse 3:
Acting in a noble cause,
He abolished cruel laws,
Set the mind and body free,
He's the son of liberty.

Verse 4:
Sent unto a foreign court,
There he firmly did support,
His country's rights and dignity,
Like a son of liberty.

Verse 5:
And at home his actions tell,
That he filled his station well,
Bold intriguers foiled we see,
By the son of liberty.

Verse 6:
Reason, knowledge, truth combined,
Deep research with learning joined,
Virtue, mild philosophy,
Form the son of liberty.

Verse 7:
Public virtue, private worth,
In his character shine forth,
Jefferson the great is he,
And the son of liberty.

Verse 8:
Few like Jefferson we find
'mong the sons of human kind,
Friend of peace and honesty
Is the son of liberty.

Verse 9:
Hark! What voices rend the sky!
Lo, the sovereign people cry,
Jefferson shall leader be,
Honored son of liberty.

As found in *Songs America Voted By: From George Washington to Richard Nixon—
the Gutsy Story of Presidential Campaigning* by Irwin Silber
Published by Stackpole Books (Harrisburg, PA), 1971

In many ways "The Son of Liberty" could be thought of as a singing biography of the candidate; this in-depth treatment of the candidate's personal characteristics gives it more specificity than the Adams' campaign song, making it potentially more persuasive to the electorate. Unlike other campaign songs of this era, "Jefferson and Liberty" went into the significant details of Jefferson's life and explained why he would make a good president.

While we see campaign music used in this election, it was not with the force that one might expect. In fact, as with Washington, many of these songs in 1800 were still not "campaign" songs in the modern sense of the term. Most of the songs that survive were written for the inauguration, and subsequent years in office, to promote the current president.[12] Thus, these songs were written for the winners after the fact, acting to boost presidential approval. One might look to these songs as very early "campaign" songs for a second term, as can be seen with "Adams and Liberty," which was written in 1798 and subsequently used in the 1800 election. One of the more notable songs of this type is "Jefferson and Liberty," which, like "Adams and Liberty," was also written by Robert Treat Paine Jr. The song's title gives reference to the previous rendition of Paine's "Adams and Liberty." This could be viewed as a jab at Adams, who came in third in the election, thus losing both the presidency and the vice presidency. It could also be a reflection of Paine's loss of support for Adams (interestingly, Paine's father, Robert Treat Paine, signed the Declaration of Independence with both Adams and Jefferson). The song was set to the tune of "Gobby-O," an old Irish tune popular at the time.

Verse 1:
The gloomy night before us flies,
The reign of terror now is o'er;
Its gags, inquisitors, and spies,
Its herds of harpies are no more!
(Chorus)

Chorus:
Rejoice! Columbia's sons, rejoice!
To tyrants never bend the knee;
But join with heart and soul and voice,
For Jefferson and Liberty.

Verse 2:
O'er vast Columbia's varied clime,
Her cities, forests, shores and dales,
In rising majesty sublime,
Immortal Liberty prevails.
(Chorus)

Verse 3:
Hail, long expected, glorious day!
Illustrious, memorable morn,
That freedom's fabric from decay
Rebuilds, for millions yet unborn.
(Chorus)

Verse 4:
His country's glory, hope, and stay,
In virtue and in talents tried,
Now rises to assume the sway,
O'er freedom's temple to preside.
(Chorus)

Verse 5:
Within its hallowed walls immense,
No hireling shall e'er arise,
Arrayed in Tyranny's defense,
To crush an injured people's cries.
(Chorus)

Verse 6:
No lordling here, with gorging jaws,
Shall wring from industry the food;
Nor fiery bigot's holy laws
Lay waste our fields and streets in blood.
(Chorus)

Verse 7:
Here strangers, from a thousand shores,
Compelled by tyranny to roam,
Shall find, amidst abundant stores,
A nobler and a happier home.
(Chorus)

Verse 8:
Here art shall lift her laureled head,
Wealth, industry, and peace divine;
And where dark, pathless forests spread,
Rich fields and lofty cities shine.
(Chorus)

Verse 9:
From Europe's wants and woes re-
mote,
A friendly waste of waves between,
Here plenty cheers the humblest cot,
And smiles on every village green.
(Chorus)

Verse 10:
Here, free as air's expanded space,
To every soul and sect shall be
The sacred priv'lege of race,
The worship of the Deity.
(Chorus)

Verse 11:
These gifts, great Liberty, are thine;
Ten thousand more we owe to thee—
Immortal may their mem'ries shine
Who fought and died for Liberty.
(Chorus)

Verse 12:
What heart but hails a scene so bright,
What soul but inspiration draws,
Who would not guard so dear a right,
Or die in such a glorious cause?
(Chorus)

Verse13:
Let foes to freedom dread the name;
But should they touch the sacred tree,
Twice fifty thousand swords would
flame
For Jefferson and Liberty.
(Chorus)

Verse 14:
From Georgia to Lake Champlain,
From seas to Mississippi's shore,
The sons of Freedom loud proclaim,
The Reign of Terror now is o'er.
(Chorus)

As found in *The New Green Mountain Songster: Traditional Folk Songs of Vermont*
    by Helen Hartness Flanders
Published by Yale University Press (New Haven, CT), 1939

The song reflects the joyous atmosphere of the country at Jefferson's election to the presidency in 1800. The opening verse notes how the "reign of terror now is o'er." This referred to the Alien and Sedition Acts, passed in 1798, which limited speech critical of the Federalist-controlled government.[13] Once he took office, President Jefferson pardoned those who had been prosecuted under the Acts. "Jefferson and Liberty" also speaks of Jefferson as one who will defend our country from the "tyrants" who wish to do the country harm. Bob Waltz has noted about this song that "it never went into tradition [referring to the oral tradition of passing down music from generation to generation]. . . but it stayed 'in print' better than any campaign song prior to 1860."[14] After being used to celebrate Jefferson's 1800 victory, it was used again as a reelection campaign song in 1804.[15] Still, the level of specificity about the candidate (or the elected president) expressed in "The Son of Liberty" and "Jefferson and Liberty" was rare for this time period.

From Liberty to Good Feelings and the Man

Like "Adams and Liberty" the songs of the 1808 election did not bring to the forefront the name of the candidate running for office in any way other than to briefly mention them in the body of the song. This can be seen in "Madison, Union and Liberty," which also continues the trend of presidential songs with the word "liberty" in the title.

Verse 1:
As yon effulgent orb of light
With beaming glory sinks to rest,
Veiled in a gloomy cloud of night
His splendors vanish from the West,
So Jefferson to shade retires,
But Madison, like morn, appears,
Fresh confidence and hope inspires,
And light again the nation cheers
Huzza for Madison! Huzza!
For Union and America!

Verse 2:
Late have the foes to freedom sought
Our happy Union to divide;
For which our heroes bravely fought,
For which our patriots bravely died.
But vain their efforts yet have proved,
The temple, still unshaken, stands,
Nor by the power of faction moved,
Nor leveled by rebellion's hands.
Huzza for Liberty! Huzza!
For Union and America!

Verse 3:
For should the Tories all unite,
And join again with British foes,
Hell would rejoice at such a sight,
But heav'n in justice interpose;
Millions of freemen, firm and brave,
Would grasp the keen avenging steel,
Lightning would storm o'er every wave
And thunders from our Navy peal.
To blast the wretch who dare betray
The PEOPLE OF AMERICA

Verse 4:
Then join, ye friends of Freedom, join!
For lo! Sedition marches forth;
With whom infernal fiends combine,
The South to sever from the North;
To crush the traitors of our land,
Be ready at a moment's call,
United—safely shall we stand—
Divided—we are sure to fall:
Long may Columbians live to see
Pow'r, Union, Peace and Liberty.

As found in *Songs America Voted By: From George Washington to Richard Nixon— the Gutsy Story of Presidential Campaigning* by Irwin Silber
Published by Stackpole Books (Harrisburg, PA), 1971

While the song compares Madison to the morning in his readiness to take his position in the White House, the text serves more as a tribute to the outgoing president, Thomas Jefferson. It also reminded the electorate of those who fought for the liberty of the country and what is needed to defend that liberty, which is in this case the election of Madison. Indeed, the song is more about the country and its people than any particular candidate. Within the context of that message, Madison is held up as the next person within the Democratic-Republican Party who will move the country in the right direction, continuing the work of Jefferson. The other known campaign song for Madison in 1808, "Huzzah for Madison, Huzzah," also spoke in general terms about the candidate. It was effectively a shorter version of "Madison, Union and Liberty," using several of the same lines. In both cases, the use of the term "huzza" or "huzzah" was the nineteenth-century equivalent of "hurrah" or "hooray" today. If there were campaign songs of Madison's Federalist opponents in 1808 and 1812, Charles Cotesworth Pinckney and DeWitt Clinton, no evidence of their music has survived. Madison easily won both elections.

For the next few decades, presidential campaign songs followed this method—they briefly mentioned the candidate for whom they were written, but each song was more of a patriotic rallying cry. Another example of this was in James Monroe's campaign song, "Monroe Is the Man." Written to the tune of Joseph Mazzinghi's "Young Lochinvar,"[16] the song's lyrics are as follows:

> Oh say sov'reign people whose voice is the law,
> Whose will is supreme, and keeps factions in awe;
> Who shall o'er the Union dear vessel preside,
> Shall sit at the helm and course wisely guide?
> Among the best pilots say who leads the van,
> O! say sov'reign people which, which is the man?
>
> Is it him whose whole life has so constantly shewn,
> That the cause of the people was ever his own?
> The firm friend of freedom in every sphere,
> Whose conscience 'mong kings and 'mong courts still was clear.
> Whose actions grow brighter the nearer we scan,
> O! Say sov'reign people—which—which is the man?
>
> Who cares not for office for pow'r or for place,
> But whose merits and virtues the highest would grace,
> Whose country's his Idol, her good all his care,
> And in the worst times who did never despair;
> In Peace and in War—who can act and can plan,
> O! Say sov'reign people—which—which is the man?
>
> O! 'tis easy to tell without speaking his name,
> So well is he known in the records of fame,
> To him much we owe, and on him we depend,
> We can ne'er be deceived in so faithful a friend;
> He's the Man that we love—for to hate him who can,
> MONROE—yes MONROE—he indeed is the man.

As found in *Songs America Voted By: From George Washington to Richard Nixon— the Gutsy Story of Presidential Campaigning* by Irwin Silber
Published by Stackpole Books (Harrisburg, PA), 1971

Much like the respective songs for Adams and Madison, "Monroe Is the Man" is partly a patriotic song about the country and partly vague praise for the candidate. Combine this with the fact that the song does not even mention Monroe's name until the very end, and this might seem like a poorly constructed campaign song. After all, part of the goal of a campaign song would seem to be to get the listener to learn about the candidate and like him or her. The composition of "Monroe Is the Man" does not appear to do this very well. In another time, this may have been a problem for Monroe. However, when he ran for the presidency in 1816, Monroe, a Democratic-Republican, faced little real opposition from the Federalist Rufus King, winning the Electoral College 183-34.[17] Indeed, the Federalist Party was dying, and the country was entering what historians would later refer to as the "Era of Good Feelings," where the country was basically a one-party state. Monroe easily cruised to victory in 1820, winning all but one Electoral College vote.[18] During this period, campaign music did not have to be very specific or even refer much to the candidates, as the races were not very competitive. That, though, would soon change.

Power to the People

In 1824, there were four major contenders for the presidency, each one representing the Democratic-Republican Party: John Quincy Adams, Andrew Jackson, William H. Crawford, and Henry Clay. The main thing that divided the candidates was that they each represented a different geographical area of the country. The only known song that was used in the 1824 campaign was Jackson's "The Hunters of Kentucky" (set to the tune of "Miss Bailey"), which extolled the candidate's virtues. The song became quite popular, and Jackson would use it again when he ran for the presidency in 1828.[19]

Although Jackson had more Electoral College votes and a higher percentage of the popular vote than any of the other candidates, he did not have a majority in the Electoral College. This threw the election into the House of Representatives, which, under the leadership of Speaker of the House Henry Clay, eventually gave the presidency to John Quincy Adams. When Adams then appointed Clay secretary of state, Jackson was less than pleased and returned to run against Adams four years later.[20]

Given the background, it is quite understandable why the election of 1828 was a bitter one. Political parties reformed around the two main candidates, with Jackson nominated by the Democrats and Adams nominated by the new National Republican Party. Beginning in this era, suffrage was slowly being expanded to white men who were property-less, a class that had largely been denied the franchise. The 1828 election also marked the beginning of a new era, whereby more average voters, not just congressional caucuses, would have a say in nominating presidential candidates.[21] In 1800, members of Congress from both the Federalists and the Democratic-Republicans started nominating presidential candidates. This practice was known as the congressional nominating caucus, and eventually came to be called the "King Caucus" because it was seen by many people around the country as an undemocratic way to nominate presidential candidates. In 1824, only 66 members of Congress attended the caucus, and they nominated William Crawford, who finished third in the Electoral College and fourth in the popular vote that year. This was largely the case because Crawford suffered a debilitating stroke in August of 1823, but this fact was concealed from the King Caucus, and they still nominated him. The failure of the King Caucus to fulfill its duty to the satisfaction of most voters resulted in no congressional caucus being held in 1828. Instead, in 1828 both Jackson and Adams were nominated by various state legislatures.[22]

This resulted in emotional appeals that had not been seen since the election of 1800, and each side was knee-deep in the mud it was slinging at the other candidate. For instance, one of Jackson's campaign songs, "Jackson Toast," decried the 1824 deal that Henry Clay struck to give Adams the presidency. Similarly, Jackson's "The Hickory Tree" not only described why Jackson was a war hero at the Battle of New Orleans; it also made several disparaging remarks toward President John Quincy Adams:

> While Jonny was lounging on crimson and down,
> And stuffing both pockets with pelf,
> Brave Andrew was pulling John Bull's colors down,
> And paying his army himself.
>
> While Jonny was gorging the fat of the land
> And bartering for Cod, d'ye see—
> Brave Jackson was feeding his patriot band,
> On nuts of the Hickory tree.
>
> While Jonny made journeys, yet never stirred out,
> At twenty-five dollars per day,
> Bold Jackson o'er mountains and swamps took his rout,
> And mortgaged his lands for the pay.
>
> When Jonny had bought his commission of Clay,
> And mounted the throne, d'ye see,
> Brave Jackson disgusted at rouges turn'd away
> And again sought his Hickory tree.
>
> From the original sheet music "The Hickory Tree"
> Published by Elton, Printer (New York) 1828

Note the greater level of specificity about Jackson that was involved in "The Hickory Tree" when compared to the earlier campaign songs. The level of negativity toward the opponent is also striking, even to the point of disparagingly referring to a sitting president by first name only.

Adams fought back with mudslinging songs of his own. For instance, "Adams and Clay," in addition to speaking to the virtues of the president, referred to Jackson as a potential "tyrant." Even more insulting was "Little Wat Ye Wha's A-comin'," set to the traditional Scottish tune, "Highland Muster Roll."[23] The song's title, "Little Wat Ye Wha's A-comin'," is roughly translated from traditional Scottish as "Little know you who is coming."[24] The song predicted what America would be with Jackson as president:

Little wat ye wha's a-comin',
Little wat ye wha's a-comin',
Little wat ye wha's a-comin',
Murder wi' gory han's a-comin',
Fire's a-comin', swords a-comin',
Pistols, guns an' knives are comin',
Nero's comin', Hero's comin',
Forbye the second section's comin',

Little wat ye wha's a-comin',
Little wat ye wha's a-comin',
Little wat ye wha's a-comin',
Martial an' Lynch's Law are comin',
Slavery's comin', Blunder's comin',
Robbing's comin', Jobbing's comin',
An' a' the plague o' War's a-comin'.

Little wat ye wha's a-comin',
Little wat ye wha's a-comin',
Little wat ye wha's a-comin',
JUGGERNAUT himsel' is comin',
He'll fret and fume, he'll shoot and stab,
He'll stamp an' swear "like any drab,"
He'll play Jack Cade—hang honest men,
An' after that Calhoun's a-comin'.

As found in the *Cincinnati Gazette*
Published July 30, 1828

Indeed, this pro-Adams song compares Jackson to the infamous Roman emperor Nero and claims Jackson is a corrupt, pro-slavery murderer who will take the law into his own hands if elected. Again, the level of specificity against Jackson is much greater than what voters had been accustomed to in most early campaign songs. More voters bought into Jackson's negative lyrics than Adams' negative lyrics, as Jackson handily defeated Adams in 1828, with 56% of the popular vote and an Electoral College margin of 178-83.[25] In any event, this increased competition among an expanded electorate began a change in musical campaign usage. Such changing use of song would continue and come into fruition in 1840.

Tippecanoe and the Music Too!!!

Although the election of 1828 included greatly expanded and in-depth use of music compared to most prior presidential elections, it was not a watershed moment in electoral music history. The 1828 election was mired in personal mudslinging, which helped spur on additional use of songs to create emotional appeals. The election was not a "singing campaign" as much as it was one of defamation and denigration.

Indeed, it was not until the election of 1840 that music took a central place in American presidential campaigns. As noted by Studwell and VandeCreek:

> Most songs created by the fertile minds of humans have a much shorter life than that of the species which brought them to life. This is particularly true for most special occasion compositions, and when the subject of the pieces is a volatile presidential campaign which often focuses on ephemeral issues, the cultural life of the song is indeed short. Yet some campaigns are of tremendous historical significance and the songs which added spice and energy to the political process are as a result of lasting interest.[26]

Most campaign music up until the 1840 election fell into the former category: the songs were written for a given campaign, but they were soon forgotten. In this sense, pre-1840 campaign music was in the background. However, the introduction of "Tippecanoe and Tyler Too," or "Tip and Ty" for short, in the 1840 election, brought about music's grand entrance into the political forefront. Set to the tune of "Little Pigs,"[27] the song sang the praises of the Whig presidential candidate William Henry Harrison and his running mate John Tyler. "Tippecanoe and Tyler Too" painted them as the down-to-earth candidates of the people, while demeaning their opponent, the incumbent Democratic President Martin Van Buren:

Verse 1:
What's the cause of this commotion, motion, motion,
Our country through?
It is the ball a-rolling on
For Tippecanoe and Tyler too.

Chorus:
For Tippecanoe and Tyler too.
And with them we'll beat little Van, Van, Van,
Van is a used up man.
And with them we'll beat little Van.

Verse 2:
Like the rushing of mighty waters, waters, waters,
On it will go!
And in its course will clear the way
For Tippecanoe and Tyler too.
(Chorus)

Verse 3:
See the Loco standard tottering, tottering, tottering,
Down it must go!
And in its place we'll rear the flag

Of Tippecanoe and Tyler too.
(Chorus)

Verse 4:
The Bay State boys turned out in
thousands, thousands, thousands,
Not long ago,
And at Bunker Hill they set their seals
For Tippecanoe and Tyler too.
(Chorus)

Verse 5:
Have you heard from old Vermont,
mount, mount
All honest and true?
The Green Mountain boys are rolling
the ball
For Tippecanoe and Tyler too.
(Chorus)

Verse 6:
Don't you hear from every quarter,
quarter, quarter,
Good news and true?
That swift the ball is rolling on
For Tippecanoe and Tyler too.
(Chorus)

Verse 7:
Now you hear the Vanjacks talking,
talking, talking,
Things look quite blue,
For all the world seems turning round
For Tippecanoe and Tyler too.
(Chorus)

Verse 8:
Let them talk about hard cider, cider,
cider,
And Log Cabins too,
It will only help to speed the ball
For Tippecanoe and Tyler too.
(Chorus)

Verse 9:
His latchstring hangs outside the door,
door, door,
And is never pulled through,
For it never was the custom of
Old Tippecanoe, and Tyler too.
(Chorus)

Verse 10:
He always had his tables set, set, set,
For all honest and true,
To ask you in to take a bite
With Tippecanoe, and Tyler too.
(Chorus)

Verse 11:
See the spoilsmen and leg-treasures,
treasures, treasures,
All in a stew!
For well they know they stand no
chance
With Tippecanoe and Tyler too.
(Chorus)

Verse 12:
Little Matty's days are numbered, numbered, numbered,
Out he must go!
And in his place we'll put the good
Old Tippecanoe and Tyler too.
(Chorus)

As found in *Tippecanoe Song of the Log Cabin Boys and Girls of 1840,* edited by
    Anthony Banning Norton
Published by A.B. Norton and Co. (Mount Vernon, OH), 1888

This song has been recognized by many scholars as playing a very influential role in the 1840 election. It helped Harrison win the presidency and began the great singing campaigns of the 1800s. Journalist Irwin Silber wrote that this song, "firmly established the power of singing as a campaign device"[28] within the United States. Writing in *The North American Review* at the time, Helen Johnson said that the song "was to the political canvass of 1840 what the Marseillaise was to the French Revolution. It sang Harrison into the Presidency."[29] Johnson went on to say in her article that, "[t]hrough this half-martial, half-rollicking melody the pent-up feelings of a people whose banks were suspended, whose laborers were out of work, who were pinched by hard times, and to whom the Whigs promised "two dollars a day and roast beef," had found expression, and the song was sung throughout the country as if by madmen."[30]

As noted by Danny O. Crew in his book *Presidential Sheet Music*, "to quote an anonymous Democrat of the day, upon losing the election: 'We have been sung down, lied down [and] drunk down.'"[31] Anthony Norton, a casual observer of the election in 1840, wrote of the election in his 1888 book, *The Great Revolution*: "The songs waked [*sic*] the people up in 1840 and played a very important part on the great Revolution. In the cabins, upon the roads, in the towns and cities, everywhere, sweet voices were singing the songs for 'Tippecanoe and Tyler Too.'"[32]

The lyrics emphasize the virtuous qualities of Harrison and Tyler as the candidates of the people, with references to the "log cabin" and "hard cider." The song also painted Harrison as a war hero with the reference to his victory at the 1811 Battle of Tippecanoe, while at the same time denigrating the vices of Van Buren. At its core, the song attempts to appeal to the listener and persuade that person to have a positive view of the candidate associated with the song. It tries to do this by giving the impression that Harrison and Tyler have all of the qualities necessary for the presidency, while indicating that Van Buren does not. The song does this over twelve verses, which is quite long compared to most previous campaign songs. Another interesting point about "Tippecanoe and Tyler Too" is that it does not touch on any of the issues associated with the campaign. The song in essence is used to help the candidate gain popularity while avoiding the questions circulating around the campaign, which was likely the goal of those who had supported Harrison in his presidential bid. In fact, it mentions some potentially negative personal aspects about the candidate (such as the fact that Harrison was accused of drinking too much) and turns them into positives for the voting public by mocking them. This was perhaps an intentional strategy on the part of the Harrison campaign, as Whig leaders had previously blamed defeats on a lack of "appeal to the masses" from their candidate.[33] Richard Houghton expressed this in his editorial in the 1838 Frankfort (KY) *Commonwealth*, where he suggested criteria that should be used for selecting for their candidate, "that man. . . who can bring into the contest the greatest capital in popularity, with the smallest drawback of popular dislike. . . . [o]nly General

Harrison. . . has yet given evidence. . . of capacity, integrity, sound sense, and genuine patriotism; and who possesses above all, that essential requisite. . . to wit, the favor and goodwill of the mass of the people—in other words popularty."[34] Houghton claimed that the presidential election had essentially been turned into a popularity contest, an idea that would carry into future elections.

Prior to 1840, the campaign music was not widespread and, in many cases, was typically used in a satirical fashion. There was not necessarily a great deal of value to these songs for the candidates, especially considering the way in which these songs were usually constructed, oftentimes not focusing on the candidate enough. What happened in 1840 that made music such a powerful force within the election?

As noted above, the King Caucus system ended in 1824. In 1828, state legislatures nominated the presidential candidates, thus meaning more people were involved in the process. Four years later in 1832, all three candidates had been nominated by national conventions: Jackson of the Democrats (by this time the Democratic-Republicans were known simply as the Democrats), Henry Clay of the National Republican Party, and William Wirt of the Anti-Masonic Party.[35] This allowed for even more people to be included in presidential nominations, thus lending itself to more use of music to appeal to these participants.

By the mid to late 1830s more citizens were also taking part not just in the nomination but also in the election of U.S. presidents. Old restrictions on the right to vote related to property qualifications were being abolished in the late 1820s and throughout the 1830s as part of Jacksonian reforms. As noted by one scholar, the right to vote and democracy was developing "by fits and starts" during this era.[36] Because the right to vote was being granted to all white men, regardless of whether they owned real estate, the electorate expanded an astonishing sixty percent during the short period of 1836 to 1840![37] Accordingly, Irwin Silber suggests that "1840 is a tidewater mark in American politics for a variety of reasons, and the development of mass campaign techniques, of which singing may have been the flamboyant, reflected more deep-going changes in the American electoral pattern—namely, the institutionalization of the party system and the popular selection of presidential electors."[38] As voting qualifications were no longer limited to those who owned property, more and more men were being granted the franchise during the early decades of the nineteenth century.

In addition, more than just men were participating within the election. Although women were still not allowed to vote, by the middle of the nineteenth century they were becoming increasingly involved in American politics. According to one contemporary observer, 1840 was "the first campaign in which women generally engaged, and, by their smiles and songs and encouragement, promoted the election."[39] Indeed, during this era women were increasingly entering the political realm in the United States. By the early 1840s, Lucretia Mott and Margaret Fuller were becoming active in the suffrage movement, and one of the crowning achievements of the early women's rights movement was the 1848

Seneca Falls Convention. Thus, by the 1840s politics was democratizing in leaps and bounds in the United States, quickly moving away from an interest of the landed gentry.

At the same time, by 1840 the United States had developed into a full two-party system, in which the Democrats and the Whigs were competing for power. Although the United States briefly had a two-party system emerge in the late 1790s, the Democratic-Republican Party quickly began dismantling the Federalists in 1800 and subsequent elections. Adams, who lost in 1800, was the last Federalist elected president. Beginning in 1800, the Democratic-Republican Party won a majority of congressional seats in every election for decades. From 1800-1820, they controlled between 63% and 86% of House seats; during the same period, the party controlled between 53% and 86%.[40] As noted above, by the early 1820s, the Federalist Party was dead, America was effectively a one-party state, and the Era of Good Feelings was in full swing. This did not last long, however. The fissures that developed within the Democratic-Republican Party in 1824 led to a party realignment in 1828 between the Democrats and the short-lived National Republican Party; during the 1830s the Democratic opposition became the Whigs, a party which remained the alternative to the Democrats until Lincoln's Republicans emerged in the 1850s. Thus, by 1840, not only were more people able to vote. In addition, there were two viable political parties once again competing for votes. These changes in the American political system required presidential candidates to bring their messages to the people in ways that were unnecessary for George Washington a half century earlier. In any changing political environment, successful campaigns tend to be the ones that most quickly and most fully adapt to the transformed conditions, and the vast sea change occurring in the early to mid-nineteenth-century made 1840 a year where some major adaptations became necessary.

Indeed, music became an important new vehicle for politics in an era where the electorate was expanding and parties were fully competitive. A song set to a catchy melody could spread campaign ideas across the land in ways that speeches could not. It is one thing to memorize a candidate's speech and repeat the gist of it to others you meet. It is quite another to hear a catchy tune and sing it to others (think of the *Cheers* Albania song from the introduction). A song, as a mnemonic device, is much easier for the casual listener to remember later when compared with a speech. According to one witness of the time, songs in support of Harrison did more than help the listener remember about the candidate; they also had a profoundly negative influence on the electorate as a whole:

> Whig songs were so riveted upon the mind. . . that they can correctly quote from memory that which was so distasteful. . . Men, women and children did nothing but sing. . . The writer can remember of many wives and daughters of Democrats joining in the singing, and how mad the husbands and fathers were, and what fantastic tricks some of them cut in their rage, and all to no purpose; the singing still went on. We know of daughters being locked up to prevent

their singing Whig songs, and of their company being unceremoniously turned out of houses to which they had been invited by irate parents.[41]

While this might have been a bit of hyperbole written by a Whig opponent, it is more evidence of the music's impact by someone who was there. Even if no one was "locked up" or "turned out" for singing these songs, the fact remains that the 1840 election was a turning point for electoral songs in this country, and one where music was now infinitely more important to campaigning.

One other aspect that may have made "Tippecanoe and Tyler Too" so effective is that it used the campaign slogan (or perhaps the campaign slogan was derived from the song) giving it further potency than other campaign songs to this time. The slogan and the music were thus working hand in hand to help constituents remember the names of the candidates and their traits. This technique would be used sporadically in a few other nineteenth-century elections. We will not, however, see this technique used consistently until the 1924 election of Calvin Coolidge. One may wonder why songwriters for campaigns would not think to utilize this method considering the effectiveness in which it was implemented within the campaigns of Harrison and Tyler. Regardless, the effect of campaign music in influencing the electorate had been established and would continue to be used in significant ways with political campaigns for the future.

Don't Judge a Songbook by Its Cover

The use of music of this period went well beyond the use of just a song or two, extending itself also into entire songbooks that were written for a political party or a specific candidate. From 1788-1836, political songbooks were available with titles from "The American Songster" to "The American Patriotic Songbook." Most of these songbooks were generalized, presenting a variety of politically motivated songs (some associated with political candidates) for public consumption. However, with the 1840 election of Harrison, a more specialized songbook began to come into prominence for each election. With titles like "The Harrison and Log Cabin Songbook" and "A Miniature of Martin Van Buren," it is obvious that the tactic was not just to have a main political theme song, but rather a variety of songs that one's supporters could sing to spread the word. Like a good political slogan, a useful song can be remembered easily by the masses (many of whom still could not read at that time), making the message easy to transport from locale to locale and disseminate among the populace. Just like having any campaign music is better than having none, having multiple songs to tell people of your candidate only increases the odds that your candidate will be remembered favorably on election day. This technique was not in full use until 1840, as it was in that year that the number of songs used in presidential campaigns exploded.

Another strong explanation for the growth of the songbook during this era involved the technological developments surrounding the printing press. In the early nineteenth century, the printing press had undergone few major changes since Johannes Gutenberg's invention of a manual moveable type machine and subsequent printing of the Bible in 1455. One of the more significant changes that occurred prior to the nineteenth century was made by Ottaviano Petrucci. Petrucci devised a way to print using multiple impressions, which consists of printing on the same piece of paper two or three times, in the late fifteenth century. This allowed him to print the staves, followed by the notes, followed by the song text. This made music much clearer on the page and, consequently, easier to read as compared to the traditional single impression method of Gutenberg.[42] However, by 1814, Germans Friederich Koenig and Andreas Bauer had invented for London printers a moveable print bed that was run by steam power. This greatly increased the speed at which newspapers, books, and other works could be printed and published. In the 1820s and 1830s, this technology began taking off in the United States. These technological innovations culminated in 1840, when R. Hoe & Company created a revolving press that could print eight pages at one time.[43]

This evolution of printing technology had an immediate impact on the use of songs for political purposes. Indeed, politicians soon saw that this new technology could be used in elections. With these faster presses in the middle of the nineteenth century, songbooks could be printed at a rapid rate and then quickly distributed during a quickly changing campaign. This became another way for candidates to disseminate their songs beyond having them sung at rallies and then reproduced orally by those who had been at the event.

This trend of "songbooks" continued well into the twentieth century. The election of 1900 produced 23 songsters (12 Republican, 10 Democrat, and one Prohibition Party) including "The Democratic National Campaign Song Book for 1900" and the "Republican Hot Shot: A Campaign Songster for 1900."[44] The 1904 election produced only seven songsters (five Republican and two Democrat) including the "Roosevelt Campaign Songster" and the "Parker Campaign Song Book."[45] The 1908 election produced just four including the "Socialist Campaign Songs" and the "Taft and Sherman Campaign Songster, 1908" (there is no Democratic campaign songster of record for the 1908 election).[46] The 1912 campaign would again produce only seven songsters with them evenly divided: one Democrat, two Republican, two Progressive Party, and two Socialist Party, while the 1916 campaign would produce only five total songsters.[47] Compare this with the election of 1864 in which no fewer than 28 songsters were produced and one can see that the use of the songbook had been slowly in decline leading into and during the early part of the twentieth-century. It was with the election of 1924, however, the year of the first radio election, that we see the use of campaign songbooks and songsters become almost non-existent, with some years producing none at all as can be seen in 1932.[48] As we will discuss in more detail in chapter three, this decline in use of songbooks, is likely due to candidates moving their musical campaigns to the radio airwaves.

As mentioned earlier, the early campaign songs relied on the use of popular or familiar tunes with new texts added by the authors of the songs. The use of popular/familiar songs was essential to these early campaign songs. As is true today, popular tunes are known by many of the people and are more than likely sung by them with some regularity. This allows the population to grab onto a campaign song with relative ease. Imagine if campaigns had an original musical score written for every campaign song. Perhaps it might make the discussion of campaign music far more interesting from a musical perspective, but it loses its effectiveness as a type of propaganda. If people attend a campaign stop and hear an unknown tune one or perhaps two times, they may walk away curious, and even liking what they heard. But more than likely, they would be unable to remember the tune, and consequently the text of the song. However, using a tune that the electorate hears and sings on a regular basis gives the candidate the advantage of a tune they will most assuredly remember. This is also of particular importance when considering the length of many of these campaign songs after 1840, as many of them have six, eight, ten or more verses of text that are used to inform voters about the candidates.

The second part of this formula is text. In the early campaign songs examined heretofore, the lyrics almost always mentioned the candidate's name, but usually no more than once or twice. By the 1840s, songs mention a candidate's name repeatedly throughout the song. Indeed, each verse in "Tippecanoe and Tyler Too" refers to the candidates' names; the chorus also refers to them and negatively mentions the opponent, Martin Van Buren. Since the public already knows the tune to the song, they are able to join in with the words and easily take the song home with them, prepared to hum it to themselves or even sing it in the presence of others. In fact, the idea probably was to use one of the more catchy tunes, so a person might sing the songs all the way home. Putting these two elements together gives a campaign a combination that will greatly increase the chance that people will remember the candidate's name and keep it on the tip of their tongues throughout the election cycle. As we see with elections of the modern era, name recognition and the ability of a candidate to keep his or her name active among the electorate is of great importance when running a political campaign. Before the birth of the modern mass media, there was not twenty-four-hour news coverage on cable television or the radio, so being able to spread a candidate's name and bring forth admirable qualities in song was an invaluable tool, and one that most candidates and supporters were eager to exploit. This formula of using a popular tune and inserting the candidate's name and qualities frequently within the text was a necessity for early campaign songs to make sure that they could be remembered long after that campaign stop had ended. It remained a staple of campaigns well into the 1970s.

Indeed, this formula is employed by the majority of all campaign songs that were written well into the twentieth century. Examining the songbooks for Harrison and Tyler reveals songs such as "Harrison" set to the tune of "Yankee Doodle," "The Log Cabin and Hard Cider Candidate" set to the tune of "Auld Lang Syne" and "Little Vanny" set to the tune of "Rosin the Beau." A sampling of some of the other popular and/or familiar tunes that were used regularly for campaign songs were: "John Brown's Body," "Old Dan Tucker," "The Star-Spangled Banner," "Marching Through Georgia," and "Wait for the Wagon." This trend truly began in 1840.

Accentuate the Negative?!?

This does not mean that the only songs written were ones designed to positively introduce a candidate's name to the public. Just like politics of today, candidates have been using a "negative" campaign strategy for centuries, something we have already seen in 1800 and 1828. In the 1840 election there was substantial evidence that the Democratic Party was showing signs of frustration with Harrison and Tyler's use of music to persuade the electorate without substantially touching on the major issues. This led them to use music to fight back against Harrison and the Whig Party. Songs such as "The Last Whig Song" set to the tune of "Old King Cole," "When This Old Hat Was New" set to a tune of the same name, and, a song that attacked the Log Cabin and Hard Cider appeal of Harrison, "Bullet Proof (or The Hero Who Never Lost a Battle)" set to the tune of "Auld Lang Syne":

Verse 1:
Oh, no, he never lost a flight!
He's even bullet proof!
For why? When e'er the battle raged,
He always kept aloof!
    He always kept aloof, my friends,
    He always kept aloof,
    And that's the reason why Old Tip
    Was always bullet proof!

Verse 2:
'Twas very cautious in Old Tip,
'Twas very brave and fair—
The more our British foes came on,
The more he wasn't there!
    The more he wasn't there, my
    friends,
    The more he wasn't there,
    And that's the reason why Old Tip

Was always bullet proof!

Verse 3:
'Twas very lucky for him too,
It was, it was indeed!
The more he didn't get a wound,
The more he didn't bleed!
    The more he didn't bleed, my
    friends,
    The more he didn't bleed,
    And that's the reason why Old Tip
    Was always bullet proof!

Verse 4:
But while retreating through the wood,
And through the tangled fern,
He tore his mustn't-mention-'ems
And had to put on her'n.
    And had to put on her'n, my friends,

And had to put on her'n,
And that's the reason why Old Tip
Was always bullet proof!

Verse 5:
And thus the war path he did tread,
Through all the fearful fray;
But always (as old settlers said),
He ran the other way.
   He ran the other way, my friends,
   He ran the other way,
   And that's the reason why Old Tip
   Was always bullet proof!

Verse 6:
But he had high authority
To thus preserve his tallow,
For Falstaff says "discretion is
The better part of valor."
   The better part of valor, my friends,
   The better part of valor,
   And that's the reason why Old Tip
   Was always bullet proof!

Verse 7:
Then here's a health to Tip-Canoe,
"The hero of defeat,"
As safe a generalissimo
As ever beat retreat!
   As ever beat retreat, my friends,
   As ever beat retreat,
   And that's the reason why Old Tip
   Was always bullet proof!

Verse 8:
For oft his gallant troops, tis' said,
Paternally he'd tell,
To "stand a little farther off,
And they could see as well!"
   And they could see as well, my friends,
   And they could see as well,
   And that's the reason why Old Tip
   Was always bullet proof!

Verse 9:
And many a prudent soldier, who,
To his advice gave heed,
Went off without a single wound
To carry home for seed,
   To carry home for seed, my friends,
   To carry home for seed,
   And that's the reason why Old Tip
   Was always bullet proof!

Verse 10:
And thus the mighty General,
Through all the bloody war,
Escaped with bare a bramble scratch
His sole and only scar!
His sole and only scar, my friends,
His sole and only scar,
And that's the reason why Old Tip
Was always bullet proof!

As found in the *Albany Argus*
Published May 18, 1840

The song used here by the Democratic Party attempts to explain that Harrison is not a hero, but rather a coward who would much rather run away from a fight with the enemy than actually engage them. Worse, he would do this at the cost of his own soldiers. Through the use of his "retreat" in battle it also expresses the frustration of the campaign in the fact that Harrison had "retreated" from answering any question that was pertinent to the campaign or the office of the presidency.

Harrison and the Whig Party were also in the business of negative campaigning. Their song entitled "Van Buren" has been described by Jerry Rodnitzky as possibly "the most caustic song ever written."[49] Whether it was more negative than 1828's "Little Wat Ye Wha's A-comin'," is left in the eye of the beholder. What is true, however, is that, due to the growth in popularity of music during the 1840 campaign, it is likely that the song was heard by far more people than was its 1828 predecessor. Perhaps this widespread nature added to the potency of the song. "Van Buren" poses a number of unflattering questions and answers them all with the Democratic candidate's name.

Verse 1:
Who never did a noble deed?
Who of the people took no heed?
Who is the worst of tyrant's breed?
Van Buren!

Verse 2:
Who, while but a little boy,
Was counted, crafty, cunning, sly,
Who with the wily fox could vie?
Van Buren!

Verse 3:
Who, when an urchin, young at
school,
Would of each classmate make a tool,
In cheating, who the roost would rule?
Van Buren!

Verse 4:
By scheming who to England went?
By intrigue who is President?
By proxy who has millions spent?
Van Buren!

Verse 5:
Who wants to bring the poor man
down
To work a week for half a crown?
(Such twenty seven monarchs own)?
Van Buren!

Verse 6:
Who when distress and want was
ours,
Profusely scattered golden showers?
To buy French Artificial Flowers?
Van Buren!

Verse 7:
Who never had an honest thought?
Who to their senses others brought?
And has himself a Tarter caught?
Van Buren!

Verse 8:
Who like the wily serpent clings,
Who like the pois'nous adder stings,
Who is more base than basest Kings?
Van Buren!

Verse 9:
Who rules us with an iron rod,
Who moves at Satan's beck and nod,
Who heeds not man, who heeds not
God?
Van Buren!

Verse 10:
Who would his friend, his country
sell,
Do other deeds too base to tell,
Deserves the lowest place in Hell?
Van Buren!

As found in *A Miniature of Martin Van Buren*
Published in 1840 (unknown publisher)

Although there is quite a bit of negative campaigning today, the song "Van Buren" is more evidence that this technique is nothing new.

Whether one looks at positive music or negative music, songbooks or isolated tunes, it is clear that music came into its own by the 1840 presidential campaign. No longer was music something written after the election to coronate the winner, nor was it something that was occasionally done. Due to changes in the electorate and in printing technology, music had become central to campaigns. This trend would continue for many subsequent elections, something we continue to explore in chapter two.

Notes

1.   Jordan M. Wright, Campaigning for President: Memorabilia from the Nation's Finest Private Collection (New York: HarperCollins: 2008), 6.

2.   Irwin Silber, *Songs America Voted By: From George Washington to Richard Nixon—the Gutsy Story of Presidential Campaigning* (Harrisburg, PA: Stackpole Books, 1971), 21.

3.   "God Save Great Washington," *Philadelphia Continental Journal*, April 7, 1786.

4.   Oscar Brand and Anthony Seeger, Liner notes from *Presidential Campaign Songs 1789-1996*, Oscar Brand, Smithsonian Folkways Recordings, 45052, released in 1999, compact disc, 7.

5.   Henry Clay Watson, *Camp-Fires of the Revolution* (New York: James Miller, 1850), 258.

6.   George Washington, "The Address of General Washington to the People of The United States on his declining of the Presidency of the United States," *American Daily Advertiser*, September 19, 1796.

7.   John Ferling, *Adams vs. Jefferson: The Tumultuous Election of 1800* (New York: Oxford University Press, 2004).

8.   William Miles, Introduction to *Songs, Odes, Glees and Ballads: A Bibliography of American Presidential Campaign Songsters*, (New York: Greenwood Press, 1990), ix.

9.   Silber, *Songs America Voted By*, 23.

10.   Robert Treat Paine, *The Works, in Verse and Prose, of the Late Robert Treat Paine, Jun Esq.* (Boston: J. Belcher, 1812), 245.

11.   Silber, *Songs America Voted By*, 25.

12.   Silber, *Songs America Voted By*, 25.

13.   Brand and Seeger, *Presidential Campaign Songs*, 8.

14.   Bob Waltz, "Remembering the Old Songs: Jefferson and Liberty," accessed June 17, 2010, http://www.lizlyle.lofgrens.org/RmOlSngs/RTOS-JeffersonLiberty.html.

15.   Brand and Seeger, *Presidential Campaign Songs*, 8.

16.   David Ewen, *All the Years of American Popular Music* (Englewood Cliffs, NJ: Prentice-Hall, 1977), 17.

17.   David Leip, "Atlas of U.S. Presidential Elections," accessed May 14, 2011, http://uselectionatlas.org/.

18.   Leip, "Atlas of U.S. Presidential Elections."

19.   John William Ward, *Andrew Jackson: Symbol for an Age* (New York: Oxford University Press, 1955), 13-16.

20.   L. Sandy Maisel and Mark D. Brewer, *Parties and Elections in America: The Electoral Process* (Lanham, MD: Rowman & Littlefield, 2008), 35.

21.   Florin Fesnic, "Election Types," in *Encyclopedia of U.S. Campaigns, Elections, and Electoral Behavior, Volume 2*, ed. Kenneth F. Warren (Thousand Oaks, CA: Sage Publications, 2008), 210-12.

22.   Frederic Austin Ogg, *The Reign of Andrew Jackson: A Chronicle of the Frontier in Politics* (New Haven, CT: Yale University Press, 1919), 68-94; Robert A. Dahl, "Myth of the Presidential Mandate," in *Politicians and Party Politics*, ed. John Gray Geer (Baltimore: The Johns Hopkins University Press, 1998), 239-258.

23.   "Media Construction of Presidential Campaigns Teacher Guide 1828 Doc. #4: 'Little Wat Ye Wha's A-Comin' Song," Project Look Sharp, accessed May 14, 2011, http://www.ithaca.edu/looksharp/mcpcweb/unit2_1828_1840/pdfs/1828/tguide1828doc4. pdf.

24.   "Media Construction," Project Look Sharp.

25.   Leip, "Atlas of U.S. Presidential Elections."

26.   William E Studwell and Drew E. VandeCreek, Preface to *"Forward! Forward! Is the Word": Republican Presidential Campaign Songs of 1856 and 1860* (S.I.: s.n., 2000).

27.   Helen Kendrick Johnson, "The Meaning of Song," in *The North American Review, Vol. CXXXVIII*, ed. Allen Thorndike Rice (New York: 1884), 494.

28.   Silber, *Songs America Voted By*, 37.

29.   Johnson, "The Meaning of Song," 494.

30.   Johnson, "The Meaning of Song," 494.

31.   Danny O. Crew, Introduction to *Presidential Sheet Music: An Illustrated Catalogue* (Jefferson, NC: McFarland & Company, Inc., Publishers, 2001), 5.

32.   A.B. Norton, *The Great Revolution of 1840: Reminiscences of the Log Cabin Hard Cider Campaign* (Mount Vernon, OH: A.B. Norton & Co., 1888), 3.

33.   Robert Seager II, ed., *The Papers of Henry Clay Volume 9: The Whig Leader January 1, 1837-December 31, 1843* (Lexington: University of Kentucky Press, 1988), 229.

34.   Seager, *The Papers of Henry Clay*, 230.

35.   James S. Chase, *Emergence of the Presidential Nominating Convention, 1789-1832* (Champaign: University of Illinois Press, 1973).

36.   Sean Wilentz, *The Rise of American Democracy: Jefferson to Lincoln* (New York: Norton, 2005), xxi.

37.   Michael F. Holt, *Political Parties and American Political Development: From the Age of Jackson to the Age of Lincoln* (Baton Rouge: Louisiana State University Press, 1992), 163.

38.   Silber, *Songs America Voted By*, 33.

39.   Norton, *The Great Revolution of 1840*, 7.

40.   *See* Kenneth C. Martis et al., *The Historical Atlas of Political Parties in the United States Congress, 1789-1989* (New York: MacMillan, 1989).

41.   Norton, *The Great Revolution of 1840*, 375.

42.   Stanly Boorman, "Petrucci, Ottaviano: Publications," in Oxford Music Online, Oxford University Press 2007-2011, accessed August 31, 2010, http://www.oxford msiconline.com.floyd.lib.umn.edu/subscriber/article/grove/music/21484?q=petrucci&sea rch=quick&pos=2&_start=1#firsthit.

43.   David A. Copeland, *The Media's Role in Defining the Nation: The Active Voice* (New York: Peter Lang Publishing, 2010), 86-87; William Sonn, *Paradigms Lost: The Life and Deaths of the Printed Word* (Lanham, MD: Scarecrow Press, 2006), 125-32.

44.   Miles, *Songs, Odes, Glees and Ballads*, 118-125.
45.   Miles, *Songs, Odes, Glees and Ballads*, 126-127.
46.   Miles, *Songs, Odes, Glees and Ballads*, 128-129.
47.   Miles, *Songs, Odes, Glees and Ballads*, 129-133.
48.   Miles, *Songs, Odes, Glees and Ballads*, 135-136.
49.   Jerry Rodnitzky, "Popular Music," in *The American President in Popular Culture*, ed. John W. Matviko (Westport: Greenwood Press, 2005), 36.

~ 2 ~

Campaign Music Post-Tippecanoe
(1844-1916)

The use of music as a driving force in presidential campaigns began with "Tippecanoe and Tyler Too" in 1840. It would remain a driving force in presidential campaigns throughout the remainder of the nineteenth century and into the twentieth century. Campaign songs would continue to get more creative and move vindictive as well, with negative songs focusing on personal attacks of character at times. In addition, we would see the advent of campaign songs that were nonpartisan in nature that served to inform the public about the candidates or speak in general terms about the stereotypes associated with each of the candidates rather than persuade the listener to vote one way or another.

In this chapter we will concentrate on a few major elections during three different periods of this era. The 1856-1864 elections represent the rise of the Republican Party, the electoral success of Abraham Lincoln, and the prospect of an election in the middle of a civil war. The 1884-1892 elections involved one candidate, Grover Cleveland, winning the popular vote three times in a row. Finally, the rise of Tin Pan Alley compositions coincided with a period of great change in American elections at the turn of the century, from the elections of McKinley and Bryan to the great three-way race among Theodore Roosevelt, Woodrow Wilson, and William Howard Taft.

Freedom Song

By the 1850s, music had firmly established itself as a campaign mainstay. For instance, after the seminal election of 1840, numerous songs were again written for the 1844 contest between the Democratic candidate James K. Polk and the Whig candidate Henry Clay. Songs on behalf of Polk included "Jimmy Polk of Tennessee," "Polk, Dallas and Texas" (Polk's running mate was George M. Dallas), "Hard Times," and "Two Dollars a Day and Roast Beef," while songs for Clay included "Great Henry Clay," "Harry of the West," "Clear the Way for Harry Clay," "Farmer Clay," and "Clay and Frelinghuysen" (Clay's running mate was Theodore Frelinghuysen).[1] The 1848 and 1852 elections followed a similar path, with numerous songs written in a similar style to that of 1840.

Something else was occurring in America during this period though that was having a major impact on politics and would soon exert its influence on campaign music. The issue of slavery was driving wedges among abolitionists, relativists, and supporters. It was particularly devastating to the Whig Party. After Whig President Millard Fillmore signed the Fugitive Slave Act in 1850, requiring that law enforcement officials assist slave owners who were trying to capture runaway slaves, the issue tore the party apart. Fillmore was the last Whig elected president. Members of the party left to join the Democrats, the Know Nothing Party, the Free Soil Party, or the newly formed Republican Party. Even Fillmore left the Whigs and ran for reelection as a member of the Know Nothing Party. The Republicans would quickly gain traction as one of America's two parties. Formed in 1854, the party quickly rose to national prominence, running John C. Frémont in 1856. Frémont finished second in the race, behind Democrat James Buchanan but ahead of the incumbent, Fillmore.[2]

Although there were other issues at stake, including immigration and the annexation of Cuba, the main concern of the 1856 election was slavery. This was evident in Frémont's songs, including "Huzza for the Railroad!" and "Frémont and Freedom."[3] Even more notable was Frémont's "We'll Give 'Em Jessie." The song, set to the tune of "Wait for the Wagon," refers in the title to the candidate's wife, Jessie Benton Frémont, and is a play on the phrase, "We'll give 'em hell."[4] The lyrics are as follows:

Verse 1:
Ye friends of freedom rally now,
And push the cause along;
We have a glorious candidate,
A platform broad and strong;
"Free Speech, Free Press, Free Soil, Free Men,
Frémont," -- we have no fears,
With such a battle-cry, but that
We'll beat the Buchaniers.

Chorus:
We'll give 'em Jessie,
We'll give 'em Jessie,
We'll give 'em Jessie,
When we rally at the polls.

Verse 2:
Our leader scaled the mighty hills,
'Twixt East and West the bars,
And from the very topmost peak
Flung out the stripes and stars;
Nor cold, nor heat, thirst, hunger, naught
Of horror moved his fears;
With such a captain can we fail
To beat the Buchaniers?
(Chorus)

Verse 3:
In after time his dauntless arm
Unlock the Golden Gate;
His eloquence to Freedom gave
The El Dorado State.
In every word, in every deed,
Such manliness appears,
Frémont's the man to lead us on
To beat the Buchaniers.
(Chorus)

Verse 4:
Where e'er clear heads and gallant hearts
Are wanted, foremost he;
And ever true in word or deed,
He's proved to Liberty.
Survey him every way you will,
The noble man appears,
So shout Frémont and Liberty-
Down with Buchaniers!
(Chorus)

Verse 5:
Then rally, rally, every man
Who values Liberty,
Who would not see our fair land given
To blighting Slavery.
Our cause: "Free Speech, Free Press, Free Soil,
Free Men"—So now three cheers
For the people's candidate, Frémont,
Who fights the Buchaniers.
(Chorus)

As found in *The Freemen's Glee Book: A Collection of Songs, Odes, Glees and Ballads, with Music, Original and Selected, Harmonized and Arranged for Each*
Published by Central Freemont and Dayton Glee Club (New York), 1856

"We'll Give 'Em Jessie" continues in the tradition of "Tippecanoe and Tyler Too," in that it refers to specific campaign issues and makes use of Frémont's campaign slogan: "Free soil, free labor, free speech, free men, and Frémont." This linking together of music and slogan would be a rarity until the early twentieth century. In addition, the song makes use of alliteration, much like "Tip and Ty." Furthermore, like "Tip and Ty," "We'll Give 'Em Jessie" used Frémont's name repeatedly throughout the entire song. It also demonstrates the accepted role of women's involvement in politics (even if women did not have the right to vote yet), as the song repeatedly referred to the candidate's wife. Overall, it was a great piece of campaign music, even though it was not the key to victory for Frémont. It was also part of many more songs for Frémont. Indeed, a publication called *The Republican Campaign Songster* was produced by a New York company in 1856 and sold for fifteen cents per copy.[5]

The Buchanan campaign had plenty of songs of its own. The most notable of these referred to the presidential candidate and his running mate, John C. Breckinridge; it was appropriately titled "Buchanan and Breckinridge" and set to the music of the "Star-Spangled Banner."[6] Although this song emphasized one of Buchanan's planks, that he would unite the various factions dividing the country, other Democratic songs in 1856 were not so positive. One song in particular, "Empire Club Song," was an anti-Frémont song that highlighted the issue of slavery and played on racial prejudices:

> Come Democrats and listen,
> While I sing to you a song,
> 'Tis about the Nigger-Worshippers,
> And it will not take me long.
>
> Frémont is on their platform,
> And their principles endorse,
> To worship Niggers night and morn,
> And ride the Woolly Horse.
>
> Free speech, free niggers, and Frémont,
> Now seems to be the go. . .
> But these crazy Nigger-Worshippers
> The Union would destroy.
>
> For there's balm in Gilead,
> We hear the people say—
> With Buchanan and Breckinridge
> We will surely win the day.
>
> From the "Empire Club Song" as found in *The Campaign Democrat*
> Published by John C. Noble (Louisville, KY), July 30, 1856

The "Wooly Horse" apparently referred to in the song was in actuality a horse that P.T. Barnum had purchased while on tour with Tom Thumb. However, when Frémont went missing temporarily during his exploration of the Rocky Mountains in 1849, Barnum used the public excitement that was generated by the story to bring forth this creature that he claimed Frémont has sent back East from his exploration. According to the legend, the beast was part antelope, buffalo, camel, elephant, horse, and sheep.[7] Putting aside this odd story, "Empire Club Song" clearly attempted to whip up the prejudices of Democratic voters and those who were bigoted against African Americans.

Overall, the changing political landscape of the 1850s was reflected in campaign music. A competitive two-party system remained in place, even if one of the parties had changed. In addition, the great political issue of the day, slavery, worked its way into the campaign lyrics, from the Frémont campaign's use of the phrase "free men" to music by racist opponents that referred to the new Republicans as "crazy Nigger-Worshippers." This race baiting strategy was part of a winning campaign, as Buchanan won the White House with over 45% of the popular vote and over 58% of Electoral College votes in a three-way race.[8] Still, Frémont made a good showing, with 33% of the popular vote and a second place finish in the Electoral College. This was an excellent start for the new Republicans and a harbinger of things to come in 1860.

Simply the Best

Some of the best remembered campaign songs tend to be from the most contested elections. Others come from elections where great presidents were elected. The 1860 election contained both of these elements. It was a four-way race among Republican Abraham Lincoln, Democrat Stephen Douglas, Constitutional Union Party candidate John Bell, and Southern Democrat John C. Breckinridge. Lincoln won, and in the ensuing five years presided over a country that descended into civil war; Lincoln's successful tenure in holding the country together during its darkest moments has earned him the distinction of America's greatest president by many historians. None of that would have come to pass without a victorious run in 1860, and music was an important part of Lincoln's success.

Slavery was again the most controversial issue in the election, ultimately not being resolved until the North and South fought each other in the Civil War. One example of the issue's relevance during the campaign can be seen in "The Lincoln Flag," which, like many campaign songs before it, uses the tune of "Yankee Doodle" for its setting (to this point in history the song was used for, among others, "American Sprit" from the 1800 election, "Harrison" from the 1840 election, "Farmer Clay" from the 1844 election, and "Wide-Awake Yankee Doodle" from the 1856 election).[9]

Verse 1:
Unroll, the Lincoln flag, my boys,
Where freemen's sons are speeding,
And wave it, while a rag, my boys,
Remains where Freedom's bleeding.
    Our hearts are true as steel, my boys,
    And every man's a brother;
    While we have hearts to feel, my boys,
    Our hands will help each other.

Verse 2:
Up with the tapering mast, my boys,
As high as any steeple;
Then make our banner fast, my boys,
The standard of the people.
    Our hearts are true as steel, my boys,
    And every man's a brother;
    While we have hearts to feel, my boys,
    Our hands will help each other.

Verse 3:
Free labor and free speech, my boys,
And LINCOLN for our leader,
And a free press to teach, my boys,
America, God speed her!
    Our hearts are true as steel, my boys,
    And every man's a brother;
    While we have hearts to feel, my boys,
    Our hands will help each other.

As found in *The Wide-Awake Vocalist, or, Rail Splitters' Song Book: Words and
    Music for the Republican Campaign of 1860*
Published by E.A. Dagget (New York), 1860

"The Lincoln Flag" not only unveiled the candidate's name within the context of
a popular tune, but several campaign issues are also represented in the song.
Most notably, the song attempted to show the moral superiority of the North
over the slave owners of the South and the fact that God will be on the side of
those for freedom. This continues a trend we saw in 1856—after 1840, presidential campaign songs became increasingly more complex, intertwining more
campaign issues into their lyrics. Furthermore, "The Lincoln Flag" continued
Frémont's themes of freedom: freemen, free labor, free speech, and free press
are emphasized in the lyrics.

This, however, was not the most prominent campaign song that is typically
associated with Lincoln in 1860. "Lincoln and Liberty" was considered to be
Lincoln's main campaign song during the election. It is set to the tune of "Rosin
the Beau" and given its text by Jesse Hutchinson, a member of the famous singing group "The Hutchinson Family Singers," who had modeled themselves after

the four-part European singing troupes of the 1830s. Their repertoire consisted of "sentimental ballads, comic songs, martial airs, and patriotic and topical songs."[10] The Hutchinson family was also known to "proselytize: [as] they passionately espoused Causes,"[11] including that of abolitionism, making their alliance with Lincoln a natural fit. As with the first Lincoln campaign song above, the writer is attempting to associate Lincoln with the side of righteousness and justice:

Verse 1:
Hurrah for the choice of the nation!
Our chieftain so brave and so true;
We'll go for the great Reformation-
For Lincoln and Liberty too!
(Chorus)

Chorus:
We'll go for the son of Kentucky
The hero of Hoosierdom through;
The pride of the Suckers so lucky
For Lincoln and Liberty too!

Verse 2:
Our good David's sling is unerring,
The Slavecrat's giant he slew;
Then shout for the Freedom-preferring
For Lincoln and Liberty too!
(Chorus)

Verse 3:
They'll find what by felling and mauling,
Our railmaker statesman can do;
For the people are everywhere calling
For Lincoln and Liberty too!
(Chorus)

As found in *Hutchinson's Republican Songster for the Campaign of 1860*
Published by O. Hutchinson (New York), 1860.

Lincoln's campaign, much in the style of mid-nineteenth-century campaigns, used many other songs, including "Honest Abe of the West," "Ole Abe's Preliminary Visit to the White House," "Old Abe the Rail Splitter," "Hurrah for Lincoln," "We'll Vote for Lincoln," "Lincoln and Hamlin—God Bless Them!," "Lincoln Is the Man," "Give Us Abe and Hamlin, Too," "Lincoln Banner Song," "Old Abe and His Fights," "Abe Lincoln's Excelsior," and "The Lincoln Wedge."[12] Although there were a few other songs which did not heavily emphasize Lincoln's name (and/or the name of his running mate, Hannibal Hamlin), most Republican songs in 1860 used "Abe" "Lincoln" or both names in the title and throughout the song. A representative example of this is Linda Lindon's "We'll Vote for Lincoln," set to the tune of "Wait for the Wagon."[13] The first verse and chorus are as follows:

Verse 1:
Come, all ye friends of freedom
In every noble State,
Come vote for Abra'm Lincoln,
Our worthy candidate.
A statesman true and honest,
He's proved himself at home,
But now we'll send him from us

For four long years to come.

Chorus:
We'll all vote for Lincoln,
We'll all vote for Lincoln,
We'll all vote for Lincoln,
Our country's steadfast friend.

As found in *Lincoln's Campaign or the Political Revolution of 1860* by Osborn
    Hamiline Oldroyd,
Published by Laird & Lee (Chicago), 1896

The trend begun in 1840 of name emphasis was in full swing twenty years later
with Lincoln. It would be quite difficult to leave a rally where these songs were
sung and not have "Abe Lincoln" replying in one's head.

Similar to the elections of 1840 and 1856, campaign songs in 1860 were not
all positive and espousing the candidates' beliefs and values. There were also
attack songs presented by both sides. In this sense, Stephen Douglas had campaign firepower of his own. Douglas understood that if he was to have a chance
to win the election of 1860 or a future challenge in 1864, he would need to "re-
invigorate the northern party and again win the northern states that had once
hoisted the Jackson banner."[14] Douglas firmly believed that conciliation, or concession, alone would be able to save the country from civil war by ensuring the
sanctity of the Union and the eventual erosion of slave power.[15] This was a strategy that had worked for Buchanan and the Democrats in 1856 and one that
Douglas hoped would work again. This approach was exemplified by a negative
Douglas campaign song entitled "Stand by the Flag." Like many other campaign
songs of the era, it was set to the tune of the "Star-Spangled Banner":

Verse 1:
May patriots defend our flag to the last,
As proudly it streams from the national mast;
And ages to come, as it gracefully waves,
May no star e'er be lost 'mid the storm that it braves;
Against foreign foes ever gallantly borne,
By the hand of a traitor, let it never be torn.
    Come freemen, then rally, to the flag let's be true,
    'Gainst the treason of Lincoln, and Breckinridge too.
    "And conquer we must, for our cause it is just,
    And this be our motto: *In God is our Trust.*"

Verse 2:
Let Lincoln proclaim "the irrepressible" flight,
To spread o'er his country its withering blight,
And water the soil with the blood of her sons,
By myrmidons shed, with knives, pistols, and guns.
Let us swear the blest Union we'll bravely defend,
And assassins in flight to their holes we will send.

Come freemen, then rally, to the flag let's be true,
'Gainst the treason of Lincoln, and Breckinridge too.
"And conquer we must, for our cause it is just,
And this be our motto: *In God is our Trust.*"

Verse 3:
Let Breckinridge follow where Yancey may lead,
That Douglas may be crushed and his country may bleed;
Let him take his command from a traitorous mouth,
And his party betray for revolt in the South;
Still as patriots we'll move in an unbroken band,
Our standard to guard, and to save the dear land.
  Come freemen, then rally, to the flag let's be true,
  'Gainst the treason of Lincoln, and Breckinridge too.
  "And conquer we must, for our cause it is just,
  And this be our motto: *In God is our Trust.*"

Verse 4:
Brave Douglas shall bear our banner on high-
The flag of the Union, let the people draw nigh;
From the North and the South, the blest Union to save,
He will rally a band with hearts honest and brave;
And sectional factions, North and South in dismay,
He'll scatter in shame on the next voting day.
  Come freemen, then rally, to the flag let's be true,
  'Gainst the treason of Lincoln, and Breckinridge too.
  "And conquer we must, for our cause it is just,
  And this be our motto: *In God is our Trust.*"

As found in *The Democratic Campaign Songster, No. #1*
Published by American Publishing House (Cincinnati, OH), 1860.

The song attempts to align Douglas with the side of freedom and righteousness according to the candidate's vision of the U.S. Constitution. The song went further, referring to Lincoln as a "traitor" and a man who was willing to "water the soil with the blood of her sons," while Douglas would fight to keep the Union together and avoid a blood-filled conflict. In a sense, the song was characterizing Douglas as the great "uniter," while Lincoln would only split a divided nation further. This perception is interesting, especially considering the fact that "southern Democrats were determined to deny him [Douglas] the nomination"[16] due to his "opposition. . . to a federal slave code for the territories [which] had convinced southern slave owners that they would be unable to control a Douglas administration."[17] However, Douglas' spirit of compromise was on display when he authored the "Doctrine of Popular Sovereignty," which allowed territories to vote if they were going to be slave or free[18] (a law that was overturned by the Dred Scott Decision in 1857, which declared that the Constitution protected slavery for all federal territories). It was a "formula that he hoped would bridge the differences between the North and South on the slavery question, thus preserving the Union."[19] Thus, Douglas' song may have been an accurate depiction of his political strategy.

This is a good point to discuss some of the difficulties that arise when a campaign writes new song lyrics for an otherwise existing "popular" tune. The practice was quite common from 1840 until the radio era. Since this strategy involves inserting text that was not necessarily designed to fit with the music being presented, oftentimes there are places that are difficult to sing because the accentuation of the words does not line up with the accentuation of the text. This can be seen in the final verse of the song above. In the "Star Spangled Banner," the relevant lyric is "And the rockets' red glare, the bombs bursting in air;" in "Stand By the Flag," the relevant line is, "And sectional factions, North and South in dismay." The text that the songwriter chose here expressed the exact sentiment that Douglas and the Democrats wanted to articulate, but the accent now occurs on the "tions" of the word "factions," as opposed to the word "glare" of the original text, which is awkward because the stress or accent of the music and the stress of the word do not align in the same place:

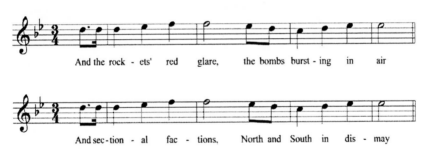

Consequently, it makes it quite difficult for the general public to sing, since we have a built-in desire for accented syllables to end up on accented beats in the music. This may not necessarily affect the popularity or the effectiveness of the song, but it is a factor to keep in mind when we consider that the means of spreading this message is still by word of mouth during this era. If the text does not easily translate into the song, making the song difficult to sing, it also makes the song difficult for the next party to learn and be able to carry as a message for the candidate when they move down the road.

This idea can be equated to the idea of the "hook" in popular song today. A "hook" in music is defined as "a musical or lyrical phrase that stands out and is easily remembered."[20] Campbell and Brody explain that hooks are valuable to a songwriter because "they become embedded in listeners' memory much as the hook at the end of a line gets snagged in the mouth of a fish."[21] It is noteworthy that the most common and recognizable hook in a song will tend to be the chorus or refrain which often details the main "message" of the song. A song might have revealing lyrics, but if the hook is awkward, people will not remember it as easily because it fails to stick in their head. Conversely, a song might have near-ly incoherent lyrics, but if it has a great hook, people will find themselves singing the song all the way home even though they do not like it. Of course, the most effective method is to write text and music that work together to make a more powerful hook for the electorate to grab on to as they walk away from a campaign stop.

Don't Swap Horses in the Middle of the Stream

Lincoln won the 1860 election with just under 40% of the popular vote but with nearly 60% of the Electoral College votes. Soon thereafter, South Carolina seceded, beginning a trend in which several Southern states followed to later form the Confederate States of America. When Southern forces attacked Fort Sumter in April 1861, little more than one month after Lincoln was sworn in as president, the Civil War began. It was still raging on when Lincoln was scheduled to run for reelection in 1864.[22]

Lincoln's Democratic opponent in 1864 was George McClellan, a former General-in-Chief of the Union Army whom Lincoln removed from his post in 1862. This drama only heightened what was already an almost untenable proposition: holding a presidential election in the middle of a civil war.

McClellan's campaign produced numerous songs which spoke to very specific issues about the war effort. McClellan had several positive songs, including 'McClellan Is the Man," which used a similar style as other songs of past campaigns with the title and lyrics stating that "Candidate X Is the Man;" "Soon We'll Have the Union Back," which promised peace and a restoration of the Union; and "Little Mac Shall Be Restored," which discussed vindicating the fired general. Each of these songs made repeated reference to McClellan and to the Civil War; most of them were reused musical compositions with new lyrics added specific to the campaign's issues. Democrats, much like in 1856, also produced negative songs. Some of them, such as "White Soldiers' Song," decried Lincoln's suspension of the writ of habeas corpus and his unilateral decision to free slaves in Confederate states. Other Democratic songs played on even more overtly racist sentiments, including the Copperhead song "Fight for the Nigger," which claimed that blacks were being liberated while whites were being enslaved by Lincoln.[23] These types of songs hit a new low, even surpassing the vile rhetoric of 1856. Indeed, virtually all songs by and for the McClellan campaign either criticized Lincoln's handling of the war effort, condemned his policies on race and slavery, or did both simultaneously. In this way, the Democratic songs of 1864 were driven by both policy and personality.

Lincoln's reelection songs were generally of a different sort, as they tended to be much more positively focused on Lincoln and the cause of Union. For instance, Enos B. Reed wrote "Rally for Old Abe" and set it to the tune of "Rally Round the Flag, Boys" According to the song's text,

Verse 1:
Let's rally for "Old Abe," boys, let's rally once again,
Fighting for our homes and our Union;
We will cast our votes for "Abe," boys, and cast them not in vain,
Fighting for our homes and our Union.

Chorus:
It's "Old Abe," forever! hurrah, boys! hurrah!
We are no traitors—all for the war;
Then we'll rally for "Old Abe," boys, rally once again,
Rally for "Old Abe" and for freedom!

Verse 2:
He has done the best he could, boys—the best could do no more,
Fighting for our homes and our Union;
And he'll fight the battle through, boys, until the fight is o'er,
Fighting for our homes and our Union!
(Chorus)

Verse 3:
We want no traitors' aid, boys, but only ask the brave
To fight for our homes and Union;
And in the land of freedom we do not want a slave;
Then fight for our homes and our Union!
(Chorus)

Verse 4:
Then we'll rally for "Old Abe," boys—come, rally ounce again—
Fighting for our homes and our Union;
We'll try him once again, boys, and try him not in vain,
Fighting for our homes and our Union!
(Chorus)

As found in *The Republican Campaign Songster, for the Campaign of 1864*
Published by J.R. Hawley & Co. (Cincinnati, OH), 1864

Other pro-Lincoln songs from 1864 included "Lincoln Chorus," "A Health to Thee, Abe Lincoln," "Lincoln, Pride of the Nation," and a reprisal of "Lincoln and Liberty."[24] No less than three campaign songsters were printed for Lincoln that year.[25] Although there is a stark contrast in the tenor of Lincoln's songs when compared to those of McClellan, Lincoln's music maintains the emphasis on his name, much like those songs used in 1860. The difference from the past campaign is that Lincoln's 1864 songs tended to be much more general praises of the man and support for the war effort. This would buck the general trend of the era, but with good reason, as there was no musical precedent for campaign songs during a civil war. Lincoln and his supporters played it safe concerning music, not taking the more toxic path of their opponents. Lincoln won the election handily, although he was assassinated six weeks after his second inauguration.

The Day After

After the Civil War, the elections of 1868 and 1872 went to Ulysses S. Grant. Campaign music for Grant tended to emphasize his military achievements. Music supporting Democratic opponent Horatio Seymour in 1868 worried about Grant becoming a military dictator and complained that he was a foolish tool of other Republican politicians; these songs also played on racial prejudices. Pro-Seymour songs in 1868 that used bigoted lyrics included "The White Man's Banner," which proclaimed that voters needed to "vindicate our Fathers' choice, A White Man's Government." Similarly, "Captain Grant of the Black Marines" had lyrics which satirically stated "I am Captain Grant of the Black Marines, the Stupidest man that ever was seen." By 1872, the songs in support of Democratic candidate Horace Greeley tended to emphasize the personal character of Greeley himself. Each side had negative songs in these two elections. In both elections, name usage was high as was specificity. Songs almost always tended to be new lyrics adapted to old tunes.

One major development that occurred between 1868 and 1872 was the ratification of the Fifteenth Amendment in 1870. This amendment guaranteed that "The right of citizens of the United States to vote shall not be denied or abridged by the United States or by any state on account of race, color, or previous condition of servitude." This extended voting rights to African American men, and this led to political empowerment of these voters in the South during Reconstruction.

Indeed, the Census of 1870 demonstrated that African Americans made up a majority of voters in Louisiana, Mississippi, and South Carolina, and they made up more than 40% of the population in Alabama, Florida, Georgia, and Virginia. African Americans controlled a majority of some Southern legislatures during Reconstruction, with hundreds of African Americans elected to these offices. Several African Americans were elected to Congress.[26]

This change in voting rights led to a transformation in presidential politics. With voting rights extended and relatively safe in 1872, the war hero Grant had no problem securing the Republican nomination again. Horace Greeley was nominated as a member of the Liberal Republicans, a short-lived political party that broke away from the more radical wing of the Republicans. This liberal group supported civil service reforms, equality, and the Civil War Amendments (including the Fifteenth Amendment), but they also favored amnesty toward confederates and an end to Reconstruction. Once the Liberal Republicans nominated Greeley, the Democrats followed suit, hoping to capitalize on this division among the Republicans. This failed, and Grant won a resounding victory in 1872, carrying over 81% of Electoral College votes.[27]

Although the election of 1876 would result in a bargain that ended Reconstruction and brought about the Jim Crow legislation that denied African Americans the vote for nearly another century in the South, in 1872 voting rights of African Americans were relatively protected. Thus, the Democratic Party's campaign tactic since 1856, of race baiting and using racial epithets in music, was not used again in 1872. The dominant mood of the country was in favor of the Civil War Amendments, African Americans were voting in high numbers, and both major party presidential candidates supported political equality for newly freed slaves. In fact, the only major campaign songs that mentioned race were from the *Greeley and Brown Campaign Songster*; these songs, such as the minstrel "Kingdom Coming," championed Greeley because of his pre-Civil War support for abolition.[28] Much like the changes seen when voting rights were expanded to non-propertied white men earlier in the eighteenth century, the extension of voting rights to African American men during Reconstruction resulted in a change in campaign music. Even after African American men were denied the right to vote in many places after Reconstruction, there is little evidence that racist lyrics returned to national presidential campaign music.

Two Out of Three Ain't Bad

The number of campaign songs was growing substantially in the post—Civil War era. This likely reflected another trend during the 1870s and 1880s, which was a general increase in the amount of music published in America. As more time passed since 1840, it also demonstrated the increased realization of the importance of campaign music.[29]

The 1884 general election pitted Democrat Grover Cleveland against Republican James G. Blaine. Cleveland would be the first Democrat to win the White House since Buchanan in 1856. This long trend of Republican victories was reflected in the Democratic campaign song, "Let's Have a Chance." The song, written by Thomas P. Culiar, began with the following lines:

> We have grown so sick and tired
> of Republicans and fraud,
> We've resolved they shall be fired
> from the nation's bed and board,
> And along with many thousands,
> we are praying to the Lord
> to let us have a change,
> Do you wonder, do you wonder
> Is the thing absurd or strange?
> After twenty years of plunder,
> We should want a little change.

As found in *Cleveland and Hendricks Campaign Songster*
Published by John Church & Co. (Cincinnati, OH), 1884.

Although Cleveland would eventually win a relatively close victory over Blaine (Cleveland won the popular vote 4,914,482-4,856,903 and the Electoral College 219-182),[30] there was plenty of mudslinging during the campaign. An example of this occurred in the song "Ma! Ma! Where's My Pa?" which was also the campaign slogan used by James Blaine's 1884 campaign. The slogan referred to the supposed illegitimate child of Grover Cleveland (he claimed possession of the child as all the other men involved with the mother of the child at the time were married).[31] The song's chorus says "Ma! Ma! Where is my pa? Up in the White House darling" with the verse implying that, by the child's behavior, he was in dire need of a father figure in his life because he was "fat" and a "brat" and would catch insects and "pull off [their] wing." This integration of song lyric and slogan was still relatively rare during this era. The song would ultimately backfire, though, perhaps because it gave Cleveland the sympathy vote, or perhaps it made the Republicans look as if they were overly vicious in their attacks. Regardless, following Cleveland's victory the Democrats responded to the Republican anthem of "Ma, Ma, Where's My Pa" with the new tagline of "Gone to the White House Ha, Ha, Ha."[32]

Each candidate had a substantial songster that year. Interestingly enough, some of the publications for 1884 were for neither candidate. There were electioneering band books, designed for bands that could be hired to play for either party, or give equal time to both.[33]

When Cleveland ran for reelection in 1888, he faced Republican Benjamin Harrison, the grandson of William Henry Harrison. Cleveland won the popular vote again, but Harrison won where it counted, in the Electoral College. Like his grandfather, Benjamin Harrison knew how to involve music in his campaign. Propelling Harrison to victory were songs such as "Tippecanoe and Morton, Too," (a play on "Tippecanoe and Tyler, Too," this time referring to Benjamin Harrison and his running mate, Levi Morton), "Harrison's Victory March," and the negative campaign song, "When Grover Goes Marching Home."[34]

Once Cleveland lost the White House in 1888, his wife is said to have remarked to a staff member at the White House, "I want you to take good care of all the furniture and ornaments in the house, and not let any of them get lost or broken, for I want to find everything just as it is now, when we come back again. . . . We are coming back just four years from to-day."[35] When Cleveland was renominated by the Democratic Party in 1892, it set up a titanic rematch between Harrison and Cleveland, pitting a sitting and former president against each other. This became another election where music played an important role. From a purely political perspective, it also marked the only time in U.S. history that a president was unseated and then managed to win back the presidency four years later. Populist Party candidate James Weaver also threw his hat into the ring.

One of the issues surrounding Cleveland's presidential bid four years earlier was that of the popular vote, which Cleveland had secured, versus the Electoral College vote, which went to Harrison 233 to 168.[36] This issue was reflected in the campaign songs used by Cleveland in his successful bid in 1892. A song that called into question the "legitimacy" of Harrison's presidency was "Turn the Rascals Out." This song is of interest because it departs from the traditional "formula" of taking a popular tune and inserting text relating to the candidate. With words and text written by Philip H. Bruck, this well-known campaign song states how Cleveland and party will "turn the rascals out" of the White House just as he had done in 1884 when the Republicans held the presidency:

Verse 1:
What is the cry throughout our land?
It's turn the rascals out,
And with our gallant Cleveland
We'll turn the rascals out;
To prove the G.O.P.'s a bluff,
Four years of Harrison's enough;
With Cleveland and with Stevenson
We'll turn the rascals out.
(Chorus)

Verse 2:
We want a man for President,
We'll turn the rascals out.
We want a head and not a hat,
We'll turn the rascals out.
Reform and honesty we want,
Not words deceptive full of cant;
With Cleveland and with Stevenson,
We'll turn the rascals out.
(Chorus)

Verse 3:
No Harrison nor Reid will do,
We'll turn the rascals out,
But Cleveland brave and Stevenson true,
We'll turn the rascals out;
So all you voters, workman all,
Join hands and push them to the wall,
With Cleveland and the Stevenson,
We'll turn the rascals out.
(Chorus)

Verse 4:
What did we do in Eighty-four?
We turned the rascals out.
What will we do in Ninety-two?
We'll turn the rascals out.
Poor Ben can leave the White House then,
And Grover will move back again;
And Steve will run the Senate when
We turn the rascals out.
(Chorus)

Chorus:
We'll turn the rascals out,
We'll turn the rascals out;
We'll turn the rascals out,
We'll turn the rascals out.

From the original sheet music "Turn the Rascals Out"
Copyright © 1892 by Philip H. Bruck

The text of the song makes it clear that the Democrats felt that Harrison and the Republicans were "deceptive and full of cant," perhaps an indication of the previous elections, but more than likely a reference to the type of administration this "empty hat" was running at the time. The song also insinuated that a phony party was able to obtain the White House in an election where the popular vote indicated that they were not the people the country wanted occupying the Oval Office. Thus, the song claimed that 1892 was the time to take the White House back from the "rascals." In essence, the song was a rallying cry to fellow Democrats to right the perceived injustice that removed Cleveland from the White House four years previous. Although the popular vote margin was again narrow in 1892 (only 363,000 votes separated Harrison and Cleveland out of more than 10,000,000 earned by both men), the vote of the Electoral College was not close at all with Cleveland winning 277 to 145.[37] Overall, the song represents the beginning of a changing trend in campaign music at the end of the nineteenth century. The song involved both new music and new lyrics, demonstrating more active involvement by songwriters in presidential campaigns during this period.

Harrison was not without his own songs during the 1892 election. While running for the presidency in 1888, Harrison looked to capitalize on the image his grandfather's campaign had made forty-eight years earlier of being the "log cabin" and "hard cider" candidate. In the younger Harrison's 1888 campaign, this generated a wealth of songs, but a contested election result. The election of 1892 would find the Republicans trying to use the same philosophy to reelect Harrison for a second term. This connection is evident in the song "Grandfather's Hat." Here, D.E. Boyer summoned up the tune of "Rosin the Beau" in an attempt to sway the electorate to vote for the 1892 version of "Tippecanoe":

Verse 1:
Ye Jolly young lads of the nation,
And all ye sick Democrat, too,
Come out from the Free-Traders Party,
And vote for our Tippecanoe.
   And vote for our Tippecanoe,
   And vote for our Tippecanoe,
   Come out from the Free-Traders Party,
   And vote for our Tippecanoe.

Verse 2:
Old Tippecanoe, in the forties,
Wore a hat that was then called a bell;
His grandson, our leader, now wears it,
And it fits him remarkably well.
   And it fits him remarkably well,
   And it fits him remarkably well
   His grandson, our leader, now wears it,
   And it fits him remarkably well.

Verse 3:
Our battle-cry still is protection,
Our flag is the red, white and blue;
We're marching straight forward to vict'ry,
Again with young Tippecanoe.
   Again with young Tippecanoe,
   Again with young Tippecanoe
   We're marching straight forward to vict'ry,

Again with young Tippecanoe.

Verse 4:
Remember, November is coming,
Free-Traders begin to look blue;
They know there's no chance for Grover,
For grandfather's hat will sail through.
    For grandfather's hat will sail through,
    For grandfather's hat will sail through,
    They know there's no chance for Grover,
    For grandfather's hat will sail through.

As found in *The Harrison Campaign Songster, 1892* by D.E. Boyer
Published by The Home Music Company (Logansport, IN), 1892

The elections of 1888 and 1892 may perhaps mark the first time in U.S. history that the relative of a former president attempted to exploit that relationship to win political office. As was the case, Benjamin Harrison attempted to refer to the "hat" his grandfather wore as a symbol of his relation and perhaps his similar temperament. Cleveland's song fought back by stating that the electorate should "want a head not a hat" for their president. This is likely an allusion back to the election of 1840 when William Harrison was able to attain the White House without satisfactorily addressing many of the relevant issues at hand. Perhaps the real insinuation was that William Harrison had no head on his shoulders and so neither did his grandson. Regardless, Cleveland was successful in the 1892 election in both the popular and Electoral College votes, eliminating any possible "dispute" of the presidency.

Cleveland's use of "Turn the Rascals Out" began another shift in presidential campaign music that would continue for multiple election cycles into the twentieth century. Up until this point, the songs used in presidential campaigns primarily utilized existing popular and/or common tunes to which a new text would be written. However, as we saw with "Turn the Rascals Out," a new trend of songwriters composing completely new songs began to usurp the position of this old formula.

Tin Pan Alley and Ragtime Compositions

What happened around the turn of the twentieth century to make new compositions superior and more abundant than the "parodied" songs of the previous century? (The use of the word "parody" will come up numerous times throughout this book. The term, as typically used by the general public, often refers to an existing song in which new text has been written that is intended to be satirical in nature. An example of this would be Weird Al Yankovic, who took the rap "Gangsta's Paradise" by Coolio and changed it to "Amish Paradise," a satirical play on the rigors of the Amish lifestyle. However, throughout much of musical history the term "parody" has also referred to "a work in which new text has been substituted for the original, often without humorous intent."[38] For the purposes of this text, the word "parody" simply means that a new text, either satirical or serious in nature, has been substituted in whole or in part for the original text of the song.)

Perhaps the best explanation for this new trend of parodied campaign songs involved the developing musical styles of the times and candidates' desires to tap into what was then the "popular" music. For example, around the turn of the twentieth century, Ragtime music was very popular and was perhaps one of the first distinctly American musical genres.[39] The music combined the traditions of the European classical styles and the polyrhythms and syncopation of African cultures to create a new and unique-sounding music that was ideal for dancing. The roots of Ragtime can also be seen within the "Cake Walks" of the mid-1800s. (The Cake Walk was a dance whose origins are said to have originated from slaves mocking the high manners and fancy dances of white slave owners. However, more than likely the origins truly stem from the 1890s when contests were organized for couples who would strut and march in a circle presumably to win the prize of a cake. The music for the Cake Walk was highly syncopated leading to much flare in the dance.)[40] As noted by Martin and Waters, "Beginning in the 1890s and lasting two decades, ragtime swept the nation,"[41] hitting full stride around 1897 when the first "mature" rags were published. The most popular of these early rags today is the "Maple Leaf Rag" of Scott Joplin who began publishing rags in 1899 with great success. Also during this time, Tin Pan Alley was establishing itself as the musical center of publishing popular music. Tin Pan Alley was the "jocular name for a district on West 28th Street in New York where, beginning in the late 1880s, numerous publishers specializing in popular songs were located."[42] The composers of Tin Pan Alley initially specialized in melodramatic ballads and comedic novelty songs with topics that ranged from love and heartbreak to satire and baseball. However, it would later embrace the Cake Walk and "experience major growth through promoting ragtime."[43] Subsequently the composers would also embrace Jazz and the Blues as they developed in the 1910s and 1920s combining the "popular tunes" of Tin Pan Alley with the jazz styles of the day. Tin Pan Alley would boast names such as Harry Von Tilzer, Irving Berlin, and George Gershwin among the composers publishing with them.

As Tin Pan Alley and the Ragtime style developed and grew in popularity across the United States, the use of these popular musical genres could have significant benefits for a candidate. A familiar tune can assist with the memorization of a song, but having a new composition in the style of the latest and greatest craze can effectively establish one's position as a candidate who is with the times and aware of the issues that are important to the electorate. In a sense, adopting the newest popular music style served as a way to attract younger voters and appeal to the notion of the "common man," which is a trend that we will see continue in various forms throughout the following century.

Campaign songs during this era also served as outlets for professional songwriters and composers to turn a buck in any given election year through the sale of sheet music. Sound recording was still in its infancy, so music was disseminated mainly through publishing and live performances. In the late nineteenth and early twentieth centuries, "affordable pianos and printed music broadened the market for home music, encouraging a torrent of songs and piano pieces."[44] Consequently, parlor music became a common aspect of home life in America. Many families owned pianos and most had at least one member of the family who was literate enough in music to play for family gatherings or just a quiet evening at home.[45] The sale of these higher quality songs that were associated with the presidential campaigns was a great way to get a popularized message out to the public who would utilize them as their home entertainment. They also served as a great way for professional songwriters to find employment. Much like how advertisements have been an economic boom for newspapers and radio and television stations in more recent elections, campaigns a century ago allowed songwriters to capitalize financially. Given the higher voter turnout rates of a century ago (and the lack of distracting "reality show" entertainment such as *American Idol* or *Survivor*), there was a public appetite for political songs, and songwriters began to see that they could help satisfy it.

The election of 1892 was not the first time in history that fully composed songs had been used (think of "Van Buren" from the 1840 election), but it was the beginning of their prominence on the campaign trail. This also does not mean that it was the end of the use of popular/familiar tunes being used as the canvas for new lyrics supporting a particular candidate either. It does, however, indicate that the candidates and/or their staffs were beginning to think in terms of the electorate as an advertiser might think of them. . . as consumers of a product. By the early twentieth century, campaigns understood candidates as the "product" that needed to be "sold." The use of popular music thus became a great marketing tool. This also feeds into the assertion that beginning with the Harrison election of 1840, the perceived popularity of the presidential candidate begins to become elevated within the campaign. By utilizing the popular genres of music, a candidate can feed into this notion of their popularity. These concepts revolving around marketing would become even more prevalent as mass communication became more established later in the century.

We can see the more common use of this modern popular music format in the Ragtime campaigns of the early 1900s. The election of 1904 was in many ways fairly lackluster with respect to the campaigns and the music associated with them. It was considered a foregone conclusion that Theodore Roosevelt would win the election, leading Democrats and their candidate, Alton B. Parker, to be less than enthusiastic during the campaign. Given Roosevelt's popularity, Parker was a reluctant candidate who did not even go on a speaking tour until the end of October 1904. By that time, Parker's Democratic Party strategists had already told him that Roosevelt would win the election. For these reasons, one of Roosevelt's leading biographers has called the 1904 presidential election the most absurd political campaign of our time.[46] The many predictions of Roosevelt's impending victory were accurate: Roosevelt beat Parker by over 2.5 million popular votes (it was the largest popular vote margin of victory to that point in U.S. history, and it would retain that distinction until 1920), and he had a resounding victory in the Electoral College of 334-140.[47]

This massive triumph could not have been foretold four years earlier, when President William McKinley agreed to put Roosevelt on the Republican ticket as the vice presidential candidate. McKinley needed to select a new vice presidential candidate in 1900 after Vice President Garrett A. Hobart died in office in 1899. Roosevelt later took over the presidency from McKinley after he was assassinated in 1901. The Republicans initially had had no intention of Roosevelt being president, merely offering him the vice presidency to keep him in a position where they felt he could do no harm at the time:

> The party leaders were not ignorant of his phenomenal popularity. It was evident on the surface of political affairs and below the surface. They could not hide or ignore it. It knocked at their very doors; it thrust itself upon them at every turn. They wanted a running mate for McKinley who would not be a drag upon him, a man who would add strength to the ticket. The two shrewdest politicians in the United States, Senators Piatt and Quay, favored his nomination after they had carefully looked over the situation. He was too independent and headstrong to nod his subservience to any political "boss," and it was thought the Vice Presidency would be a comfortable, easy berth for him where he would be harmless.[48]

However, upon taking over the helm of the presidency, Roosevelt quickly ascended in popularity, supervising unprecedented American growth throughout the Western Hemisphere and reforming blatant abuses of capitalism. Due to the popularity of the Republican candidate among the electorate, it appeared as if the Democratic Party was merely going through the motions of a campaign realizing that Teddy Roosevelt was a shoo-in for the presidency. Consequently, the music was not an important part of the election.

Still, there are some interesting songs that came from 1904. "Parker! Parker! You're the Moses Who Will Lead Us Out of the Wilderness" was composed by Paul Dresser. Like many other election songs that year, it was not intended to be taken too seriously, and often "poked some good-natured fun. . . [or] committed some atrocious puns"[49] at the expense of the various candidates.

Verse 1:
Oh, the eight of next November
Is a day you must remember,
There will be a great uprising of the people know you why?
We searched the country over
And from out the fields of clover
Comes a leader of the people "by the people" hear the cry.

Refrain:
Parker, Parker,

The days are growing darker,
Your country needs you badly in its hour of distress;
Parker, Parker,
You're not a side-show barker,
You're the Moses who will lead us out of the wilderness.

Verse 2:
There will be no brag or bluster,
No military fluster,
No more mountain lion shooting, no more wild and wooly fun,
A Democracy united
Will see that things are righted,
Everyone will be *deelighted*, for we have them on the run.
(Refrain)

Verse 3:
There will be a great hosanna
When New York and Indiana
Go Democratic, it will be a case of hip hooray!
So up and down the middle
Taggert has them on the griddle,
On the Icebanks of the Fairbanks of the Washbanks far away.
(Refrain)

As found in the original sheet music "Parker, Parker" by Paul Dresser
Published by James H. Curtin (New York), 1904

When Roosevelt declined to run again in 1908, the reins of the Republican Party were left to William Howard Taft. He ran against William Jennings Bryan, a candidate who was making his third run as the Democratic Party's nominee for the presidency. This election continued the Tin Pan Alley music trend, with such catchy songs as "B-I-Double L-Bill" (a ply on Taft's first name), "Get on the Raft with Taft" (a catchy rhyme), and "Line Up for Bryan." Bryan, much like his previous two runs, could not defeat Taft or the national popularity of the Republican Party. The election was not very close in 1908, with Taft holding an 8% margin in the popular vote and winning two-thirds of the Electoral College votes. Similar to 1904, this relatively lopsided victory led to less serious use of music.

The Three-Way Race of 1912

It was not until the "Bull Moose" Campaign of 1912 that the use of campaign song again became central in the election of a presidential candidate. While elections with more than two candidates were common throughout our electoral history, in the 1912 election three high-powered candidates were running for the presidency. They included the Republican incumbent Taft, the Democratic challenger Woodrow Wilson, and former President Roosevelt, a progressive Republican who had grown dissatisfied with the more conservative policies of Taft's presidency. Fresh off of world travels that had mesmerized the American people, Roosevelt sought a third term in office. Having lost this bid for the Republican nomination to Taft, Roosevelt formed his own party, the Progressive or "Bull Moose" Party, to enter the election.

A great deal of the campaign music in this election focused around the in-house fighting of the Republican Party between Roosevelt and Taft. Roosevelt's success in his two terms made him a welcome sight to many Republican voters. This sentiment was reflected in Roosevelt's campaign music. Songs such as "Teddy, Come Back" reflect the growing angst that the public had with Taft and the direction he was taking the Party and the country:

Verse 1:
Guess we've got the sleeping sickness since you went,
For it don't seem like when you were President;
So we send this C.Q.D. to wherever you may be,
And be sure that ev'ry word of it is meant:

Chorus:
Teddy, come back!
Come and take up the slack,
You can wake us up and shake us up
And put us on the track.
We miss your nerve, we miss your smile,
We miss your daring, dashing style,
So Teddy, oh Teddy, come back!

Verse 2:
Used to be that every day you swung your stick,
Making some bold grafter feel almighty sick;
Can't you hustle back and bust every high and mighty trust,
We'll be standing at your back through thin and thick.
(Chorus)

Verse 3:
Let the lions and the tigers roam the earth,
Come and tighten up your old rough-rider girth;
We are waiting here for you, and we need you P.D.Q.,
So come back and pitch right in for all you're worth.
(Chorus)

From the original sheet music "Teddy, Come Back" by Nesbit & Lombardi
Published by New York & Chicago Music Publishing House, 1910

The song articulates how some in the Republican Party felt like they had been taken off the proper course steered by Roosevelt when he was in office. It also makes reference to some of the famous mottos of Roosevelt, such as "speak

softly, and carry a big stick"[50] which can be seen in the line "used to be that eve-
ry day you swung your stick." Also referencing the African safaris that Roose-
velt had been on, the song calls on him to come back and put the Republican
Party back on course "P.D.Q." Other Roosevelt songs in 1912 included "When
Teddy Comes Marching Home" (words by Irving B. Lee and music by W.R.
Williams), "We're Ready for Teddy Again" (words by Harry D. Kerr and music
by Alfred Solman), and "Teddy's Comin' Back Again" (words and music by
A.T. Hendricks). Of these songs, the first two had their lyrics penned by two of
Tin Pan Alley's finest lyricists.

Taft also had his supporters, as was indicated by his winning the Republican
nomination. Even though Roosevelt picked up many of Taft's followers, those
who remained loyal to the incumbent president did so with increased vigor. In
fact, Taft's supporters had a variety of their own songs which set to assail the
virtues of their conservative candidate. And, as with many songs before them,
these songs attempted to paint the opposition, in this case Roosevelt, as the faux
candidate. Take, for example "Taft the Leader" written by Fox and Strauss,
which says:

Verse 1:
The real leader we have found
Who'll never sound retreat,
Who'll take his stand and hold his
ground
Nor ever meet defeat.
He's steadfast 'mid the battle's roar,
He's true in trial's hour,
So we will keep him four years more
Upon the seat of pow'r.

Chorus:
Taft the real, our ideal,
Taft, the tried and true,
Where you lead we will go,
Taft we're all for you.

Verse 2:
Oh, statesman of the winsome smile,
We're happy, for we feel
We'll sail with you for many a mile
Upon an even keel.
The whole world hails you as a man
And wise, not ever bold,
A stalwart true American
Of patriotic mold.
(Chorus)

Verse 3:
A man of peace you are, oh yes,
You'd put an end to war,
And have us grow in happiness
With no wild strife to mar.
But we'll back you for vigor true
To riddle every sham,
They cannot honey-fugle you,
Staunch son of Uncle Sam.
(Chorus)

From the original sheet music "Taft the Leader" by Strauss & Fox
Published by Willis Music Co. (Cincinnati, OH), 1912

The song indicates that Roosevelt was not the true leader of the Republican Party and that in Taft they had found a "real leader." With lines such as "We'll sail
with you for many a mile" and "But we'll back you for vigor true," it was obvious that those supporting Taft were true believers in his cause. The song also

takes shots at Roosevelt, calling him "ever bold" and indicating that he is a "sham."

Finally, Wilson's campaign also made use of Tin Pan Alley. Foreshadowing a practice that would become more common in the middle of the twentieth century, Wilson's campaign made use of a popular whiskey advertising slogan with "Wilson—That's All!"[51] With words by Ballard MacDonald and music by George Walter Brown, the song was another original composition in the 1912 campaign. Wilson was ultimately victorious in this hotly contested election, as he cruised to victory with Roosevelt and Taft splitting the Republican vote.

In the Jungle, the Nonpartisan Jungle. . .

There are also times in history when campaign songs are written about an election in general. The controversy that was created in this three-way election served as wonderful fodder for the composers of Tin Pan Alley and created a great occasion to use song to describe the situation. As Silber notes, "During this time, Tin Pan Alley was enjoying a vogue of 'jungle' songs"[52] with compositions such as "Congo Love Song" and "Under the Bamboo Tree." Some of these songs were even in reference to the African safaris of Teddy Roosevelt, which made their use all the more appropriate within the context of the election. A. Seymour Brown teamed up with songwriter Bert Grant to write an interesting nonpartisan song about the election of 1912 entitled "The Election in Jungle Town," in which each of the major players is represented by a specific animal: Roosevelt by the "Monkey," Taft by the "Baboon," James Clark as a "Leopard" who is "speaker of the house," Bryan as a "Lion from the plains," and Wilson as a "Kangaroo."[53] The song spoke of the election in terms of these jungle characters. None of the "candidates" felt they should bow out of the race, creating a great deal of dissention between the animal delegates. Furthermore, as was the case within the election, it spoke to how the candidates were "slinging mud" and "berating" the others, making it quite difficult to nominate a candidate for each of the animal parties:

> Verse 1:
> The moon looked down and softly smiled
> At a sight he saw in a Jungle wild,
> One night not long ago,
> Far and near the air resounds
> With weird and most uncanny sounds
> That came from down below,
> Ev'ry animal delegate,
> From each state, None were late
> Casting votes for ev'ry candidate
> For the President.
> The baboon said, "I won't retire,

Although my term will soon expire
I'd like to run again!"
But another monkey he got sore,
Seems he'd been elected twice before,
And he said, "I'll try it just once more,
For the party must have me!"

Chorus:
And Pandemonium hit the jungle with a dull and sick'ning thud,
When each candidate
Started to berate,
One another and to slinging mud,
Ev'ry beast and bird made their feelings heard,
Some of them would only frown,
There was consternation
At the nomination
Of the president of Jungle town.

Verse 2:
And in the other party, too,
Dissension started in to brew,
Which made the donkey sore.
The leopard argued with the mouse
And said, "I'm speaker of the house,
So I should have the floor."
Then the lion came from the plains,
With flowing mane, to explain,
Said, "If I will only use my brains,
I'll be President."
The elephant began to shake
And called upon his aide, the snake,
To see what he could do.
Then the tiger said, "There is a course,
We'll pursue it as a last resource,
Make the kangaroo our old dark horse,
And he'll hop right in the chair."
(Chorus)

From the original sheet music "The Election in Jungle Town" by Brown & Grant
Copyright © 1912 by Remick Music Corp.

Although nonpartisan use of music dates back to at least the electioneering band books of 1884, those previous works were compilations of songs that tried to give equal, positive time to each candidate. "The Election in Jungle Town" is of a different sort, as it is one song that pokes fun at all candidates running. This type of music would remain something of an oddity until approximately one century later.

Looking to the Media Eras

We have until this time focused on elections from earlier in American history, which were limited by the ways in which information could be disseminated to the public. The way that songs were used was driven by the styles of campaigning and the production of song sheets and songbooks. In the next chapter we will continue our chronological progression through the twentieth century and reveal that new technology brought about the need to change campaign strategies. Just as the evolution of the printing press altered the way that music was used in campaigns, technological advancements in the twentieth century led to campaign music evolving once again. We have already alluded to one example of this, as there was a sharp decline in the use of "songbooks" with the inception of radio in the 1920s. We will also see a change in the way campaigns focus their message as the television becomes a more household item in the 1940s and 1950s. And as we move from the twentieth into the twenty-first century, the development of cellular telephones and the Internet become a major part of the way in which candidates musically communicate their messages. In each of these instances, songs will continue to play a central role in the dissemination of a candidate's name to the electorate.

In addition, changes in the franchise would lead to evolution in the use of campaign music. The extension of voting rights in the nineteenth century to non-propertied white men and to African Americans during Reconstruction led to changes in campaign music.In the twentieth century, the extension of voting rights to women and to voters aged 18-20 would have similar effects on campaign songs.

Notes

1. Irwin Silber, *Songs America Voted By: From George Washington to Richard Nixon—the Gutsy Story of Presidential Campaigning* (Harrisburg, PA: Stackpole Books, 1971), 48-52.

2. Heather Lehr Wagner, *The History of the Republican Party* (New York: Chelsea House, 2007); George Washington Platt, *A History of the Republican Party* (Cincinnati, OH: Krehbiel, 1904).

3. Silber, *Songs America Voted By*, 70-72.

4. Stuart Schimler, "Singing to the Oval Office: A Written History of the Political Campaign Song," accessed June 10, 2010, http://www.presidentelect.org/art_schimler_singing.html.

5. Beryl Frank, *The Pictorial History of the Republican Party* (Secaucus, NJ: Castle Books, 1980), 15.

6. Oscar Brand and Anthony Seeger, Liner notes from *Presidential Campaign Songs 1789-1996*, Oscar Brand, Smithsonian Folkways Recordings, 45052, released in 1999, compact disc, 14.

7.   A.H. Saxon, *P.T. Barnum: The Legend and the Man* (New York: Columbia University Press, 1989), 10.

8.   David Leip, "Atlas of U.S. Presidential Elections," accessed May 14, 2011, http://uselectionatlas.org/.

9.   Silber, *Songs America Voted By*, 13.

10.   Gage Averill, *Four Parts, No Waiting: A Social History of American Barbershop Harmony* (New York: Oxford University Press, 2003), 23.

11.   Vera Brodsky Lawrence,*Strong on Music: The New York Music Scene in the Days of George Templeton Strong, 1836-1975* (New York: Oxford University Press, 1988), 228.

12.   Osborn HamilineOldroyd, *Lincoln's Campaign or the Political Revolution of 1860* (Chicago: Laird & Lee, 1896), 150-182.

13.   Oldroyd, *Lincoln's Campaign*, 156-58.

14.   James L. Huston, *Stephen A. Douglas and the Dilemmas of Democratic Equality* (Lanham, MD: Rowman& Littlefield Publishers, Inc., 2007), 169-170.

15.   Allen Johnson, *Stephen A. Douglas: A Study in American Politics* (Charlston, SC: Bibliobazaar, 2008), 380.

16.   John M. Murrin et al., *Liberty, Equality and Power: A History of the American People, Fifth Edition* (Canada: Cengage Learning, 2008), 555.

17.   Murrin et al.,*Liberty,Equality and Power*, 555.

18.   Robert W. Johannsen, *The Frontier, the Union and Stephen A. Douglas* (Champaign: University of Illinois Press, 1989), 95.

19.   Johannsen, *The Frontier*, 96.

20.   Bob Monaco and James Riordan, *The Platinum Rainbow: How to Succeed in the Music Business Without Selling Your Soul* (Sherman Oaks, CA: Swordsman Press, 1980), 178.

21.   Michael Campbell and James Brody, *Rock and Roll: An Introduction, Second Edition* (United States: Thompson Schirmer, 2008), 14.

22.   Harry Hansen, *The Civil War: A History* (New York: Penguin Putnam, 1961).

23.   Silber, *Songs America Voted By*, 87-91.

24.   *The Republican Campaign Songster, for the Campaign of 1864* (Cincinnati: J.R. Hawley& Co., 1864), 10, 12, 32, 41.

25.   Silber, *Songs America Voted By*, 92-94.

26.   Gabriel J. Chin and Randy Wagner, "The Tyranny of the Minority: Jim Crow and the Counter-Majoritarian Difficulty," *Harvard Civil Rights-Civil Liberties Law Review* 65 (2008), 80-83.

27.   Earle Dudley Ross, *The Liberal Republican Movement* (New York: Holt, 1919).

28.   *The Greeley & Brown Campaign Songster* (New York: Fisher & Denison, 1872).

29.   "Music for Public Occasions," Library of Congress,accessed May 17, 2011, http://memory.loc.gov/ammem/smhtml/smessay2.html.

30.   Leip, "Atlas of U.S. Presidential Elections."

31.   Richard E. Welch, *The Presidencies of Grover Cleveland* (Lawrence: University Press of Kansas, 1988), 36-39.

32.   Wesley O. Hagood, *Presidential Sex: From the Founding Fathers to Bill Clinton* (New York: Carol Publishing Group, 1998), 63.

33.   Library of Congress, "Music for Public Occasions."

34.   Frank, *The Pictorial History of the Republican Party*, 53; Beryl Frank, *The Pictorial History of the Democratic Party* (Secaucus, NJ: Castle Books, 1980), 72.

35.　Paul F. Boller Jr., *Presidential Wives*, (New York: Oxford University Press, 1988), 174.

36.　Leip, "Atlas of U.S. Presidential Elections."

37.　Leip, "Atlas of U.S. Presidential Elections."

38.　Don Michael Randel, *The Harvard Concise Dictionary of Music and Musicians* (Cambridge: The Bell Knap Press of Harvard University Press, 1999), 493.

39.　John Edward Hasse, *Ragtime: Its History, Composers and Music* (New York: Palgrave Macmillan, 1986), 1.

40.　H. Wiley Hitchcock and Pauline Norton. "Cakewalk," In *Oxford Music Online*, Oxford University Press 2007-2011, accessed June 9, 2011, http://www.oxfordmusicon line.com.ezp1.lib.umn.edu/subscriber/article/grove/music/04568.

41.　Henry Martin and Keith Waters, *Essential Jazz: The First 100 Years* (Boston: SchirmerCengage Learning, 2009), 31.

42.　J. Peter Burkholder, Donald Jay Grout, and Clause V. Palisca, *A History of Western Music*, (New York: W.W. Norton & Company, 2006), 753.

43.　Martin & Waters, *Essential Jazz*, 69.

44.　Burkholder, *A History of Western Music*, 567.

45.　Burkholder, *A History of Western Music*, 597.

46.　Edmund Morris, *Theodore Rex* (New York: Random House, 2002), 339-363.

47.　"Historical Election Results: Electoral College Box Scores, 1789-1996," Office of the Federal Register, accessed June 25, 2010, http://www.archives.gov/federal-register/electoral-college/scores.html#1904.

48.　Frederick E. Drinkere and Jay Henry Mowbray, *Theodore Roosevelt: His Life and Work* (Washington, D.C.: National Publishing Co., 1919), 156.

49.　Silber, *Songs America Voted By*, 186.

50.　Donald J. Davidson, ed., *The Wisdom of Theodore Roosevelt* (New York: Kensington Publishing Company, 2003), 9.

51.　Silber, *Songs America Voted By*, 205.

52.　Silber, *Songs America Voted By*, 208

53.　A. Seymour Brown and Bert Grant, "The Election in Jungle Town," (New York: Remick Music Corp., 1912.

Part Two

The Mass Media Era

~ 3 ~

Women's Suffrage &
"Wireless" Technology (1920-1948)

I'm a Suffragette

As noted in chapter one, there is a long history of women being involved in American politics and elections. This predates when women earned the rights to vote, and, of course, includes the suffrage movement as well. After the Fifteenth Amendment protected the right to vote irrespective of race, the women's suffrage movement focused on seeking similar protections based on sex. A constitutional amendment protecting women's right to vote was written by Susan B. Anthony and first introduced in Congress in 1878 by California Senator Aaron A. Sargent, a close friend of Anthony's. During that and succeeding sessions of Congress, the amendment either died in committee or was defeated on floor votes. Southern senators voiced the strongest opposition. Undeterred, those supporting women's suffrage took their campaign to the state level. By 1920, most Western states had granted women full suffrage, and many Midwestern and Eastern states extended the right to vote to women in some, but not all, types of elections. For instance, some states protected women's right to vote in only presidential elections or only in primary elections.[1]

The suffrage movement finally achieved national success in August of 1920, when the Nineteenth Amendment was ratified by the requisite number of states. The Amendment states "The right of citizens of the United States to vote shall not be denied or abridged by the United States or by any state on account of sex." Thus the 1920 election became the first one in which women across the country, in every state, could cast a ballot for the U.S. presidency. Just like the Fifteenth Amendment fundamentally changed the language that presidential campaigns used in their music, so would the Nineteenth Amendment. As stated by Silber, beginning in 1920 there were references "to both sons and daughters" in campaign songs.[2] This process began even before the ratification of the Nineteenth Amendment though, in the 1916 song for Woodrow Wilson, "Be Good to

91

California, Mr. Wilson (California Was Good to You)." At one point in the song, respect is given to the building women's suffrage movement, when the lyrics state to President Wilson, "And don't forget 'twas votes for women, Helped to make the vict'ry too."[3] Of course, it is no surprise that these lyrics supportive of women voting appeared in a 1916 campaign song based out of California, as California was one of the Western states which had guaranteed women the full right to vote by 1916.[4]

Once women's right to vote was established nationwide in 1920, song lyrics became even more accommodating toward women. For an example of this, one can turn to a campaign song by Republican presidential candidate Warren G. Harding and his running mate, Calvin Coolidge. One of their songs, "The Campaign Hymn of the Republic," set to the tune of "John Brown's Body," used the lyric, "America is calling: Sons and Daughters brave, arise!" Likewise, another Harding song in 1920, "The Little Snug Old White House in the Lane," has a line referring to "Columbia's loyal sons and her daughters brave and true." (It is of perhaps of some interest to note that the song "John Brown's Body," along with tunes such as "Yankee Doodle" and "The Star Spangled Banner" was a tune often used for political parodies. The song was about abolitionist John Brown and was made popular during the Civil War.[5] The tune itself was said to be based off the early Methodist hymn "Say, Brothers, Will You Meet Us" but would be more commonly known today as the chorus from the "Battle Hymn of the Republic."[6] (It is also perhaps of interest to note that the "original" lyrics to the song made people uncomfortable and, as such, there are a number of variations on the original theme of the song.[7])

Of course, there had been suffragette songs in American politics for decades leading into the 1916 and 1920 elections, such as "Columbia's Daughters," "Let Us All Speak Our Minds," Taxation Tyranny," and "Winning the Vote."[8] However, these songs were used by those in the women's suffrage movement to convince people of the righteousness of their cause, usually in an attempt to convince citizens to support women's suffrage. The difference between these songs and the two Harding songs above is that the suffrage songs were not used by a major party candidate to win the presidency. These types of lines, including women as well as men in the lyrics, were a rarity before the 1916 and 1920 elections. Indeed, in preceding elections, lyrics tended to refer only to men. These included 1912's "Taft and Sherman" (That every man that knows what's right Will vote for Taft and Sherman"), 1912's "Wilson—That's All" (When a fellow meets a fellow"), 1908's "Line Up for Bryan" (We'll fall in line for Bryan, boys, Hip, hip, hooray"), or 1908's "Get on the Raft with Taft" (We'll save the country sure, boys").[9]

The 1920 election was different, due to the change in voting rights and the corresponding new voters to which songwriters needed to appeal. What sense would it make to refer to the country's voters as "boys" or "men" when women were voting? Smart songwriters took this change in electoral law into account, and they penned more inclusive lyrics accordingly. The fact that women were voting in every state in 1920 was reflected in new lyrics which referred to women as the daughters of Columbia or America. There are several songs in subsequent elections which referred to both men and women, or they referred to family members of both sexes. Although electoral lyrics after 1920 did not always emphasize women's involvement in such an overt way, the norm after 1920 was for song lyrics to use gender neutral terms such as "people," "we," or "our."

Turn Up the Radio

Until the 1920s, campaigns made their headway by traveling the country, usually via train, and speaking at various locations along the way. The print news media carried information across America, but these reports spread only as fast as the relatively slow transportation of the day could carry them. Consequently, candidates had to engage in extensive travel to get their name, face, and campaign messages out to the general public. Many of the songs from the previous chapter were used to energize the crowds and to offer them a way to easily remember a candidate's name as the crowd departed from a stump speech by the visiting candidate. The advent of radio, and eventually television, would change all of this. Politicians would take advantage of these technological advancements as a way to influence voters via music.

Through the use of radio, candidates would be able to travel less (and to more targeted areas), while still delivering the messages of their campaign by song and speech to the populace at large. This powerful new medium also caused a change in campaign music. Radio produced a shift in campaigns, involving them much more with the music's selection and use, while also allowing the music to more closely represent respective presidential candidates. Politicians could now more closely integrate a campaign slogan with music, and that music could easily be broadcast across the country.

Radio did not instantly arrive on the political scene in the 1920s, however. Rather, the scientific principles which govern radio waves came to be known in the latter half of the nineteenth century. In 1864, James Clerk Maxwell discovered the wavelike properties of light.[10] He also noted the same similarities in both electrical and magnetic fields, which would lead him to hypothesize that light is made of electromagnetic vibrations.[11] Maxwell developed equations that would describe light and radio waves in terms of electromagnetism that travels through space.[12] In 1888, Heinrich Hertz demonstrated how to set the radio waves in motion, how we could detect them, and how they would pass through solid objects, releasing the results of his early experiments.[13] In fact, it is after Hertz that we would name the way in which we measure of the frequencies on the electromagnetic spectrum. It was the Italian Guglielmo Marconi, however, who would take Hertz's research and turn it into far more practical applications.

In its early stages, wireless radio technology was used primarily for two-way communications via telegraphy (wireless telegraphy began to show its functionality in about 1895 and was in full use around the turn of the twentieth century). This application is precisely what Marconi is most remembered for in the development of radio technologies. In 1896, Marconi used radio waves to carry Morse code messages; his Wireless Telegraph Company shortly thereafter set up shore-based radio stations to send and receive telegraph signals to ships at sea.[14] Since no telegraph lines could exist at sea, radio waves found a perfect niche in telegraphy. Furthermore, radio's early application was most obviously seen at sea for other purposes, such as for communications between ships and to coordinate rescue efforts in sea disasters.[15] One historical event that bears this out was the sinking of the *Titanic* 1912, as the telegraphy played a role in the attempted rescue of the passengers aboard the ship.[16]

Even during these early stages of use, there were ongoing experiments involving the transmission of music using these radio waves. Lee de Forest turned this idea of telegraphy into telephony, which is the basis for radio communications. He was the inventor of the *audion*, the early form of the vacuum tube capable of modulating, amplifying and detecting radio energy, which improved both the transmission and reception of radio waves.[17] In 1908, Forest began experimenting with the transmission of phonographic music from the Eiffel Tower.[18] Two years later he would be broadcasting the voice of Enrico Caruso from the Metropolitan Opera in New York.[19] The development of radio was halted during World War I in order to focus energies on applications more pertinent to the military efforts of the war. However, following the war, the radio would begin to make giant steps toward becoming a major form of communication and entertainment in the United States and abroad.

Politics and Music on the Radio
During the Roaring Twenties

During the interwar period, radio began to show its practical applications for the average American family, as many individuals began making their own home radios to listen to music broadcasts.[20] At the same time, radio began to make its appearance on the political scene. The first use of radio for explicitly "political" means occurred in 1920 when Pittsburgh's KDKA radio station broadcast the returns of the presidential election over the airwaves.[21] After many years of amateur radio operators making broadcasts, KDKA was the first commercial radio station, and its first broadcast was the announcement of Warren Harding's victory over James M. Cox on November 2, 1920.[22] But it was four years later with the 1924 election that political campaigns started to take advantage of the technology at their disposal.

Early on, political campaigns did not see that value in using radio broadcasting. This may have initially been due to the novelty of the new medium or to the fact that few households had radios. But as the popularity of radio spread between the 1920 and 1924 presidential elections, political strategists began to see how they might be able to use the wireless. In 1921, President Harding began making occasional speeches over the radio.[23] When he died in 1923, Coolidge continued to speak on the radio as a way to communicate with the electorate and shape public opinion.[24] According to Coolidge, "I am very fortunate that I came in with the radio," because "I can't make an engaging, rousing, or oratorical speech. . . but I have a good radio voice, and now I can get my message across."[25] President Coolidge's perceived success could not keep his challengers at bay, however. As described in more detail below, the 1924 presidential election was stained by the politics of the Teapot Dome scandal. The election pitted the Republican Coolidge against the Democratic candidate John W. Davis, one of the last true conservatives nominated by the Democratic Party for the presidency. Coolidge also faced opposition from a former member of his own party, as Wisconsin Senator Robert M. La Follette broke away from the Republicans and ran as the nominee of the Progressive Party.

By 1924, many candidates and other party operatives were talking about how they could use the radio as a part of their campaigns. Due to these discussions, radio stations began to worry that they would be inundated with requests for speech time by all of the primary candidates. This caused Owen Young, chairman of the Board of Directors for General Electric and RCA, to proclaim that "No citizen of this great country need say that he has not heard the pronouncements of the presidential candidates of the two great parties."[26] As noted by Don Moore in his article about the "1924 Radio Election":

> [The] *New Republic* Magazine predicted that the upcoming campaign would be mainly fought by radio. *Nation* agreed, editorializing that 1924 would be looked back on as 'the radio year', but thought that by 1928 the broadcasting fad could be over. William McAdoo, the most likely Democratic candidate, went as far as to apply for a license to set up a station at his home in Los Angeles. His plans were to do most of his campaigning by radio from his living room![27]

According to many accounts of the 1924 election, music did not play a vital role. In fact, Jerry Rodnitzky has noted that "[p]opular music ignored the three boring presidents [Warren Harding, Calvin Coolidge and Herbert Hoover]."[28] Although we will describe in more detail below how music was still quite relevant during this era, it was also the case that politicians supplemented their radio speeches with a popular singer of the day, more than likely performing one of their popular tunes and campaign songs. Furthermore, radio ended up becoming a large part of the campaigns as both the Republican and Democratic National Conventions were aired live. The Republicans in particular took the use of a radio very seriously during the election, keeping vice presidential nominee Charles Dawes on the radio every evening through election day. In addition to Dawes,

> For the final two weeks before the election, they [the Republicans] bought all the time on two stations, WAHG, Richmond Hill, Long Island and WHBF, Providence, RI. With programming originating from Republican offices in

Manhattan, Republican politicians spoke morning noon and night from October 21 to election day. . . . For the grand finale, the Republicans set up three big radio rallies. The first, on October 29, brought together several major speakers on WJZ and six other stations. The following night they put together a 'Midnight Theatrical Review' of political speeches and entertainment with stars including Al Jolson and Elsie Ferguson. . . . Finally, on the Saturday night before the election, WEAF and sixteen other broadcasters carried a huge rally of speeches and music from New York's Metropolitan Opera House."[29]

Consequently, campaigns realized that through radio they could reach the masses without the need to travel, and they realized that electioneering by radio could be a great tool for a candidate to disseminate his or her message. The Republican radio blitz paid off, as the Coolidge/Dawes ticket netted 382 Electoral College votes compared to Davis' 136 and La Follette's 13.[30]

Coolidge declined to run for reelection again in 1928. That year saw Republican Secretary of Commerce Herbert Hoover running against Democratic New York Governor Al Smith, who was the first Catholic nominated for president on a major party ticket. According to David Clark, 1928 would mark the "emergence of radio as a full grown campaign device," which is evidenced by the fact that the "Republicans went on to reserve the major share of their publicity budget for radio campaigning in [the] 1928 [elections]."[31] In the 1928 presidential election, the Republican Party spent $435,894 on radio campaigning with the Democrats spending over $200,000 more than their Republican counterparts. This money was put to good use as the Democrats received "250,000 letters, 10,000 telegrams and, most welcome of all, $600,000 in cash contributions," while the Republicans "admitted radio secured them 100,000 letters and 'heavy contributions.'"[32]

Politicians during this period seemed split over whether the inception of radio as a campaign tool was a welcome invention. In a 1928 debate, Senator Pat Harrison, a Democrat from the state of Mississippi, believed radio was indeed a good thing because it gave candidates an easier way to spread their messages to the electorate. According to Harrison, "Radio will purify politics. The blatant demagogue once sought the little hamlet where not even a newspaper account of his speech would be circulated so that he might display his goods and waves in demagoguery. Radio has come to do away with that. The venomous darts of scurrilous archers cannot pass through the air. Religious intolerance cannot pass."[33]

Senator George Moses, a Republican from New Hampshire, disagreed. Instead, he claimed that "[r]adio has played havoc with politics." He indicated that the Democratic broadcasting fund exceeded the cumulative amount spent less than three decades earlier for a president to be elected for two terms. He also noted that the use of radio required that more than one "stump" speech be written for a candidate, which was a departure from the past as well. Moses further indicated that the radio would have a tendency to magnify the defects of a person in political office stating that "[r]eputations have been made and destroyed by radio and the politicians have suffered more from it than anyone else." But Moses did think that in the long run "politics will be benefitted by radio and politics will be purged by it."[34] Both politicians were able to agree, however, that "radio had changed political values by enforcing a higher standard from political speakers."[35] Regardless of the opinions of those in public office or those running political campaigns, the radio became a political fixture during elections of the 1920s. And as radio came to be an ever more important part of presidential elections, music also followed as a campaign device that was disseminated over the air.

Radio (Almost) Killed the Singing Campaign Star

As the campaigns began to move their message to the airwaves, they also sought to utilize campaign songs in a different manner. This would change the way in which campaign songs were produced and by whom. As Stuart Schimler has noted, "the 1920's would serve as the start for the fall of the popularity of this long tradition [of campaign music]. It was harder to survive in the scrutiny of the new mass media."[36] With the inception of radio, the old singing campaigns of the nineteenth century began to come to an end. George S. Jackson has stated, "[W]hen politics served as a staple form of entertainment for the long winter evenings and when elections were usually a cross between debauchery and circus day; when there were no radios to emphasize the futility of campaign oratory, and no moving pictures to impress upon the voters the prosaic appearance of candidates, then there was romance; then people sang songs."[37] With the radio becoming an integral part of the political campaign, people no longer needed to sing for a candidate's message to be heard or to be reminded of the candidate. The message could be heard over the airwaves, as songs could be heard as a part of radio broadcasts; the message could also be performed by the most popular singers of the day at campaign rallies. People stopped relying so heavily on the use of songbooks and families singing together around the fireplace for their evening entertainment. The radio offered them all the entertainment they would need and a link to the outside world.

Schimler notes, though, that "there were some songs that caught on and were popular."[38] Irwin Silber takes a similar view to that of Schimler, stating:

> To be sure, the passing into history of campaign singing did not signify the death of the campaign song. Songwriters, both amateur and professional, continued hopefully to launch new musical manifestoes by way of sheet music and popular parodies, but these ventures were, for the most part, largely ineffectual. Occasionally a song would become part of the identifiable decor of a political candidate. . . but in general there was no market for such material and little inspiration.[39]

Consequently, these scholars saw the 1920s and the radio as the beginning of the death of the campaign song.

There is an alternate explanation to Schimler and Silber's theory of the decline of campaign song, however. Although the elevation of radio within political campaigns signified the end of the large number of campaign stops, and consequently the "singing" campaigns of the 1800s, this does not mean that there was a lack of music or of quality music, nor does it mean that politicians stopped using music as a way to sway the electorate. Instead, the music that a campaign chose to associate itself with needed to be more focused and serve more specific purposes. As noted by William Miles,

> The song itself could no longer rhythmically carry the party's message or imbue the candidate with an image that could be reduced to a community chant or slogan. After the radio presented the actual voice of the candidate to the electorate and eventually, by means of movies and television, a living picture of the nominee himself, no song could create a believable image that was at direct odds with that which the voter actually saw and heard.[40]

Because of this, campaign music entered a period where it was in flux and at odds with the new desire to communicate through the radio. Indeed, *New Republic* writers from that time period could see these former campaign strategies being utilized on the airwaves, stating:

> It remains a question how long the political use of radio will be merely as a transmitter of the direct campaign utterances of candidates. When the battle is definitely transferred to the air, may we not expect all the familiar features of the usual campaign reproduced there? Will not the voice of the radio agent fill the air as the typewriter of his brother in the press agent fills the newspapers? We may then expect bedtime stories burbling with anecdotes of some candidate's boyhood, tenors expanding on his favorite lullaby, radio orchestras playing his special march directly after the Star Spangled Banner, even the voice of his aged mother now and then quavering out a tribute.[41]

Thus, much like during earlier eras, campaigns saw music as a way to create a positive connect to America for a candidate. The radio simply became a new medium to help convey this message. During this period, Luther A. Huston Washington commented on the fruition of campaign songs for radio and recording, stating that "changed times are reflected in the use of campaign songs. Once they were for the mass meetings; they tended to be whistled and sung whenever two or three of the same party were gathered together."[42] Huston Washington went on to say that, "[s]ince the world war the radio has come into general use as a medium for campaign music and oratory. The sound truck has come familiar. . . . It is possible that the radio will start a new wave of campaign music rolling up. . . ."[43]

As the campaigns desired to implement these strategies, they needed to change many aspects of the way they promoted their candidates, and they began to shift their focus in the direction of advertising. Much of radio's music play was sponsored by particular companies or products, many of which had very catchy jingles to go along with them. For example, there was the Champion Spark Plug Hour, which presented music by the Champion Sparkers Male Quartet with an orchestra which also played the "March of the Champions" for the spark plug manufacturer.[44] Other examples include the Eveready Hour (a variety show sponsored by Eveready Batteries), the Palmolive Hour (a concert show sponsored by Palmolive Soap), and the Dodge Victory Hour (one of radio's first variety shows sponsored by Dodge's "Victory Six" automobile).[45] Presidential campaigning would take on a similar focus. As campaigns' attention shifted to the airwaves, they began adopting the advertising model, seeing themselves as "sellers" and the electorate as "buyers" of candidate "products." However, this trend would take some time to develop. Radio would not utilize music within presidential elections to its fullest extent until after World War II because the musical productions of Tin Pan Alley continued to serve as the primary musical vehicle to promote candidates through sheet music.

The enduring influence of Tin Pan Alley and the emergence of radio prompted a change in the way campaign songs were written. No longer was the majority of "popular" campaign songs derived from existing popular tunes (although candidates occasionally continued to make use of this practice). Rather, the trend of composing new songs for a campaign, which slowly began with the Cleveland election in 1892, developed into the practice of current popular genres with the "Ragtime" elections around the turn of the twentieth century. By this era, songs were usually written specifically for the candidates, mentioning the candidates' names more often and espousing their virtues. On the one hand, a candidate lost the ability to associate himself with an existing popular tune, making it potentially more difficult for the electorate to "catch on," as it were, to their song. However, with songwriters such as Al Jolson penning songs for political campaigns, the quality of the music increased when compared to previous campaign songs. For instance, the lyrics genuinely fit the music, making them far less awkward to sing. Even though both the music and lyrics were new, the tunes were catchy and appealing to the general public. Campaigns were also able to alter their campaign music and the musical styles changed by using these popular songwriters to their advantage. An example of this can be seen in a song written for Warren G. Harding's campaign by Al Jolson. Jolson was a famous vaudeville singer/songwriter, actor, and comedian who was said to have "invented the role of the pop music superstar,"[46] and was famous for the pizzazz for which he approached his singing. Jolson was also the star of what many consider to be the first "talkie" film, *The Jazz Singer* in 1927.[47] The song Jolson wrote, "Harding, You're the Man for Us," utilized the newly developed jazz style of the day and was known as the "official Republican campaign song"[48] of the 1920 election:

Verse 1:
We need a man to guide us

Who'll always stand beside us,
One who is a fighter through and through
A man who'll make the White House
Shine out just like a lighthouse
And Mister Harding, we've selected you.
Harding, lead the G.O.P.
Harding on to victory!
We're here to make a fuss!
Miser Harding, you're the man for us!

Verse 2:
We know we'll always find him
With Coolidge right behind him,
And Coolidge never fails, you must agree,
We know he will be guarding
The Nation just like Harding
When they are both in Washington, D.C.
Harding, Coolidge is your mate,
Harding, lead the ship of state,
You'll get the people's vote,
And you'll also get the Donkey's goat!

> From the original sheet music "Harding, You're the Man for Us"
> Copyright © 1920 by Al Jolson   Published in New York, 1920

The song spoke of Harding as the man who would "stand beside us" and the one who could make the White House a beacon to the country. It also promised that Harding would "lead the G.O.P." and "get the Donkey's goat" by winning the election. Furthermore, it referenced Coolidge as the man who would "be guarding" the nation along with Harding, as they could both be "fighters" for the citizens of the country. Kevin Kusinitz notes of Jolson's song in his 2008 article "Celebrity Endorsements" that, "Interestingly, it was a Republican, Warren Harding, who seemed to have been the first 20th century candidate to seduce show business. . . . Harding must have been savvy enough to realize that having Al Jolson appear at his rallies was a good way to bring a crowd. Jolson, one of the biggest stars of his time, worked his magic singing "Harding, You're the Man for Us" to enthralled audiences."[49]

As we will discuss in more detail below, radio and other forms of media were producing a phenomenon of celebrity in the early to mid-twentieth century. Harding was quick to capitalize on this phenomenon by selecting one of the biggest songwriters of the day to promote his campaign. By bringing Jolson with him, Harding was able to capture rally goers who wanted to see the presidential candidate *and* those who wanted to hear Jolson's music. The ability to bring in a larger audience certainly has the potential to pay large dividends for a candidate.

The Republican Party did not have a monopoly on the use of famous songwriters to compose new campaign songs. In 1928, Irving Berlin, "who was swept up in the heady atmosphere of the inflated property which had given the era much of its cultural style,"[50] got into the political mix for Democratic presidential candidate Al Smith. Berlin was a famous Tin Pan Alley composer of songs, Broadway shows, and Hollywood films.[51] His songs made him a legend before he turned the age of thirty. Some of his hit songs included "Alexander's Ragtime Band" (his first hit song in 1911), "What'll I Do" (1924), "Blue Skies" (1927), "God Bless America" (1940), and "White Christmas" (1942).[52] Berlin composed the campaign song "(Good Times with Hoover) Better Times with Al," which spoke of the prosperity the country would have with Al Smith as the president:

Verse:
Whether we elect a GOP
Or the man who comes from Albany,
We'll remain OK
In a business way,
Looking at the future, we can see:

Chorus 1:
Good times with Hoover,
Better times with AL;
Blue skies with Hoover,
Bluer skies with AL.
Prosperity does not depend on who's in the chair,
We're bound to have prosperity no matter who's there.
So we'll have Good times with Hoover,
Better times with AL!

Chorus 2:
Good times with Hoover,
Better times with AL;
Blue skies with Hoover,
Bluer skies with AL.
They tell us that the future will be rosy and bright,
But they don't have to tell us, we admit that they're right.
That we'll have good times with Hoover,
Better times with AL!

"Better Times With AL" by Irving Berlin
© Copyright 1928 by Irving Berlin - © Copyright Renewed
International Copyright Secured   All Rights Reserved   Reprinted by Permission

Putting aside the irony of using this song in 1928, just one year before the beginning of the Great Depression, "(Good Times with Hoover) Better Times with Al," continued the practice since 1840 of mentioning the name of the candidate repeatedly. In fact, as music is expressed more over the mass media, it becomes more important to make sure that the candidates' names are mentioned numerous times during a song, as the listener would not be in the physical presence of the candidate. Indeed, during the nineteenth century, a smaller voting

population and geographical area allowed presidential candidates to largely engage in retail politics, where they could take their message to the people and
meet with the electorate directly. However, as the size of the country and the
number of voters were on the increase, retail campaigning became ever more
laborious for the candidates because it involved ever more traveling, hand shak-
ing, and stump speeches. Radio, and the wholesale politics it represented, allowed candidates to make fewer stops because their speeches could be heard live
by audiences all over the country. But this wholesale campaigning came at a
price, as the more intimate connection between the candidate and the voter was
lost. Thus, the candidate's name was often used in songs many times as part of
the "hook," so the electorate could walk away singing not only the tune, but the
name of the candidate as well. Al Smith made use of this same tactic in another
1928 campaign song, "Good-Bye Cal, Hello Al,"[53] "He's Our Al," and "Al
Smith for President."[54]

Slogan Song

In addition to the better fit between text and music, one other aspect served to
make campaign songs a useful tool in the interwar elections: the songs were
frequently written around the campaign slogan associated with a particular candidate. This is not the first time in history we saw this method used in campaign
music, as it occurred occasionally in earlier elections. "Tippecanoe and Tyler
Too" was the first campaign song to incorporate the campaign theme into the
campaign music, and James Blaine's 1884 slogan, "Ma! Ma! Where's My Pa?,"
was also the title of his campaign song. That point notwithstanding, it was not
the common practice to use the campaign slogan as the basis for a campaign
song during the nineteenth century. In other nineteenth-century elections where
campaigns used slogans within songs, the slogans were often altered slightly
within those songs. This alteration was likely done to make the slogans fit better
with the music. Another explanation could have been that there were multiple
renditions of the campaign slogan circulating the electorate. At a time when
songs and slogans were transmitted orally, it would have been common for a
variation or two to develop as the word was spread from person to person and
town to town. This would have been just a slight variation, but a variation nonetheless. One song that referenced an altered slogan was "We'll Give 'Em Jessie," which included a more articulated version of John C. Frémont's 1856 slogan of "Freedom, Freemen and Frémont!"[55] The song did not use the campaign
slogan as the title phrase but expanded the slogan where it was used in the song
to further articulate what Frémont stood for, saying "Free soil, Free labor, Free
speech, Free men, and Frémont."[56] The title, "We'll Give 'Em Jessie," was slang
for "We'll give 'em the business," or "We'll give 'em hell;" it also served as a
reference to the candidate's initials, J.C., and his wife's name, Jessie.[57] Another
example of this was in the election of 1900 which produced the song "The Full

Dinner Pail" for the William McKinley campaign. The slogan "The Full Dinner Pail" was actually used as part of McKinley's 1896 campaign and was revived in 1900 as "Four More Years of the Full Dinner Pail."[58] In this song, the campaign slogan was shortened back to its original form from 1896. Although it was used in the title figure of the song, the slogan "Dinner Pail" is the only remaining portion of the slogan mentioned within each verse.[59]

While this method was used sparingly throughout the nineteenth century, the introduction of the radio into elections in 1924 accelerated the use of campaign slogans in campaign songs. That year, Calvin Coolidge had a campaign slogan of "Keep Cool and Keep Coolidge," which was turned into an original campaign song for the candidate. With lyrics written by Ida Cheever Goodwin and music by Bruce Harper, this song was described as "The Official Campaign Song of the Home Town Coolidge Club of Plymouth, Vermont":[60]

Verse 1:
In a quaint New England farmhouse on an early summer's day,
A farmer's boy became out Chief in a homely simple way,
With neither pomp nor pageantry, he firmly met the task,
To keep him on that job of his, is all the people ask.

Refrain:
So "Keep cool and keep Coolidge" is the slogan of today,
"Keep cool and keep Coolidge" for the good old U.S.A.
A lot of politicians cannot do a thing but knock,
But Calvin Coolidge is a man of action and not talk.

So just "Keep cool and keep Coolidge" in the White House four years more,
We have a chance to do it in this year of "twenty-four,"
He's been tried, he's never wanting, He is giving of his best,
"Keep cool and keep Coolidge" is our country's mighty test.

Verse 2:
With a private life of virtue and a public record clean,
He stands upon the summits with a countenance serene,
Defender of the righteous and a juggernaut to wrong,
We'll make him stay in Washington—a hundred million strong.
(Refrain)

From the original sheet music "Keep Cool and Keep Coolidge"
Published by Home Town Coolidge Club (Plymouth, VT)

The song's reference to keeping it "cool" was not just a play on Coolidge's last name. Silent Cal, as governor of Massachusetts, gained a positive national reputation of being calm when he successfully handled the 1919 Boston police strike.[61] After succeeding the presidency, he became well known for his relaxed, carefree demeanor, and this even extended to his golf game, where his consistently poor play never resulted in so much as a complaint or a swear word out of the president.[62] In fact, upon hearing the news that Harding had died of a heart attack, Coolidge was sworn in and promptly. . . [and]went to sleep for the evening![63] "Keep Cool and Keep Coolidge" was an accurate musical reflection of Coolidge's ability to handle adversity without losing his composure.

Much like he did for Harding four years earlier, Al Jolson performed for Coolidge at campaign rallies, this time singing "Keep Cool and Keep Coolidge."[64] The song accomplished what "Tippecanoe and Tyler Too" did nearly a century earlier. It spoke about the virtues of Coolidge and how he was the candidate who showed he could act on behalf of the will of the people. The song also articulated with disdain how other "politicians" (including Coolidge's political opponents) could talk a great game but were reluctant to act. Furthermore, the song touted Coolidge as the "defender of righteousness" and as the "juggernaut to wrong," attempting to solidify him firmly on the moral high ground of the election. What's more, the fuller integration of the music with the campaign (including the slogan) was probably another direct consequence of the growth of radio. The more attenuated connection between the candidate and the voter was necessitating campaigns to have unifying themes; in modern jargon, the campaigns began to see a need to "stay on message." Before radio, it was easier for candidates to change their speeches, and their music, as they traveled from place to place around the country to suit the local political climate. However, if the same speech a candidate gives in Boston can also be heard over the radio in New York, Atlanta, Chicago, Houston, and San Francisco, a candidate would need to craft a speech that appealed not just to the local crowd but also to all of the potential radio listeners. Campaign music would fall under the same rules, needing to be evermore connected to the themes of the campaign. Uniting the slogan and the song into one was an effective way of accomplishing this goal. Perhaps this also explains why another one of the president's campaign songs in 1924 had a catchy slogan as its title: "Coolidge and Dawes for the Nation's Cause."[65]

Coolidge was not the only candidate to have his slogans turned into song in the 1924 election. John W. Davis' slogan of "Remember the Teapot Dome" was adapted into song with lyrics by J.J. Carney and music by P.B. Story. The song, actually entitled "John W. Davis," reminded people about the Tea Pot Dome scandal during the Harding administration (of which Coolidge was the vice president) and emphasized Davis' theme of reform. Furthermore, the song speaks to the moral compass that Davis would provide to the country that his predecessors lacked and spoke of how he would reclaim the lost navy oil lands for the American people:

Verse 1:
John W. Davis is the name we shout,
The Old Republican Party we'll show "this way out"
This last administration Just surprised our dear old Nation,
Remember the Teapot Dome.

Chorus:
Hurray, Hurray, we'll have good times once more,
When Davis gets behind the White House door.
When we're under honest rule,
And no Politician's tool,
Gee, won't republicans be sore.
Let's hope he takes the rotten Ku-Klux-Klan
And wipes them out to ev'ry living man.
Hurray, Hurray for Davis,
The only man to save us.
Remember the Teapot Dome.

Verse 2:
John W. Davis the choice to make,
And we will never regret it for our welfare's at stake,
We need his good protection and insist on his election,
Remember the Teapot Dome!
(Chorus)

Verse 3:
Our Davis upholds all that is good and true,
West Virginia says, "We are proud of you,"
Our Nation's losses he'll retrieve,
He'll spurn all bribes, he'll not deceive,
Remember the Teapot Dome!
(Refrain)

Verse 4:
John W. Davis without spot or stain,
Will help to get all the Navy oil lands back again,
He'll win in this election,
And through his wise direction,
He'll save the Teapot Dome!
(Refrain)

From the original sheet music "John W. Davis"
Published by J. J. Carney (New York), 1924

The "Teapot Dome" was the name given to the 1922 oil bribery scandal and ensuing investigation of the Harding administration. Teapot Dome was a Wyoming oil reserve that was known by that name because of a teapot-shaped stone formation on the site. It was administered in the early 1920s by Secretary of the Interior Albert Fall, who was also a close friend of President Harding. The Teapot Dome reserve and another one in Elk Hills, California, had been under the control of the navy. However, Secretary Fall was able to transfer control of those lands to the Department of the Interior in the early 1920s. Shortly thereafter, Fall secretly leased drilling rights to the reserves to two oil companies.

These leases had been awarded without competitive bidding, and Fall became the recipient of large loans from the companies, which did not charge him interest.[66] After *The Wall Street Journal* broke the story in 1922, Republican Senator La Follette led an investigation of the affair.[67] The scandal was a poster child for corporate-created government corruption, one of the issues that eventually drove La Follette to break away from the Republicans and run for the presidency as the Progressive Party nominee in 1924. For his part in the scandal, Albert Fall was later convicted of accepting bribes, sentenced to a year in prison, and fined $100,000.[68] Up until the Watergate scandal in 1972, the Teapot Dome scandal was considered to be the "greatest and most sensational scandal in the history of American politics" and is now "used to symbolize the power and influence of oil companies in American politics."[69]

Despite the fact that Coolidge was only the vice president when this incident occurred (he did not take office until 1923 upon the death of Harding), the Teapot Dome incident was used by the Davis campaign in "Remember the Teapot Dome" to brand Coolidge as corrupt. One can also notice in Davis' song, as with Coolidge's, that the lyricist attempted to give the candidate the moral high ground in the campaign. Furthermore, in using the scandal to paint Coolidge as a part of scandal bribery-laden administration, Davis' song also utilized negative campaign tactics in the same song. This tactic is also quite popular in our electoral system today, especially with the use of commercials that begin by announcing the virtues of a given candidate before describing the political sins of an opponent.

Finally, "Remember the Teapot Dome" included a bit of irony when considered over the long term. The song, while decrying the failings of Coolidge and other Republicans, tells the listener that it hopes Davis "takes the rotten Ku-Klux-Klan, And wipes them out to ev'ry living man." Davis, an attorney by trade, served for a time as Woodrow Wilson's solicitor general, the person who represents the federal government in cases before the United States Supreme Court, and he would eventually argue over 100 cases before the U.S. Supreme Court. Three decades after Davis ran for president, he appeared before the Court in a companion case to *Brown v. Board of Education*, where he argued in favor of the now-overruled "separate but equal" doctrine.[70] Thus, the fact that his 1924 campaign song extolled as one of his virtues that he would wipe out the KKK is rather ironic when he would later argue that the Constitution allows for racial segregation in public schools. Regardless of the accuracy of Davis' song, it was another example of putting a campaign slogan to music.

Celebrities Become Vogue

In order to make them more effective, many of the campaign songs of the 1920s were produced in a "professional" manner, oftentimes being orchestrated for performance by professional musicians, making them acceptable for broadcast performance and for live performance in a large venue. Coolidge's "Keep Cool and Keep Coolidge" for example, was written to be performed by either a band or orchestra with a male or mixed quartet of singers, and, as stated earlier, was performed live on numerous occasions by Al Jolson.[71]

As radio was becoming more commonplace, it also created the phenomenon of celebrity. People could become overnight sensations simply by appearing on this medium, as the radio created a common sense of "community," whereby people could tune in and all listen to the same voice or hear about the same person. Although those of us living in the twenty-first century may think this celebrity deification is a cable television—inspired phenomenon, celebrity worship in the United States and elsewhere certainly predates the age of CNN, Fox News, and reality television programs. As noted by one media scholar, "[t]he television age took further something which radio had begun—the manufacturing of fame largely through appearances on the electronic media. From the late 1920s onward radio made celebrities out of bandleaders and comedians. . . radio newsreaders of the early 1940s were eminent examples of media celebrity."[72]

Politicians soon saw that they could capitalize on this celebrity phenomenon. Not only would candidates attempt to associate themselves with the famous songwriters who were writing and singing campaign songs for them, but they would also try to align themselves with popular figures of the day. This would work itself into campaign songs too. One example of this noted above was the use of Al Jolson by Harding and Coolidge. For another example, one only needs to turn to the election of 1928, when Herbert Hoover teamed up with Charles Lindbergh. Lindbergh had come to world fame after his solo flight across the Atlantic in 1927, even to the point that a popular dance of the era, the Lindy hop, was named after him. Lindbergh endorsed the presidential campaign of Herbert Hoover on October 3, 1928, telling Hoover, "[t]he more I see of your campaign, the more strongly I feel that your election is of supreme importance to the country."[73] Hoover hoped to use this connection with Lindbergh to boost his notoriety with the electorate (a move that was apparently part of Hoover's success, as he won the 1928 presidential election over Al Smith). This connection with Lindbergh was turned into the Hoover campaign song "If He's Good Enough for Lindy (He's Good Enough for Me)," which may have been the first endorsement song in U.S. campaign history.[74] The song began by describing Lindberg's famous transatlantic flight. It then referred back to its title, reflecting the well-known pilot's endorsement of Hoover. Basically, the song told the electorate that if such a great American hero supported this candidate, the rest of the country should as well. The song also went on to note Hoover's service during World War I, when as director of the U.S. Food Administration he led a food conservation drive that sent rations to American soldiers and allies in Europe.[75]

Overall, then, several developments become apparent in presidential campaign music during the 1920s. Songs became more professionalized, songwriters largely penned both the lyrics and the melodies to campaign music, slogans and music became one, and celebrity was exploited in song. Having songs professionally written was not always a good thing, however:

[T]he commercial publisher who, not wishing to risk economic loss, continued to rely upon relatively well-known Tin Pan Alley and ASCAP [American Society of Composers, Authors and Publishers] writers. They, however, were not usually tied to any particular party or candidate, thus their songs lacked the sharp edge and personal partisan involvement so common to their. . . predecessors. In fact, the lack of partisanship resulted in at least several incidences of a writer releasing two songs supporting opposing candidates.[76]

Consequently, the new trend of composed campaign songs did not mean the end of the more "amateur" songs or the songs that were set to the popular tunes of the day. Although these trends were fading, they had not completely disappeared. For instance, the 1920 Harding campaign produced "The Little Snug Old White House in the Lane" set to the tune of "Little Old Log Cabin in the Lane" and "The Campaign Hymn of the Republic" set to the tune of "John Brown's Body."[77] The 1928 campaign of Al Smith produced a song of the same title set to the tune of "Sidewalks of New York," which used much of the same text, but personalized portions to Smith.[78]

Nonpartisan songs also continued to be composed around the presidential elections of this period. For instance, Herb Magidson and Robert King commented on the 1928 election with their song, "Mr. Hoover and Mr. Smith." Although this was done in a slightly less colorful way than Brown and Grant had some sixteen years earlier with "The Election in Jungle Town," Magidson and King offered useful satire nonetheless. "Mr. Hoover and Mr. Smith" involved the listener seeing the two candidates in a dream. The song then depicted the two candidates continually jabbing barbs at each other through backhanded comments. Through these snide remarks, the listener is able to understand how each candidate is cynically viewed by the public, and some of the campaign issues were also described:

> I had a dream that other night,
> I saw two famous men,
> They met each other on the street,
> Shook hands awhile and then
> They started talking in a friendly way.
> And here's exactly what I heard them say:
>
> Who's the grandest greatest man this country ever knew?
> Oh! It's you, Mister Hoover
> No, it's you, Mister Smith.
> Excepting Georgie Washington, he was a good man, too
> He's not running, Mister Hoover,
> What a break, Mister Smith.
> Are you dry? You can't remember!
> But you'll know, know, know in November?
> Well, anyhow you'll get one vote, because I'll vote for you.
> Be yourself, Mister Hoover,

Keep the change, Mister Smith.

I've heard politicians say that you have got technique.
What technique, Mister Hoover?
It's the bunk, Mister Smith.
Why don't you bring your family to visit me next week?
Great idea, Mister Hoover.
Bring your lunch, Mister Smith.
Do you trust in your supporters?
I did once, but now I use garters.
I'm feeling kind of hoarse today,
Why I can hardly speak,
Try some oil, Mister Hoover,
No, I'm cured, Mister Smith.

This dream was such a funny sight,
It certainly was queer,
I watched but neither cracked a smile,
For they were both sincere.
I listened and I didn't miss a word,
Now here's some more of what I heard:

How will you treat the farmers if they put you in the chair?
Once a week, Mister Hoover;
Applesauce, Mister Smith.
I think you'll like the capitol, they'll give you lots of air,
Hot or cold, Mister Hoover,
Just hot air, Mister Smith.
Oh! I hear you're from the East Side,
No, you're wrong, old top, it's the WET side;
What will we give the people who have done more than their share?
Vacuum cleaners, Mister Hoover?
Why not cough drops, Mister Smith?

I've got some new ideas that I'd like to use next fall,
Hope you do Mister Hoover,
Yes, you do, Mister Smith.
I hear you've got some wrinkles up your sleeve, and that ain't all,
Lots of wrinkles, Mister Hoover,
Press your pants, Mister Smith.
You look swell in your brown derby,
Shows I'm not high-hatting you, Herbie.
Well Anyhow, I've got to go, I hear my Party call,
Reservoir, Mister Hoover,
Skip the gutter, Mister Smith.

"Mr. Hoover and Mr. Smith" poked fun at the candidates, portraying them as full of themselves and referencing potentially divisive issues. For instance, the offer for Hoover to "Try some oil," to which he replies "No, I'm cured," is almost certainly a reference to the Teapot Dome oil scandal, something that plagued the last Republican presidential candidate. The line for Smith, where he states he is from the "WET side," denotes Smith's anti-Prohibition stance (in fact, Smith's campaign slogan in 1928 was "Liberty we want beer."

First Depression, Then Happy Days Are Here Again

The prominence of campaign music, which was in a state of flux with the inception of radio, would succumb to hard times, falling off, especially for Republican candidates, in the 1930s and 1940s following the election of Franklin D. Roosevelt (whose main campaign song for his elections, "Happy Days Are Here Again," will be explored in chapter five because of its relevance to modern pop music in presidential campaigns). In part, the lack of campaign music can be attributed to the simple fact that there was comparatively less to sing about during the Great Depression. This does not mean that there was a lack of music during this time period, however.

Upon taking office in 1933, Roosevelt created the "Works Progress Administration" which, among other things, created the Federal Music Project to employ musicians on the relief roles who had been working relief projects.[79] These musicians were employed in a number of capacities including teachers, performers and composers/songwriters.[80] A great deal of this program was centered on classical musicians and educating the public. However, folk singers such as Woody Guthrie, Pete Seeger, and Jenny Vincent benefitted from the Federal Music Project as well, writing songs that contained a pro-union stance and progressive social messages.[81] Lawrence Epstein notes of these folk singers:

> They were naïve. Their songs were meant to be splinters under society's skin, causing pain and requiring attention. They were as young in thought as they were in years, readier to create than to evaluate. They wanted to build graveyards to encrypt the past. Their caution had been amputated. They were, to adapt T.S. Eliot's comment in another context, people "dreaming of systems so perfect no one will need to be good." The folk singers saw the horrors of the Great Depression, but they also saw the Roosevelt Administration using the federal government to fix economic problems.[82]

Consequently, a number of these songs also sang in support of Roosevelt and acknowledged the support he had for the labor movement, thus continuing to solidify his popularity among the electorate. Epstein also notes a fundamental issue with these folk singers, noting that:

As artists, in many cases as musical geniuses, they didn't understand that sur-
rendering their art to a larger principal was a form of suicide. The ideology
could either limit their overall subject matter or limit their views within the political subjects they wrote about. Their ideology stopped them from exploring
other political views. . . . The ideology made them listen to political ideas for
lessons on art, not to the audiences they to whom they were singing or wished
to reach.[83]

Whatever the shortcomings may have been as songwriters, their music was popular among the labor movement, particularly in the American South. However,
as the goal of the Roosevelt administration's Federal Music Project was ultimately one of educating the public about the arts, these types of folk artists were
"exceptions to the nonpolitical thrust of the program."[84]

Following the Great Depression, WWII was in full force with songs that
"focused on soldiers and separation from loved ones."[85] In fact, the music during
the campaign and early years of Roosevelt's presidency was the last music of
any prominence until the end of the war. Perhaps another reason why campaign
music receded during this era can be attributed to Roosevelt's high popularity.
Given his landslide victories in all four of his elections, there was not as much of
a need for Roosevelt to use music, nor were his opponents as inclined to pour
time and money into music at a time when there was not much money available
for campaigning. This fact was borne out in the 1936 election. As observed by
one reporter of the time, "[c]ampaign song-writers are again at work. Republican headquarters has been flooded with songs, despite the announcement that
the party intends to adopt no official anthem. Democratic headquarters, apparently, is less interested in singing, for few reports of new songs are heard."[86]
Thus, songs played a smaller role during this time, although interest in campaign
music appeared to be slightly on the rise in the years leading up to World War
II.

Jerry Rodnitzky has noted that the strength of Franklin Roosevelt was in his
inherent ability to connect on an emotional level with the American public.[87] His
emotional appeal was largely tied to the medium of radio, as Roosevelt made
frequent use of his "fireside chats" to connect with the American public. His use
of the media would not arguably be equaled until Ronald Reagan's effective use
of television led him to be dubbed the "Great Communicator." Despite Roosevelt's emotional connection, the songs from the 1932 campaign were not overly
specific to Roosevelt, nor were they necessarily emotional. Some examples of
these songs include "Row, Row, Row with Roosevelt," "Everything will be
Rosy with Roosevelt" and "On the Right Road with Roosevelt." Note how these
songs make extensive use of Roosevelt's name, a common campaign song tactic
during the radio era. Another song that fits this category would be "We Want a
Man Like Roosevelt" by Kenneth Wardall.

Verse 1:
A Democratic vic'try is on its way,
'Twill reach us in November when the vote will say,

From Maine to California, from the mountains to the sea,
F.D. Roosevelt's been elected, our next president he'll be.

Chorus:
We want a man like Roosevelt,
We want a man that knows,
How to pull the country from depression's pit,
How to furnish work for men who crave for it.
We want a man like Roosevelt,
One with proven grit and courage rare,
He'll knock out prohibition with repeal, not resubmission,
When he's seated in the Presidential chair.

Verse 2:
Throughout our glorious nation a sign appears,
It tells of want and hunger and our children's tears,
But greed will soon be routed and the poor forgotten man
Will have all that God intended when our chief drafts his plan.

Copyright © 1932 by Kenneth Wardell
Published and Sold by Charles Coleman (Brooklyn, N.Y.), 1932

All of these songs, including "We Want a Man Like Roosevelt," talk about the future president in glowing terms, but in a very generic sense. Despite the "lack of emotional" connection associated with the campaign, in 1932 Roosevelt would have no problem winning over the electorate because Hoover had comparatively little credibility during the Great Depression after promising "chicken in every pot and a car in every garage" in his 1928 campaign slogan. "When partisans of Roosevelt sang the Democratic theme song of the year, 'Happy Days Are Here Again,' it seemed as though change was possible."[88] The song was also a reference to Roosevelt's promise to repeal prohibition, thus bringing "happy hour" back[89] (other Roosevelt campaign songs that exemplified the "wet" theme were "Kiss Yourself Goodbye!" and "Gone Are the Days[90]"). And in 1934, when Roosevelt adopted "Happy Days Are Here Again" as his economic recovery theme song, the president began making more of an emotional connection to the electorate. As he brought his New Deal reforms to the American public, his popularity among the voters was sealed. Roosevelt would continue to use "Happy Days" for his future presidential campaigns with much success.

These would not be the only songs used, however, as prominent singer/songwriters of the day, such as Bill Cox, Jay Gorney, and Henry Myers wrote and performed new songs for Roosevelt in his successful campaigns of 1936, 1940, and 1944 as well.[91] This was a continuation of the trend that developed in the 1920s of presidential candidates attaching themselves to celebrities who had gained fame through the radio. For instance, in 1932, prominent singer Eddie Cantor attached himself to Roosevelt by singing, "Roosevelt, Garner, and Me" (another song with significant name references).[92] Not only was Garner a singer, but he was also a major Broadway and film star. Also in 1932, up-and-coming movie star/singer Dick Powell sang "The Road Is Open Again," which described Roosevelt's proposed National Recovery Administration.[93] It appears that Roosevelt understood quite well the importance of celebrity in presidential campaigns.

Roosevelt and his campaign staff also knew that the radio age demanded songs that repeatedly mentioned the candidate's name. In addition to the songs he used like this in 1932, Roosevelt also had "Franklin D. Roosevelt's Back Again" and "Mister Roosevelt, Won't You Please Run Again" in 1940,[94] as well as 1940's "Let's Re-Re-Re-Elect Roosevelt."[95]

As for Roosevelt's Republican opponents, they attempted a slightly different strategy, but one that was still prominently used in the radio age. In addition to using songs that emphasized their names, Alfred Landon and Wendell Willkie tied their campaign slogans into their campaign songs. In 1936, the official Republican campaign song was "Happy Landin' with Landon,"[96] which was a play on one of Landon's campaign slogans, "Land Landon with a Landslide."[97] In an attempt to have a complete match, in 1940 Wendell Willkie's song had the same title as his slogan: "We Want Willkie."[98] Although each of these Republican challengers also used a theme of alliteration, they ultimately failed to defeat the ever-popular Roosevelt, as did Dewey in 1944.

Finally, as a precursor to campaigning on a visual medium (something that we will describe in the next chapter), in 1944 Roosevelt began dabbling in animated film. The thirteen-minute cartoon short *Hell-Bent for Election* depicts Roosevelt as a streamlined diesel train engine, named "Win the War Special," racing against an old-fashioned Republican train, named "Defeatist Limited." The voters are represented by a longshoreman, Joe, who is encouraged to sidetrack the "Defeatist Limited" and get the "Win the War Special" to Washington. This is to be done without falling asleep at the switch, something the cartoon Joe did in 1942, when Republicans gained seats in both houses of Congress. A well-dressed Republican operative attempts in multiple ways to make Joe fall unconscious. In addition to the cartoon's background music, there is a sing-along at the end, titled "We're Going to Win the War," that encourages voters to cast their ballot for Roosevelt:[99]

> There'll be a job for everyone,
> Everyone - everyone,
> There'll be a job for everyone
> If we get out and vote.
>
> You want to have security,
> Security - security,
> You want to have security
> You've got to get out and vote.
>
> They're growing big red apples
> That Hoover is promoting.
> If you don't want to sell those apples,

Start voting, man! Start voting!

Oh! Get behind the President,
President - President
Get behind the president
If you want to win the war.
Right behind the president 1944.
Vote![100]

This was the first known use of a presidential campaign song in a cartoon short. Although the combination of cartoons and music in presidential campaigns was still in its infancy in 1944, by the 1950s other candidates, particularly Eisenhower, would make much more extensive use of this method of appealing to voters.

Wild Thing

It has been said that the election of Harry Truman in 1948 was not notable for its campaign music; in fact, it has been suggested by some that the postwar elections represented the final decline, and perhaps death, of the campaign song's importance within presidential campaigns.[101] If one is comparing these songs to those of the "singing campaigns" of the nineteenth century that might be an accurate assessment. However, if one looks at the music through the eyes of a campaign attempting to market its candidate, this is not true at all. Truman, for example, was able to take "I'm Just Wild About Harry," and exploit the fact that the song used his first name in the title. The song was written by Noble Sissle and Eubie Blake and made popular in the 1921 musical "Shuffle Along," the first completely African American production on Broadway.[102]

The song contains an up-beat ragtime theme and was an instant success with the public. Truman's campaign changed the words of the original song to focus more on the campaign message. However, at the same time, the song was short and to the point, a recipe that was perfect for the radio age. The modified lyrics spoke of how wild the singer was about Truman and conversely how Truman was just as excited about both the country and each individual citizen. In addition, the song references Roosevelt's "New Deal" and indicates that Truman will continue those policies in his administration if elected.[103] "I'm Just Wild About Harry" mentioned Truman's name (first and/or last) a total of six times within this short span. Truman most assuredly benefited from having an existing popularized song that already contained his first name that he could manipulate in this way without changing the song's existing "hook." This is a benefit that other campaigns would not necessarily have.

However, a shift was under way toward the use of popular song more in the coming decades, as campaigns continued to "market" their candidates in the most effective way possible. One way of accomplishing this was by finding a song with the candidates' name already in it (such as was done by Truman); an alternative method was finding a song with a hook containing a campaign message about a candidate with verses that could be altered slightly to speak more to the candidate's message. The shift back to popular songs may simply have to do with the ability of the electorate to associate a popular tune with a candidate. While a new song gives a candidate more of a chance to "say what one needs to say," it does not have the preexisting popular appeal and consequently the popular association that even a parodied song can give you despite the flaws inherent in a parodied song. One other factor that might have led to this trend was the attempt to associate a candidate with not only what was popular, but also with who was popular during any giving election. This would lend popular credibility to a candidate and allow him or her to appeal to the electorate through a song or performing artist that already had won the popularity of the general public. This effect will also be seen to a greater extent when campaigns start making use of television.

Overall, the radio age marked a shift away from the singing campaigns and retail politics to mass marketing and wholesale politics. This meant a greater need of songs that frequently repeated the candidate's name to help foster name recognition. Another increasingly common way to accomplish this goal and "stay on message" was by using campaign slogans as song titles, song lyrics, or both. Finally, as the radio helped develop national celebrities, especially singing stars, politicians began to ask for endorsements and songs from these new icons, as a way to connect with the public.

Notes

1. Alexander Keyssar, *The Right to Vote: The Contested History of Democracy in the United States* (New York: Basic Books, 2000), 149-71; The National Archives, *Our Documents: 100 Milestone Documents from the National Archives* (New York: Oxford University Press, 2003),152-53; Marjorie Shuler, "Out of Subjection Into Freedom," in *The Woman Citizen* (September 4, 1920), 360.

2. Irwin Silber, *Songs America Voted By: From George Washington to Richard Nixon—the Gutsy Story of Presidential Campaigning* (Harrisburg, PA: Stackpole Books, 1971), 239.

3. Andrew B. Sterling and Robert A. Keiser, "Be Good to California, Mr. Wilson (California Was Good to You)" (New York: Shapiro, Bernstein & Co., Inc., 1916).

4. Danny O. Crew, *Suffragist Sheet Music: An Illustrated Catalog of Published Music Associated with the Women's Rights and Suffrage Movement in America, 1795-1921* (Jefferson: MacFarland, 2002), 341.

5. Franny Nudelman, *John Brown's Body: Slavery, Violence & the Culture of War* (Chapel Hill, NC: The University of North Carolina Press, 2004), 14.

6. George Kimball, "Origin of the John Brown Song," *The New England Magazine*, December 1889, 317-377; 372.

7. Kimball, "Origin of the John Brown Song," 374.

8.   James Douglas Sporborg, *Music in Every Classroom: A Resource Guide for Integrating Music across the Curriculum, Grades K-8* (Englewood, CA: Libraries Unlimited, 1998), 94.

9.   George E. Fairbanks, "Taft and Sherman," in *Fairbanks' Republican Campaign Songs* (South Cornish, NH: George E. Fairbanks, 1912); Ballard MacDonald and George Walter Brown, "Wilson—That's All!" (New York: Shapiro, Bernstein & Co., Inc., 1912); George W. Gale, "Line Up for Bryan" (Cincinnati, OH: The Gale and Mullane Music Company, 1908); Harry D. Kerr and Abe Holzmann, "Get On the Raft with Taft" (New York: Leo Feist, Inc., 1908 and 1912).

10.   Antti V. Räisänen and Arto Lehto, *Radio Engineering for Wireless Communication and Sensor Applications*, (Norwood, MA: Artech House, Inc., 2003), 6-7.

11.   Räisänen and Lehto, *Radio Engineering*, 6-7.

12.   Räisänen and Lehto, *Radio Engineering*, 6-7.

13.   Räisänen and Lehto, *Radio Engineering*, 7.

14.   Joseph Straubhaar, Robert LaRose, Lucinda Davenport, *Media Now: Understanding Media, Culture, and Technology* (Belmot, CA: Wadsworth, 2009), 159.

15.   Lewis Coe, *The Telegraph: A History of Morse's Invention and Its Predecessors in the United States*, (Jefferson, NC: McFarland & Company, Inc., Publishers, 2003), 145.

16.   Tom Kuntz, ed., *The Titanic Disaster Hearings: The Official Transcripts of the 1912 Senate Investigation*, (New York: Pocket Books, 1998).

17.   Coe, *The Telegraph*, 147.

18.   W.J. Stanton, "The Independent Exchange at Prairie City, Ia," *Telephony, Volume 17, No. 5* (January 30, 1909): 126.

19.   James A. Hijiya, *Lee De Forest and the Fatherhood of the Radio*, (Cranbury, NJ: Associated University Press, 1992), 71.

20.   Edward C. Pease and Everette E. Dennis, ed., *Radio: The Forgotten Medium* (New Brunswick, NJ: Transaction Publishers, 1995), 6.

21.   Edward W. Chester, *Radio, Television and American Politics*, (New York: Sheed and Ward, Inc., 1969), 9.

22.   John Fass Morton, *Backstory in Blue: Ellington at Newport '56* (Piscataway, NJ: Rutgers University Press, 2008), 46.

23.   Morton, *Backstory in Blue*, 15.

24.   Morton, *Backstory in Blue*, 16.

25.   Michael X. Delli Carpini, "Radio's Political Past," in *Radio: The Forgotten Medium*, ed. Edward C. Pease and Everette E. Dennis (New Brunswick, NJ: Transaction Publishers, 1995), 21.

26.   Eunice Fuller Barnard, "Radio Politics," *The New Republic* (March 1924): 91-93; 91.

27.   Don Moore, "The 1924 Radio Election," accessed June 8, 2010, http://www.pateplumaradio.com/genbroad/elec1924.html.

28.   Jerry Rodnitzky, "Popular Music," in *The American President in Popular Culture*, ed. John W. Matviko (Westport, CT: Greenwood Press, 2005), 40.

29.   Moore, "The 1924 Radio Election."

30.   "Historical Election Results: Electoral College Box Scores, 1789-1996," Office of the Federal Register, accessed July 13, 2010, http://www.archives.gov/federal-register/electoral-college/scores.html#1924.

31.   David G. Clark, "Radio in Presidential Campaigns: The Early Years (1924-1932)," *The Journal of Broadcasting, Volume 6 Issue 3 (Spring 1962)*: 229-238; 229-230.

32.   Clark, 235.

33.   "Agree Radio Raises Plane of Politics: Senators Moses and Harrison in Debate Find an Issue on Which They Are in Accord," *The New York Times*, October 25, 1928, p. 8.

34.   *The New York Times*, "Agree Radio Raises Plane of Politics."

35.   *The New York Times*, "Agree Radio Raises Plane of Politics."

36.   Stuart Schimler, "Singing to the Oval Office: A Written History of the Political Campaign Song," accessed June 10, 2010, http://www.presidentelect.org/art_schimler_singing.html.

37.   George Stuyvesant Jackson, *Early Songs of Uncle Sam* (Boston: Bruce Humphries Publisher, 1933), 103-104.

38.   Schimler "Singing to the Oval Office."

39.   Irwin Silber, *Songs America Voted By*, 236.

40.   William Miles, Introduction to *Songs, Odes, Glees and Ballads: A Bibliography of American Presidential Campaign Songsters* (New York: Greenwood Press, 1990), Xliii.

41.   Barnard, "Radio Politics," 92.

42.   Luther A. Huston Washington, "The Voters Still Sing, Though Faintly," *The New York Times*, September 27, 1936, 13.

43.   Huston Washington, "The Voters Still Sing," 13.

44.   Jim Coxx, *Sold on Radio: Advertisers in the Golden Age of Broadcasting* (Jefferson, NC: McFarland and Company, Inc. Publishers, 2008), 161.

45.   Coxx, *Sold on Radio*, 24, 126; William David Sloan and James D. Startt, *The Media in America: A History* (Scottsdale, AZ: Publishing Horizons, Inc., 1990), 424.

46.   Roy Hemming and David Hajdu, *Discovering Great Singers of Classic Pop: A New Listeners Guide to 52 Top Crooners and Canaries with Extensive Discographies, Videographies and Recommendations for Collectors* (New York: New Market Press, 1991), 12.

47.   Hemming and Hajdu, *Discovering Great Singers*, 12.

48.   Nan Britton, *Honesty or Politics* (New York: Elizabeth Ann Guild, Inc., 1932), 211.

49.   Kevin Kusinitz, "Celebrity Endorsements," *Weekly Standard* May 23, 2008, accessed July 11, 2010, http://www.weeklystandard.com/Content/Public/Articles/000/000/015/127joosu.asp.

50.   Silber, *Songs America Voted By*, 249

51.   Judith Tick and Paul Beadoin, ed., *Music in the USA: A Documentary Companion*, (New York: Oxford University Press, 2008), 378.

52.   George Frazier, "Irving Berlin," *Life*, April 5, 1943, 80.

53.   Beryl Frank, *The Pictorial History of the Democratic Party* (Secaucus, NJ: Castle Books, 1980), 112.

54.   Silber, *Songs America Voted By*, 248-50.

55.   Robert North Roberts and Scott John Hammond, *Encyclopedia of Presidential Campaigns, Slogans, Issues, and Platforms* (Westport, CT: Greenwood Press, 2004), 36.

56.   Silber, *Songs America Voted By*, 69.

57.   Irwin Silber, ed., *Songs of the Great American West* (Mineola: Dover Publications, 1995), 30; Irwin Silber, ed., *Songs of the Civil War* (Mineola: Dover Publications, 1995), 169.

58.   Silber, *Songs of the Great American West*, 64-65.

59.   Silber, *Songs America Voted By*, 176-177.

60.   Danny O. Crew, *Presidential Sheet Music: An Illustrated Catalogue,* (Jefferson, NC: McFarland & Company, Inc., Publishers, 2001), 124.

61.   Robin S. Doak, *Calvin Coolidge* (Minneapolis, MN: Compass Point Books, 2004), 19-21.

62.   Don Van Natta Jr., *First off the Tee: Presidential Hackers, Duffers and Cheaters from Taft to Bush* (Cambridge, MA: Public Affairs Books, 2003), 153-56.

63.   Doak, *Calvin Coolidge*, 26.

64.   Kusinitz, "Celebrity Endorsements."

65.   Beryl Frank, *The Pictorial History of the Republican Party* (Secaucus, NJ: Castle Books, 1980), 105.

66.   Kim Long, *The Almanac of Political Corruption, Scandals and Dirty Politics* (New York: Delacorte Press, 2007).

67.   Barbara J. Davis, *The Teapot Dome Scandal: Corruption Rocks 1920s America* (Minneapolis, MN: Compass Point Books, 2008), 48.

68.   Long, *The Almanac of Political Corruption.*

69.   Robert W. Cherny, "Graft and Oil: How Teapot Dome Became the Greatest Political Scandal of its Time." *History Now.* Gilder Lehrman Institute of American History, accessed June 10, 2010, http://www.gilderlehrman.org/historynow/historian5.php.

70.   Richard Kluger, *Simple Justice: The History of Brown v. Board of Education and Black America's Struggle for Equality*, (New York: Knopf, 1976).

71.   Crew, *Presidential Sheet Music*, 124.

72.   Jeremy Tunstall, *The Media in Britain* (New York: Columbia University Press, 1983), 1.

73.   Leonard Mosley, *Lindbergh: A Biography* (Mineola, NY: Dover Publications, 1976), 135.

74.   Silber, *Songs America Voted By*, 251.

75.   Oscar Brand, vocal performance of "If He's Good Enough for Lindy (He's Good Enough for Me)," by an unknown composer, on *Presidential Campaign Songs 1789-1996*, Smithsonian Folkways Recordings, 45052, released in 1999, compact disc.

76.   Miles, *Songs, Odes, Glees and Ballads*, xlv.

77.   Thomas Andrew Bailey, *Voices of America: The Nation's Story in Slogans, Sayings, and Songs* (New York: The Free Press, 1976), 360.

78.   Jerry Silverman, *New York Sings: 400 Years of the Empire State in Song* (Albany: State University of New York Press, 2009), 90.

79.   Kathryn A. Flynn and Richard Polese, *The New Deal: A 75th Anniversary Celebration* (Layton, Utah: Gibbs Smith, 2008), 56.

80.   Flynn & Polese, *The New Deal*, 56.

81.   Flynn & Polese, *The New Deal*, 62.

82.   Lawrence Jeffery Epstein, *Political Folk Music in America from Its Origins to Bob Dylan* (Jefferson, NC: McFarland & Company, Inc., Publishers, 2010), 121.

83.   Epstein, *Political Folk Music*, 121.

84.   Flynn & Polese, 62.

85.   Rodnitzky, "Popular Music," 40.

86.   Washington, "The Voters Still Sing,"13.

87.   Rodnitzky, "Popular Music," 40.

88.   Silber, *Songs America Voted By*, 256.

89.   Frank, *The Pictorial History of the Democratic Party.*

90.   Silber, *Songs America Voted By*, 259-60.

91.   Rodnitzky, "Popular Music," 41.

92.   Frank, *The Pictorial History of the Democratic Party*, 119.

93.   Frank, *The Pictorial History of the Democratic Party*, 121.

94.   Silber, *Songs America Voted By*, 269-72.

95. Frank, *The Pictorial History of the Democratic Party*, 135.

96. Frank, *The Pictorial History of the Republican Party*, 122.

97. Eric Swartz, "U.S. Presidential Campaign Slogans," (2011), accessed May 2, 2011, http://www.taglineguru.com/campaignsloganlist.html.

98. Frank, *The Pictorial History of the Republican Party*, 125-27.

99. *Hell-Bent for Election, Part One*, (October 28, 2007), accessed May 2, 2011, http://www.youtube.com/watch?v=xhykCuN_BpY, and *Hell-Bent for Election, Part Two*, (October 28, 2007), accessed May 2, 2011, http://www.youtube.com/watch?v= 3U3A6DWQ0zY&feature=related.

100. *Hell-Bent for Election, Part Two.*

101. Silber, *Songs America Voted By*, 281.

102. Steven Gould Axelrod, Camille Roman, and Thomas Travisano, eds., *The New Anthology of American Poetry: Modernisms: 1900-1950* (Piscataway, NJ: Rutgers University Press, 2005), 596.

103. Sissle, Noble and Eubie Blake. "I'm Just Wild About Harry" (Los Angeles: Warner Bros. Inc., 1921).

~ 4 ~

Good Night, and Good Luck
(1952-1968)

Just as radio had done before it, television had humble beginnings but then slowly began to create a larger and larger market share for itself in the United States. The advent of television did not mark the first time that presidential campaigns had used the visual medium as a part of their campaign strategy. As noted in the last chapter, for years candidates had used the cinema to project their image on the big screen for all to see, as in the film short *Hell-Bent for Election*. However, television represented the first time that candidate images could be sent directly into the home of the electorate, making it a powerful tool for presidential candidates just as the radio had been and would continue to be.

Also like the radio before it, the technological developments that would bring the television began in the nineteenth century. The earliest experiments with the transmission of image revolved around the use of optical, mechanical, and electronic technologies. By the 1920s, however, optical and electronic technologies had been shown to have the most promise with optical technologies the center of the modern television today.

In 1873, Willoughby Smith, an English electrical engineer, discovered the effects that light had on selenium.[1] Smith noticed that the resistance of selenium varied with the amount of light that the material was exposed, thus changing the electrical current of the material based on the amount of light that it was exposed to.[2] This photoconductivity, or change in electrical current, discovered by Smith would begin the voyage which brought television to the world. It would also be the basis of early television designs. The first of these was done eleven years after Smith's discovery, when, in 1884, a 23-year-old German university student named Paul Gottlieb Nipkow invented and patented the first electromagnetic television, employing the use of a scanning disk.[3] While this technology would allow for the transmission of still images, the transmission of moving images presented difficulties. Scottish inventor John Logie Baird is credited with having the world's first true demonstration television on October 30, 1925, although it was through the use of mechanical scanners which are no longer used today.[4] Baird also developed the first video recording device in 1927, the same year that Philo Farnsworth made the first working television system. Thus, just as radio was becoming a staple in U.S. political campaigns and in transmitting music, the technology of television was just developing. This would eventually lead to television becoming the dominant medium in American politics, and campaign music would also be a part of this transformation.

The first practical use of television occurred in Germany with regular broadcasts established in 1929. While experimental mechanical television broadcasting began in the United States in the 1920s, it was not until 1941 that commercial television broadcasting began.[5] During the late 1920s and 1930s, televisions were being sold in the United States and programming was available via local stations. It was during this time that television began to see the tentative steps toward becoming an intrigue part of presidential campaigns. In the 1928 presidential campaign, Governor Alfred Smith stood in front of television cameras in Albany, New York, to accept his party's nomination, which was carried on the General Electric Station in Schenectady.[6] Four years later in the election of 1932, the Democratic National Committee produced a television program over station W2XAB in New York.[7] And in 1940 the first television coverage of a national convention took place with anywhere between 40,000 and 100,000 viewers watching the Republican National Convention, which took place in Philadelphia, over stations in eastern Pennsylvania and in New York.[8]

It was not until the 1952 election, however, that the television began to assume its prominent role in presidential campaigns (and all of politics for that matter).[9] By that year, there were enough television sets in circulation in the United States to make advertising on the medium an effective way to communicate a campaign's message to the electorate.[10] As with the development of the radio, television has had a major effect on the way campaigns go about selling their candidates. The radio allowed candidates to spread the message of their campaign to a larger group of potential voters with one address. The upside and downside to the radio were one in the same. The electorate could hear the candidate speak, but they could not see the candidate. Consequently, candidates would need to be well spoken or, in other words, they would need to have a voice that would communicate well over the radio. With the development of the television, the electorate could now not only hear the candidates, but see them as well. No longer was it enough to have a candidate who simply spoke well, but there was a need for a candidate to be well mannered and have a television presence. Candidates from this point on would need to be visually appealing, which might include possessing physical attractiveness, having the right dress, and projecting favorable nonverbal communication. Music could be one way of accentuating these visuals or compensating for a lack of them.

The introduction of television into American politics offered candidates all of the benefits of radio along with the ability to be seen by voters in much the same way as at a campaign rally (and usually seen better than at a campaign rally, as many persons at a large campaign stop are a significant distance from the candidate). As noted by Kaid and Johnston, the television medium offered multiple advantages over other modes of communication. First, like radio before it, television could reach more viewers than traditional campaign stops or the newspaper (which, unlike television or radio, requires the ability to read). As television became more popular in the 1950s and 1960s, it surpassed radio in its increased ability to reach the electorate. Second, and again like radio, the message was under the control of the candidate. Unlike a campaign stop that might be hampered by crowd noise or even disrupted by hecklers, messages on the mass media were not disturbed by such factors. Third, presentation was controlled by the campaigns. With radio, this meant that a candidate with a hoarse voice could wait to record a speech or advertisement until his or her voice was healed. With television and its visual images, this manipulation allowed for a tired candidate to tape and to retake until the clip met with the candidate's approval, or to use makeup and lighting to alter one's appearance.[11] All of these factors would also drive how campaign music, both in the form of full songs with lyrics and background music, would be heard on television. For instance, a performer taping a song for radio or television use no longer had to worry about stage fright or forgetting lines because a poorly sung song could simply be retaped.

The addition of the television might lead an astute observer to one of a few conclusions. First, that campaign music simply stayed as a radio-based medium and did not have influence on the television campaigns of presidential candidates. Second, that music made drastic changes in order to adapt to the television medium. Or, third, that music continued to wither as a campaign tool, as suggested earlier by Irwin Silber, Jerry Rodnitzky and William Miles. The reality is that campaign music made a very smooth, albeit limited, transition from live performances and radio to the early stages of television. The distinguishing factor was that the music in television spots may not have been the same as was used at campaign stops as they were designed specifically as a marketing tool for the television. Considering the advertising nature of these songs, it is more likely that these songs may have had radio airplay. In addition, many of the early uses of campaign music on television looked more like a radio spot with an accompanying animated cartoon, or they were simply like a live performance of the song. Looking at the early advertisements that feature music prominently, one often finds that the music plays a more important role than the image viewed on the television. These "musical" advertisements do the speaking that would normally be associated with the issue ads a candidate may have produced during this time, as the images were used as a visual stimulus for the viewer. The 1952 election between Democratic candidate Adlai Stevenson and Republican candidate Dwight (Ike) D. Eisenhower was an excellent example of this.

"I Like Ike" but "Love the Gov"

The 1952 election featured numerous songs that were used on the television. One of the most memorable is "I Like Ike" (or "You Like Ike" depending
on the source). The song does not talk about Eisenhower in any specific way,
but serves as a call to the electorate to elect Eisenhower to the presidency:

Ike for President. Ike for President. Ike for President.

You like Ike, I like Ike, everybody likes Ike for President.
Bring out the banners, beat the drums, we'll take Ike to Washington.
We don't want John or Dean or Harry. Let's do that big job right.
Let's get in step with the guy that's hep. Get in step with Ike.

You like Ike, I like Ike, everybody likes Ike for president.
Bring out the banners, beat the drums, we'll take Ike to Washington.
We've got to get where we are going, travel day and night.
Let Adlai go the other way. We'll all go with Ike.

You like Ike, I like Ike, everybody likes Ike for President.
Bring out the banners, beat the drums, we'll take Ike to Washington.
We'll take Ike to Washington![12]

The one-minute advertisement that showcased this song featured a cartoon in
which most of the images were people marching to the tune and carrying signs
that say "Ike," all the while being led by Uncle Sam. Other imagery included the
elephant, the traditional symbol of the Republican Party, carrying a sheet on its
back with Eisenhower's picture and having a sheet tied to its trunk with the
word "Ike" written on it. The elephant also pulled a drum which it was pounding
with a mallet held in its tail. In addition, when the song and the ad depicted three
prominent Democrats as donkeys with identifying features such as glasses and
facial hair: John (Vice Presidential nominee of Stevenson, John Sparkman),
Dean (Secretary of State Dean Acheson), and Harry (President Harry Truman).[13]
The crowd of supporters was constantly moving forward (toward the right of the
screen from the viewer's perspective). At one point, a silhouette of a man on a
donkey can be seen in the background riding backward (to the left); this is presumably meant to be Adlai Stevenson, whose name is sung in the song at that
point. If one views the advertisement while listening to the song, it is obvious
that the two were written together, as the parade of supporters march in unison
to the driving beat of the song, and the lyrics depict what is occurring in the cartoon. Much like the use of slogans in songs during the period when radio dominated presidential campaigns, by the 1950s television was creating more integration. By this time, the music, message, slogan, and pictures were all being
merged together to offer multiple visual and audio components about the candidate. Overall, the song and the cartoon were relatively short in duration, but the
tune used was very catchy and repetitive, making it easy to remember and, thus,

easy to associate with the candidate. In fact, the song was so repetitive, that it used the name "Ike" approximately 30 times in about 60 seconds. Clearly, the song tried to pound Eisenhower's nickname into voters' heads, continuing a trend that became common during the radio era. In addition, the song utilized Eisenhower's campaign slogan, "I Like Ike," continuing the early to mid-twentieth-century trend of integrating a presidential campaign's slogan into its music.

Another song written for the 1952 campaign was the identically named "I Like Ike," composed by Irving Berlin. Stuart Schimler says "the song was popular and was probably the last famous song for elections."[14] The song did not have television airplay, but would more than likely have been used via recording, radio or live performance during the campaign. (It was common during the period for campaigns to record campaign songs and use trucks to play them around various cities.)[15] The lyrics of the song state,

I like Ike
I'll shoot it over a mike,
Or a phone
Or from the highest steeple
I like Ike
And Ike is easy to like,
Stands alone,
The choice of We the People.

A leader we can call without political noise,
He can lead us all
As he led the boys,

Let's like Ike,
A man we all of us like,
Makes no deals,
His favors can't be curried
And Uncle Joe is worried 'cause "we like Ike."

"I Like Ike" by Irving Berlin
© Copyright 1950, 1952 by Irving Berlin
© Copyright Renewed
International Copyright Secured   All Rights Reserved   Reprinted by Permission

The song does not speak about Eisenhower in specifics but describes him as a good leader who is above the politics of the day, a man who can't be bought, and a person who would scare "Uncle Joe" (a reference to Soviet dictator Joseph Stalin). Considering that Eisenhower was one of the generals who played a key role in the Allied victory in World War II, it is no surprise that Berlin attempted to foster this the sentiment about Eisenhower the politician to conform to the popular notion at the time of Eisenhower the general. Finally, like the other Eisenhower song above, this one also incorporated the campaign slogan, "I Like Ike," within the campaign song. Another 1952 Eisenhower song, "Hike with Ike," continued the theme of rhyming the candidate's name.[16] Eisenhower apparently incorporated numerous songs like this into his campaign because he believed that it would appeal to younger voters.[17]

The Democratic nominee in 1952, Illinois Governor Adlai Stevenson, used the relatively new medium of television to promote his candidacy through the use of music as well. His advertisements were not as sophisticated as "I Like Ike," however. According to one source, "Stevenson's spot ads were little more than illustrated radio spots," whereas Eisenhower used the television spots to highlight many of his political positions in addition to the advertisement-based material he used.[18] In fact, several of Stevenson's advertisements featured a single speaker on the screen and nothing more. One of the more memorable spots his campaign ran was "I Love the Gov." The song was likely a cheap knock-off of the "I Like Ike" television advertisement. Using the same rhyming scheme in the title as "I Like Ike," the "I Love the Gov" advertisement featured a singer who is unknown (so are the composer and lyricist, whom one author notes have all "gone to their graves thankful for the anonymity"[19]) performing the song for an audience.

> I'd rather have a man with a hole in his shoe
> Than a hole in everything he says.
> I'd rather have a man who knows what to do
> When he gets to be the Prez.
> I love the Gov', the Governor of Illinois.
> He is the guy that brings the dove of peace and joy.
> When Illinois the GOP double-crossed,
> He is the one who told all the crooks, "Get lost."
> Adlai, love you madly,
> And what you did for your own great state,
> You're gonna do for the rest of the 48.
> Didn't know much about him before he came,
> But now my heart's a ballot that bears his name.
> 'Cause listen to what he has to say,
> I know that on Election Day,
> We're gonna choose the Gov' that we love.
> He is the Gov' nobody can shove.
> We'll make the Gov' president of the you, the me and the U.S.A.[20]

The text of the song indicated that Eisenhower had a "hole in everything he says" and that Stevenson was trustworthy and a man who could bring peace to the nation. The song also attempted to paint the Republican Party as a bunch of "crooks" who "double-crossed" the state of Illinois but were rebuked by Stevenson (this was likely a reference to former Republican Illinois Governor Lennington Small, who had been previously indicted for embezzlement, or it may have been a general pejorative reference to the Republican Party as "crooks"). The song, through the use of the singer and the text, attempted to influence its listeners emotionally as well by stating that "my heart's a ballot that bears his name" and "gonna choose the Gov' that we love." Stevenson's campaign also had a musical cartoon advertisement in 1952 titled "Adlai to You." It used a theme of "You say potato, I say potahto," with Stevenson's first name, alternating between a pronunciation of Adlai as Ad-LIE and Ad-LEE. According to the song's lyrics,

> It's Adlai to you, Adlai to me,
> I don't care how you quote it.
> Adlai, Adlai—don't pronounce it.
> Just go out and vote it!
> STEVENSON![21]

The tune was set to a catchy piano jingle. The cartoon character was emphasizing the spelling of "Adlai" at a chalkboard. The commercial focused on getting viewers to remember Stevenson's first and last name, telling the voter nothing about the candidate's policy positions. Stevenson also ran a parody of "Old MacDonald Had a Farm," that was titled "Let's Not Forget the Farmer."[22] The advertisement reminded voters what life was like during the Great Depression (which was also the last time that Republicans controlled the White House), and asked them to cast their ballots for Stevenson.[23] Another campaign song for Stevenson, "Don't Let 'Em Take It Away," was another reference to the 1929 stock market crash, as "it" referred to in the song title was economic prosperity.[24]

The positive description of Stevenson in "I Love the Gov" and the catchy songs from "Adlai to You" to "Let's Not Forget the Farmer" to "Don't Let 'Em Take It Away" notwithstanding, Stevenson went on to lose to Eisenhower in November 1952. Indeed, Eisenhower won 55% of the popular vote; the former general triumphed in 39 of 48 states for 83% of Electoral College votes.[25] Both men won their respective party's nominations again in 1956. Stevenson's campaign produced several new songs, including "We're Madly for Adlai," "Believe in Stevenson," "Adlai's Gonna Win This Time," "Stevenson, Stevenson," and "Let's Go with AD-A-LAI." Each of these songs made extensive use of Stevenson's first or last name. Most of these songs also used a rhyming technique with his name, and some of them adopted lyrics to previously existing tunes. Examples of the latter point were "Adlai's Gonna Win This Time," which was set to the tune of "Get Me to the Church on Time," from the show, *My Fair Lady*; similarly, "Stevenson, Stevenson" was set to the tune "My Pony Boy," and "Let's Go with AD-A-LAI" used the music of "Ta-ra-ra Boom-de-ay."[26] Although Stevenson's campaign produced a host of new music, Eisenhower relied primarily in 1956 on his successful songs from 1952, especially the two "I Like Ike" songs.[27] The 1956 general election produced the same result as 1952. Eisenhower won a second term with an even bigger victory than 1952:

57% of voters cast ballots for Eisenhower, leading to the incumbent prevailing in 41 of 48 states with 86% of the Electoral College votes.[28]

High Hopes

The 1960 presidential election pitted Democratic Massachusetts Senator John F. Kennedy against Republican Vice President Richard Nixon. Television took a new political step that year, as it marked the first televised debates between presidential candidates. The contrast between the two men in the debates could not have been starker. According to one source, the "handsome, poised Kennedy came across very well on television, especially in comparison to Nixon's shifty eyes and five-o'clock shadow."[29] At least in the debates, it appeared that Kennedy was making the transition to the television age quite well, while Nixon was still mired in the age of radio. In fact, it has become well-recognized common knowledge that those who listened to the debates on the radio (and could only judge the candidates on their words, not their looks) thought Nixon had won, while those who watched on television declared Kennedy the winner.[30] Although there is little empirical evidence to substantiate the notion that radio listeners favored Nixon and television watchers liked Kennedy, the widespread belief in this notion has likely been based on the very different personas that the two men had in front of the cameras. Their respective campaigns' use of music was also quite varied in 1960. Indeed, when looking through the various advertisements that were produced by the Nixon campaign, it is obvious that the use of music on television was not a major part of the campaign's strategy. Instead, the ad spots from the Nixon campaign mainly featured the candidate in about sixty second clips discussing his views on various issues within the campaign (which has remained a fairly common approach to television commercials in presidential campaigns). Music was not even in the background for Nixon in 1960—it was nonexistent.

Of course, Kennedy also described his policy positions in his television advertisements just as his opponent did. However, Kennedy's campaign also used one of its television ads to run a song that was not given an official title, but which could simply be called "Kennedy":

Kennedy, Kennedy, Kennedy, Kennedy, Kennedy, Kennedy, Kennedy for me, Kennedy! Kennedy! Kennedy! Kennedy!

Do you want a man for President who's seasoned through and through, But not so dog-goned seasoned that he won't try something new? A man who's old enough to know, and young enough to do? Well, it's up to you, it's up to you, it's strictly up to you.

Do you like a man who answers straight, a man who's always fair? Well measure him against the others and when you compare,

You'll cast your vote for Kennedy and the change that's overdue.
So it's up to you, it's up to you, it's strictly up to you.

Yes, it's Kennedy, Kennedy, Kennedy, Kennedy, Kennedy, Kennedy, Kennedy for me, Kennedy! Kennedy! Kennedy! Kennedy! Kennedy! Kennedy! Kennedy![31]

The song does several things that make it effective. First, it mentions the last name of the candidate repeatedly in both the opening and closing moments of the song. In fact, "Kennedy" is mentioned 26 times in the 60 second song. Although "I Like Ike" used the nickname Ike a few more times, many of those instances were sung by the background chorus. In contrast, each use of the name "Kennedy" in the present song was loud and forceful, making it impossible for a viewer of the advertisement to walk away not knowing the candidate's name. Second, the advertisement was set to a light-hearted, upbeat tune that was easy to remember. In other words, this repetition of the name "Kennedy" acts as a hook for the song that people would more than likely have stuck in their heads following the advertisement. Third, the song noted the candidate as a man who was "young enough" to "try something new," but at the same time was a "seasoned" candidate who was "old enough to know." This was a reference to two things. First, it noted Kennedy's relative youth; at 43 years of age, he was the youngest candidate elected U.S. president. Second, the song balanced this against his experience; by the time he was elected president in1960, Kennedy had served three terms in the U.S. House of Representatives and more than one full term in the U.S. Senate, for a total of almost 14 years in Congress. (This notion of a veteran politician who is still relatively young was later put to song by Robert Griffin when running for the U.S. Senate in 1966. A Detroit-based rock band, Doug Brown and the Omens, performed a song for Griffin entitled "Give Bob the Ball," which made repeated reference to the candidate's "youth and experience.")[32] "Kennedy" also described Kennedy as a fair, straight shooter.

The television is not the only place where campaign music could be heard during the 1960 election. While the amount of music present at campaign rallies was in decline, the songs that were produced and used were effective within the campaigns. In addition to the "Kennedy" song that was used in his television advertisement, a version of the song "High Hopes" (tune by James Van Heusen) was adapted for the Kennedy campaign. The song "High Hopes" was from the film *A Hole in the Head* and won the 1959 Academy Award for Best Original Song. The song was a hit in 1959, spending the entire summer on the Billboard Hot 100 chart, peaking at number 30.[33] Much like the "Kennedy" song, this adaptation of "High Hopes" tried to differentiate Kennedy from his opponents and emphasize that his election as president would usher in a new, more productive era. The song had a new text, which was written by Sammy Cahn that stated:

Everyone is voting for Jack,
'Cause he's got what all the rest lack,
Everyone wants to back—Jack,
Jack is on the right track.

'Cause he's got high hopes,
He's got high hopes,
1960's the year for his high hopes,
Come on and vote for Kennedy,
Vote for Kennedy,
And we'll come out on top.

Oops! There goes the opposition—ker -
Oops! There goes the opposition—ker -
Oops! There goes the opposition Kerplop!

K—E—Double N—E—D—Y
Jack's the nation's favorite guy,
Everyone wants to back—Jack,
Jack is on the right track.

'Cause he's got high hopes,
He's got high hopes,
1960's the year for his high hopes,
Come on and vote for Kennedy,
Vote for Kennedy,
He'll keep America strong,

Kennedy, he just keeps rolling—a -
Kennedy, he just keeps rolling—a -
Kennedy, he just keeps rolling along.

High Hopes (Campaign Version)
Words by Sammy Cahn
Music by James Van Heusen
Copyright © 1959 (Renewed) Maraville Music Corp.
All Rights Reserved   Used by Permission
Reprinted by permission of Hal Leonard Corporation

The song was effective for a few reasons. First, like many songs of the past, it parodied a popular song of the day that people would easily remember and associate with the candidate. Second, the text of the song mentioned both his first and last name many times (Jack is stated six times, and Kennedy is stated or spelled eight times), making it apparent whom the song is describing. The use of these parodied songs in which portions of the original text are kept, make the song more memorable (since an entirely new text does not need to be learned). These songs become more of a factor as we transition to the modern uses of campaign music in the 1970s and 1980s (we will say more about this in chapter five).

The Kennedy campaign did not just alter lyrics for the song "High Hopes." When they made use of the song, they employed star power by asking Frank Sinatra, who had sung the original song in *A Hole in the Head*, to perform the song with altered lyrics. Convincing Sinatra to do this was not a difficult task for the Kennedy campaign, as Sinatra was a huge supporter of JFK. In 1960, Sinatra raised $2 million for Kennedy's campaign by arranging $100-a-plate dinners and political rallies where he performed for those in attendance.[34] (Sinatra remained an admirer of Kennedy for the remainder of the politician's life. Reportedly, when Kennedy was assassinated in November 1963, Sinatra was so devastated that he left the set of the movie he was filming and refused to see anyone for several days.[35]) Thus, singing for Kennedy was only a small part of the entertainer's contribution to the campaign. Kennedy also continued the tradition that had taken off during the radio era of capitalizing on musical celebrity. In addition to soliciting Sinatra's help, Kennedy ran a television commercial in which Harry Belafonte (who most famously sang the calypso tune "Banana Boat Song") introduced Kennedy and then stated that he would be voting for him.[36]

The 1960 Republican candidate, Richard Nixon, was quite conservative compared to Kennedy and, consequently, much of the music that was written for his campaign reflected those conservative leanings. However, considering the use of the double entendre, one song could have caused quite a stir within the campaign. "Click with Dick" was written by Olivia Hoffman, George Stork and Clarence Fuhrman. Little is known about the composers of the song that was chosen as the Republican campaign song of 1960. The song's lyrics include the following:

> Come on and click with Dick,
> The one that none can lick,
> He's the man to lead the U.S.A.
> In Dick we have the one,
> Who truly gets things done,
> Ev'ry time he has his say.
>
> He's a man of peace and reason
> For the job in ev'ry season,
> And he knows how to fight,
> When he is in the right,
> So let's all lick with Dick.

Click With Dick
Music by George Stork and Clarence Fuhrman, words by Olivia Hoffman
Copyright © 1960 by Elkan-Vogel, Inc.
International copyright secured   All rights reserved
Used with permission

If there were any misgivings by the Republican National Committee about the line used as the hook of the song, there is no evidence that it was made public. Looking beyond the hook, the song speaks of Nixon as the man of "peace and reason" and says that he will be the man who can get "things done." The song is original for Nixon's campaign and does a good job of indicating the first name of the candidate numerous times within. However, as stated above, the use of his abbreviated name "Dick" could be taken in a number of different ways and possibly even go against the more conservative nature of the candidate. On election day, the voters gave Kennedy a razor thin popular vote victory of 120,000 votes (out of more than 68,000,000 votes cast), although Kennedy did score a convincing victory in the Electoral College over Nixon of 303-219.[37]

Hello, Lyndon. . . Goodbye, Barry

Another song that was adopted by a candidate in the 1960s was "Hello Dolly!" from Lyndon Johnson's 1964 presidential campaign. As was the case with many of the songs of this era, the composers of Tin Pan Alley reworked the title song of the 1964 Tony Award–winning Broadway show *Hello, Dolly!* into the campaign song "Hello, Lyndon." Among the ten awards the show took home were: Best Musical, Best Composer/Lyricist, Best Book of a Musical, and Best Musical Director, implying that not only the story, but the music from the show was critically acclaimed.[38] In addition, the title song's cover, done by Louis Armstrong, reached number one on Billboard's Hot 100 in May 1964, showing the huge popularity of the song just as Johnson was mounting his campaign to retain the presidency.[39]

The song was adapted for Johnson by the original composer, Jerry Herman, and, surprisingly, retained a number of the original lyrics from the song. Most notable in the changes is the insertion of "Lyndon" for "Dolly" in the song. In addition, some of the later lines were adapted to have more reference to the candidate and the election, a natural progression to make the song usable for the campaign. The text of the song says:

> Hello Lyndon,
> Well, hello, Lyndon
> We'd be proud to have you back where you belong
> You're lookin' swell, Lyndon,
> We can tell, Lyndon,
> You're still glowin', you're still crowin',
> You're still going strong.
>
> We hear the band playing
> And the folks saying,
> That the people know that you've got so much more

So flash that smile, Lyndon,
Show us that winning style, Lyndon
Promise you'll stay with us in sixty-four!

We hear the band playing
And the folks saying
"Let's all rally 'round the one who knows the score!"
So, be our guide, Lyndon,
Ladybird at your side, Lyndon,
Promise you'll stay with us in sixty-four!

Hello Lyndon
A parody of "Hello Dolly"
From HELLO, DOLLY!
Music and Lyric by Jerry Herman
© 1963 (Renewed) JERRY HERMAN
All Rights Controlled by EDWIN H. MORRIS & COMPANY,
A Division of MPL Music Publishing, Inc.
All Rights Reserved
Reprinted by permission of Hal Leonard Corporation

Johnson had assumed the presidency upon the death of John F. Kennedy in 1963. The song, thus, makes reference to how his supporters would be "proud to have you back where you belong" as he had served for a short time as president by the time the 1964 campaign was in full swing. In addition, the song spoke of Johnson as someone who understood the "score" and was thus the man who should stay in the White House to finish the business of the Kennedy administration. "Hello, Lyndon" received extensive radio and television airplay in 1964.[40]

Johnson also integrated the use of his name, rhyming, and a campaign slogan in 1964's "All the Way. . . with L.B.J." The song was sung for him by Laura Lane at the Democratic National Convention in Atlantic City and sheet music was later reproduced for campaign use.[41]

The Republican challenger in 1964 was the very conservative Arizona Senator Barry Goldwater. Although there is little evidence of music being used in the Goldwater campaign, one song, "Go with Goldwater" was distributed on sheet music throughout the campaign.[42]

Johnson's campaign proved successful in the elections of 1964 as he soundly defeated Goldwater. Johnson won over 60 percent of the popular vote, earning nearly 16 million more votes than Goldwater out of over 70 million total votes cast. Johnson's victory in the Electoral College was even more impressive, as he beat Goldwater 486 to 52.[43]

Music Recedes on the Campaign Trail
and in the Television Ad

The old usages of campaign music were beginning to change by the late 1960s. There was only one major campaign song in 1968, "Nixon's the One," which extolled the virtues of the former vice president and claimed that he could fix the nation's problems.[44] Beyond this, songs with words did not figure prominently into the campaign. Indeed, the growth of television advertising was changing the nature of music in presidential elections.

By the 1968 election, the use of music on the television ads of presidential candidates had been greatly altered. Instead of using a song as the ad with the song's text talking about that candidate, the music became more background to a political message. Evidence of this is borne out in the television advertisements produced by the Nixon campaign. Perhaps learning from the campaign eight years earlier (where all of Nixon's television advertisements were short speeches that incorporated no music), the Nixon television advertisements of 1968 were topical in nature with background music used to associate the mood of the images with the feeling they were meant to produce. One such advertisement was entitled "The First Civil Right." The ad shows various images of protests and that descended into riotous violence. Depicting this unrest was part of Nixon's "law and order" campaign in 1968. Nixon banked on many moderate and independent white voters being fed up with the perceived radicalism of the 1960s. Arguing that lawlessness had been caused by the previous eight years of Democratic leadership and reinforced by liberal Supreme Court rulings on the rights of the accused, Nixon appealed to what he termed the "silent majority" of Americans by promising a return to stability, order, and traditional values.[45] Attempting to motivate the silent majority, the advertisement "The First Civil Right" involved a voice-over by Nixon stating:

> It is time for an honest look at the problem of order in the United States. Dissent is a necessary ingredient of change, but in a system of government that provides for peaceful change, there is no cause that justifies resort to violence. Let us recognize that the first civil right of every American is to be free from domestic violence. So I pledge to you, we shall have order in the United States.[46]

Supporting the images and narrator was a musical tapestry that might best be described as something out of an Alfred Hitchcock horror movie or a George Romero zombie film. The music used dissonant chord clusters that were played at uneven intervals over a snare drum (which could be construed as militaristic) almost giving it a feel like the work "The Banshee" by Henry Cowell. In addition to this use of dissonance, the sound engineer utilized an almost hollow echo effect to increase the eerie quality of the music by sustaining the clusters and percussion. The music successfully put the listener in a state of unease and nervousness about the lawlessness depicted in the advertisement. In fact, most of the ads Nixon employed in his 1968 presidential campaign used a similar methodology in an attempt to appeal to the emotions of the electorate by showing the Democrats as the party that courted anarchy. For instance, a Nixon advertisement entitled "Convention," began with still photographs of Humphrey speaking at the Democratic National Convention, and it was set to a rousing, patriotic march, "Hot Time in the Old Town Tonight"; the advertisement then cut away to pictures of riots, Vietnam War casualties, and people living in rural poverty, set to eerie music that was similar to that in the advertisement "The First Civil Right."[47] The "Convention" advertisement had no voice-over words. Instead, the only audio in the advertisement were the dueling musical themes. Nixon's use of music in television advertisements was part of an effective campaign strategy, as he won the presidency that year. Although Nixon's margin of victory in the popular vote was by just over 500,000 votes (less than 1% more votes than Humphrey), Nixon scored a decisive victory of over 100 votes in the Electoral College.[48]

Later campaigns would take a route similar to Nixon's advertisements of 1968, relegating music on television advertisements to the background. By 1972, Nixon used comparably less music in his television advertisements than in 1968, with most of Nixon's advertisements in 1972 having no music at all. When Nixon did have music that year, it included a single snare drum playing in the advertisement "McGovern Defense" when speaking about Nixon's opponent, followed by the playing of "Hail to the Chief" when the advertisement discussed Nixon; it also included a rather cheesy rendition of a song entitled "Nixon Now" in an advertisement of the same name.[49] Democratic nominee George McGovern, on the other hand, had no music in his television advertisements in 1972.

By 1976, music in television advertisements had firmly receded into the background. For instance, that year, Jimmy Carter used music in several of his advertisements, but none of the songs included lyrics; instead, a narrator, sometimes Carter himself, spoke lines about the candidate, while the music was part of the setting, not the centerpiece. President Gerald Ford only used music as a background jingle in two of his television advertisements. In both cases, the song played for a few seconds before its volume decreased so a narrator could speak about Ford's laudable qualities.[50]

This background music on television ranged from brooding dissonance in negative advertisements to upbeat happy songs in advertisements about the candidate running the advertisement. For instance, in 1984, President Ronald Reagan's reelection campaign ran an advertisement entitled "Prouder, Stronger, Better." The ad famously began with the narrator stating, "It's morning again in America. . . " before going on to describe how much better the economy was compared to 1980. The music used in "Prouder, Stronger, Better" was tranquil, almost Coplandesque, featuring a solo clarinet flowing over a peaceful orchestral tapestry, giving the listener a feeling of ease with the state of the country in 1984.[51]

Conversely, in 2004, the George W. Bush campaign ran an advertisement called "Wolves," which described Democratic candidate John Kerry as weak on defense "in an increasingly dangerous world"; the visual images were of a forest, with the final shot depicting a pack of wolves (likely representing terrorists) getting up and running toward the camera, prepared to attack. The music in this advertisement is, unsurprisingly, ominous and foreboding.[52]

Of course, instead of using fear in a negative advertisement, a campaign can also be negative by making the opponent out to be a fool. In that same 2004 campaign, George W. Bush ran an anti-Kerry advertisement entitled "Windsurfing." The ad featured footage of Kerry windsurfing back and forth in two different directions. During the advertisement, the narrator described Kerry as flip-flopping on various issues, including the Iraq War, education reform, and increasing Medicare spending; each time the narrator described Kerry's purported "flip-flop," the images showed him surfing in the opposite direction. This rather flippant ad had as its background music Johann Strauss' *The Blue Danube* waltz.[53] The song fits rather nicely with the theme of the advertisement, as the waltz is quite lighthearted in nature.

All of these 1984 and 2004 examples involve music staying somewhat relevant on television, but also music that is no longer the most important part of the ad. In this sense, television advertisements, beginning with 1968, involve the total integration of music with the ad, but with that integration music is now being utilized as part of the scenery instead of in a leading role. The music continues to serve as an important function in this form of communication, but not nearly as important as in other contexts, and not nearly as important on television as was the case when commercials played full campaign songs without a voice-over coming in and cutting away from the music.

Finally, much like was the case in the 1950s and early 1960s, later elections saw many television advertisements which used no music at all. In these cases, music did not just regress into background music—it was thought to be so unimportant or distracting to the advertisement that it was abandoned altogether.

With music in television ads now relegated to use more as background effect, it did not have the same importance in television use in later campaigns as it did in the 1952 and 1960 elections. Not since "I Like Ike," "I Love the Gov," and "Kennedy" have we seen television advertisements that were driven by music. Instead, it appears that once the novelty wore off of using music in television advertising, the music took a backseat to voice-overs about character, experience, and the issues (although this increased focus on the issues is not necessarily a bad thing!). The radio also became less and less of a musical tool for candidates in the later part of the twentieth century, with campaigns choosing to use it in the same background method as the television ads and favoring the candidate or another announcer speaking about various campaign issues.

Candidates, however, would continue to utilize campaign music as a part of their campaign rallies and party conventions. Thus, even when music recedes on radio and television advertisements, during the same time the use of campaign song experiences something of a resurgence when candidates are meeting the voters face-to-face. Although these campaign theme songs would often wind up on the radio or television due to media coverage of rallies and conventions, they were not used in the same way as music in paid advertisements. With the paid ads, the message moved primarily to the spoken words and the images, thus leaving music as mere filler. But at rallies and conventions, the music stood on its own as a way to pump up the crowd either before or after a candidate spoke. Paid advertisements became shorter over the last few decades, as the price of advertising time increased exponentially. In a 60 second or even 30 second paid advertisement, there is only time to get the message out through the use of words and pictures, leaving little to no time for music to stand on its own. But at a rally or convention, candidates have time to play music that stands alone, pushing the songs out of the background and into the forefront, utilizing these songs for association with the candidate or as a part of the campaign's message. For these reasons, music became more important in one form of campaigning and less important in another.

We have now looked at presidential campaign music from the singing campaigns for the nineteenth century through the development of the radio and television in the twentieth century. While the amount of music decreased over this period, the importance of that music within the election remained high, and in certain respects, increased. The way in which the music was used changed with the technology and the needs of the campaigns. In the next chapter we will examine the transition of music which started with songs like Roosevelt's use of "Happy Days Are Here Again," in which campaigns will focus less on using a song parody or a new campaign song, but rather associate themselves with popular songs and artists. This trend slowly began in the 1930s and remained quite rare as a campaign tactic for several decades before becoming the primary way that presidential candidates used music by the mid-1980s.

Notes

1. R.W. Burns, *Television, an International History of the Formative Years*, (London: The Institution of Electrical Engineers, 1998), 35.

2. Burns, *Television*, 35-37.

3. Burns, *Television*, 85.

4. Burns, *Television*, 143-149.

5. "Television History—The First 75 Years," TV History, accessed July 14, 2010, http://www.tvhistory.tv/index.html.

6. Edward W. Chester, *Radio, Television and American Politics*, (New York: Sheed and Ward, Inc., 1969), 70.

7. Chester, *Radio, Television and American Politics*, 70.

8. Chester, *Radio, Television and American Politics*, 70.

9.   Chester, *Radio, Television and American Politics*, 70.

10.   Lynda Lee Kaid and Anne Johnston, *Videostyle in Presidential Campaigns: Style and Content of Televised Political Advertising* (Westport, CT: Praeger, 2001), 1.

11.   Kaid and Johnston, *Videostyle in Presidential Campaigns*, 1-2.

12.   "Dwight D. Eisenhower TV Ad I Like Ike: 60 1952," 4President Corporation, accessed July 14, 2010, http://tv.4president.us/tv1952.htm.

13.   "The Living Room Candidate: Presidential Campaign Commercials from 1952-2008," Museum of the Moving Image, accessed July 14, 2010, http://www.living roomcandidate.org.

14.   Stuart Schimler, "Singing to the Oval Office: A Written History of the Political Campaign Song," accessed June 10, 2010, http://www.presidentelect.org/art_schimler_ singing.html.

15.   Luther A. Huston Washington, "The Voters Still Sing, Though Faintly," *The New York Times*, September 27, 1936, 13.

16.   Beryl Frank, *The Pictorial History of the Republican Party* (Secaucus, NJ: Castle Books, 1980), 146.

17.   Frank, *The Pictorial History of the Republican Party*, 146.

18.   "The Living Room Candidate," 1952.

19.   Eric Burns, *Invasion of the Mind Snatchers: Television's Conquest of America in the Fifties* (Philadelphia: Temple University Press, 2010), 198.

20.   Burns, *Invasion of the Mind Snatchers*, 198.

21.   "The Living Room Candidate," 1952.

22.   "The Living Room Candidate," 1952.

23.   "The Living Room Candidate," 1952.

24.   Beryl Frank, *The Pictorial History of the Democratic Party* (Secaucus, NJ: Castle Books, 1980), 144.

25.   David Leip, "Atlas of U.S. Presidential Elections," accessed May 14, 2011, http://uselectionatlas.org/.

26.   Irwin Silber, *Songs America Voted By: From George Washington to Richard Nixon—the Gutsy Story of Presidential Campaigning* (Harrisburg, PA: Stackpole Books, 1971), 290-293.

27.   Silber, *Songs America Voted By*, 293.

28.   Leip, "Atlas of U.S. Presidential Elections."

29.   Nelson W. Polsby, Aaron B. Wildavsky, *Presidential Elections: Strategies and Structures of American Politics* (Lanham, MD: Roman & Littlefield, 2008), 79.

30.   Polsby&Wildavsky, *Presidential Elections*, 79.

31.   Polsby&Wildavsky, *Presidential Elections*, 79.

32.   "Robert Griffin," Serving History, accessed August 11, 2010, http://www. servinghistory.com/topics/Robert_Griffin_.

33.   "The Billboard Hot 100 for the Week Ending September 27," *The Billboard*, September 21, 1959, 58.

34.   Gene Ringgold and Clifford McCarty, *The Films of Frank Sinatra* (New York: Citadel Press, 1989), 18.

35.   John Frayn Turner, *Frank Sinatra* (Lanham, MD: Taylor Trade Publishing, 2004), 143.

36.   "The Living Room Candidate," 1960.

37.   Leip, "Atlas of U.S. Presidential Elections."

38.   Richard Tyler Jordan, *But Darling, I'm Your Auntie Mame!: The Amazing History of the World's Favorite Madcap Aunt* (New York: Kensington Books, 2004), 106; Stanley Green, *Encyclopedia of the Musical Theatre* (New York: Da Capo Press, 1976),

467; Colin Larkin, *The Encyclopedia of Popular Music* (Ann Arbor: University of Michigan Press, 1998).

39.   Fred Bronson, *The Billboard Book of Number 1 Hits: The Inside Story Behind Every Number One Single, on Billboard's Hot 100 from 1955 to the Present* (New York: Billboard Books, 2003), 146.

40.   Frank, *The Pictorial History of the Democratic Party*, 162.

41.   Frank, *The Pictorial History of the Democratic Party*, 161.

42.   Silber, *Songs America Voted By*, 298.

43.   "Historical Election Results: Electoral College Box Scores, 1789-1996," Office of the Federal Register, accessed August 12, 2010, http://www.archives.gov/federal-register/electoral-college/scores.html#1964.

44.   Silber, *Songs America Voted By*, 299.

45.   Alan Brinkley, "1968 and the Unraveling of Liberal America," in *1968: The World Transformed*, ed. Carole Fink, Philipp Gassert, and Detlef Junker (New York: Cambridge University Press, 1998), 234.

46.   Museum of the Moving Image, 1968.

47.   Museum of the Moving Image, 1968.

48.   Leip, "Atlas of U.S. Presidential Elections."

49.   "The Living Room Candidate," 1972.

50.   "The Living Room Candidate," 1976.

51.   "The Living Room Candidate," 1984.

52.   "The Living Room Candidate," 2004.

53.   "The Living Room Candidate," 2004.

~ 5 ~

Campaign Music Transitions
to the Pop Era (1972-1984)

This chapter explains how presidential campaign music underwent a transformation, largely in the 1970s and early 1980s. Prior to this era, almost all music used by campaigns fit neatly into two different categories. First, there existed music that was sung at campaign events which was written for the candidates by popular songwriters and other composers. These songs were crafted specifically with the candidates in mind, and their lyrics referred to the candidates and their issues. Second, there were songs used on radio and television. In the 1950s and early 1960s, these songs were similar to the music written for the campaign trail, but by the late 1960s, music on these mediums began evolving into instrumental background pieces. In the 1970s and 1980s, use of music on the campaign trail would change as well. The emerging trend was to simply adopt, word-for-word and lyric-for-lyric, entire pop songs for use on the campaign. By 1984, this transition was complete, with the use of pop songs being the dominant method of campaign music use.

The movement of campaign music to the uses we are accustomed to seeing in the modern election cycles was under way long before the elections of the 1970s and early 1980s, however. To varying degrees, popular music has been used in presidential campaigns since George Washington through the use of the parody song. Recall chapter one, which discussed "God Save Great Washington," a song set to the tune of "God Save the King." This song was certainly known at the time, but considering the recently fought Revolutionary War, one could argue just how popular the song actually was at the time. These parodied songs, which set new text to popular or well-known tunes of the day, were sung over and over again throughout both the eighteenth and nineteenth centuries in presidential campaigns. This raises an interesting question: what transitional force moved candidates from using these parodied songs to simply using the popular song itself as the campaign music? Like many things, this transition did not occur overnight. Instead, it slowly began as a trickle with elections earlier in the twentieth century, eventually progressing into the flood of popular music we see in U.S. presidential campaigns from the 1980s to the present.

Early, Happy Beginnings to the Pop Era

The four presidential campaigns of Franklin Delano Roosevelt represent the beginning of the transition to pop music. The song that was chosen by the Democratic Party in 1932 as Roosevelt's official campaign song was "Happy Days Are Here Again," which had previously been used in the 1930 film *Chasing Rainbows*. The song, written by Milton Ager and Jack Yellen, was popular before Roosevelt made use of it. The song was chosen to inspire the electorate and show them that, with Roosevelt, the return of better days for the country was just around the corner. Only a few years earlier, the song would have been a terrible choice for a campaign, as the country was experiencing the economic boom of the 1920s. In fact, while governor of New York in the late 1920s, Roosevelt and his closest political advisor, Louis Howe, initially began planning for Roosevelt to run for the presidency in 1936 because they assumed that Herbert Hoover was going to be easily reelected in 1932.[1] Of course, the stock market crash of 1929 and the ensuing Great Depression changed this calculus. Roosevelt ran in 1932 and won the nomination of the Democratic Party. His goal of turning the country around was displayed in "Happy Days Are Here Again": The text of the entire song spoke of the troubled times of the past vanishing with more pleasant times on the immediate horizon.[2] And with lines that specifically spoke of the worries that people had been experiencing leaving for good, it is evident that the song was designed to resonate with an electorate that was in the throes of the Great Depression. That the whole song maintained a message that the Democratic Party was attempting to portray about Roosevelt makes it that much more effective, and might explain why it was used, lyric-for-lyric, during an era when this practice was otherwise rare. Although the song, because it was taken word-for-word, failed to mention the candidate's name or any planks in his policy platform, it reflects, in its entirety, a strong and positive message that was associated with Roosevelt every time the popular song was heard via radio or in live performance. Of course, that goes to another important point when using a "prepackaged" or "canned" popular song—if still popular, the song will continue to receive regular radio airplay during the election season. This airplay often has nothing to do with the campaign, as it is simply part of a radio station's attempt to play popular music to attract listeners. When a song is known to be a staple of a campaign, informed listeners who hear it as part of regular radio airplay will immediately think of the candidate. This then becomes a supplement to the use of the song by the campaign at rallies, conventions, and in its own paid radio and television advertisements.

Roosevelt, however, came very close to choosing a different song in 1932. While at the Democratic National Convention in Chicago, Roosevelt was trying to select a song to accompany his nomination. Assisting him in this endeavor were Howe and Bronx Democratic boss Edward Flynn. Since Roosevelt served as Secretary of the Navy before being elected governor of New York, the future president suggested that his nomination be complemented by "Anchors Aweigh." Flynn turned to Howe and declared: "That sounds like a funeral march. Why don't we get them to play something peppy, like 'Happy Days Are Here Again'?" Howe agreed, and the two of them convinced Roosevelt to use the song. Flynn immediately contacted the convention floor manager and requested that "a lively rendition of 'Happy Days'" be played. When Flynn heard the song played by the convention band, he is claimed to have remarked that "it certainly sounded more cheerful and appropriate to the occasion."[3]

As this short story demonstrates, the use of music, and its effect on voters' moods, has long been on the minds of candidates and their advisors. Roosevelt, Flynn, and Howe wanted to exercise power over those at the convention, and those listening on the radio, by associating Roosevelt's run for the presidency with a cheerful outlook toward the future. The use of this song was part of a successful campaign for FDR in 1932, as he handily beat Hoover in the popular vote and the Electoral College. As for "Happy Days Are Here Again," the song remained a staple for Roosevelt throughout his presidency. In 1934 he adopted it as the theme of his economic recovery plans.[4] It was also his official campaign song through three additional elections that would make him the only president in United States history to be elected to the office four times. This song then transcended Roosevelt, and became a standby for the entire Democratic Party. Indeed, when Jimmy Carter received the party's nomination at the 1976 convention, party officials tried to make the delegates and viewers think of Roosevelt's successes by playing the song that will forever be associated with FDR, "Happy Days Are Here Again."[5]

But it is also important to point out that the approach of using a preexisting song, note-for-note and lyric-for-lyric, was still an oddity in the 1930s and 1940s. As noted in the last chapter, Roosevelt made use of several other songs that had lyrics tailored to his campaigns. In addition, none of Roosevelt's four Republican challengers (Herbert Hoover, Alf Landon, Wendell Willkie, and Thomas Dewey) employed the same tactic in any known official capacity within their campaigns. Existing evidence suggests that Hoover's 1932 campaign recycled its use of "If He's Good Enough for Lindy." In addition, Hoover used new songs written specifically for his second campaign. These included "Whoop It Up!" by W. Hartley Gay, which was an adaptation of "Hold the Fort," and "Battle Hymn of the Republican Party," which was Alfred J. Thieme's adaptation of "John Brown's Body." In addition to "Happy Landin' with Landon," Alf Landon's campaign used an adaptation of Stephen Foster's "Oh! Susannah" at the 1936 Republican National Convention called "Landon, Oh, Landon." The song spoke of Landon as a man who believed that the Constitution of the United States was "good enough for me" (perhaps implying that Roosevelt was transgressing the document with his New Deal programs) and claimed that he had "the right solution" to keep the American ship of state from sinking.[6] Four years later, Wendell Willkie's campaign changed the lyrics of Paul Dresser's "On the Banks of the Wabash" to use in his campaign. The song recycled little if any of the original lyrics of the song, using it to advocate for Willkie as a man who has been sent from the heavens to lead the country. Finally, for the 1944 campaign of Thomas Dewey the song that would best be described as his campaign theme song was the "Republican Battle Hymn;" like the song written for Hoover's second campaign, Dewey's version was also set to the tune of "John Brown's Body." However, another song that was strongly associated with Dewey's campaign, and is a bit more colorful, was an adaptation of "Good Night, Ladies." The text of the song picked on members of Roosevelt's cabinet, Miss Frances Perkins and Harold Ikes, singing of how they would finally be leaving the White House.

Saying "Hello" While Going "Wild" with "High Hopes"

The use of popular music was seen again in the 1948 campaign of Harry Truman with the song "I'm Just Wild About Harry." The song, as mentioned in chapter three, was written by Noble Sissle and Eubie Blake and made popular in the 1921 musical "Shuffle Along."[7] The song was very effective for Truman because it already contained the candidate's first name in not just the body of the song, but also in the title and "hook" phrase of the song. In contrast to Roosevelt, the campaign for Truman opted not to use the song as it was published, but rather they made changes to the text to send more of a campaign message. This may have been necessary for one very important reason. While Roosevelt's entire song inspired hope in the future under his presidency (regardless if that was the song's original intent or not), the song Truman used did not have the same effectiveness from the initial lyrics. The original text of Noble Sissle's song was an upbeat love song from the perspective of a female who was "wild" about her man and how he made her feel.[8] The message of the electorate being "wild" about Harry is one that the Truman campaign would want to project. The remainder of the song, though, was not exactly what the campaign wished to portray about why or how the public should be wild for him. Consequently, the campaign altered some of the text (as can be seen in chapter three) to speak more to the pertinent campaign issues of the day. It attempted to align him with FDR and the New Deal economic recovery programs that were established to lift the country out of the Great Depression. It still made use of the effective hook from the original song, but with new wording it also carried through Truman's campaign message.

Thus, the song worked for Truman on two levels. Regardless of the effectiveness or memorability of the revised text, having the name recognition and association with the popular tune made it an effective tool for, at a minimum, having the electorate associate his candidacy and name with the popular tune. The fact that his name was in the song's hook only made him and the song's message more memorable to the voting public. This use of the hook, grabbing name recognition for Truman, would become a staple for future campaigns when selecting songs from the popular catalogue to use in an unaltered form. The transition was already under way, as campaigns were beginning to leave more and more of an existing song intact, making fewer changes and adding fewer new lyrics when compared to the parodied songs of the singing campaigns of the nineteenth century and those composed and arranged by Tin Pan Alley songwriters.

A similar tactic was used again in the 1960 election of John F. Kennedy with the song "High Hopes." Again, as noted in chapter four, the song had won an Academy Award in 1959 for Best Original Song and had also shown its popularity by spending the summer of the same year on the Billboard Hot 100 chart.[9] The Kennedy campaign took a different approach from the Truman campaign in picking their song though. Instead of taking a song where the hook contained either Kennedy's first or last name, they instead chose a song that was reflective of the feelings they desired the country to have about Kennedy. This was reminiscent of Roosevelt's choice of a cheery, uplifting song in "Happy Days." In the same vain as Truman, however, the Kennedy campaign decided to change some of the text of the song so it would better reflect the message of the campaign. The original song of James Van Heusen and Sammy Cahn said:

Next time you're found, with your chin on the ground
There a lot to be learned, so look around

Just what makes that little old ant
Think he'll move that rubber tree plant
Anyone knows an ant, can't
Move a rubber tree plant

But he's got high hopes, he's got high hopes
He's got high apple pie, in the sky hopes

So any time you're gettin' low
'stead of lettin' go
Just remember that ant
Oops there goes another rubber tree plant

When troubles call, and your back's to the wall
There a lot to be learned, that wall could fall

Once there was a silly old ram
Thought he'd punch a hole in a dam
No one could make that ram scram
He kept buttin' that dam

'cause he had high hopes, he had high hopes
He had high apple pie, in the sky hopes

So any time you're feelin' bad
'stead of feelin' sad
Just remember that ram
Oops there goes a billion kilowatt dam

All problems just a toy balloon
They'll be bursted soon
They're just bound to go pop
Oops there goes another problem kerplop

High Hopes
Words by Sammy Cahn
Music by James Van Heusen
Copyright © 1959 (Renewed) Maraville Music Corp.
All Rights Reserved   Used by Permission
Reprinted by Permission of Hal Leonard Corporation

The song in its original form described finding a way to lift one's spirits when one is down by looking at the positive side of life and believing that one can achieve seemingly impossible tasks. Thus, the song could have been used for the campaign in the original form because of this positive, inspiring message. Yet, since the campaign kept the title line of the song, it seems only appropriate that they would tailor the song to speak of Kennedy and the positive feelings they anticipated the nation would have of him. Since the transition to using full pop songs was not yet complete by 1960, one can easily understand why the Kennedy campaign wanted to retain the hook and title of the song but also alter it to be more in line with other campaign music of the era.

The three songs discussed to this point in this chapter—"Happy Days Are Here Again," "I'm Just Wild About Harry," and "High Hopes"—come from our previously discussed elections. They could all be considered effective campaign songs in the way they brought the candidate together with a popular song that the electorate would know. All of these campaigns either used the song in its entirety as it existed before the campaign, or made sure to preserve the song's hook and title in their original form, thus maintaining the portion of the song most recognizable to the public while altering the other material to associate the song with the campaign.

This trend continued, although to a lesser degree, with the adaptation of "Hello, Dolly!" to "Hello, Lyndon!" In this case, the adaptation changed the song's hook, but it did so by merely substituting one name for another. This song was less of a transition to the use of a song lyric for lyric because (as described in chapter four) a portion of the text was rewritten to have significance with the campaign just as had been done numerous times in song parodies before it (although many times in the past the entire song would be rewritten, not just a portion of it). This is a variance from our previous two examples where they maintained the text of the entire "hook" of the song as a part of their new parody. What is consistent about all the popular song choices represented here, including that of Johnson's, is that the songs they used were representative of the message or an integral part of the message the campaign wished to deliver. For example, "High Hopes" spoke of the high expectations for Kennedy, "I'm Just Wild About Harry" was used to generate enthusiasm among the electorate, and "Hello, Lyndon" was used as a way to promote Johnson's return to the White House. However, these songs are different from most of the pieces reviewed in chapter two and chapter three because, unlike many earlier songs, much of the song text remains the same when the piece is adopted by the campaign. This will become an important distinction as we progress into the elections of the 1980s and forward. As we move closer to the present, we will see less and less of the parodied songs of Kennedy and Truman (which are less and less variation when they are parodied), and more use of straight popular songs, such as the one used by Roosevelt in 1932.

The "Bridge" to the Pop Era

The election of 1968 saw the beginnings of a reemergence of the use of popular songs in their entirety in a way that harkened back to Franklin Roosevelt. That year, Senator Robert Kennedy sought the Democratic nomination for president, declaring his candidacy on March 16. The former attorney general entered the race only days after President Johnson squeaked out a less than convincing victory in the New Hampshire primary over his challenger, Senator Eugene McCarthy, 49% to 42%. Such a lackluster showing by the sitting president was likely a major factor in Johnson's March 31 announcement that he would not seek, nor would he accept, his party's nomination for the presidency. After Johnson's withdrawal, Vice President Hubert Humphrey entered the fray, essentially making for a three-way race among Kennedy, McCarthy, and Humphrey. Over the next few months, the three men fought their way through a nomination stalemate. By the time Kennedy won the California primary (held on June 4), Humphrey had a sizable lead in delegates (Humphrey had 561 delegates, Kennedy was second with 393, and McCarthy was a distant third with 258). Although Kennedy was behind, his victory in California gave him some momentum going into the Democratic National Convention in Chicago. Unfortunately, the world will never know how Kennedy would have fared at that convention, as he was assassinated by Sirhan Sirhan in the early morning hours of June 5 at the Ambassador Hotel in Los Angeles, shortly after completing his California primary victory speech.[10]

Until his death, Robert Kennedy's song of choice for his campaign was Woody Guthrie's "This Land Is Your Land."[11] As described in the introduction, the first verse of this song calls the listener's attention to the majestic geography of America, whereas later verses describe the country as belonging to all of its inhabitants, not just those with large amounts of wealth and political power.[12] Kennedy chose to use this song, line for line and note for note. It was a fitting choice for the candidate that year. Kennedy met with Latino civil rights activist Cesar Chavez in March 1968, and in April of that year he gave a now famous speech in Indianapolis on racial reconciliation after the assassination of Martin Luther King. Seeking racial justice and ending economic inequality were major themes of Kennedy's campaign that year.[13] The nation would have to wait another four years, however, before the first major party nominee since the Great Depression and World War II would use a popular song in its entirety.

The election of 1972 saw the utilization of popular music in the vein of Roosevelt forty years earlier. The Democratic Party nominated South Dakota Senator George McGovern for the presidency. McGovern campaigned as an antiwar, liberal candidate throughout the election, garnering strong support from women, people of color, and younger voters; McGovern's support from labor was relatively weak for a Democratic candidate though.[14] He was thoroughly defeated by Nixon. The president trounced McGovern, collecting over 60% of the popular vote; McGovern only won Massachusetts and the District of Columbia, translating to an Electoral College victory for Nixon of 520 to 17.[15]

Although McGovern used no music in his television advertisements, he did find a song for use on the campaign trail that he felt suited him quite well. In his losing effort, McGovern used Simon and Garfunkel's "Bridge Over Troubled Water" as the musical backdrop for his campaign. The song was the title track from Simon and Garfunkel's fifth and final studio album release in February of 1970.[16] When released, the album reached number one on the Billboard Music Charts pop albums list, and the single topped the Billboard Hot 100 chart.[17] McGovern tried to capitalize on Simon and Garfunkel's newfound celebrity by inviting the group to play "Bridge over Troubled Water" at a fund-raising concert at Madison Square Garden on June 14, 1972.[18] Paul Simon and Art Garfunkel, who supported McGovern, agreed to perform, and they sang the lyrics to their song.

"Bridge Over Troubled Water" described how a friend of the singer is having a streak of bad luck. The singer then lets the friend know that there is no need to worry, as the singer will help the friend. Repeated references are made to the song's title: that the singer will be a bridge over the troubled water that the friend faces.[19]

This may be a song where the lines are blurred a little as to whether the entire song was really representative of what the campaign would like to communicate. However, there was quite a bit in the song that can be used to define McGovern's campaign in 1972. As described by Charlesworth, the song evoked "images of the power of healing followed by a transcendent conclusion to life's burdensome journey."[20] In other words, the song talked about having a friend who will be the "bridge" over the "troubled waters" of your life; a person who will always be there as was reflected in the final verse of the song. But more than just this general message of hope, it discusses specifics that might hit home with the electorate, stating "When you're down and out, When you're on the street," and in the end just not laying oneself down to cross over those turbulent waters, but easing the mind of those who are troubled. It is easy to see McGovern using this song in his campaign, analogizing that he is the bridge that the country can cross; below are the "troubled waters," most notably the Vietnam War, from which McGovern would protect the nation. In fact, at one point during the election McGovern was quoted as saying "I want, indeed, to become a bridge over troubled waters. . . "[21] Given the song's release and initial popularity, it most assuredly was also played for the McGovern campaign "for free" on regular radio programming, which would have been another boost for the campaign. Again, this is the upside to selecting a campaign song that is a pre-existing pop song. While McGovern did not win the election, his campaign song serves as an important stepping stone to campaign music as it is used today. It was the first time in decades that a major party nominee in the general election used a popular song in its entirety as an official campaign song. It certainly would not be the last time this tactic was employed.

God Bless Rocky and the Children

The 1984 presidential election between incumbent Ronald Reagan and Democratic challenger Walter Mondale marked the first time that both major party candidates used unaltered popular songs as their campaign theme songs. Mondale used the theme "Gonna Fly Now" from the 1976 movie *Rocky* as well as "Teach Your Children Well." *Rocky* featured Sylvester Stallone as the title character, Rocky Balboa. It was a major commercial success, and it remains one of the highest grossing films of all time. The film also was awarded the Oscar for Best Picture.[22] The song "Gonna Fly Now" experienced similar success, peaking at number one on the Billboard Hot 100 chart in July 1977.[23] The song was played in the movie while Rocky trained, and the song climaxes as the boxer runs to the top of the steps at the Philadelphia Museum of Art. Bill Conti wrote the song's music, while Carol Connors and Ayn Robbins penned the lyrics.[24] The piece was largely instrumental, but did have a smattering of inspirational lyrics talking about working hard, growing stronger, and ultimately achieving what you desire.[25] The melody of the piece matches the motivational level of the lyrics. According to Jeff Pearlman of *Runner's World*, "so many races play Bill Conti's original *Rocky* theme near the finish line. The soaring optimism of the horn section combined with the chorus's cheesy chant of 'gonna fly now,' has an almost universal effect of sustaining the runner's energy when it's flagging the most."[26] This motivational appeal can also be applied to politics, which is exactly what Mondale tried to do several years after the film's release.

The success of *Rocky* helped propel "Gonna Fly Now" to become one of the more popular and recognizable songs of its day (and it remains quite identifiable today). The song was likely used by Mondale in 1984 to reflect a number of different images. First, Rocky was associated with the city of Philadelphia, which has great historical significance for the country. Philadelphia's connection to "Gonna Fly Now" has been capitalized upon by many, as the song is frequently played at sporting events that take place in that city. Mondale's use of the song, and his attempt to attach himself to Philadelphia, was likely part of the calculus in choosing the song (we will revisit this notion in more detail in chapter seven, where we examine the use of "Gonna Fly Now" by multiple candidates in the 2008 election). Second, the story of the first Rocky film was that of an underdog who took on the heavyweight contender, losing only by a split decision. It was a story of triumph against impossible odds, something reflected not just in the movie associated with the song but also in the lyrics themselves. This is perhaps fitting considering the popularity of Reagan in 1984. Mondale's story in 1984 was not as close of a loss as Rocky's battle in 1976, however. Mondale suffered a disastrous defeat at the hands of Reagan: the incumbent president collected nearly 59% of the popular vote and trounced Mondale in the Electoral College 525-13.[27]

Mondale made use of another popular song, "Teach Your Children" by Crosby, Stills, Nash, and Young. In a lengthy television advertisement entitled "Arms Control 5," Mondale emphasized the threat of nuclear war and the need to stop the proliferation of nuclear weapons, especially in space.[28] The ad began by showing images of children and playing the Crosby, Stills, Nash, and Young song. Although the song was largely background music, the following lyrics could be overheard on the commercial:

Teach your parents well,
Their children's hell will slowly go by. . .
Don't you ever ask them why, if they told you, you would cry,
So just look at them and sigh and know they love you.

You who are on the road
Must have a code that you can live by
And so become yourself
Because the past is just a good bye. . .
Don't you ever ask them why, if they told you, you would cry,
So just look at them and sigh and know they love you.

TEACH YOUR CHILDREN
© 1970 Nash Notes. All rights administered by Sony/ATV Music Publishing LLC,
8 Music Square West, Nashville, TN 37203
All Rights Reserved   Used by Permission

"Teach Your Children" was not as recent of a release in 1984 as "Gonna Fly Now," nor was it as popular when it hit the charts. Indeed, the song, released in 1970, only reached number sixteen on the Billboard Hot 100 chart.[29] That point notwithstanding, there is no doubt that the song was familiar to most voters in

1984, as was the super group that originally sang the song. Furthermore, the song promoted a message of idealistic peace, something that fit well with Mondale's advertisement and his campaign generally. This theme, however, did not win over the public as well as Reagan's motto of "peace through strength."[30]

Part of Ronald Reagan's successful reelection bid was choosing the campaign song "God Bless the U.S.A." by Lee Greenwood. In contrast to the song Mondale's campaign used, which relied heavily on association, "God Bless the U.S.A." had a text that glorified the country:

Verse 1:
If tomorrow all the things were gone,
I'd worked for all my life.
And I had to start again,
with just my children and my wife.
I'd thank my lucky stars,
to be livin' here today.
'Cause the flag still stands for freedom,
and they can't take that away.

Chorus:
And I'm proud to be an American,
where at least I know I'm free.
And I won't forget the men who died,
who gave that right to me.
And I gladly stand up,
next to you and defend her still today.
'Cause there ain't no doubt I love this land,
God bless the U.S.A..

Verse 2:
From the lakes of Minnesota,
to the hills of Tennessee.
Across the plains of Texas,
From sea to shining sea.
From Detroit down to Houston,
and New York to L.A.
Well there's pride in every American heart,
and it's time we stand and say.

Chorus:
And I'm proud to be and American,
where at least I know I'm free.
And I won't forget the men who died,
who gave that right to me.
And I gladly stand up,
next to you and defend her still today.
'Cause there ain't no doubt I love this land,
God bless the U.S.A..

God Bless the U.S.A.
Words and Music by Lee Greenwood
Copyright © 1984 SONGS OF UNIVERSAL, INC. and Universal – SONGS OF POLYGRAM
    INTERNATIONAL, INC.
All Rights Controlled and Administered by SONGS OF UNIVERSAL, INC.
All Rights Reserved   Used by Permission
Reprinted by permission of Hal Leonard Corporation

This simple message was one that could easily appeal to the American public at large and especially to those who served in the armed forces. It is no surprise that Reagan chose this song. By the summer of 1984, "God Bless the U.S.A." was a popular country western song, having already found wide use as a sign-off on many television stations, and as a supplement to "Take Me Out to the Ball Game" during the seventh inning stretch at many baseball parks.[31] The song, which was nominated for a Country Music Award for Song of the Year in 1984,[32] spent 10 weeks on *Billboard*'s Country Singles Chart in 1984, peaking at number seven.[33] The song was also part of a winning strategy for Reagan, who only lost the state of Minnesota (Mondale's home state) and the District of Columbia (which has supported the Democratic presidential nominee in every election where the metro area's voters have been able to vote for the presidency, beginning in 1964).

By the time Reagan made use of Greenwood's song, the harshness of the economy in 1982 had turned into 1984's "morning in America." Unemployment plummeted, the poverty rate leveled off, interest rates began to decline, and inflation remained low. Reagan parlayed this economic recovery into a monumental victory against Mondale that year, and Reagan would be the first president since Eisenhower to serve two full terms as president. Although Reagan's policy of cutting taxes while increasing federal spending led to significant increases in the national debt, the fact that people were working again and that prices were no longer spiraling out of control at the supermarket sealed Reagan's victory in 1984.[34] Having a popular patriotic theme song didn't hurt either.

Unlike the typical Tin Pan Alley song, "God Bless the U.S.A." was not a song that Reagan used to highlight his own virtues or what he perceived to be Mondale's shortcomings; the song did not speak directly to either candidate, nor was it written with a particular candidate in mind. Instead, "God Bess the U.S.A." was taken word-for-word from the lyrics penned by Greenwood, who wrote the song with no preconceived notions that it would ever be used in Reagan's reelection campaign. After the song's enormous success had led the organizers at the 1984 Los Angeles Summer Olympics to use the piece at the closing ceremonies, Greenwood received a call from President Reagan. According to Greenwood,

> As heartwarming as it was to have my song included in a televised patriotic event, I was really surprised when, not long afterwards, President Reagan called me, asking if he could include it at his film presentation at the [Republican] national convention. . . . It's difficult to say no to the President. Anyway, I

thought it would be alright. . . . I really hadn't planned for it to be used to endorse a candidate. But I guess we all should feel lucky that we can be involved in the political process without being afraid of reprisals.[35]

Thus, like the composers of "Happy Days Are Here Again," "This Land Is Your Land," "Gonna Fly Now," and "Bridge over Troubled Water" before him, Greenwood's song was not written with a politician in mind. . . but that is exactly how it was used.

Regardless of Greenwood's original intent, this "prepackaged song" nevertheless served Reagan well by delivering a political message of support for America and the troops who have fought and died for the country. Reagan made use of these lyrics because they appealed to Americans' sense of patriotism; in this sense, Reagan and his advisors must have thought the song was also attractive to a large segment of voters. Consequently, the song as a whole was reflective of Reagan's message and his position that he was a proud American who believed he could lead the country forward. The song's subtle, yet continually present, religious imagery also allowed Reagan to appeal to the Moral Majority without doing so in an overtly "preachy" way. There is no question that Reagan thought the average listener would have a positive view of this song, especially given the song's popularity in 1984. Furthermore, given how much the song had already been used at various sporting events and in other venues, it was a song with which many people were already familiar, and it was one that was still receiving regular radio airplay.

Explaining the Changing Musical Trends

Candidates in every presidential election since the 1984 election have used popular songs, lyric-for-lyric as a staple of their campaigns. What will be explored in chapters six and seven is how that music has been used, in what ways, and how the use of music has changed with new technologies. Before moving on to that discussion, it is important to assess and understand why candidates in the 1970s and early 1980s largely changed from the use of parodied songs and new compositions to using all of a preexisting popular song as the musical centerpiece for their respective campaigns.

One of the most reasonable explanations for this change had to do with musicians endorsing, and performing for, candidates. As was mentioned in chapter three, Al Jolson was known not only for composing original songs for presidential candidates, but was also known to travel to the candidate's campaign rallies and perform those and other songs on behalf of his preferred candidate. The same trend continued into future elections. For example, in the subsequent elections for Roosevelt following his 1932 victory, a popular singer/songwriter was on the scene writing and performing a campaign song on the radio in addition to the "Happy Days Are Here Again" that was already being employed in the campaigns. In 1936 country singer Bill Cox performed "Franklin D. Roosevelt's

Back Again."[36] "In 1939, Jay Gorney, who had written the music for 'Brother Can You Spare a Dime,' collaborated with Henry Myers on a musical plea for a third term, titled, "Mister Roosevelt, Won't You Please Run Again?"[37]

This trend would carry into the elections of the 1960s and 1970s. In fact, it was not uncommon for musicians to travel the campaign trail with the presidential candidate of their choice. "Thus, Frank Sinatra stumped for John Kennedy in 1960," as did Harry Belafonte. In the 1968 election, "Phil Ochs and Peter, Paul and Mary stumped for Eugene McCarthy, while several country singers, including Ernest Tubbs and Merle Haggard, helped Richard Nixon."[38]

Jerry Rodnitzky has argued that the 1970s marked the end of campaign songs or of songs that mention the president as a general principal.[39] However, we contend that the 1970s and early 1980s did not mark the end of campaign songs, but rather served as a period of transition between the parodied songs of the past and the straight use of popular music as the campaign theme song of the future. Candidates were already using popular singers of the day on the campaign trail performing campaign songs. It was the logical progression to abandon the parodied song on the campaign trail in favor of a popular song that was primarily associated with the artists who were supporting your campaign. From there, it is only a very small jump to making use of a song that has a popular hook with a few lines that are relevant to the candidate's campaign, even if the songwriter/performer otherwise has nothing to do with the candidate. This trend does have its pitfalls. Most notably, the candidate's full name would no longer be mentioned within the song. Occasionally, a candidate's first or even last name might be already located within a preexisting song, but this is a rarity. In addition, there would be no direct talk of issues associated with the campaign in the songs either. Thus, choosing a good song starts to require a candidate's staff to search through the repertoire of an artist or artists to determine which song would best associate itself with the campaign's message.

There are benefits to using the repertoire of the artists associating themselves with your campaign, however. First, the songs are already well known by the public. With this new strategy, songs can simply be performed in a way that would associate them with the candidates. That could be accomplished by performing them at prominent points during campaign stops. Second, it allows a candidate to have an automatic association with a particular artist. This would allow the candidate to enjoy some of the popularity of the artist through this musical association, whether that artist actually had the intention of supporting that candidate or not, such as the case of Ronald Reagan using "Born in the U.S.A."

During the same 1984 campaign in which Reagan used "God Bless the U.S.A.," his campaign also attempted to associate him with artists who would have seen screen time on MTV. Continuing a tradition begun by candidates during the rise of radio, the president tried without success to convince the pop stars Billy Joel and John Cougar Mellencamp to join his campaign (although he was able that year to convince Michael Jackson to appear with him in an anti-drunk driving effort aimed at teenagers).[40] Reagan's handler, Michael Deaver, contacted Bruce Springsteen's agent, asking if the pop star could appear with the president on the campaign trail; Springsteen's agent declined on his behalf.[41] Nevertheless, in September, Reagan invoked Springsteen's name at a rally in New Jersey: "America's future rests in a thousand dreams inside your hearts. It rests in the message of hope in songs of a man so many Americans admire—New Jersey's own, Bruce Springsteen. And helping you make those dreams come true is what this job of mine is all about."[42] Most assuredly, Reagan was referring to Springsteen's megahit in 1984, "Born in the U.S.A.," a song whose title appeared to play on a strong theme of patriotism. Of course, if Reagan had spent some time listening to more of the song than the title and hook, he would have realized that the song was not trumpeting the hopes and successes of America; rather, the lyrics reflected the negative experiences of a Vietnam veteran:

> Born down in a dead man's town
> First kick I took was when I hit the ground
> End up like a dog that's been beat too much
> Till you spend half your life just coverin' up
> Born in the U.S.A. . . .
>
> Got in a little hometown jam
> So they put a rifle in my hand
> Sent me off to a foreign land
> To go and kill the yellow man. . .
>
> Come back home to the refinery
> Hiring man says, "Son, if it was up to me. . . "
> Went down to see my VA man
> He said, "Son, don't you understand now. . . "
>
> Had a brother at Khe Sahn
> Fighting off the Viet Cong
> They're still there, he's all gone
> He had a woman he loved in Saigon
> I got a picture of him in her arms now.

"Born in the U.S.A." by Bruce Springsteen
Copyright © 1984 Bruce Springsteen (ASCAP)

Instead of embodying a message of "hope" as the president claimed, Springsteen's "Born in the U.S.A. is one of despair. A young man with no future gets himself in trouble, and is offered the chance to serve in Vietnam rather than go to jail. When he returns home, he cannot find a job, he has lost his patriotism, and he is reminded of his fallen comrade (this type of musical misrepresentation will be discussed further in chapter six). That point notwithstanding, Reagan referred to the Boss in his reelection campaign, hoping to capitalize on this singer-songwriter's popularity and the perceived message in the title of his well-liked song. As for Springsteen, it turns out that he is fairly liberal and had no intention of providing assistance to Reagan's reelection campaign. Years later, Springsteen publicly endorsed, and actively campaigned for, Democratic nominees John Kerry in 2004 and Barack Obama in 2008.[43]

Another factor leading to the change in the dominant way campaign music is used relates to shifts in political party identification. Beginning in 1932, Franklin Roosevelt forged the New Deal coalition of voters, which largely included urban voters, organized labor, Northerners, African Americans, Jewish voters, liberal intellectuals, and white Southern moderates/conservatives.[44] Many members of this coalition, including urban voters, Northerners, and African Americans, had high levels of support on a consistent basis for the Republican Party before the Great Depression. Although keeping together the New Deal coalition was a daunting task, it largely held until the late 1960s, when Nixon's "Southern Strategy" peeled off many white Southerners; with that exception, several groups in the New Deal coalition have largely remained loyal to the Democratic Party through the 2008 presidential election.[45]

The straight-up use of popular music is something that the Roosevelt campaign likely thought would be a more effective way of communicating a campaign message to members of the New Deal coalition when compared with other groups. For instance, it is unlikely that those who largely remained loyal to Hoover in 1932, such as business owners and rural voters in the North and West, would find as much appeal in the use of popular music as groups in the New Deal coalition. Since Roosevelt was looking to court voters who eventually settled into the coalition, it is no surprise that using "Happy Days Are Here Again" was a part of his campaign's strategy. Although no major party nominee would employ this strategy again until the New Deal coalition lost its Southern white block of voters, Roosevelt did introduce a new method of using music in presidential campaigns. Once the tactic is put into use again in the later 1960s and early 1970s, it was the Democratic candidates Robert Kennedy and George McGovern who also used music in this way.

Looming larger than party identification, the success of protest music in the 1960s and 1970s helps explain the change from original and parodied campaign songs to the use of existing popular songs. As Courtney Brown has noted, "[t]he dominant factor that influenced the genesis of the contemporary genre of political protest music in the United States, Britain and much of Europe is the political tumult associated with the Vietnam War and the Civil Rights Movement. . . "[46] Why might this music be influential in the future of presidential campaign music? The simple answer is that the protest music of the Civil Rights Movement and Vietnam showed the power that music had to connect on an emotional level with the public and the influence that it could have to sway public opinion. As Brown has stated, the music and musicians "both riveted and taught a large segment of an entire generation, as well as many others across generations."[47] Craig Hurst has noted that, "[i]n addition to entertainment and aesthetic edification and enlightenment, one of the many functions music serves is to unify people."[48]

Protest music was around in the United States long before the 1960s and 1970s. However, the genre that most often contained the music of protest was not a member of the mainstream music until this later time. Rock and roll would serve as the foundation from which protest music would find its way to the public, most notably in the form of folk music and the folk revival of the 1960s. What separated rock and roll from the popular music (especially those of Tin Pan Alley) that came before it was its focus on youth culture and the sensibilities of the working class. It had sprung up from the rural blues of the South, but moved to the urban centers of the country as it developed, incorporating a wide variety of new technologies, all the while embracing the African American musical influences from which it originated. Consequently, while the composers of Tin Pan Alley avoided the recording technologies available to them in favor of printing their music, the genres that would later form the basis of rock and roll (jazz, country/rockabilly, and rhythm and blues) embraced recording, leading to a widespread growth in popularity. Further, the music of Tin Pan Alley seemed to target the upper middle and upper classes with references to the finer things in life, while rock and roll focused on the average American, giving the music more universal appeal.

After the establishment of rock and roll as "popular" music in the 1950s, it seems only natural that music would evolve to speak about major social issues. With songs that spoke more explicitly about love and sex, rock and roll challenged the conservative nature of the culture of the 1950s, eventually leading the way to the political and social revolution of the 1960s.[49] Folk music was revived within the rock and roll genre to fill this role of social change and political protest. Folk music "drew from a long tradition of simple, straightforward songs about real life, hard times, and personal and public struggles, often with simple acoustic accompaniment."[50] A music that had been so strongly associated with the labor unions in the past, would now seek to sway public opinion on war and social injustice. And the music did so with surprising effectiveness. Some of the lasting songs that come from the civil rights era include: Bob Dylan's "Blowin' in the Wind," Pete Seeger's "We Shall Overcome," and Peter, Paul and Mary's "Where Have All the Flowers Gone?"

As stated earlier, the folk music that would serve as the foundation of protest music in the formative years was not overly complicated or complex, but relied on the simple settings of a powerful text to deliver its message. For example, Bob Dylan's "Blowin' in the Wind" is essentially a one man show, just a singer and his guitar laying down a simple harmonic accompaniment so as not to impede the powerful message of the song. The song's writer sought to ask a series of rhetorical questions about equality and social justice to the listener, finishing each series of questions by stating that the answer is the same as the title of the song: "Blowin' in the Wind."[51] The music was influential on a number of levels. As Hurst notes:

> Soon other songs flourished within the civil right movement, bringing solidarity and strength to members. The Student Non-Violent Coordinating Committee

(SNCC), formed in 1960, the Congress of Racial Equality (CORE), and Martin Luther King's Southern Christian Leadership Conference (SCLC) all used songs. The fervor for civil rights led directly into university campuses with the founding of organizations such as Students for a Democratic Society in 1960 and the University of California Berkley Free Speech movement in 1964. Folk music would also remain a fixture of campus organizing, and in the face of escalating fighting in Southeast Asia, folk music served as a rallying cry for the mounting peace movement and a focus for the enlarging crowds at anti-war rallies.[52]

Protest music was not limited to folk music, however. With the rising escalation in the Vietnam War came more animosity toward the war and music led the way. Rock singer Edwinn Starr came out with "War" in 1970 simply asking, rhetorically, if war is good for anything, and answering in the negative.[53] The song does not speak about Vietnam specifically, but references war in general giving it a universal message. Another popular song of the Vietnam protest movement was "I Ain't Marchin' Anymore" by Phil Ochs. Here, Ochs speaks from the position of a young soldier who is refusing to fight in another war because of the horrible atrocities that he has witnessed. The song projects a universal message about all wars and the devastation they cause. Songs like these were powerful because "[m]usicians had a captive audience during those Vietnam War years: young people and their loved ones who were going to be sent to fight—and possibly die—in a war no one really understood."[54] According to Brown, "[t]he Vietnam War enabled protest music to evolve to a state of sophistication that it otherwise would never have achieved."[55] Further, the music had a strong popular following and had succeeded in swaying the popular opinion of America's youth. Indeed, by 1969, the influence of rock music was so great that hundreds of thousands of young people were drawn to the Woodstock music festival, which was billed as three days of peace and music.

The music associated with civil rights struggles in the 1950s and 1960s also helped shape public opinion. As noted in the introduction, songs that attempted to sway people to the cause of desegregation included "We Shall Overcome," "Oh Freedom," "We Shall Not Be Moved," and "Ain't Gonna Let Nobody Turn Me Round." Marchers sang these songs, and they were played at various types of civil rights protests as a way to inspire those who took part in the events. Organizers ensured that music would be part of the movement because they knew the influence of music.

Given the success that pop, rock, folk, and gospel music was having at drawing people to the causes of civil rights and opposition to the Vietnam War, it should come as no surprise that politicians took notice in the United States and started to look for ways to also make use of this music. This trend began as a trickle in 1968, with Robert Kennedy's use of "This Is Your Land." This Woody Guthrie song was well known to most Americans, and given the patriotic connotations in the song, changing the lyrics to suit Kennedy's campaign might have backfired. Thus, Kennedy made use of the song with its existing music and lyrics.

This trend accelerated in 1972 with McGovern's use of "Bridge over Troubled Water." Another factor at this point was driving McGovern's use of this popular song. The 1972 presidential election was the first one in the United States in which the national voting age was lowered from 21 to 18. Thus, there were younger voters casting their ballots. Much like expanding electorates in the 1840s and 1920s led to campaigns changing their use of music, the lowering of the voting age changed campaign music use in the 1970s.

Based on research done of college students' political orientations and music preferences in the early 1970s, it would be a good campaign strategy indeed to use music to sway younger voters. The important question for campaigns, however, was which type of music might help motivate these younger voters. According to Fox and Williams' 1974 study, certain types of music appealed to students of different political persuasions. For instance, 52% of liberal students and 31% of moderates claimed to like protest music, while only 17% of conservative college students liked that type of music.[56] Conversely, 74% of conservative students and 68% of moderates claimed to like current popular hits, whereas only 46% of liberals claimed the same.[57] Between 72% and 78% of each group claimed to like rock music.[58] Thus, if a liberal like McGovern was looking for music to help accentuate his campaign and attract younger voters, he would have wanted to choose a preexisting rock song that appealed to young people of all political ideologies, or he would have wanted to choose a genre such as popular hits, that would have appealed to a group of voters, such as moderates, that the well-known liberal would have wanted to attract on election day. Thus, Simon and Garfunkel was an obvious, good choice for McGovern.

It is also no surprise that the first presidential candidates to use preexisting songs in their entirety were Democrats. They were harkening back to a tradition begun by a giant in their party, Franklin Roosevelt. Given that many people who took part in the civil rights and the antiwar movements would have been more likely to vote for Democratic candidates anyway, it was a logical choice for candidates from this party to begin using similar types of music to motivate these protestors to begin voting for them.

By 1984, the politics of music had evolved so that it was ready for both parties to use it. Just as conservative interest groups in the 1970s and 1980s began making use of the same tactics that liberal interest groups had success with in the 1960s and 1970s, so Republican candidates began using preexisting songs in the same way that Democratic candidates had been using. Since by the 1980s members of the electorate who experienced the 1960s and who grew up on pop and rock music (most notably, the baby boomer generation) was older and paying more attention to politics, it was easier to use this type of music to motivate a larger segment of the population. Indeed, studies have shown that voter turnout generally increases when an individual's age increases, up until approximately 75 years of age.[59] As those who came of age in the 1960s (and came of age with the popular music of that era) aged and started voting more, it is quite reasonable that presidential candidates saw that using this type of music could be used to influence more and more voters. Thus, "Gonna Fly Now" and "God Bless the

U.S.A." could be used to appeal to many more voters than similar songs would have been able to do even a decade or so earlier.

With popular music showing its ability to appeal to the American public and serve as a rallying cry to the people, it was only logical that political candidates would see the benefit in using songs that had already established their popularity with the American public. How they chose to use that music within their campaigns changed again in the late 1980s and would remain fairly consistent until the 2008 election, when the Internet began to become a large factor in bringing back the "singing" campaign styles of the nineteenth century. This is not to say that the Internet has completely displaced the use of preexisting music, but it is to say that like Tin Pan Alley, radio, and television before it, the Internet is a new technological development which has altered the ways in which politicians use music to their advantage. Before we turn to the World Wide Web, however, let us first examine how preexisting music was used by politicians to influence elections from 1988 through 2004.

Notes

1.   Sean J. Savage, *Roosevelt the Party Leader, 1932-1945* (Lexington: University Press of Kentucky, 1991), 11.

2.   Jack Yellen and Milton Ager, "Happy Days Are Here Again" (New York: WB Music Corp., 1929).

3.   William Safire, *Safire's Political Dictionary* (New York: Oxford University Press, 2008), 305.

4.   Jerry Rodnitzky, "Popular Music," in *The American President in Popular Culture*, ed. John W. Matviko (Westport, CT: Greenwood Press, 2005), 40.

5.   Safire, *Safire's Political Dictionary*, 305.

6.   "Landon Version of 'Oh, Susannah' Holds Constitution is "Good Enough for Me,'" New York Times, June 8, 1936, 8.

7.   Steven Gould Axelrod, ed., *The New Anthology of American Poetry: Modernisms: 1900-1950* (Piscataway: Rutgers University Press, 2005), 596.

8.   Sissle, Noble and Eubie Blake. "I'm Just Wild About Harry." (Los Angeles: Warner Bros. Inc., 1921).

9.   Randy Miller et al., *Harry the K: The Remarkable Life of Harry Kalas* (Philadelphia: RunningPress Book Publishers, 2010), 20-21; "The Billboard Hot 100 for the Week Ending September 27," *The Billboard*, September 21, 1959, 58.

10.   Thurston Clarke, *The Last Campaign: Robert F. Kennedy and 82 Days That Inspired America* (New York: Holt Paperbacks, 2008); Mel Ayton, *The Forgotten Terrorist: Sirhan Sirhan and the Assassination of Robert F. Kennedy* (Dulles, VA: Potomac Books, 2007).

11.   Safire, *Safire's Political Dictionary*, 97.

12.   David R. Shumway, "Your Land: The Lost Legacy of Woody Guthrie," in *Hard Travelin': The Life and Legacy of Woody Guthrie*, ed. Robert Santelli and Emily Davidson (Hanover, NH: University Press of New England, 1999), 129.

13.   Clarke, *The Last Campaign*.

14.   Richard Michael Marano, *Vote Your Conscience: The Last Campaign of George McGovern* (Westport, CT: Praeger Publishers, 2003), 11-20.

15.   "Historical Election Results: Electoral College Box Scores, 1789-1996," Office of the Federal Register, accessed August 1, 2010, http://www.archives.gov/federal-register/electoral-college/scores.html.

16.   Chris Charlesworth, *The Complete Guide to the Music of Paul Simon and Simon & Garfunkel* (London: Omnibus Press, 1997), 47.

17.   Charlesworth, *The Complete Guide*, 48-49.

18.   Rick Perlstein, *Nixonland: The Rise of a President and the Fracturing of America* (New York: Scribner, 2008), 673.

19.   Paul Simon, *Lyrics 1964-2008* (New York: Simon & Schuster, 2008), 55.

20.   Charlesworth, *The Complete Guide*, 48.

21.   Joe Morella and Patricia Barey, *Simon and Garfunkel: Old Friends* (Secaucus, NJ: Carol Publishing Group, 1991), 136.

22.   Daniel J. Leab, "The Blue Collar Ethnic in Bicentennial America: Rocky," in *Hollywood's America: Twentieth-Century America Through Film*, ed. Steven Mintz and Randy W. Roberts (Malden, MA: Blackwell Publishing, 2010), 268.

23.   Joel Whitburn, *Joel Whitburn Presents Billboard #1s, 1950-1991: A Week-by-Week Record of Billboard's #1 Hits* (Menomonee Falls, WI: Record Research, 1991), 189.

24.   Jim Piazza and Gail Kinn, *The Academy Awards: The Complete Unofficial History* (New York: Black Dog & Leventhal Publishers, 2008), 209.

25.   Bill Conti, Ayn Robbins, and Carol Connors, "Gonna Fly Now" (Los Angeles: United Artists Corporation, 1976, 1977).

26.   Jeff Pearlman, "Gonna Fly Now," *Runner's World*, July 2008, 82.

27.   "Historical Election Results"

28.   "The Living Room Candidate: Presidential Campaign Commercials 1952-2008," Museum of the Moving Image, accessed July 20, 2010, http://www.livingroomcandidate.org.

29.   Fred Bronson, *The Billboard Book of Number 1 Hits: The Inside Story Behind Every Number One Single, on Billboard's Hot 100 from 1955 to the Present* (New York: Billboard Books, 2003), 308.

30.   Ronald Reagan, *An American Life* (New York: Simon & Schuster, 1990), 549.

31.   Irwin Stambler and Grelun Landon, *Country Music: The Encyclopedia* (New York: St. Martin's, 1997), 191.

32.   Stambler and Landon, *Country Music*, 191.

33.   Joel Whitburn, *The Billboard Book of Top 40 Country Hits* (New York: Billboard Books, 2006), 144.

34.   John Ehrman, *The Eighties: America in the Age of Reagan* (New Haven, CT: Yale University Press, 2005), 49-89.

35.   Lee Greenwood and Gwen McLin, *God Bless the U.S.A.: Biography of a Song* (Gretna, LA: Pelican Publishing, 1993), 157.

36.   Richard Carlin, *Country Music: A Biographical Dictionary* (New York, Routledge, 2003), 85.

37.   Rodnitzky, "Popular Music,"41.

38.   Rodnitzky, "Popular Music,"42.

39.   Rodnitzky, "Popular Music,"42.

40.   Jim Cullen, *Born in the U.S.A.: Bruce Springsteen and the American Tradition* (Middletown, CT: Wesleyan University Press, 1997), 6-7.

41.   Cullen, *Born in the U.S.A.*, 7.

42. Jaap Kooijman, *Fabricating the Absolute Fake: America in Contemporary Pop Culture* (Amsterdam: Amsterdam University Press, 2008), 31.

43. Rachel Sklar, "The Boss Picks a Boss: Bruce Springsteen Endorses Obama," *The Huffington Post*, April 16, 2008, accessed June 4, 2011, http://www.huffingtonpost .com/2008/04/16/bruce-springsteen-endorse_n_96933.html.

44. M.J. Heale, *Franklin D. Roosevelt: The New Deal and War* (New York: Routledge, 1999), 7.

45. Henry C. Kenski and Kate M. Kenski, "Explaining the Vote in the Election of 2008: The Democratic Revivial," in *The 2008 Presidential Campaign: A Communication Perspective*, ed. Robert E. Denton, Jr. (Lanham, MD: Rowman & Littlefield, 2009).

46. Courtney Brown, *Politics in Music: Music and Political Transformation from Beethoven to Hip-Hop* (Atlanta: Farsight Press, 2008), 135.

47. Brown, *Politics in Music*, 135.

48. Craig W. Hurst, "Twentieth-Century American Folk Music and the Popularization of Protest," in *Homer Simpson Goes to Washington: American Politics through Popular Culture*, ed. Joseph J. Foy (Lexington: The University Press of Kentucky, 2008), 217.

49. Hurst, "Twentieth-Century American Folk Music," 151.

50. Hurst, "Twentieth-Century American Folk Music," 229.

51. Bob Dylan, *Lyrics: 1962-2001* (London: Simon & Schuster UK, Ltd., 2006), 53.

52. Hurst, "Twentieth-Century American Folk Music," 231.

53. Edwin Starr, vocal performance of "War," by Norman Whitfield and Barrett Strong, recorded 1970, on *War and Peace*, Motown Records, 33 rpm.

54. Brown, *Politics in Music*, 141.

55. Brown, *Politics in Music*, 142.

56. William S. Fox and James D. Williams, "Political Orientation and Music Preferences Among College Students," *The Public Opinion Quarterly* 38, No. 3 (Autumn 1974): 352-371, 368.

57. Fox and Williams, "Political Orientation," 368.

58. Fox and Williams, "Political Orientation," 368.

59. M. Margaret Conway, *Political Participation in the United States* (Washington, D.C.: CQ Press, 1991), 17.

Part Three

The Popular Music Era and Beyond

~ 6 ~

The "Canned" Campaign Song
(1988-2004)

By the late 1980s, music in presidential elections had made a long journey in the two centuries that it had been in use in the United States. To that point, it had been used in several different ways. Politicians made use of music in the form of song parodies in the singing campaigns of the nineteenth century. At the end of the nineteenth century and beginning of the twentieth century, there was an increase in the use of original compositions in campaigns that coincided with the rise of the Tin Pan Alley composers. The campaign song traversed the new media of radio and television in the twentieth century, changing and adapting in those media. Eventually music would become a staple of the political rally and convention once again, leaving the use of music in the media of radio and television to be used in more of a background role, serving as an emotional tie to the images and spoken message being delivered to the listener and viewer. All the while, these songs changed to reflect the addition of new groups of voters in American presidential elections. The journey has led presidential campaign music from parodies and original compositions of the past, to the straight use of songs that are popular and well known within the culture. The trend of using popular songs in their existing format has become a staple of presidential elections since the presidential election of 1984, carrying through to the most recent presidential elections in 2008.

As documented in chapter five, the move to using an existing popular song without alteration slowly began with the 1932 election of Franklin Delano Roosevelt, eventually culminating with Ronald Reagan and Walter Mondale in 1984 and the permanent establishment of the trend. That popular singers had been traveling with campaigns for many years singing campaign songs and popular songs to endorse their candidate, and that protest songs in the 1960s and 1970s had a cultural impact, made it even more clear that this trend could potentially be an effective one for use at campaign rallies and other live appearances. Why would this trend have solidified itself in the elections of the 1980s, however? There is an additional factor that may have contributed to the development of the popular song within the presidential campaign: the enhancement of music within popular culture through the use of the music video, especially on Music Television (MTV).

Living in a Material World

The 1980s were marked by a number of significant events both in and out of music. In 1980, John Lennon was murdered while returning home from a recording session with his wife Yoko Ono.[1] His death was felt worldwide, as he had embodied the dreams of hope and peace of the 1960s, and his death marked a symbolic end to the idealistic views the 1960s had represented.[2] The decade saw the development of rap/hip-hop, glam metal, new wave, and synthpop among others. The decade also saw the music of protest turn from the Vietnam war to hunger, farmers and apartheid with "Band Aid" and "USA for Africa" in 1984 and "Live Aid," "Farm Aid," and "United Artists against Apartheid" in 1985.[3] Nineteen Eighty Six would see the first Rock and Roll Hall of Fame bash in New York as well as Amnesty International's "Conspiracy of Hope" tour featuring several prominent rock artists, including U2 and Sting.[4] The decade would also see the rise of superstars such as Michael Jackson, Madonna, Prince and Whitney Houston, among countless others.[5] It also saw the death of several prominent musicians including Bon Scott (AC/DC), Bob Marley, John Belushi (Blues Brothers), Muddy Waters, Marvin Gaye and Roy Orbison.[6]

Outside the specific sphere of music, the free love attitudes that had evolved out of the 1960s into the 1970s quickly reversed themselves with the realization of HIV/AIDS and the devastation that it could cause. America's young adults "rejected the hippie looks and concentrated on smart business dress and became yuppies."[7] The decade was not without its share of United States involvement in wars with the invasion of Grenada in 1982 and the invasion of Panama in 1989, in addition to the ongoing Cold War with the Soviet Union that had begun in the 1950s. Electronics and computers continued to develop, seeing the forming of Nintendo Entertainment Company in the video game industry and the battle between IBM and Apple home computers. U.S. space exploration suffered a devastating loss with the *Challenger* explosion in 1986. And in 1989 a shocking blow was struck to communism when the Berlin Wall would finally come down, paving the way for the reunification of Germany. Also in the late 1980s, the Singing Revolution in Estonia, involving mass gatherings and song protests, helped lead to Estonian independence from the Soviet Union.[8]

The election of Ronald Reagan signified a change in the political direction of the country that had seen unemployment, interest rates, inflation, and the poverty rate soar under the Gerald Ford and Jimmy Carter administrations.[9] This recession worsened in the first few years of the Reagan administration. The new president's solution had multiple facets. First, Reagan advocated tax cuts; since these were expected by the administration to take some time to "trickle down," Reagan looked for an interim solution as well. He turned to Federal Reserve Chairman Paul Volcker, a Carter appointee. Volcker advocated raising higher interest rates even higher as a way to curb inflation. Reagan supported this policy, which did lower inflation. A side effect of higher interest rates, however, was an ever greater increase in unemployment, which rose from seven percent to almost eleven percent in 1982. Businesses closed, farms were foreclosed on, the poverty rate increased, and homelessness ballooned. Although painful, Reagan advocated staying the course. In the meantime, the president's popularity rating fell to 35 percent, and the Republicans lost 26 House seats in 1982.[10]

The music industry was not immune from the economic downturn of the 1970s and early 1980s. It too was in the midst of its first major recession in nearly thirty years. This resulted in many companies restructuring their hiring practices and laying off employees in an attempt to save on costs. The economic downturn would also prompt a change in the way the music industry had contracted with artists, moving from a model where they would have many artists with niche popularity, to a model where they would have fewer artists who were very marketable and could achieve widespread popularity in an attempt to consolidate profits.[11]

At the turn of the twentieth century, the "popular" music of the day was coming out of Tin Pan Alley. As noted in chapter two, the focus of Tin Pan Alley was on published music, as opposed to recorded music. This made sense for Tin Pan Alley at the time, as the new recording technologies that were being developed had a limited sound quality.[12] The fact that "publishers did not receive royalties from the sale or use of recorded music; and the demand for prerecorded cylinders could not compete with the demand for sheet music" also affected the decision within Tin Pan Alley to publish music and not record it. [13] Conversely, jazz, country, and rhythm and blues embraced recording and the sale of records as the method to bring their music to the public; these genres formed the basis of rock and roll and its subsequent offsets. Some scholars even credit audio recording as the reason for the popular rise of rock and roll in the 1950s. In fact, according to Garofalo, "[j]ust as record companies would come to replace publishing houses as the center of the music industry, rock n' roll would push aside Tin Pan Alley pop as the dominant style of popular music."[14]

Through 1980, the music industry had based their business model on the sale of records and promotion of artists through radio play. While the television had been a part of mainstream America since the 1950s, the music industry had never fully sought to capitalize on the potential of airing music on television in a format similar to that of radio before the 1980s. However, artists, especially new acts, used television to promote their careers by appearing on programs like *The Ed Sullivan Show*. Programs such as these were television's way of bringing the vaudeville stage to the country through the use of mass media which was also referred to in the industry as "vaudeo."[15] While a record company may potentially have increased record sales from an artist's appearance on one of these shows, the artists themselves would assuredly receive a much greater benefit from this type of promotion than the record labels. However, in the early 1980s television would aid in the music industry's economic recovery, by bringing music to the people in a completely new way. On August 1, 1981, at 12:01 a.m., John Lack spoke the words, "Ladies and Gentlemen, Rock and Roll," and MTV was launched.[16] MTV was the brainchild of Mississippi disc jockey turned programmer Robert Pittman.[17] His concept was essentially that used on the radio: through the use of the video jockey or VJ, music would be played on the television as music videos. Just like on radio, Pittman planned for these music videos to play on the air twenty-four hours a day, seven days a week (This is something which may come as a bit of a shock to younger Americans viewing MTV in the early twenty-first century, as the original MTV channel now barely plays any music videos at all!). The station had instant popularity for the small numbers of people who were able to receive the initial broadcasts; the network spread to the entire country in 1985, creating a pop culture icon that is still thriving, although the formatting has changed substantially over the years.[18]

MTV was able to open the world of music to a new generation through a medium that they were more in tune with. Music videos, while relatively simple at first, would become more complicated, telling the stories of songs and bolstering the fashion trends of the music stars that were shown in them. Combining the renewed vigor of the music industry, with its collective focus on a fewer number of talents and the music video, would make pop culture icons, the most notable of which was Michael Jackson. Indeed, Jackson revolutionized the music video industry with "Thriller" in 1983.[19] The video was not only popular on MTV, but ranked third in all video cassettes sold in 1984, according to Billboard, and is the bestselling music video ever.[20] The increasing popularity of popular music, both new and old, due to the new pop culture identity and status of music, made the 1984 election the point from which popular music, many times without alteration, would find itself as a permanent fixture within the presidential campaign. Now what was left to determine was how that popular music would be used.

In the last chapter, we examined Ronald Reagan's choice in 1984 of "God Bless the U.S.A." by Lee Greenwood. This election, in which Mondale also used the pop song "Gonna Fly Now," would mark the permanency of the popular song in presidential elections. With respect to "God Bless the U.S.A," the entire piece represented a message the campaign desired to associate with their candidate, in this case that Reagan believed in America, supported the country and the troops, and was proud of the country in which he lived. The fact that the entire song clearly communicated that message left no room for error with the electorate. The song conjured up patriotic images for the listener, and any part of the song represented a patriotic position that Reagan wanted to portray. Although "God Bless the U.S.A." was not a song one would have seen on MTV in 1984, it marked the dawn of a new era in campaign music. Pop music would be the norm from this election. That Reagan, a Republican, chose a patriotic country western song should not be surprising, given the conservative leanings of country music generally. Mondale's choice in "Gonna Fly Now," was not as effective as Reagan's, since it contained fewer relevant political themes, and it expressed no prominent political message.

While using an entire preexisting popular song marked the beginning of popular music in the campaign, this practice also marked a change away from a campaign song being clearly representative of a campaign's more specific policy messages. That is not to say that there are not songs where the entire work cannot be associated with the campaign, but rather that campaigns would begin to favor a single hook line that presented the campaign's message, many times not worrying about the remainder of the song. Sometimes, when looked at from the correct perspective, these songs could be seen as repetitive of the campaign in their entirety or at least larger chunks. At other times, what remained of the song might not be a representative message at all, instead leaving just the one line that represented the song's hook that was relevant to the campaign. This can be seen with the Reagan campaign's use of Bruce Springsteen's "Born in the U.S.A.," which was discussed in chapter five.

Coming to America, Which Is Your Land

The 1988 election, involving George Herbert Walker Bush and Michael Dukakis, marked a shift in campaign songs to the approach of the "one-line-wonder." By this time, political minds were far more concerned with delivering a quick, easily remembered message to the general public, largely due to the rise of the news media and television. Indeed, between 1968 and 1988, the average media sound bite (a block of uninterrupted speech by a candidate on television news) decreased from approximately 42 seconds to less than 10 seconds.[21] Presidential campaigns were shortening their messages in every way they delivered them, because they knew that media coverage was becoming ever more focused and significantly shorter. If a message took longer to communicate, candidates risked that important parts would not be replayed in the media, or certain parts of the message could be taken out of context in a shorter sound bite. The need to be more precise began to infect every part of the candidates' campaigns, including music selection. Thus, the concept of using an entire song to espouse a value of the candidate was replaced by a specific catch phrase that most often represented the song's hook/title phrase so that the electorate might more easily remember and thus associate it with the candidate. As discussed in chapter two, the hook is designed to be the most memorable and catchy point of the song. It is many times the most repeated music and text in the song and, consequently, the portion of the song that a person would remember quite easily after the first hearing. Thus, since the hook of a song is the portion that is most identifiable to the electorate, it stands to reason that campaigns would begin to think of music and the message they wish to send to the electorate through the music in these terms. Candidates who did not follow this trend and instead chose songs (and song clips) that "went off message," risked being punished by the media or giving rise to unneeded controversy.

Another reason campaigns may have moved in this direction was due to the difficulty in finding an existing song that, in its entirety, would fully express the message of the campaign. When campaigns were having songs written for them or when they tended to have parodied lyrics, this task was relatively easy to accomplish. However, the composition of new songs can be daunting and difficult for the public to associate with the candidate if the song is not well remembered, and, as indicated in chapter two, the results of parodied songs can oftentimes be of a relatively poor quality. Consequently, if a campaign wanted to use a preexisting song in its entirety, it was now faced with a daunting task of looking through thousands of songs to find not only the message that the campaign would want to send with the entire song, but one that was both popular with the electorate and in a genre that the electorate would find appealing. With these considerations in mind, the use of a song's hook to express a campaign's message seems like the best choice, as it is the portion of the song that tends to be best remembered by the listener. Thus, beginning in the 1980s, candidates attempted to create an association between themselves and the hook of a popular song.

This premise was put into use repeatedly for the 1988 presidential election. Running for the Republicans, George H.W. Bush's campaign saw the song "This Land Is Your Land" by Woodie Guthrie as a song whose hook could deliver an important message about the values of the campaign. Recall that this song and its message were discussed in the introduction. The 1940 folk song is well known by most Americans. Its lyrics proclaim that the land belongs to all of us, from coast-to-coast, across different regions of the country. More particularly, the chorus speaks of the country being not for one class of people, but for all people.[22] This is a very positive message to deliver to an electorate who desire to feel that this country is not only for those who have monetary wealth or the correct skin color, but rather for all people no matter who they are, how much they own, or where they live. In fact, it was this very opinion that caused Guthrie to write songs such as "This Land Is Your Land." Guthrie once stated, "I hate a song that makes you think that you are not any good. I hate a song that makes you think that you are just born to lose. Bound to lose. No good to nobody. No good for nothing. Because you are too old or too young or too fat or too slim too ugly or too this or too that. Songs that run you down or poke fun at you on account of your bad luck or hard traveling."[23]Bush's campaign was trying to capitalize not only with the text of the song, but with the songwriter and his beliefs as well. The choice of this song, however, might also be considered a bit ironic for a Republican candidate. As described in the introduction, while Guthrie claimed to have no political view other than a desire to fight for the workingman, he often performed at Communist Party functions and was strongly associated with the Communist Party.[24] However, Guthrie saw them as the only ones fighting for worker's rights at the time, and when asked if he had any problems with the Communist Party or his association with them, he merely said, "left wing, right wing, chicken wing—it's the same thing to me."[25] The song "This Land Is Your Land" was also used by Robert Kennedy when he ran for the presidency in 1968.

Bush's main competitor in 1988 (there were several third party candidates who ran in the election, including Congressman Ron Paul, who was then the nominee of the Libertarian Party) was Democrat Michael Dukakis. The Massachusetts governor chose the song "America" by Neil Diamond to serve as his campaign song. It was originally released in 1981 and reached number one on the adult contemporary chart. This song was a more intriguing choice for a campaign when compared to George H.W. Bush's selection for multiple reasons. First, the song's hook, which talks about immigrants coming to the United States, can be looked at in a couple of different ways for the Dukakis campaign. First, one might assume that the campaign was referring to a hopeful change from the Republican establishment of the previous eight years which, while had seen a recovering economy, had also seen the national debt soar to over 2.6 trillion dollars.[26] The ads run by the Dukakis campaign, such as "Hey, Pal," bear this theme out in the campaign.[27] (The ad shows a man in a suit who is representative of the Republican Party. He opens by saying "Hey, pal. How about a couple hundred billion? I'll pay you right back." The man then laughs and later asks "What's another trillion between friends?" Meanwhile, the narrator talks about the rising debt under the Reagan administration and mismanagement of the economy. The narrator ends by saying "Sorry, pal" with the text on the screen saying "We can't afford the Republicans.")[28] The song's hook could also imply the coming of new citizens to the United States, which was implied by the lyrics of the song which talk about people coming to America who have traveled long and hard to reach this country to pursue their dreams.[29] These same thoughts could also have been in reference to Dukakis' Greek heritage, implying that he understood the plights of those who immigrate to this country and work hard to make their American success story.[30]

Second, when looked at from the right perspective, the entire song, not just the hook, could be seen as a political message that was associated with the Dukakis campaign. The text speaks of how those with dreams take them to the United States because that is where they are free to pursue those dreams. Further, the song talks about America as a beacon of freedom shining brightly.[31] The song finishes with the opening lines of "My Country 'Tis of Thee" or "America" which says:

> My country 'tis of thee
> Sweet land of liberty
> Of thee I sing[32]

While, as stated previously, the song was obviously written to discuss immigration to America, the text can also be looked through the light of a coming home of the values of the Democratic Party that had been absent for the previous eight

years under ·Reagan. With the return of these values through the election of
Dukakis, the Democrats of the country would have had a chance to immigrate
back to power and remake America through those Democratic values. Taking a
view such as this might be stretching the text of the song a bit; however, the case
can be made for it and, on the whole, makes the song a potentially powerful
choice to express a campaign message. Under this interpretation, one can easily
understand why Dukakis chose the song.

The election, however, was not to be for Dukakis in 1988. G.H.W. Bush
won convincingly in both the popular vote (by over seven million votes) and the
Electoral College vote (by over 300 votes); Dukakis was only able to carry 10
states in the election.[33] This was, however, better than the two Democratic candidates that had run in the 1980 and 1984 elections.[34] Earlier in the campaign
season, it looked as though Dukakis might win the election, as he had a 17-point
lead over Bush in the polls during the summer of 1988. However, shortly thereafter, Bush campaign manager Lee Atwater created the now infamous "Willie
Horton" advertisement. The ad described Horton, a convicted murderer and rap-
ist, who committed rape again while out of prison in Massachusetts on a fur-
lough program. The advertisement injected the issue of race into the campaign
(Horton is an African American) and also made Dukakis appear soft on crime,
both of which helped lead to the governor's electoral demise.[35]

"Don't Stop" Being "Crazy"

Four years later, Bill Clinton's 1992 campaign employed a similar musical philosophy to President Bush in the 1988 presidential election. There are some important differences in their approaches, however. For instance, while the Bush
campaign picked a song whose hook would convey a particular value of their
campaign, the hook of Clinton's campaign song also served as the campaign's
slogan (Don't stop thinking about tomorrow) during the election. During the
Democratic National Convention, the party played the song "Don't Stop (Thinking About Tomorrow)" by Fleetwood Mac. This song blared over the speakers
at Madison Square Garden when Clinton was nominated for the presidency,[36]
and it would continue to be associated with Clinton for the remainder of his
campaign. The lyrics of the song's first verse and chorus state,

> If you wake up and don't want to smile,
> If it takes just a little while,
> Open your eyes and look at the day,
> You'll see things in a different way.
>
> Don't stop thinking about tomorrow. . .

Don't Stop
Words and Music by Christine McVie

With these lines, Bill Clinton told the public not to ignore their future, and attempted to establish with the voting public that he was the man who could refocus the country and move it in the correct direction, leaving behind the years dominated by Republicans Ronald Reagan and George H.W. Bush. This was one simple message that people could easily associate with Clinton and his campaign, conveyed in a song by Fleetwood Mac. Donald Bracket notes in his book *Fleetwood Mac: 40 Years of Creative Chaos* that Clinton's use of "Don't Stop" was "a brilliant tactic that may have cemented his image in the public's mind as a forward thinker fixed on that perpetual 'tomorrow' that makes the song so catchy."[37] The group originally recorded "Don't Stop" in 1977, with the song rising all the way to number three on the *Billboard* charts that year.[38] This is another example of a song chosen because its message and history indicate that the listener is likely to have a positive view of the song due to its popularity. Given that Bill Clinton and Al Gore in 1992 were the first baby boomers to be nominated for the presidency and vice presidency by a major party ticket, "Don't Stop" was an excellent way to convince other baby boomers that their time was now, and that they needed to seriously consider their future when they entered the voting booth in November of 1992. In addition, the song played to the emotions of an electorate who were tiring of the Republican Party and the direction of the country by promising through the song that "It'll be better than before" because "Yesterday's gone." Since the country was still in the midst of a recession in the fall of 1992, this message resonated with many voters. In many ways, "Don't Stop" was the culmination of decades of popular music taking over presidential campaign theme music: successful protest music for baby boomers, which was noticed by politicians, led to popular music being used lyric for lyric, and was eventually used by baby boomers running for president. Perhaps this is one of the reasons that "Don't Stop" remains one of the most recognizable preexisting presidential campaign theme songs and why it is still so easily associated with Bill Clinton.

"Don't Stop" symbolized another important message of the Clinton-Gore campaign in 1992, that of the "New Democrats." Winning over the votes of the white working class and middle class, a group that has been more likely to support the Democratic Party since the New Deal Coalition was formed in the 1930s, was part of the Reagan-Bush strategy of success in the 1980s. Many of these voters supported the fortieth president in 1980 and 1984 and came to be known as "Reagan Democrats." Although they began slowly returning to the Democratic Party in the 1986 midterm elections, many Reagan Democrats also supported George H.W. Bush in his 1988 presidential campaign.[39]

Some within the Democratic Party feared that the party was seen as too liberal and would continue to lose presidential elections unless it changed its approach. This group, led by the Democratic Leadership Council (DLC), referred to itself as "New Democrats" and advocated a third way to American politics, which included continuing to advocate for liberal social issues but also more moderate/centrist positions on fiscal issues. Bill Clinton became the poster child for the New Democrats, as he took liberal social positions while also advocating for tax cuts, tax credits, and free trade. Clinton was also a former chair of the DLC.[40]

With this understanding of New Democrats in mind, once can see how "Don't Stop" was also meant to send a message to Reagan Democrats. The notion that "[y]ou'll see things in a different way" and that things will be "better than before" imply the new, third way direction taken by Clinton and the DLC in 1992. This major portion of the Clinton message was aptly expressed in song.

Clinton made use of music in other ways in 1992, including by playing his saxophone. As a child, Clinton took up the tenor saxophone and became an accomplished player in school.[41] His inspiration was apparently based in his experience of hearing live jazz music performed by Al Hirt in New Orleans as a child.[42] During the campaign, Clinton made an appearance on *The Arsenio Hall Show*; he donned sunglasses and jammed on his saxophone with the house band, playing Elvis Presley's "Heartbreak Hotel."[43] Clinton also appeared on *The Tonight Show* with Johnny Carson and played "Summertime" on his saxophone.[44] The Arkansas governor became the first presidential candidate to appear on MTV when he took part in a televised forum, on which he famously answered an audience member's question about the type of underwear he wore.[45] Informal public appearances like these, which also involved the use of music, changed campaigning forever, allowing candidates to have direct access to the public without being filtered by the news media.[46] Candidates could now appear on these casual programs and expect more of a softball line of questioning than journalists would tend to pitch to them, making such performances advantageous to politicians. Although this type of campaigning on talk shows was a rarity for presidential candidates in 1992, it has now become commonplace (In 2003, Arnold Schwarzenegger went so far as to announce his candidacy to be California's governor on *The Tonight Show*, a move that would have been unthinkable before Bill Clinton paved the way for it.[47]) It all began with Bill Clinton, and his saxophone playing was likely the "hook" that got him onto these shows. Indeed, this casual use of music was likely another way, like playing "Don't Stop," that the Clinton campaign thought would be beneficial in connecting with undecided voters of the baby boomer generation and those of subsequent generations. Indeed, much like great campaigners of the past, such as Franklin Roosevelt and Ronald Reagan, Clinton pulled together a powerful song and other musically oriented pop culture elements to produce a well-integrated campaign.

Of course, there are times when the candidate or members of their campaign do not choose the music that gets associated with them or their run at political office. Instead, the song "chooses" the candidate for one of any number of reasons which may include: being purely by accident, because it fits a stereotype that is held about the individual, or because the song potentially fits the personality of the individual. Consequently, H. Ross Perot is a unique case when it comes to campaign music. Perot, a self-made Texas billionaire, appeared on the *Larry King Live* show in February 1992 to announce that he would run for the presidency as an independent candidate if supporters secured his name on the ballot in all 50 states.[48] Perot's platform included support for congressional term limits, a pro-choice position on abortion, an increase in the gasoline tax, decreased military spending, a national health care plan, opposition to international free trade agreements[49] (he once famously remarked that the North American Free Trade Agreement would result in a "giant sucking sound" of jobs leaving for Mexico),[50] and ending the budget deficit.[51] In early June of that year, polls showed Perot leading a three-way race: according to a *Time*/CNN poll, Perot would have been supported by 37% of voters in a general election, while Bush and Clinton both polled at 24% support.[52] Even with this momentum, Perot abruptly dropped out of the race on July 16th; he then changed his mind again and reentered the race on October 1st, little more than one month before election day.[53]

While most candidates for office pick their song in an attempt to convey a positive message about their campaign, Perot was essentially handed a song, Patsy Cline's "Crazy," because it described what many in the public thought of him, on both sides of the political spectrum. Former President Jimmy Carter referred to Perot as a demagogue, and George F. Will labeled Perot "an intellectual sociopath."[54] President Bush's press secretary, Marlin Fitzwater, called Perot "a paranoid person who had delusions."[55] After Perot stated that Republicans under Bush had tried to disrupt his daughter's wedding and tap his telephones, President Bush responded by stating that such charges were "crazy."[56] David Brinkley remarked that political professionals thought Perot was "half-crazy" for the way he ran his campaign.[57] "Comedians and Perot's critics routinely brand him as 'crazy,' and Perot himself acknowledged the charges, rather gracefully, by dancing with his wife to Patsy Cline's song 'Crazy.'"[58] at a campaign rally in Dallas, Texas, just days before the 1992 election.[59] On election night in 1992, Perot told supporters, "We're crazy again now. . . We've got busses lined up outside to take you back to the insane asylum after all this is over."[60] When Perot gave his concession speech on election night, he also played the song and encouraged supporters to sing along.[61] With messages like these, Perot's use of "Crazy" appears to be a rather lighthearted attempt to poke fun at the use of campaign theme songs themselves. This theory takes on some traction when compared to the very serious and driving message of Clinton's "Don't Stop (Thinking About Tomorrow)." "Crazy" was also perhaps an ironic reflection of the impression those associated with the two major parties had of Perot and his supporters. Perhaps this was also how Perot thought he could cleverly call attention to his "crazy," unconventional ideas. Regardless of how it might look politically, it was an interesting way of handling the public view held of him in a carefree way. One could even argue that Perot was attempting to find a song that would elicit a positive reaction from the public by choosing an amusing piece of music to associate with his campaign instead of a more serious campaign song designed to speak to a particular issue or belief.

In the end, the use of "Crazy" was not part of a winning strategy for Perot. Instead, the song was a poor choice by an unconventional campaign. Although it was an amusing attempt by Perot to poke fun at himself (or perhaps even an attempt to be "crazy like a fox" and retake his earlier lead in the polls), the song was a very bad idea. It did not do what many other candidates' songs do. It failed to portray the candidate in a positive light, it neglected to mention any of the candidate's policy positions, and it said nothing negative about his opponents. The song is slow rhythmically. It left little to inspire supporters. And for a man who had already demonstrated some instability by dropping out of the race and reentering, reminding the electorate that some people thought he was crazy was not a good tactic.

The "crazy" moniker stuck to Perot, which was not helped by his use of the song of the same name. During the post-1992 debate on NAFTA, Perot's theories on the trade agreement were referred to by members of the Clinton White House as a "crazy conspiracy" and he was called "fanatical."[62] When Perot announced he was running for the presidency again in 1996, James Carville quipped that the "only thing Perot ought to run for is a psychiatrist's office."[63]

The Bush campaign was not without its own musical selections during the 1992 presidential campaign. In addition to using "This Land Is Your Land" again within the campaign, Bush, in an attempt to show the "kinder, gentler" candidate, used Bobby McFerrin's "Don't Worry, Be Happy."[64] However, McFerrin demanded that the campaign cease the use of his song as he did not support Bush in his bid for reelection.

In addition to "This Land Is Your Land" and "Don't Worry, Be Happy," Bush turned to country music and country musicians in an attempt to bolster his campaign. Just as Reagan had done in the 1984 election, Bush called on Lee Greenwood and "God Bless the U.S.A." to be a part of his reelection bid.[65] Both Naomi Judd and Tanya Tucker performed at the Republican National Convention further solidifying the Bush campaign's ties with the conservative roots of country music.[66] In addition to this use of country songs and singers, "Bush's speeches late in the campaign we peppered with phrases from country song lyrics that, Bush felt, presented his opponent in a bad light."[67]

The 1992 election did not see President Bush follow in his predecessor's footsteps and win reelection to the presidency, nor did it see an upstart third party challenger gain a surprise victory. Rather, the Democrats would win back the White House behind their smooth-talking candidate Bill Clinton and his theme song of "Don't Stop (Thinking About Tomorrow)," borrowed from Fleetwood Mac. In fact, Clinton would beat Bush by six million votes in the popular election while taking 69% of the Electoral vote. Although there was much more to the Clinton-Gore '92 campaign than their use of music, the music did not hurt. Indeed, many voters identified with the campaign's slogan, and there is no doubt that the song of Fleetwood Mac's went a long way in delivering this message to those attending campaign rallies and watching the Democratic National Convention. In addition, some credit Clinton's saxophone performance on *Arsenio* as helping him win,[68] and Clinton himself acknowledged that "MTV had a lot to do with the Clinton-Gore victory."[69]

"Dole Man" v. "Beginnings"

The Republican nominee in 1996, Kansas Senator Bob Dole, looked to the practices of the past with his campaign song. Instead of taking on a popular song verbatim into his campaign, Dole chose instead to use a song parody to represent his campaign. This does not mean that the trend of using pop music lyric for lyric and note for note was on the way out. Instead, that strategy remained dominant during and after the 1996 election. Just as was the case in previous eras, there are always some anomalous campaign practices. In 1996, the Dole campaign engaged in such a practice, although its use of song was only a small rewrite of lyrics to an existing song.

Originally a 1967 hit of Sam and Dave, "Soul Man" was cleverly altered to "Dole Man" in an attempt to use the song's catchy hook phrase to create name recognition. Two versions of "Dole Man" appear to have been used during the campaign. The first was written by Joyce Moore, the wife of Sam Moore who was the tenor voice in the Sam and Dave duo. In fact, Moore sang and recorded this version for the Dole campaign. The version by Joyce Moore spoke of how Dole had worked his entire political career to make the United States a better place and that the country should no longer worry as Dole had given up his seat in the Senate in order to keep making the United States a better place by becoming the president.[70]

The Dole campaign ran itself into a public relations problem with the use of this song, however. One of the original writers of "Soul Man" objected to Dole's use of the song. Furthermore, it came to light that Dole had never asked for permission to appropriate the song from the song's publishers and owners, Rondor Music and Warner/Chappell, who then demanded compensation. Although the campaign maintained that it had done nothing wrong, use of the song was suspended by the campaign in September 1996.[71]

The second version was written by William Tong, a geologist and professor by trade, and a political parodist who runs the "Boot Newt Sing Along Page."[72] According to the website where this song was first discovered by the authors, the lyrics are "as sung by a Dole supporter.[73] The text of this version said:

Coming to you	And when you get 'em
On a muddy road	Give back some
Insults	So don't you worry
I got a truck load	'Cause Bob's running

I'm a Dole man	I'm a Dole man
I'm a Dole man	I'm a Dole man
I'm a Dole man	I'm a Dole man
I'm a Dole man	I'm a Dole man

Got where he got   Just go to vote
The easy way   And he'll get in
And he gets richer   You got no hope
Each and every day   The Congress is Republican
                                    Yeah! Yeah! Yeah! Yeah!
And he hates Bill
From Little Rock   I'm a Dole man
And when he starts   I'm a Dole man
He can't stop   I'm a Dole man
                                    I'm a Dole man

There are some aspects of this song that might lead one to believe that it was sung by a Dole supporter about the campaign. The song did not refer to any specific attributes or qualities that Dole had to be president, but rather talked about him in very vague generalities. The song also referred to the difficult path that Dole had while running for office, speaking of "insults" and how Republicans should "give some back." It also made reference to the fact that in 1994 the Republicans won back both the House and Senate to have control of Congress for the first time in over forty years. Consequently, the song told the Democrats that "you got no hope" because of the Republican domination in the Congress.

However, according to Tong, the song was "intended to be sarcastic."[74] It was meant to be a slap at the Republican candidate through the use of the very song that Dole's campaign had been using on the campaign trail to support his candidacy. While the song mentioned Bob Dole's name (either first or last) 13 times throughout the song, the text of the verses clearly paints Dole in a negative light, claiming that the Republican candidate had gotten where he was the "easy way" while it accused Dole of slinging mud from the "muddy road." In addition, the final verse served as a rallying cry to Democrats. The thought of the Republicans having control over both houses of Congress as well as the presidency was more than enough motivation for the Democrats and liberal-minded independents to cast their votes for Clinton that November. For anyone who was listening to more than just the song's hook, it served as a reminder of this fact. In this sense, the final verse may have served as a subtle reminder for any members of the electorate who desired to prevent one party government from coming to fruition.

In the end, however, most listeners probably only remembered the clever hook from the song, thus making even this parody a positive song for the Dole campaign. Those who did listen to the lyrics that followed were certainly reminded of the nation's political situation. The song "Dole Man" also tied into the theme that Dole was "the man," which was also expressed in his campaign slogan, "A Better Man for a Better America."[75]

One benefit that Bob Dole's campaign may have had from their use of a parodied version of Sam and Dave's "Soul Man" was an association with what was by 1996 a pop culture icon in the Blues Brothers. Originally designed as an act on *Saturday Night Live*, the Blues Brothers (played by Dan Aykroyd and John Belushi) recorded fourteen total albums, beginning with their 1978 hit record "Briefcase Full of Blues" which reached number one on Billboard's top 200 charts and had been a top forty hit with Sam and Dave's "Soul Man." The Blues Brothers became a pop culture icon largely through their *Saturday Night Live* skit and subsequent 1980 movie, *The Blues Brothers*. The film detailed a tale of redemption for paroled convict Jake (Belushi) and his brother Elwood (Aykroyd), who took on "a mission from God" to save from foreclosure the Catholic orphanage in which they had grown up. In order to complete their "mission" they had to reunite their rhythm and blues band, the Blues Brothers, and organize a performance to earn the $5,000 owed by the orphanage to the tax assessor. Along the way they are targeted by a destructive "mystery woman" (who turns out to be Jake's former fiancée), Neo-Nazis, and a country and western band, all while being pursued by the police.[76] Although the song was not used in the film, the fact that this group had recorded it and had a strong association with it due to its popularity on the Billboard charts could only be an asset to the Dole campaign as they would now have an association with these two figures who were well known in the pop culture scene by 1996.

This is not to say that the Dole campaign did not pick the song to be associated with its original performers as well. In choosing a parody of "Soul Man," Dole was able to associate himself with what the Rock and Roll Hall of Fame describes as "the greatest of all soul duos."[77] From 1961 to 1981, Sam and Dave had several songs break the top 50 on the Billboard Chart's Hot 100 including, "I Thank You" (number nine), "Hold On, I'm Comin'" (number 21), and "When Something Is Wrong With My Baby" (number 42).[78] In culmination of a twenty-year duo career they were inducted into the Rock & Roll Hall of Fame in 1992, the Grammy Hall of Fame in 1999 (for their song "Soul Man"), and the Vocal Group Hall of Fame in 2007.[79] Thus, in many ways, the Dole campaign was able to achieve two pop music associations for the price of one with their choice of "Soul Man." How much a factor like this played into the decision to use the song (rather than the fact that "soul" and "Dole" had a similar rhyme scheme) is unknown. However, these associations were recognizable to the public in general.

Change was afoot for Bill Clinton's campaign in the 1996 election as they changed their musical message from Fleetwood Mac's "Don't Stop (Thinking About Tomorrow)" to Chicago's "Beginnings." The song was played throughout the Democratic National Convention as a theme of Clinton's reelection bid,[80] and it tied into Clinton's 1996 campaign slogan, "Building the Bridge to the 21st Century."[81] Clinton's idea in using the song was to demonstrate that if reelected, his presidency would begin the twenty-first century and all of the promise of a new millennium. In addition, one can understand the song as representing the strides that the administration had made within its first term as only the "beginning" of the changes that Clinton's administration would make to the country if he were reelected to the White House. As the song's chorus says,

> Only the beginning of what I want to feel forever.
> Only the beginning. Only just the start.
> I've got to get you into my life.
> Got to get you next to me.
> Only the beginning. Only just the start.

Beginnings
Words and Music by Robert Lamm
Copyright © 1969 Primary Wave Lamm (ASCAP) and Spirit Two Music, Inc.
Copyright Renewed
All Rights Reserves
Reprinted by Permission of Hal Leonard Corporation

"Beginnings"
Written by Robert Lamm
Copyright © Spirit Catalogue Holdings, S.à,r,l, and Lamminations Music
All Rights for Spirit Catalog Holdings, S.à.r.l.
Controlled and Administered by Spirit Two Music, Inc. (ASCAP)
International Copyright Secured.   All Rights Reserved.   Used By Permission

The verses of the song were clearly intended by the artist to be about love, as they speak of the beginning of a romantic relationship. Thus, the song's later lyrics really had no bearing on the message the campaign wished to deliver through the song's hook. However, by projecting the message that it is "only the beginning, only just the start," the song delivered a powerful message to the electorate that, if elected, change would continue as had happened in the first four years of Clinton's presidency.

The song had one distinct advantage over that of the Dole campaign. The song was "appropriated with the blessing of the band's management, if not the band itself."[82] In fact, Peter Schivareli, who co-manages the band Chicago with Robert Kaufman, is active in Chicago politics and was in touch with the organizers of the Democratic National Convention about the band performing at the event.[83]

This use of association with popular figures in the music scene has become quite common in the political arena. Previous chapters have demonstrated that since the radio era, great artists like Al Jolson, Frank Sinatra, and Harry Belafonte have associated themselves with political campaigns as a way to lend their "star power" to a particular candidate or political party. The same can be said of candidates who are looking to bolster a particular view of themselves or their campaign with the electorate. For example, many candidates want to be seen as on the side of the working man and woman. In such a case, the use of a song by Bruce Springsteen would be desirable, as he is pro-union and projects an image of working-class solidarity and social consciousness with songs like "Johnny 99."[84] Ronald Reagan attempted to associate his 1984 campaign with Springsteen's song, "Born in the U.S.A.," only for the management for the more liberal Springsteen to rebuff his request.[85] Also as noted earlier in the chapter, George H.W. Bush associated himself with the song "This Land Is Your Land," whose writer, Woody Guthrie, was noted for his support for the working class and equality, two themes that Bush likely would have wanted to project. Court-ing working-class and middle-class voters thought the use of these icons was likely part of the electoral strategies of these two presidents to appeal to Reagan Democrats. In this sense, an artist's political beliefs (or perceived political be-liefs) may be just as important as which song a campaign chooses and the mes-sage the song's hook delivers to the voters.

These associations can make choosing a song difficult for a candidate at times. While a candidate may find a song whose hook contains a political mes-sage they may wish to send about their campaign, if the songwriter's political beliefs are not popular with the electorate at large, a candidate may wish to search for a different song to avoid association with a particular artist or group. An example of a group that falls into this category is Rage Against the Machine (described in the introduction), whose members espouse communist and anti-capitalist views, claiming that America practices cultural imperialism.[86] Con-versely, a candidate may find a musician he or she wishes to associate with the campaign, but may not be able to find a song that has a message appropriate to that campaign. This may occur when a popular artist is still relatively new with a small catalog of songs to their name. A hypothetical example might be an artist such as Carrie Underwood, who rose to fame through season four of *American Idol* in 2006 but did not have the extensive repertoire of songs for a candidate to select from by the 2008 presidential campaign. In such a case, a song may be used as warm-up music for a rally, but could not serve well in a prominent spot in the rally as a theme song.

There are other associations that a successful campaign will consider when choosing a popular song. Most notable among these is who is the target audience of the campaign. Returning again to the 1992 election, Bill Clinton chose to use "Don't Stop" by Fleetwood Mac. Given when the song was released (1977), this song was likely chosen to resonate with baby boomers, a group from which Clinton wanted to solicit votes. A similar type of association can be made with a genre of music. In general, country music and musicians tend to be more associ-ated with Republican/conservative political views. Consequently, a Republican candidate may want to choose a song from this genre, especially during a prima-ry campaign, when the voters showing up at the polls are statistically more con-servative. Conversely, a Republican candidate may wish to choose a more liber-al genre of music during the general election campaign, when most voters are moderate or centrist. Alternatively, a Republican may see an advantage to still choosing music from a more conservative genre, even during the general elec-tion, as a way to shore up the base of the party. These same theories apply for a

Democratic candidate, who faces a more liberal electorate in the primaries and a more moderate one in the general election. Thus, it becomes a balancing act for a candidate when deciding which song to select, which genre of music to choose from, what era the song should be from, and the political leanings of the musical artist. All of these factors can affect how the electorate might react to the campaign's song choice.

While many candidates have attempted to coordinate these factors when picking campaign songs, it appears that Bill Clinton in 1992 and 1996 was a master at it. His selection of "Don't Stop" and "Beginnings" incorporated many of these themes. Both songs were by bands that found success as the Baby Boomers were coming of age, both bands were fairly close to Clinton ideologically, both songs and the genre of music appealed to voters on the left and in the middle of the electorate, each song respectively tied into one of Clinton's campaign slogans, and in both cases there was some level of support for the candidate from the artists themselves (Fleetwood Mac went so far as to reunite as a band to perform for Clinton as his first inauguration.[87]) Since Clinton also incorporated music that he played on popular talk show programs, he no doubt understood, and fully took advantage of, the importance of using music in a presidential campaign. If Ronald Reagan was the "Great Communicator," Bill Clinton might be termed the "Great Performer."

One final aspect that should be considered by a campaign is whether an artist will not permit use of its song by a campaign. This may occur because the artist wants to be paid for use of the song or because the artist disagrees with the political beliefs of the candidate. The Dole campaign in 1996 suffered because of this when Dole made use of "Soul Man" without permission and had to eventually stop using the piece. Something similar occurred with Mike Huckabee in the 2008 presidential primary elections. Huckabee chose to use "More Than a Feeling" by Boston, but the group then gave the candidate bad press because they felt they had been "damaged" by a faulty political association; Boston argued that Huckabee's use of their song went against their target demographic for sales and promotion.[88] Although one could argue that "any press is good press," that was not the case for Huckabee in 2008. Indeed, if music is important to presidential campaigns (and over two centuries of history demonstrates it is), then having songwriters and pop artists decrying the use of their song in your campaign is the equivalent of one denouncing your entire campaign to the nation (or at least the group of voters who are among their fan base). At a time when pop culture figures, and especially those in the musical world, seem to have so much sway over the political opinions that are held by the public, it makes the choice of campaign songs all the more important and all the more tricky at the same time.[89]

The Music of the Millennium:
"Let the Day Begin" "Right Now" for
"We the People" as "I Won't Back Down" Because
"You Ain't Seen Nothin' Yet"

The 2000 election pitted the son of former President G.H.W Bush, George W. Bush, against the man who had served as Bill Clinton's vice president for the previous eight years, Al Gore. Bush was serving his second term as governor of Texas when he became the Republican nominee, winning a crowded primary field that also featured 2008 Republican nominee John McCain. Gore, the son of a U.S. senator, had previously served as a House member and senator; the vice president only had one serious opponent in the Democratic primaries, former Senator Bill Bradley. During the fall campaign, the race became a dead heat. As the polls opened on election day, it was unclear who would win. According to the Gallup tracking poll, Bush and Gore shared nine lead changes in over the last two months. Final polls by Zogby/MSNBC, Gallup, the *Washington Post*, and CBS showed either candidate in the lead by no more than two percentage points; in all four polls, this was within the margin of error.[90]

Musically, the election was significant because for the first time in the popular music era each candidate used multiple pieces as theme songs at various points during the campaign season. This is significant because in every other election during this era, no more than one candidate engaged in this practice, and often neither major party candidate did so. This use of multiple popular songs by each campaign in 2000 was part of a new trend that has extended through 2004 and 2008. It was likely caused by multiple factors, which range from the proliferation of popular music of various genres that may contain one-line messages to the relative ease of being able to play compact discs and music files at political rallies in the twenty-first century. Whatever the primary cause of this new trend, it has developed over the last decade, and is the logical extension of using popular music songs in the 1970s, 1980s, and 1990s.

What makes the 2000 election even more of an anomaly is that the main campaign theme song representing each camp, "We the People" for Bush and "Let the Day Begin" for Gore, was not an overly popular song. Furthermore, while one camp would have a relatively unknown group outside of the West Coast music scene, the other would rely on a former musical icon who had achieved great popularity but, by the 2000 election cycle, was known as a "one hit wonder" in the music industry. However, both songs delivered a positive and representative message for their respective candidates.

Republican nominee George W. Bush used three songs within his campaign: "We the People" by Billy Ray Cyrus, "Right Now" by Van Halen, and "I Won't Back Down" by Tom Petty. Each of these songs had a different message that could be delivered based on what events occurred on the campaign trail, what the poll numbers were showing, and what the target demographic of a certain rally might have been, among other factors.

"We the People" was played at the Republican National Convention as George W. Bush's theme song for the evening. The song was written with a political intent. While the lyrics do not talk about Bush directly, they do express views that one would expect to resonate well with the American public.

The song embodies many of the ideas held within the U.S. Constitution, a document that certainly appeals to many voters. The song speaks of how the people are the ones who run the country and expresses the idea that since the people are the ones who pay taxes to support the government, the government should listen to what we have to say. The song also refers to working-class citizens, speaking of farmers, factory workers, middle-class white collar works, etcetera, a group whom Bush was attempting to win away from the Democratic Party, similar to the courting of "Reagan Democrats" in the 1980s.[91] This is also consistent with Bush's portrayal of himself as a "compassionate conservative" during the 2000 campaign, a line which also served as one of his slogans. In this sense, the song was a great choice for the Bush campaign.

One aspect that makes this song unique, however, was that Billy Ray Cyrus offered it to both the Bush and Gore campaigns for their use.[92] The practice of amateur and professional songwriters submitting songs to the presidential candidates for consideration is not a new one. However, as far as the authors are able to discern, the practice of the same songwriter submitting the same song to both of the major party candidates for use had never been done before the 2000 election. What makes this case even more intriguing is that the references to working-class America are more in line with concerns of the Democratic Party, yet the Republican candidate chose to use the song "We the People." This much, at least, was stated by Cyrus's father, Ron Cyrus, a former Kentucky lawmaker and union leader who claimed, "[t]hat is a Democrat song."[93] Furthermore, the politics of Billy Ray Cyrus tend to fall more in line with the Democratic Party, according to his own admission.[94] In fact, after the Bush campaign decided to use the song, Billy Ray Cyrus began to have second thoughts about it. According to the former "Achy Breaky Heart" star and father of actress/singer Miley Cyrus, "It's struck me as different because it's a working people's song, y'know, and I've never really thought of the Republicans as the party of the working people. . . Am I wrong?"[95] In fact, Cyrus had performed at campaign rallies for Bill Clinton during the 1992 election, making a Republican candidate's use of his song even more ironic. Cyrus went on to say that the song was not about a party, but about "getting the American people to use their freedom to vote. . . . I wish both campaigns would use it."[96]

Another song utilized by the Bush campaign was "Right Now" by Van Halen. The text of the song was a rallying cry to the electorate that the solution to the problems of the past administration(s) was the presidency of George W. Bush. The lyrics of the song's hook talks about how tomorrow belongs to each person and that that tomorrow is important so each person should make their stand now.[97] The campaign likely chose the song because the hook can be interpreted to stress the importance of the presidential election, implying that this election could mean everything going forward. The song also told the American people that the election was an important one for their future saying that tomorrow and how the country is shaped belongs to them. This used a similar approach to Clinton's choice of songs in 1992 and 1996.

Unlike many of the "one line wonders" that presidential candidates have attempted to use as campaign theme songs, there is more to "Right Now" that makes it relevant to the election once one progresses past the hook. The song's lyrics emphasize how the problems of our past stand in the way of our future, how we can get swept up in a rat-race in life, how it is easy to fall behind, and how sometimes the pieces do not fall according to how we need or want them to fall. Further, it speaks of greed in the county and how the more people possess, the more they wish to possess. The song's lyrics also stress how people frequently try to take the path of least resistance, when doing so is not necessarily the right or best answer. Finally, the song refers back to the concept put forward in the hook, saying that we need to change now and make a stand to reverse our current course.[98]

When looked through the correct lens, much of this song can be seen as painting the Democratic administration of the previous eight years in a poor light, with Bush as the solution to the problems that have been created during that time. In fact, considering the scandals and the impeachment trial that plagued Clinton, a line from the song that referred to telling lies can be interpreted as a campaign reference to the Monica Lewinsky scandal and Clinton's subsequent impeachment for perjury and obstruction of justice. However, considering the one line hook or chorus mentality taken by the campaigns of the 1980s, 1990s and 2000s, it is more than likely that this was not the primary intention of the campaign, but rather a secondary benefit to those who listened to the song in its entirety with the campaign in mind. When a campaign chooses a song based on its hook, many times they are looking to the text in the body of the song to deliver a message on behalf of the campaign. Campaigns are relying on association with the song's hook, the message that it delivers about the candidate, and the campaign the song is representing. Thus, many times it is not the intent to stretch the text of the verses or even the remainder of the chorus to deliver a portion of the campaign's message. Indeed, oftentimes when a campaign plays the song at the end of a convention or rally, the crowd will begin to disperse and the press will cut away before the entire song can be played. However, if the later lyrics in a song contain useful messages, it can be a nice secondary benefit to a campaign as there are times when the remainder of the song will be played. After all, there are bound to be those who look at more than the song's hook when associating it with the campaign. One would imagine that in the fast-paced world of radio and television media coverage and ads with snappy catch-phrases that an in-depth look at a song by the electorate would not be the norm, however.

The final song that the Bush campaign used in the 2000 campaign was Tom Petty's "I Won't Back Down." While it is the final song being discussed, the song was used as staple of his campaign rallies during the primary elections.[99] In fact, "I Won't Back Down" became somewhat of a fixture at Bush events early in the campaign.[100] The song is a bit different, in that the title line, and the one that most people recognize as the hook, is also the opening lyric of the first verse. In the hook of the song, Bush attempted to deliver a twofold message to the electorate. First, in the context of the campaign itself, Bush would not back down in his fight to win the Republican nomination. Second, if elected, this would be a president who would stand up to the United States Congress and to international problems and would not back away from a fight to do what was right. The text of the song states:

Verse 1:
Well I won't back down, no I won't back down
You could stand me up at the gates of Hell
But I, won't back down

No I, stand my ground, won't be, turned around
And I keep this world from draggin' me down
Gonna stand my ground, and I, won't back down

Chorus:
(I won't back-)
Hey baby! there ain't no easy way out
(I won't back-)
Hey yea! Stand my ground
And I won't, back down

Verse 2:
Well I know what's right, I got just one life
In a world that keeps on pushin' me around
But I'll, stand my ground, and I, won't back down
(Chorus)

I Won't Back Down
Words and Music by Tom Petty and Jeff Lynne
Copyright © 1989 Gone Gator Music and EMI April Music Inc.
All Rights Reserved   Used by Permission
Reprinted by Permission of Hal Leonard Corporation

Again, we see a song whose complete text embodies a principle the presidential candidate was attempting to send to the electorate ahead of the presidential election. Yet, as was the case with Billy Ray Cyrus, although the campaign selected a song that had a positive message to send about their candidate, the song's writer and performer, Tom Petty, held political views that were in contradiction to the Bush campaign. In an interview with Warren Zanes, Petty says of the use of his music in political campaigns that, "It's very uncomfortable to hear them used when I don't agree with what's being said. But I recognize that those songs have entered into a bigger life, a life all their own. They belong to the audience. How they're used isn't always something I can control."[101] That Petty has fairly liberal views made the use of the song a potential risk for Bush, as it may have alienated the base of the Republican Party during the primaries. In the end, the Bush campaign had to cease the use of "I Won't Back Down" under the threat of lawsuit from Tom Petty.[102] According to a letter from Petty's publishing company to the Bush campaign in February of 2000, "Any use made by you or your campaign creates, either intentionally or unintentionally, the impression that you and your campaign have been endorsed by Tom Petty, which is not true."[103] In fact, by the end of the election, George Bush's campaign had come into conflict with Sting, John Mellencamp, John Fogerty, Los Lobos, and Tejano singer Emilio for using their music at campaign rallies in various capacities (such as warm-up music for the crowd) without the artists' permission.[104] With respect to "I Won't Back Down," the Bush campaign reluctantly stopped using the song, although a Bush spokesman claimed that playing a song did not imply to the public that the artist endorsed the candidate.[105] Nevertheless, when the Bush campaign stopped using the song, Bush staffer Dan Bartlett quipped, "we backed down."[106]

Like Petty, many of the artists whose music is played by political campaigns are often concerned that the playing of their music, even if only on compact disc at a campaign rally, is an endorsement of that political candidate or their political party.[107] This demonstrates two points that are relevant. First, it shows that both the musicians and the political campaigns are aware of the influence of pop culture on the voting public, especially that of the youth vote.[108] As was seen with the Bush campaign's response to Tom Petty in this case, many times a campaign will attempt to downplay or deny the fact that the playing of a song is akin to an endorsement. And perhaps they are correct in the fact that it is not a direct endorsement,[109] but it can be seen as a perceived endorsement, especially if the artist does not contest the playing of their music for the particular candidate or party. And campaigns that try to use songs without first seeking permission are certainly aware that some will perceive such action as the artist's endorsement, and campaigns will rarely, if ever, announce if an artist has not been contacted on the issue of endorsement.

Second, musicians are concerned about their political reputations among their fans. Endorsing a candidate who holds political positions that are contrary to the beliefs of their fan base could potentially be devastating to the musician's career. Similarly, if an artist attacks a candidate who holds beliefs in line with their fan base, it could result in harm to the musician's career. For an example of this, one needs look no further than the Dixie Chicks and their political commentary on President George W. Bush. Shortly before the U.S.–led invasion of Iraq in 2003, lead singer Natalie Maines asserted to the audience at one of the band's shows that the Dixie Chicks were "ashamed that the President of the United States is from [their home state of] Texas."[110] This simple remark about President Bush led to many country stations refusing to play their songs and others to boycott their music.[111] According to one source, the long-term outcome was that the trio's "country audience slowly diminished."[112] Since country music fans tend to me more conservative, it should come as no surprise that the group experienced difficulties with their fan base after being critical of a Republican president. Conversely, Pearl Jam, a rock band with a more liberal listening audience, made similar statements about President Bush and the war in Iraq with no negative effect on the band's success.[113] This notwithstanding, the Dixie Chicks made some gains by increasing listenership among adult contemporary and pop music listeners,[114] which are on average more liberal groups than country fans. The Dixie Chicks are an example of a group that invited political controversy and suffered because of it, something that other artists have shied away from. Perhaps this understanding explains why Bruce Springsteen, who has maintained a more liberal audience than the Dixie Chicks, distanced himself from Ronald Reagan in 1984, and why Tom Petty similarly wanted to separate himself from George W. Bush in 2000.

After successfully getting the Bush campaign to stop using his song, Tom Petty would later perform "I Won't Back Down" at Al Gore's home just after Gore conceded the election to Bush following the Supreme Court ruling in December of 2000.[115] In a way, this is ironic considering the message of the song, but it was also perhaps a statement by Petty that he would only lend his music and talents to the candidate with whom his political beliefs more closely coincided. (It is important to note that Petty only played for Gore at his concession speech. He did not play for any fundraising events on behalf of Gore, nor did he accompany Gore on the campaign trail at any point before the election.)

Al Gore's campaign used two songs as mainstays in 2000. The first song was "Let the Day Begin" by The Call, a popular "cult" group on the West Coast in the 1980s and 1990s; however, the group never made a successful transition to become a popular mainstream group. Because The Call was not as well-known as perhaps even Billy Ray Cyrus, it was important that the Gore campaign not just utilize the hook but also find a song with multiple verses that represented the campaign's message. This was necessary because most of the public was previously unfamiliar with the song and, as such, did not know the song's hook. Consequently, an audience might be more inclined to listen to all the text more closely upon the first few hearings to understand the song's message. The text of "Let the Day Begin" says

> Here's to the babies in a brand new world
> Here's to the beauty of the stars
> Here's to the travelers on the open road
> Here's to the dreamers in the bars
>
> Here's to the teachers in the crowded rooms
> Here's to the workers in the fields
> Here's to the preachers of the sacred words
> Here's to the drivers at the wheel
>
> Here's to you my little loves with blessings from above

Now let the day begin
Here's to you my little loves with blessings from above
Now let the day begin, let the day begin

Here's to the winners of the human race
Here's to the losers in the game
Here's to the soldiers of the bitter war
Here's to the wall that bears their names

Here's to you my little loves with blessings from above
Now let the day begin
Here's to you my little loves with blessings from above
Let the day begin, let the day begin, let the day start

Here's to the doctors and their healing work
Here's to the loved ones in their care
Here's to the strangers on the streets tonight
Here's to the lonely everywhere

Here's to the wisdom from the mouths of babes
Here's to the lions in the cage
Here's to the struggles of the silent war
Here's to the closing of the age.

Here's to you my little loves with blessings from above
Now let the day begin
Here's to you my little loves with blessings from above
Let the day begin

Here's to you my little loves with blessings from above
Let the day begin
Here's to you my little loves with blessings from above
Now let the day begin, let the day begin, let the day start

Let The Day Begin
Words and Music by Michael Been
Copyright © 1989 by Neeb Music (ASCAP)
All Rights Administered by BMG Chrysalis
International Copyright Secured   All Rights Reserved
Reprinted by permission of Hal Leonard Corporation

The song made reference to the working people of America, stating multiple job titles and what these workers do for the country. It then says, "Now let the day begin" implying that with Gore as president, it will be the start of a new day for all working people in the country. This message is similar to Ronald Reagan's slogan in 1984, "It's morning again in America." It also attempted to show that Gore valued people from all walks of life, from teachers to soldiers to doctors to winners and losers alike.

Since the group performing this song was relatively obscure, the song was not the best choice by the Gore campaign. However, in terms of message, the song hit a positive note and appealed to the electorate, especially the Democratic base and independent voters. Music programming consultant Jack Pollack commented on the Gore campaign's song choice that, "The Call's 'Let the Day Begin' is an unexpected choice but a good one. . . . It is superior not only musically but in getting a positive, optimistic message across to potential Gore voters."[116]

The second song chosen by the Gore campaign was "You Ain't Seen Nothin' Yet" by the Bachman-Turner Overdrive. The BTO, as they are also known, had a much larger fan base than The Call, and this piece of music had a much higher listenership before being chosen by Gore than was the case with "Let the Day Begin." In fact, "You Ain't Seen Nothin' Yet" saw time at the number one position on the Billboard Hot Singles Chart in 1974.[117] According to the song's lyrics,

> And said, You ain't seen nothin' yet
> B-B-B-Baby, you just ain't seen n-n-n-nothin' yet
> Here's something that you're never gonna forget
> B-B-B-Baby, you just ain't seen n-n-n-nothin' yet
> And you're thinkin' you ain't been around, that's right

YOU AIN'T SEEN NOTHIN YET
© 1974 Sony/ATV Music Publishing LLC. All rights administered by Sony/ATV Music Publishing LLC, 8 Music Square West, Nashville, TN 37203
All Rights Reserved   Used by Permission

This song is another example of the "one line wonders" that were common in the 1988-1996 campaigns. Similar to George W. Bush's selection of "I Won't Back Down," the song's hook delivered a message to the electorate that the Gore campaign was not done with the fight and, in fact, there was far more to see from the campaign than they had already given the public. Considering how close this race was through election day, this was a message that was useful to motivate both the general public and the members of the Gore campaign.

Election night 2000 was essentially a stalemate. Just before 8:00 p.m. Eastern Standard Time on November 7, 2000, the major television networks projected that Gore had won Florida, which, based on projections in other states, would have been enough to hand Gore a victory in the Electoral College. A few hours later, the networks changed their decision, claiming that Florida was too close to call. At approximately 2:15 a.m. on the morning of November 8, the networks called Florida for Bush, giving him enough Electoral College votes to win the presidency, even though Gore led the nationwide popular vote. Gore privately conceded the election to Bush, but once he learned that the vote totals in Florida had tightened up, he retracted his concession. At approximately 4:15 a.m., the networks again changed their projection on Florida, claiming it was too close to call again. Numerous machine and hand recounts ensued statewide and across various Florida counties, driven by lawsuits filed by the candidates in state and federal courts. The legal challenges ultimately led to two U.S. Supreme Court cases, both titled *Bush v. Gore*, the latter of which resulted in the Court ordering, by a vote of 5-4, an end to the recounts on the evening of December 12, 2000. This left Bush a small lead in Florida of 537 votes (out of approximately 6 million total voters cast in the state), giving him enough to win the state and a majority in the Electoral College. On December 13, a full 36 days after election day, Al Gore finally conceded the presidency to George W. Bush.[118]

The 2004 Campaign:
A "Beautiful Day" "Only in America"

The final campaign discussed in this chapter is the 2004 election between incumbent George W. Bush and his Democratic challenger, Massachusetts Senator John Kerry. This election again saw the use of multiple campaign songs by each of the candidates. The incumbent would summon stars of the country music world with Brooks and Dunn's "Only in America" and Pat Green's "Wave on Wave," while Kerry would use "No Surrender" by Bruce Springsteen, "Fortunate Son" by John Fogerty and "Beautiful Day" by U2. Unlike the previous election, where a number of the artists were lesser known or on the decline in their careers, this election would use musicians who were still well known in the world of music and pop culture. For the sake of discussion in the 2004 campaign, we will focus on "Only in America" for the Republicans and U2's "Beautiful Day" for the Democrats as these were, by all accounts, the most commonly played songs for each candidate.[119]

John Kerry's choice of "Beautiful Day" was a good one because the song as a whole delivered a positive and upbeat message to an electorate that was beaten and bruised by the fact that the country was fighting wars on two fronts at the time. The chorus of the song reminds people that while things may not be happy and cheery on the surface, in truth the day will be a beautiful one for them and could be potentially even better with the election of Kerry to the presidency. This use of a pop song to project a message that the future will prove brighter harkened back to Franklin Roosevelt's theme song, "Happy Days Are Here Again."

The song begins by describing how great the day will be, and it offers the advice that we should take advantage of said day.[120] This uses an analogy that the entire day is before us, and we should seize it. This is similar to Reagan's 1984 slogan, "It's morning again in America" and Gore's 2000 song choice, "Let the Day Begin." The song's bridge also serves to remind us of some of those beautiful things we should remember and be hopeful of having again in the future, including: an improved environment (one of the themes of the Kerry campaign) with reference to a greener world. The lyrics go on depict a grand view of different places across the surface of the earth. The section ends with a reference to the joyous end of the biblical flood—the rainbow and its many colors.[121] Many of the remaining lyrics of the song are also relevant to the message the Kerry campaign may have been wishing to send to the electorate. These lyrics many times set up the downtrodden situations from which we should still recognize that this beautiful day still exists.

According to U2's Bono, "Beautiful Day" is about, "a man who has lost everything, but finds joy in what he still has."[122] For the Kerry campaign, the message is powerful, uplifting, and promotes a positive view of Kerry's campaign and potentially the effect his White House could have if elected. The Democratic Party had the White House four years earlier, and it looked like they were to retain it in 2000, only to lose it all. The last two lines of the song can also be interpreted as a clever attack on President Bush, as they refer to a driver stuck in traffic that is failing to move. This indicates to the voter that a lack of progress had been achieved in Bush's first term. Thus, Kerry's choice of this song can be used in both a positive and negative sense.

The song "Beautiful Day" was a popular song. It was the lead single of U2's *All That You Can't Leave Behind* album, and the band won multiple Grammy Awards for it. One additional factor that assisted the Kerry campaign was that U2's lead singer, Bono, has long been known for humanitarian efforts around the world, something that has been acknowledged by many world leaders. To plead his humanitarian causes, Bono has met with Tony Blair, Bill Clinton, Vladimir Putin, Gerhard Schroder, Jacques Chirac, and Pope John Paul II, among others.[123] This gave credence to the Kerry campaign through the way of an implied endorsement.[124] Considering Bono's and U2's popularity, this is another factor making the choice to use "Beautiful Day" an effective one for the Kerry campaign. Furthermore, Kerry's ability to make use of a song sung by Bono was all the more useful in his campaign as the incumbent would not have the implied endorsement and the popularity and political associations that would come with the use of Bono's song that Bush had secured just two years prior. In 2002, President Bush went to great lengths to have Bono at his announcement that the United States was increasing foreign aid over a three year period; according to a *Washington Post* story, the White House "clearly craved" the support of Bono, who "looked on approvingly" when Bush made the announcement.[125] Perhaps the president sought to have Bono at that announcement because of the singer's support for aid to Africa, because he had previously met with numerous other world leaders, or because he is a devout Christian like the president.[126] Whatever the reasons why President Bush wanted Bono by his side in 2002, by 2004 Bono's music was being used for his challenger, John Kerry.

Opposite of Kerry, President Bush's campaign chose to use "Only in America" by Brooks and Dunn. At the time of the 2004 presidential campaign, Brooks and Dunn were considered to be the most successful duo in country music history. Only Simon and Garfunkel were more successful than Brooks and Dunn in record sales for a duo over their career.[127] In addition, Brooks and Dunn had won thirty-three music awards by 2004, including entertainer of the year in 1996, duo of the year on multiple occasions, and the American Music Awards

Favorite Country Group in 1997.[128] Considering that country music artists are usually connected with conservative views (artists like the Dixie Chicks and Billy Ray Cyrus being the biggest contemporary exceptions), it only makes sense that the Bush campaign chose a song from Brooks and Dunn's repertoire to represent their campaign as a way to shore up the conservative base. Indeed, the Bush campaign strategy in 2004 largely revolved around energizing the conservative base as opposed to courting more independent voters[129] (the use of country musician Pat Green's song "Wave on Wave" was also consistent with this strategy). In this vein, Brooks and Dunn performed as part of the entertainment at the 2004 Republican National Convention in New York.[130]

The song "Only in America" is another example of a one line wonder in presidential campaigns. The song's chorus, which contains the title phrase, alleges that only in this country are many of people's dreams achievable because of our freedoms. The entire chorus says:

> Only in America
> Dreaming in red, white and blue
> Only in America
> Where we dream as big as we want to
> We all get a chance
> Everybody gets to dance
> Only in America

The chorus embodies the American dream and indicates that "we all get a chance" to do what we want because of our freedoms. The body of the song exhibits this message through examples such as:

> One kid dreams of fame and fortune
> One kid helps pay the rent
> One could end up going to prison
> One just might be president

And

> A welder's son and a banker's daughter
> All they want is everything
> She came out here to be an actress
> He was the singer in a band
> They just might go back to Oklahoma
> And talk about the stars they could have been

ONLY IN AMERICA
By Randall Jay Rogers, Don Cook, Kix Brooks
© 2001 Sony/ATV Music Publishing LLC and Peermusic III, Ltd.
All rights on behalf of Sony/ATV Music Publishing LLC administered by
Sony/ATV Music Publishing LLC, 8 Music Square West, Nashville, TN 37203
International Copyright Secured   All Rights Reserved   Used by Permission

The song does not speak about the candidate in any specific way, but merely acknowledges how great the country is. Perhaps the Bush campaign was attempting to say that they have been a part of the American dream and realizing it for everyone. Perhaps they were trying to tell of the president's own success story in becoming president. Perhaps they were simply trying to appeal to patriotism in the electorate. Regardless, the campaign associated itself with a positive and popular message and a vision that many in the voting public share about this country, especially those who have immigrated to this country looking for a better life. The idea here is not to openly say "vote for me," but rather to pump up the American psyche and associate the Bush presidency with that message of hope and dreams that the song promotes successes and failures all. This song, and many of this era, are very different from "I Like Ike" or "Kennedy," which overtly and repeatedly state a candidate's name and ask the listener to vote for the candidate.

The Written and Parodied Campaign Songs Linger in the Background

The use of popular music in presidential election from 1984-2004 didn't mean the end of the parodied campaign song or the original campaign song. Songs were still being written and published on behalf of candidates. In fact, Ronald Reagan had 32 songs written and/or parodied on behalf of his candidacy between the 1980 and 1984 elections, George H.W. Bush had two songs as part of his presidential campaigns in 1988 and 1992, and Bill Clinton had 12 for his 1992 and 1996 campaigns.[131] Ross Perot even managed to have two original compositions that have association with his presidential run, "Rhythm of Reform: Song Lyrics for Reform Party Volunteers," and "Ross Perot's Swan Song."[132]

In campaigns of the past, it was not uncommon for amateur and professional musicians alike to submit songs to either the Republican or Democratic campaign offices in hopes that their song might be chosen to represent the campaign of their desired candidate, as was the case in the 1936 presidential election.[133] However, with the changes in mass media in the twentieth and twenty-first centuries and the emphasis on popular figures and popular culture within a campaign, it became less likely that a candidate would choose a song via these methods in the modern era. In fact, since the 1980s, freshly written and parodied songs were not used by the campaigns and never made it to any degree of popularity within the American public. Thus, these songs in this era were ineffective. Without a way for these musicians to get their song out to the public through aural or visual means, it is not surprising that they were unknown and had little or no impact in the elections. This trend changed again, however, with the advances in Internet-based technologies by the 2008 primaries and general election.

However, Stuart Schimler would argue that election songs that focus around issues of the campaign or personalized around the value of the candidates were no longer needed to get the message of the candidates across.[134] William Miles notes, "It is true that songs or, at the least, music still plays a role in the quadrennial electoral process, but that role is minimal compared to that which it played during the nineteenth century. Then, the song ranked with the speech, the political pamphlet, the campaign newspaper, and other assorted paraphernalia as an equal."[135] With the widespread use of television and radio, candidates were and are able to articulate their political positions in a more direct way than through the use of music. However, that does not mean the use of a theme song associated with a candidate to be used at campaign rallies and national conventions is a useless prospect. Music has the power to excite the crowd that a simple speech may not have the ability to deliver. By associating a candidate with a popular song, every time that song is heard on the radio a voter is reminded of that candidate and thus, for a moment, thinks about that candidate. It does not mean that music is necessarily less important as Schimler and Miles would argue, but that the focus of the music's use has shifted.

The era of popular music in elections has made it easier, and at the same time more difficult, for a campaign to choose the perfect song or songs to represent the candidate running. Choosing the right song can motivate those who come to your campaign rallies and watch the national conventions on television. They can give a false sense of endorsement from pop culture icons whether that endorsement is real or not. It was a trend that had been coming in the world of music and politics for a long time and one that has been proven successful from the mid-1980s to the present. What changed were the technologies involved and the interaction the electorate would come to have with the campaign process on a musical level. In chapter seven the Internet and various technologies are discussed as part of an in-depth look at the 2008 caucuses, primaries, and general election.

Notes

1.   Janna Mäkelä, *John Lennon Imagined: Cultural History of a Rock Star* (New York: Peter Lang Publishing, 2004), 207.
2.   Mäkelä, *John Lennon Imagined*, 208.
3.   Reebee Garofalo, *Rockin' Out: Popular Music in the USA, Second Edition* (Upper Saddle River, NJ: Prentice-Hall, 2002), 311-323.
4.   Garofalo, *Rockin' Out*, 311-323; Katherine Charlton, *Rock Music Styles: A History* (New York: McGraw-Hill, 2008), 264.
5.   Garofalo, *Rockin' Out*, 298-306.
6.   Charlton, *Rock Music Styles*, 264.
7.   Charlton, *Rock Music Styles*, 261.

8.   Richard Frucht, *Eastern Europe: An Introduction to the People, Lands, and Culture* (Santa Barbara, CA: ABC-CLIO, 2005), 73.

9.   Kenneth E. Morris, *Jimmy Carter: American Moralist* (Athens: University of Georgia Press, 1996), 280-81.

10.   Dinesh D'Souza, *Ronald Reagan: How an Ordinary Man Became an Extraordinary Leader* (New York: Touchstone, 1997), 104-107; Walter LaFeber, Richard Polenberg, Nancy Woloch, *The American Century: A History of the United States Since 1941* (New York: M.E. Sharpe, 2008), 232.

11.   Garofalo, *Rockin' Out*, 292.

12.   Garofalo, *Rockin' Out*, 17.

13.   Garofalo, *Rockin' Out*, 17-18.

14.   Garofalo, *Rockin' Out*, 16.

15.   Ron Simon, "The Ed Sullivan Show," The Museum of Broadcast Communications, accessed August 22, 2010, http://www.museum.tv/eotvsection.php?entrycode=ed sullivans.

16.   R. Serge Denisoff, *Inside MTV* (New Brunswick, NJ: Transaction Publishers, 1988), 54.

17.   Emily Ross and Angus Holland, *100 Great Businesses and the Mind Behind Them* (Naperville, IL: Sourcebooks, Inc., 2006), 165.

18.   Charlton, *Rock Music Styles*, 280; Denisoff, *Inside MTV*, 217.

19.   Mike Celizic, "'Triller' Video Remains a Classic 25 Years Later: Jackson Changed the Music Industry the Way Elvis, Beatles Did Before Him," *The Today Show*, accessed July 31, 2010, http://today.msnbc.msn.com/id/24282347.

20.   Lisa D. Campbell, *Michael Jackson: The King of Pop* (Boston: Branden Publishing Company, Inc., 1993), 64.

21.   George Comstock and Erica Scharrer, *The Psychology of Media and Politics* (Burlington, MA: Elsevier Academic Press, 2005), 105.

22.   Woody Guthrie, "This Land Is Your Land," in *The American Reader: Words that Moved a Nation*, ed. Diane Ravitch (New York, HarperCollins, 2000), 478-479.

23.   Ed Cray, *Ramblin' Man: The Life and Times of Woody Guthrie* (New York: W.W. Norton & Company, inc., 2004), 285.

24.   Karen Mueller Coombs, *Woodie Guthrie: America's Folksinger* (Minneapolis, MN: Carolrhoda Books, Inc., 2002), 54.

25.   Coombs, *Woodie Guthrie*, 54.

26.   "Historical Debt Outstanding 1950-1999," US Department of Treasury, Bureau of the Public Debt, accessed July 28, 2010, http://www.treasurydirect.gov/govt/reports/pd/histdebt/histdebt_histo4.htm.

27.   "The Living Room Candidate: Presidential Campaign Commercials 1952-2008," Museum of the Moving Image, accessed July 20, 2010, http://www.livingroom candidate.org.

28.   "The Living Room Candidate," 1988.

29.   Neil Diamond, vocal performance of "America," by Neil Diamond, recorded 1980, on *The Jazz Singer Soundtrack*, Capitol Records, compact disc.

30.   Frank W. Baker, *Political Campaigns and Political Advertising: A Media Literacy Guide* (Santa Barbara: ABC-CLIO, LLC, 2009), 137.

31.   Diamond, "America."

32.   Samuel Francis Smith, "America," in *Poems of Home and Country: Also Sacred and Miscellaneous Verse*, ed. Henry B. Carrington (New York: Silver, Burdett and Co., 1895), 77-78.

33.   David Leip, "Atlas of U.S. Presidential Elections," accessed July 20, 2010, http://uselectionatlas.org.

34.   Leip, Atlas of U.S. Presidential Elections."

35.   Keith Reeves, *Voting Hopes or Fears?: White Voters, Black Candidates & Racial Politics in America* (New York: Oxford University Press, 1997), 15-16.

36.   Benjamin R. Barber, *The Truth of Power: Intellectual Affairs in the Clinton White House* (New York: Norton, 2001), 45.

37.   Brackett, *Fleetwood Mac*, 167.

38.   David Marsh, *The Heart of Rock & Soul: The 1001 Greatest Singles Ever Made* (New York: Da Capo, 1999), 383.

39.   Richard Reeves, *President Reagan: The Triumph of Imagination* (New York: Simon & Schuster, 2005), 360.

40.   Jon F. Hale, "The Making of the New Democrats," *Political Science Quarterly* 110 (1995): 207-232; John F. Harris, *The Survivor: Bill Clinton in the White House* (New York: Random House, 2006).

41.   David Maraniss, *First in His Class: The Biography of Bill Clinton* (New York: Touchstone, 1995), 45.

42.   C. Edward Spann and Michael E. Williams, Sr., *Presidential Praise: Our Presidents and Their Hymns* (Macon, GA: Mercer University Press, 2008), 295.

43.   David A. Copeland, *The Media's Role in Defining the Nation: The Active Voice* (New York: Peter Lang Publishing, 2010), 260.

44.   Maraniss, *First in His Class*, 447.

45.   Jack Banks, *Monopoly Television: MTV's Quest to Control the Music* (Boulder, CO: Westview Press, 1996), 129; Richard Davis and Diana Owen, *New Media and American Politics* (New York: Oxford University Press, 1998), 14.

46.   Copeland, *The Media's Role*, 260.

47.   David A. Schultz, "From Saxophones to Schwarzenegger: Entertainment Politics on Late-Night Television," in *Lights, Camera, Campaign!: Media, Politics, and Political Advertising*, ed. David A. Schultz (New York: Peter Lang Publishing, 2004), 215.

48.   Ronald B. Rapoport and Walter J. Stone, *Three's a Crowd: The Dynamic of Third Parties, Ross Perot, and Republican Resurgence* (Ann Arbor: University of Michigan Press, 2005), 53-56.

49.   Andrew E. Martin and Brian E. Spang, "A Case Study of a Third Presidential Campaign Organization," in *Ross for Boss: The Perot Phenomenon and Beyond*, ed. Ted G. Jelen (Albany: State University of New York Press, 2001), 39.

50.   Jerrold M. Post, "The Political Psychology of the Ross Perot Phenomenon," in *The Clinton Presidency: Campaigning, Governing, and the Psychology of Leadership*, ed. Stanley A. Renshon (Boulder, CO: Westview Press, 1995), 55.

51.   Jeremy D. Mayer and Clyde Wilcox, "Understanding Perot's Plummet," in *Ross for Boss: The Perot Phenomenon and Beyond*, ed. Ted G. Jelen (Albany: State University of New York Press, 2001), 145.

52.   S. Robert Lichter and Richard Noyes, *Good Intentions Make Bad News: Why Americans Hate Campaign Journalism* (Lanham, MD: Rowman & Littlefield, 1996), 202.

53.   Martin and Spang, "A Case Study of a Third Presidential Campaign," 39.

54.   Post, "The Political Psychology of Ross Perot," 55.

55.   John Hohenberg, *The Bill Clinton Story: Winning the Presidency* (Syracuse: Syracuse University Press, 1994), 224.

56.   John Hohenberg, *Reelecting Bill Clinton: Why America Chose a "New" Democrat* (Syracuse: Syracuse University Press, 1997), 38.

57.   Lichter and Noyes, *Good Intentions Make Bad News*, 203.

58.   Mark Saltveit, "H. Ross Perot's Skeleton Closet," *Real People for Real Change* (1999), accessed February 8, 2009, http://www.realchange.org/perot.htm.

59.   John M. Broder, "Perot Winds Up Campaign with New Theme: 'Crazy,'" *The Los Angeles Times*, accessed August 7, 2010, http://articles.latimes.com/1992-1103/news/mn-1248_1_ross-perot.

60.   John Taylor, "Politics: Winners and Sinners of 1992," *New York Magazine*, December 21-28, 1992, 27.

61.   Paul E. Corcoran, "Presidential Endings: Conceding Defeat," in *Presidential Campaign Discourse: Strategic Communication Problems*, ed. Kathleen E. Kendall (Albany: State University of New York: 1995), 283.

62.   John R. MacArthur, *The Selling of "Free Trade": NAFTA, Washington, and the Subversion of American Democracy* (Berkeley: University of California Press, 2000), 232.

63.   Jacob Weisberg, "The Third Man," *New York Magazine*, April 8, 1996, 19.

64.   Jessica Letkemann, "Stump Thumping," *Spin*, September 1998, 80.

65.   Curtis W. Ellison, *Country Music Culture: From Hard Times to Heaven* (Jackson: University Press of Mississippi, 1995), 232.

66.   Ellison, *Country Music Culture*, 232.

67.   Ellison, *Country Music Culture*, 232.

68.   Laura Checkoway, "The Arsenio Hall Show," *Vibe*, May 2006, 148.

69.   Michael Paoletta, "MTV's 'Juice': Shaping Lifestyles and Attitudes Around the World," *Billboard*, September 2, 2006, 46.

70.   Melinda Newman, "Hayes Vetos Dole's 'Soul Man,'" *Billboard*, September 21, 1996, 12.

71.   Melinda Newman, "Presidential Musical Race Heats Up: Genesis Boxed Set Postponed One Year," *Billboard*, September 28, 1996, 12.

72.   Charles R. Grosvenor Jr., "Song Parodies-Authors-William Tong," *Am I Right: Making Fun of Music, One Song at a Time*, accessed June 6, 2011, http://www.amiright.com/parody/authors/williamtong.shtml.

73.   William Tong, "Song Parodies—Dole Man," *Am I Right: Making Fun of Music, One Song at a Time*, accessed June 6, 2011, http://www.amiright.com/parody/60s/samdave0.shtml.

74.   William Tong, e-mail message to author, June 2, 2011.

75.   Robert North Roberts and Scott John Hammond, *Encyclopedia of Presidential Campaigns, Slogans, Issues, and Platforms* (Westport, CT: Greenwood Press, 2004), 115.

76.   *Blues Brothers*, directed by John Landis (1980; Hollywood: Universal Pictures, 1981), DVD.

77.   "Sam and Dave," Rock & Roll Hall of Fame, accessed August 7, 2010, http://rockhall.com/inductees/sam-and-dave.

78.   "Hot 100," Billboard, March 23, 1968, 66; "Hot 100," Billboard, June 18, 1966, 18; "Hot 100," Billboard, April 1, 1967, 22.

79.   Rock and Roll Hall of Fame.

80.   Rock and Roll Hall of Fame.

81.   Roberts and Hammond, *Encyclopedia of Presidential Campaigns*, 148.

82.   Melinda Newman, "Presidential Musical Race Heats Up," 12.

83.   Melinda Newman, "Presidential Musical Race Heats Up," 12.

84.   Garofalo, *Rockin' Out*, 227.

85.   Jim Cullen, *Born in the U.S.A.: Bruce Springsteen and the American Tradition* (Middletown, CT: Wesleyan University Press, 1997), 7.

86.   Jason Ankeny, "Rage Against the Machine Bio," Vh1.com, accessed July 31, 2010, http://www.vh1.com/artists/az/rage_against_the_machine/bio.jhtml.

87.   Bob Brunning, *The Fleetwood Mac Story: Rumours and Lies* (New York: Omnibus Press, 2004), 207.

88.   Andy Green, "'More Than a Feeling' Writer Says Mike Huckabee Has Caused Him 'Damage,'" Rollingstone.com, accessed February 20, 2008, http://www.rollingstone.com/music/news/13511/70354.

89.   Nadine S. Koch, "Entertainment and Politics," review of *Entertainment and Politics: The Influence of Pop Culture on Young Adult Political Socialization,* by David J. Jackson, *Journal of Politics,* Vol. 66, No. 3 (Aug., 2004): 975-977; Diana Owen, "Entertainment and Politics," review of *Entertainment and Politics: The Influence of Pop Culture on Young Adult Political Socialization,* by David J. Jackson, *Political Communication* July 2008, Vol. 25 Issue 3: 333-334.

90.   James W. Ceaser and Andrew Busch, *The Perfect Tie: The True Story of the 2000 Presidential Election* (Lanham, MD: Rowman & Littlefield, 2001), 8.

91.   Billy Ray Cyrus, vocal performance of "We the People," by Richard Belmont Powell, Jimmie Lee Sloas and Anna Wilson, released October 17, 2000, on *Southern Rain,* Sony B00004ZDOL, compact disc.

92.   Geoff Boucher, "Songs in the Key of Presidency," *L.A. Times,* October 11, 2000, accessed July 25, 2010, http://cgi.cnn.com/2000/ALLPOLITICS/stories/10/11/latimes.campaign.songs/index.html.

93.   Boucher, "Songs in the Key of Presidency.

94.   Boucher, "Songs in the Key of Presidency.

95.   Boucher, "Songs in the Key of Presidency.

96.   Boucher, "Songs in the Key of Presidency.

97.   Sammy Hagar, et al., "Right Now" in *Van Halen–Guitar Anthology: Authentic Guitar Tab* by Van Halen (Van Nuys, CA: Alfred Publishing Company, Inc., 1995).

98.   Hagar, "Right Now."

99.   Jake Tapper, "Don't Do Me Like That," Salon.com, accessed August 1, 2010, http://www.salon.com/news/politics/feature/2000/09/16/bush/index.html.

100.   Jack Doyle, "I Won't Back Down, 1989-2008," PopHistoryDig.com, March 7, 2009, accessed August 25, 2010, http://www.pophistorydig.com/?p=932.

101.   Warren Zanes, "Interview with Tom Petty, October 23, 2008," accessed August 10, 2010, http://media.thewho.com/non_secure/pdf/TomPetty_Zanes_Interview_Oct31.pdf.

102.   Tapper, "Don't Do Me Like That."

103.   Jake Tapper, "Don't Do Me Like That"; "Petty to Bush: Don't Play My Song No More," Vh1, accessed August 1, 2010, http://www.vh1.com/artists/news/1436934/20000920/petty_tom.jhtml;

104.   Vh1, "Petty to Bush."

105.   Vh1, "Petty to Bush."

106.   Doyle, "I Won't Back Down."

107.   Doyle, "I Won't Back Down."

108.   Koch, "Entertainment and Politics;" Owen, "Entertainment and Politics."

109.   Koch, "Entertainment and Politics;" Owen, "Entertainment and Politics."

110.   Vicki Kunkel, *Instant Appeal: The 8 Primal Factors that Create Blockbuster Success* (New York: Amacon, 2009), 133-34.

111.   Kunkel, *Instant Appeal,* 134.

112.   Stephen Thomas Erlewine, "Taking the Long Way," in *Contemporary Country*, ed. Chris Woodstra, John Bush, and Stephen Thomas Erlewine (New York: Backbeat Books, 2008), 43.

113.   Gabriel Rossman, "Elites, Masses, and Media Blacklists: The Dixie Chicks Controversy," *Social Forces*, 83, No. 1 (September 2004): 61-79, 76.

114.   Rossman, "Elites, Masses, and Media Blacklists;" Geoff Mayfield, "Holiday Shifts Pace; New Realities of Dixie Chicks," *Billboard*, June 17, 2006, 65.

115.   Teri vanHorn, "Tom Petty, Jon Bon Jovi, John Popper Play for Gore: Private Concert Follows Shortly After Gore's Concession Speech," MTV, accessed August 10, 2010, http://www.mtv.com/news/articles/1424581/20001215/petty_tom.jhtml.

116.   Boucher, "Songs in the Key of Presidency.

117.   "Billboard Hot 100," *Billboard*, November 9, 1974, 60.

118.   Alan M. Dershowitz, *Supreme Injustice: How the High Court Hijacked Election 2000* (New York: Oxford University Press, 2001); Jeffrey Toobin, *Too Close to Call: The Thirty-Six-Day Battle to Decide the 2000 Election* (New York: Random House, 2001).

119.   Michael E. Ross, "Campaign Jukebox, 2004 Model: Candidate's Choice in Songs Seeks to Bond with Wide Range of Voters," MSNBC, accessed August 1, 2010, http://www.msnbc.msn.com/id/4366491; Robert Costa, "Songs for Campaign Seasons Past and Present," The Wall Street Journal Online, accessed August 1, 2010, http://online.wsj.com/article/SB122290103509796055.html.

120.   Adam Clayton et al., "Beautiful Day" (Santa Barbara, CA: Universal-Polygram International Publishing Inc., 2000).

121.   Clayton et al., "Beautiful Day."

122.   Bill Lamb, "Top 40 Pop Songs: The Best of the Best, 20. U2—'Beautiful Day' (2000)," accessed August 19, 2010, http://top40.about.com/od/top10lists/tp/top40 essentialsongsalltime.02.htm.

123.   Michka Assayas, *Bono: In Conversation with Michka Assayas* (New York: Penguin Group, 2006), 250.

124.   Laura Jackson, *Bono: His Life, Music and Passions* (New York: Kensington Publishing Corp., 2001), 192.

125.   James Bovard, *The Bush Betrayal* (New York: Palgrave Macmillan, 2004), 111.

126.   Jackson, *Bono: His Life*, 88; Višnja Cogan, *U2: An Irish Phenomenon* (New York: Pegasus Books, 2007), 79-82.

127.   Steve Huey, "Brooks & Dunn Biography," Yahoo Music, accessed August 1, 2010, http://new.music.yahoo.com/brooks-dunn/biography/.

128.   "Brook & Dunn Awards," CMT, accessed August 1, 2010, http://www.cmt. com/artists/az/brooks_and_dunn/awards.jhtml.

129.   Dana Milbank and Mike Allen, "Bush Fortifies Conservative Base: Campaign Seeks Solid Support Before Wooing Swing Voters," The Washington Post Online, accessed August 10, 2010, http://www.washingtonpost.com/wp-dyn/articles/A50296-2004Jul14.html.

130.   "GOP Convention Entertainment Sets Stage," *USA Today*, accessed August 1, 2010, http://www.usatoday.com/news/politicselections/nation/president/2004-08-23-gop-entertainment_x.htm?csp=34.

131.   Danny O. Crew, *Presidential Sheet Music: An Illustrated Catalogue* (Jefferson, NC: McFarland & Company, Inc., Publishers, 2001), 200-201, 441-446, 573-575.

132.   Crew, *Presidential Sheet Music*, 441.

133.   Luther A. Huston Washington, "The Voters Still Sing, Though Faintly," *The New York Times*, September 27, 1936, 13.

134.   Stuart Schimler, "Singing to the Oval Office: A Written History of the Political Campaign Song," accessed June 10, 2010, http://www.presidentelect.org/art_schimler_singing.html.

135.   William Miles, Introduction to *Songs, Odes, Glees and Ballads: A Bibliography of American Presidential Campaign Songsters* (New York: Greenwood Press, 1990), xlvi.

~ 7 ~

Facebook, YouTube, & MySpace, Oh My!
(2008 and Beyond)

The Internet was around long before the 2008 presidential election cycle. However, the candidates in this election expanded the use of the Internet from simply that of campaign websites to the incorporation of Facebook.com, Twitter.com, and MySpace.com pages as well as YouTube.com advertisements and commentary. In addition, the Obama campaign began to utilize other forms of telecommunications in 2008; this included using cellular phone technologies to send special text messages (such as an early alert of who the vice presidential choice would be) to those who had registered through his website.[1] As described below, Obama would reveal the contents of his iPod and Hillary Clinton would use text messaging and the Internet in an innovative and interactive way. This political use of the Internet and other electronic communicative technologies extended to music, with the Internet and other personal devices affecting candidates' use of music in various capacities.

So. . . Who Invented the Internet Anyway?

The Internet began as the brainchild of the Defense Advanced Research Project Agency (DARPA, initially called ARPA from 1958 until 1972), an agency of the United States Department of Defense. After the Soviet Union launched *Sputnik*, the world's first artificial satellite into space in 1957, the federal government became concerned about being able to quickly share information. In 1958, DARPA was created in reaction to *Sputnik*'s launch, in order to sponsor projects related to military programs. By the late 1960s, DARPA began working on what became the Internet; initially this was designed as a way for military bases to be in communications with one another in the event of a nuclear attack. DARPA initiated this process by providing grant funding to research universities and corporations to develop a communications network, which was initially called ARPANET. During the 1970s, this communications system was additionally being used by researchers at universities to correspond with one another. Also during the 1970s, the Bolt, Beranek, and Newman Technologies company invented a program that allowed users of ARPANET to send mail messages to each other, something which eventually came to be called electronic mail or "email." In the 1980s, the National Science Foundation network (NSFNET) replaced ARPANET as the communications system between university and government researchers. During the 1970s and 1980s, various networks emerged, and as they became interconnected, this grand system came to be known as the Internet. During the 1990s, the National Science Foundation effectively turned over the Internet to private enterprise, leading to extensive and largely unregulated commercial development on the Internet, which helped lead to the explosion of online users.[2]

The Internet remained largely unknown or irrelevant to the general public during its infancy. However, by the 1980s politicians were beginning to take notice. While still in the U.S. Senate, Al Gore sponsored legislation that linked Internet sub-networks. Although his initial efforts on this front during the Reagan administration were unsuccessful, in 1989 President George H.W. Bush signed into law a piece of legislation pushed by Gore, the National High-Performance Technology Act (NHPTA). The NHPTA allocated $1.7 billion for research into high-performance computer networks. In 1990, Gore began referring to the Internet as a potential "information superhighway," and he analogized it to the creation of the interstate highway system in the 1950s. During the 1992 election, Bill Clinton and Gore referred to the Internet as the "information superhighway" quite frequently. After being elected, Clinton and Gore made a high-profile visit to Silicon Valley to announce a $17 billion technology program, part of which was to pay for construction of the information superhighway. The two also announced the National Information Infrastructure, which was intended to help stimulate the growth of the Internet.[3]

By the end of the 1990s, most Americans were quite familiar with the Internet. Al Gore, however, took his involvement with the Internet to a new level when, in a March 1999 interview with Wolf Blitzer, the vice president stated that "During my service in the United States Congress, I took the initiative in creating the Internet."[4] The press, and Gore's opponent in 2000, George W. Bush, ran with Gore's exaggerated comment. During a presidential debate in October of 2000, Gore had stated that a family with an income of $25,000 or more would be ineligible for Bush's prescription drug benefit, leading Bush to state the following about Gore: "Look, this is a man, he's got great numbers. He talks about numbers. I'm beginning to think not only did he invent the Internet but he also invented the calculator. It's fuzzy math. . . "[5] When coupled with jokes by late-night comedians and others, the popular misconception soon became that Gore claimed to have "invented" the Internet.[6] Although Gore's comment was an overstatement (after all, the Internet's framework was well under way before Gore was in Congress, and others in the government took a lead role in sponsoring the legislation he helped pass), the misconception that he had "invented" the Internet made Gore seem to be even more of an embellisher on the subject. This factor may have hurt his electoral chances in the November 2000 presidential election.

YouTube and I

Regardless of who "took the initiative in creating the Internet" or who "invented" it, by the 2000 election, politicians were making use of it. During that year, all major presidential candidates maintained campaign websites during the election, as did seventy-seven percent of U.S. Senate candidates and fifty-four percent of House candidates.[7] Bush and Gore's campaign websites began using audio and video of the candidates as well.[8] Political use of the Internet expanded by 2004, as a majority of adult Americans, sixty-one percent, were using the Internet (this was a great increase from the twenty-three percent of adults who used the Internet in 1996).[9] In 2004, tens of millions of Americans were using the Internet to research candidate positions and voting records, check public opinion polls, and send emails about the election, among other things.[10] As more and more voters began using the Internet for election-related purposes, more politicians, media, and other groups began using the Internet to try to influence those voters.

Social networking websites like MySpace.com and Facebook.com were around during the 2004 presidential campaign but they were still in their infancy at the time. MySpace was developed in 2003 while Facebook.com did not make its official launch until February of 2004.[11] Consequently, they were not used prominently in the 2004 elections. However, these sites became effective tools for presidential campaigns in the 2008 elections. They can be useful devices because they allow candidates to post a variety of information about themselves and the campaigns. In addition, people can sign up to "friend" a candidate in order to get up-to-the-minute updates about campaign events on these websites. This also allows the candidate to garner a level of support on the Internet and potentially find people who are willing to volunteer for the campaign. Furthermore, these networking websites allow supporters to easily send information about a candidate on to their "friends," creating a network of seemingly endless connections for a candidate.

Perhaps more important than these social networking sites was the invention of YouTube.com in February of 2005. According to the website's own description, "YouTube is the world's most popular online video community, allowing millions of people to discover, watch and share originally-created videos."[12] The website was built to allow individuals to "connect, inform, and inspire others across the globe" via new videos and to allow small businesses a platform for advertising to the public.[13] What makes the website even more attractive is that accounts for uploading material are free, and the ability to watch material is free to the public. YouTube allows candidates a free space to run political ads, put out short clips detailing their positions on certain issues, and post footage of campaign rallies. The website was even used as the platform for both a Republican and a Democratic Primary debate leading up to the 2008 presidential elections. In 2007, YouTube teamed up with the Cable News Network (CNN) to sponsor two presidential debates before the 2008 primaries. The Democratic debate among eight contenders took place in July 2007, and the Republican debate among eight contenders took place in November 2007. In each case, video content from the debates was made available for online sharing and distribution, and questions for the candidates were submitted to CNN via videos uploaded on the YouTube website. Thousands of questions were submitted by the public for the debates.[14]

The candidates also took notice of the power of YouTube during the 2008 election and set up their own "channels" on the website, which were in addition to their main Internet pages. For instance, Barack Obama's YouTube channel, launched in September 2006, had 113,000 subscribers by November 2008, and the channel's 1,760 videos were viewed almost 94 million times.[15] John McCain's YouTube channel started operation in February 2007, eventually had 28,000 subscribers, and its 327 videos were viewed 24 million times.[16] Thus, there is no question that YouTube was a well-used tool to convey information from the candidates to the electorate in 2008.

As you will see later in this chapter, websites like YouTube also allow for the average citizen to express their opinions about candidates and campaigns, making these websites a two-way street of communication. Likewise, these types of websites permit individuals to campaign for candidates on their own with a way to distribute their messages, whether that is through the use of ads, home videos, or music. The appeal of YouTube for the general public, beginning in 2008, is that people now have a large audience that can either search for (or stumble upon) these messages, opinions, and songs. In previous years, the general public would not have been able to disseminate these opinions as widely. Consequently, these opinions did not have the same potential impact as they would by 2008. Furthermore, the 2008 election would see a candidate do what would have been nearly impossible only a few years earlier—allow campaign supporters to vote on the campaign's theme song, which eventually resulted in Hillary Clinton choosing the campaign song "You and I." In many ways, the Internet came of age politically in 2008, and this is most certainly true with respect to music on the Internet.

The use of popular music continued as a staple of campaign rallies and the national conventions for both parties during the 2008 election. Many of these songs continued to be in the vein of the "one line wonders" of the late 1980s and the 1990s. As we will explore below, some candidates also used the Internet to better connect with their supporters by incorporating them into campaign decisions. Considering the short time frame that will be emphasized in this final chapter, a discussion of the 2008 primary elections seems an appropriate place to begin our musical journey in chapter seven. Although most of our explanations and descriptions in previous chapters focused predominantly on general elections only, the quickly changing nature of campaign activities on the Internet in 2007 and 2008 warrant an extended discussion of the use of the medium during the nomination phase too. Another factor making the consideration of primaries appropriate for 2008 was the fact that music, and the total number of songs used, began to proliferate in not just the general election season but also during the period before and during the primary and caucus season. Finally, since 2008 is the most recent presidential election cycle, we give it special attention here because, as of the writing of this book, it is the closest predictor we have to the use of music in the 2012 presidential election.

This Is Our Primary Season

The 2008 primary elections and caucuses saw a race within the Democrat Party among Illinois Senator Barak Obama, New York Senator Hillary Clinton, former North Carolina Senator John Edwards, Connecticut Senator Christopher Dodd, Delaware Senator Joe Biden, Ohio Congressman Dennis Kucinich, New Mexico Governor Bill Richardson, and former Alaska Senator Mike Gravel. The Republican primaries also saw a wide group of contenders, featuring the likes of Arizona Senator John McCain, former Arkansas Governor Mike Huckabee, former Massachusetts Governor Mitt Romney, former New York City Mayor Rudy Giuliani, Texas Congressman Ron Paul, former Tennessee Senator and actor Fred Thompson, California Congressman Duncan Hunter, Colorado Congressman Tom Tancredo, and former Wisconsin Governor and Health and Human Services Secretary Tommy Thompson. This large field of candidates for each party was partly due to the fact that neither a sitting president nor vice president was running for the presidency for the first time since 1952. Thus, neither party had a presumptive nominee before primary season began, ensuring a wide open field of candidates on both sides of the aisle.

In the 2008 election cycle, multiple candidates emphasized one line messages from songs, and their musical selections were tailored toward seeking a positive reaction from the voting public. During the primaries and caucuses of the 2008 presidential election, almost every candidate made use of a song or songs that he or she believed would describe his or her political vision and motivate his or her supporters to action. These songs ranged from classic rock to adult contemporary to pop rock to country to Motown.

Texas Congressman Ron Paul was a libertarian-leaning candidate aiming for the Republican nomination in 2008. His policy positions included repealing the federal income tax, ending the federal war on drugs, closing the Department of Education, ending government subsidies to oil companies, ending an interventionist U.S. foreign policy, ending free trade, protecting privacy rights and gun rights, and abolishing Social Security.[17] Many of these policy positions put him at odds not just with the Democrats, but also with many members of his own party. When John McCain wrapped up the 2008 Republican nomination in March, Paul continued to run defiantly for more than three more months as a way to continue discussing issues that were important to him.[18] Although Ron Paul did not make much use of music while he was actively running for president in 2008, the song he chose when he spoke at the Republican National Convention in September was Tom Petty's "I Won't Back Down,"[19] a fitting choice for a candidate who had refused to throw in the towel or compromise his policy stances. Paul continued to use this song at public speeches after the 2008 election,[20] and there is no evidence that Tom Petty has objected to Paul's use of the song as he did with George W. Bush's use of it in 2000. Nor did the artist apparently object when the song, which has a desirable message for many candidates, was used as warm-up music for both Hillary Clinton and John Edwards in 2007 and early 2008.[21]

During the Democratic primaries, the main theme song of John Edwards' campaign was John Mellencamp's "Our Country," a song from the singer's 2007 album, *Freedom's Road.*[22] The 2008 campaign marked the second time that Edwards chose a Mellencamp song to represent his candidacy; when he was fighting for the 2004 Democratic presidential nomination, Edwards chose "Small Town," presumably because the tune represented Edwards' small town roots.[23] The lyrics of "Small Town" also appeal to those who have jobs with little or no opportunity for growth, a theme that squared well with Edwards' emphasis on eliminating poverty.[24] In 2008, Edwards used the same musical artist to project a similar message with "Our Country":

Well I can stand beside
Ideals I think are right
And I can stand beside
The idea to stand and fight
I do believe
There's a dream for everyone
This is our country

There's room enough here
For science to live
And there's room enough here
For religion to forgive
And try to understand
All the people of this land
This is our country

From the east coast
To the west coast
Down the Dixie Highway
Back home
This is our country

That poverty could be
Just another ugly thing
And bigotry would be
Seen only as obscene
And the ones that run this land
Help the poor and common man
This is our country

From the east coast
To the west coast
Down the Dixie Highway
Back home
This is our country

The dream is still alive
Some day it will come true
And this country it belongs
To folks like me and you
So let the voice of freedom
Sing out through this land
This is our country

From the east coast
To the west coast
Down the Dixie Highway
Back home
This is our country

From the east coast
To the west coast
Down the Dixie Highway
Back home
This is our country

OUR COUNTRY

Indeed, the song seems tailor-made for the Edwards campaign, as it talks about pluralist themes of a "dream for everyone," including room enough for science and religion. The song also emphasizes fighting against poverty and bigotry, two issues on which Edwards was outspoken. Edwards even tried to capitalize on the celebrity of John Mellencamp, as the artist put on a free concert for the candidate that preceded a campaign rally in Des Moines before the Iowa Democratic caucus; during the speech, Edwards emphasized themes from the song "Our Country" by stating to the crowd of nearly three thousand people that "Beginning in the heartland of America, right here in Iowa, you're going to rise up, stand up and say to America, 'Enough is enough. We want our country back. We want our democracy back.'"[25]

However, "Our Country" was an interesting choice for Edwards for another reason. By the time he started using the song in late 2007 and early 2008, many people who heard the song probably thought of buying pickup trucks before they thought of fighting poverty. This is because in the fall of 2006, General Motors stopped using Bob Seeger's "Like a Rock" as its theme song for Chevy Silverado advertisements; instead, the automaker unveiled Mellencamp's "Our Country" as its new anthem.[26] The advertisements were played frequently during nationally televised college and professional football games, and it was also played during the World Series.[27] That the song already had an attachment to pickup trucks and sporting events makes "Our Country" an even more fascinating selection for the Edwards campaign. Although this strong tie to commercial advertising is a potential drawback, it also ensured that Edwards chose a song that was well known among segments of the population who are interested in sports or trucks. Furthermore, the Chevrolet "Our Country" advertisements were patriotic in nature, with images of historic moments in recent American history, including Rosa Parks on a bus, Martin Luther King, Jr. speaking, the aftermath of September 11, 2001, and Hurricane Katrina's devastation.[28] Thus, what might typically be a poor strategy of tying oneself to music from a commercial advertisement was ameliorated by the fact that the commercial advertising itself played to patriotic themes.

Mike Huckabee's main song during his race for the Republican presidential nomination was "More Than a Feeling" by Boston.[29] As noted in the previous chapter, Huckabee ran into problems when Tom Scholz, group founder and chief songwriter, wrote a letter to the candidate complaining that he was using the song without permission.[30] Not everyone from Boston agreed with Scholz, however, as lead guitarist Barry Goudreau appeared with Huckabee at his rallies and helped play the song.[31] In addition to this main theme song, Huckabee played other songs at rallies, including Lynard Skynard's "Sweet Home Alabama" and the Kingsmen's "Louie Louie."[32] This put Huckabee into the growing camp of presidential candidates in recent years who have made use of multiple songs when running. Huckabee also took a page from Bill Clinton's playbook, as the fellow former Arkansas governor showed off his own musical skills, playing several songs with his band, Capitol Offense, on the campaign trail, including "More Than a Feeling," Barrett Strong's "Money (That's What I Want)," the Isley Brothers' "Twist and Shout," and Elvis's "Jailhouse Rock."[33]

Hillary Clinton used one of the more remarkable approaches to choosing a main campaign song. Early in her bid to become the Democratic nominee for president, the Clinton campaign made a decision to utilize the Internet in a unique way by allowing supporters to have input into which song would be used to represent her. Clinton emailed and texted supporters' cell phones for song ideas and then for one month allowed people to vote from a list of song choices online or via text.[34] The campaign staff put together a list of ten songs that they believed would send an appropriate message to the electorate in representing

Clinton's campaign and her message. The list included "City of Blinding Lights" by U2, "Suddenly I See" by KT Tunstall, "I'm a Believer" by Smash Mouth, "Ready to Run" by the Dixie Chicks, and "Right Here, Right Now" by Jesus Jones.[35] Clinton then gave her constituents the opportunity to vote for their choice.[36] When voting for the song ended, she encouraged people to go to her campaign website to find out which song won by appearing in a YouTube commercial with Bill Clinton that was a parody on the final episode of *The Sopranos* from 2007.[37] The commercial ended with Hillary Clinton putting a coin into a diner jukebox before the screen turns to black and tells viewers the website address to find out which song won.[38] This video was accessed on YouTube and Clinton's campaign website hundreds of thousands of times within a week of its release.[39]

This was an innovative way for Clinton to let her supporters be involved in the day-to-day decisions of the campaign by choosing a song for her which her supporters thought was appealing and representative of their candidate. While in a controlled environment (Clinton only let supporters choose from among ten options), she allowed the general populace to put a label on her campaign. This is ingenious in that it gave her supporters the feeling of ownership and a bit of a personal stake in the election. It also attempted to settle on a campaign song that is popular, at least among a group of supporters likely to vote. The idea here is that if a song is popular among those who already support a candidate, like-minded people might also find the song, and consequently the candidate, appealing. Furthermore, the online voting process Clinton chose called additional attention to her campaign and song in ways that simply playing a song at a rally or announcing a song choice in a press release or news conference would not do.[40]

Interestingly enough, however, this strategy also runs the risk of having an adverse effect on a campaign. If the song vote is tight and a relatively small majority or even plurality wins, it may mean that a candidate has a song with an indifferent or even negative perception from the electorate. The candidate could also end up with a number of supporters feeling disappointed that the song they preferred was not the one selected. Or, a biased sample of voters could give a candidate a song that is unpopular with the general public. Something like this plagued Clinton, as some bloggers criticized her for finally ending up with "You and I," sung by Celine Dion, a Canadian (not American) citizen.[41] One could even imagine opponents of a candidate voting for a song that they thought would reflect poorly on the candidate (if this sort of "cross-over" voting could be encouraged during Rush Limbaugh's Operation Chaos in 2008, it could certainly occur in online voting for a campaign song). Indeed, choosing a song in this manner could even send a campaign into a completely different direction than the candidate had planned, toward a course that only vocal minorities of candidates' supporters (or covert opponents) want it to go. Fortunately for Clinton, she was able to control some of these pitfalls by limiting the possible song choices to relatively popular ones, all of which Clinton presumably thought would represent her campaign message quite well.

As previously stated, at the end of the voting, "You and I" emerged victorious. The song talks about a person acting as a beacon of light in the world, saying that together we can do anything. As the lyrics below demonstrate, "You and
I" has an inspiring message of hopefulness:

Verse 1:
High above the mountains, far across the sea
I can hear your voice calling out to me
Brighter than the sun and darker than the night
I can see your love shining like a light
And on and on this earth spins like a carousel
If I could travel across the world
The secrets I would tell

Chorus:
You and I
Were meant to fly
Higher than the clouds
We'll sail across the sky
So come with me
And you will feel
That we're soaring
That we're floating up so high
'Cause you and I were meant to fly

Verse 2:
Sailing like a bird high on the wings of love
Take me higher than all the stars above
I'm burning, yearning
Gently turning round and round
I'm always rising up I never
Want to come back down
(Chorus)

Fly. . .

You and I
Were meant to fly
Higher than the clouds
We'll sail across the sky
So come with me
And you will feel
That you and I were meant to fly

You and I were meant to fly

You and I (Were Meant To Fly)
Words and Music by Aldo Caporuscio and Jacques Duval
Copyright © 2009 BMG Platinum Songs (BMI), Aldo Nova, Inc. (SOCAN), Songs
   of Peer Ltd. (ASCAP) and Avenue Editorial (ASCAP)
Worldwide Rights for BMG Platinum Songs and Aldo Nova, Inc. Administered by
   BMG Chrysalis
Worldwide Rights for Avenue Editorial Administered by Songs of Peer Ltd.
All Rights Reserved   Used by Permission
Reprinted by permission of Hal Leonard Corporation

Does this say something about what her constituents think of her and want the
rest of the world to see in her? That question is unanswerable here. Regardless,
her supporters had the opportunity for involvement in choosing the song that
they believe said something about their particular candidate. Despite some of the
drawbacks associated with this campaign song selection method, the idea of
allowing one's supporters this type of influence in a presidential campaign was,
at worst, a great public relations stunt that garnered plenty of media attention. It
is also quite possible that this song selection method had a lasting positive effect
on Clinton's campaign. "You and I" was also a choice by Clinton supporters that
was likely to elicit a positive response from the public, as it rose to number 16
on the *Billboard* Adult Contemporary Chart in 2004.[42] Not only that, but the
song was designed to be appealing to the public by advertisers, as it was written
for, and then heavily used in advertising by, Air Canada.[43] Thus, there was a
similarity in Clinton's and Edwards' main campaign songs, as both had previously been used in commercial advertising. For each candidate, this was another
way of having a song that was a proven winner. After all, if the song has been
successful in marketing major products, such as trucks and airlines, there is a
substantial likelihood that it will play well to voters. Of course, this represents
another example of campaigns basing themselves upon a commercial marketing
model, a trend that began with the development of radio, accelerated with the
advent of television, and shows no sign of slowing down after the invention of
the Internet.

Overall, Clinton's decision to let her song be chosen from a set of options
by her supporters is a new development in campaign music strategy. The preva-
lence of access to the Internet is what made this strategy possible. Indeed, consider how difficult it would have been for a candidate in 1988, 1948, or 1908 to
have supporters choose a campaign's theme song. It likely would have involved
mail-in ballots or one mass ballot filled out at a large event, such as a party's
national convention. Those options would have been costly to implement, difficult to coordinate, or both. With the advent of the Internet, however, new opportunities such as this are now available for campaign songs.

Candidates in the 2008 primaries would also continue the trend of using
multiple musical selections to represent varying and specific political motives.
Former Massachusetts Governor Mitt Romney saw fit to use "A Little Less
Conversation" by Elvis Presley and "You Ain't Seen Nothing Yet" performed
by Bachman-Turner Overdrive in his campaign, with each song serving a specif-

ic purpose. The first of these songs, "A Little Less Conversation," sent a simple message to the listener. Simply put, its point is that we need to stop talking about how we are going to do things and actually begin doing them; a message of urgency to the Republican base that Romney would be a man of action, not just words. Although "A Little Less Conversation" only peaked on *Billboard* at number 69 when it was released in 1968,[44] by 2008 the song had received more success and use. Indeed, the song was rereleased in 2002 on the *ELVIS 30 #1 Hits* album, and this time the song rose higher, to number 50 in the United States on the *Billboard* Hot 100 chart.[45] The song was also used in the films *Ocean's Eleven* (2001), *Bruce Almighty* (2003), and *Jackass Number Two* (2006), as well as in the hit television shows *Everybody Loves Raymond* (2003) and *Las Vegas* (2003-2008).[46] Clearly, over the last decade several television and movie producers thought the song had sufficient appeal to the public, and the Romney campaign probably had similar sentiments when choosing the musical piece.

Romney's second selection was chosen leading into the 2008 Super Tuesday elections. At this point in the campaign he used the message of "You Ain't Seen Nothing Yet" to give his supporters hope that his bid for the Republican nomination was not finished. Although Romney was behind McCain in the delegate count going into Super Tuesday, he chose to repeatedly play "You Ain't Seen Nothing Yet" after winning in Maine over the previous weekend. His campaign staff reinforced this message through statements to the media: "campaign strategists. . . point to Romney's win Saturday in Maine as a portent of surprising things to come."[47] Effectively, Romney was changing his music in the middle of his campaign to convey a new message to supporters and potential voters—I have won a small primary, but I will be winning much more on Super Tuesday. The song was an example of a campaign changing its message to inspire its supporters. Again, Romney's campaign chose a song that was popular and thought would appeal to the public. When the song was released in 1974, it rose all the way to number one on the *Billboard* Hot 100 chart.[48]

Romney was certainly not alone in the use of multiple campaign songs during the primaries. In addition to "You and I," which served as her main campaign theme, Clinton used "Takin' Care of Business" by Bachman-Turner Overdrive, "9 to 5" by Dolly Parton and "American Girl" by Tom Petty. Rudy Giuliani would use "Take Us Out" by Jerry Goldsmith (the song was the theme from the inspiring football movie *Rudy*) as well as "Rudie Can't Fail" by the Clash (clearly, in these two instances the former mayor of New York City was running on a musical theme related to his first name). Giuliani also used "Eye of the Tiger," which was written at the request of Sylvester Stallone for the movie *Rocky III* and performed by the group Survivor.[49] When adding the examples from Huckabee above, by the 2008 elections it seems that the use of multiple "theme" songs for a political campaign, something that began to proliferate with George W. Bush and Al Gore in 2000, had become a standard practice. Perhaps the best explanation for this trend is twofold. First, candidates recognize that different songs can emphasize different themes in different parts of the country. Thus, a candidate can tailor a song to a particular locale to appeal to the particular interests of voters in that area. Second, the proliferation of technology, both online and with systems to change and play music at events, now allows campaigns more opportunities to alter music with ease. In some ways this is a partial return to the great singing campaigns of the nineteenth and early twentieth centuries, where songsters were created that had dozens of songs in them for a candidate. The only difference in the Internet era is that most of the songs chosen remain preexisting popular songs that are used note for note and lyric for lyric.

From Primary to Primetime: Obama is "Signed, Sealed, Delivered" "Only in America"

The campaign of Barack Obama used several songs between the primary elections and the general election in 2008. The song that is most notably associated with the Obama campaign was "Signed, Sealed, Delivered I'm Yours" by Stevie Wonder. On the surface, Obama's one line message says "I'm here, I'm yours, and I'm ready to serve you, so pick me." This is a simple, clear message to the voters from a song out of the Motown tradition. Furthermore, if one digs a little deeper into the song, one finds that on the whole, the song conveys a message that is synonymous on many levels with Obama's dominant campaign themes of hope and change. The song notes how we are the ones that hold the future, and within the context of the campaign, how Obama is ready to be that future. Furthermore, the song can even be seen as addressing some of the youth indiscretions of Obama when the song's lyrics speak of unintended foolish things that the singer has done (this could be inclusive of Obama's admitted teenage use of alcohol, marijuana, and cocaine) but that ultimately made him the better man he is today. [50] While the lyrics of the song were certainly intended to speak about a romantic relationship, there is a double entendre that exists which seemingly makes them appropriate. Does it work perfectly? No, but just like many other "canned" songs used by political campaigns in recent decades, this song does send multiple messages that the candidate wished to convey about his campaign. And the song itself is well known today and was popular when released in 1970. Indeed, the song initially went to number three on the *Billboard* chart, and it finished at the number one position on the R&B chart that year.[51] The song's happy, upbeat tone, combined with its historical chart success, makes it a musical selection likely to be found appealing by the average voter who listened to it during the campaign.

Other notable songs used by Obama's campaign in the 2008 election were "City of Blinding Lights" by U2 (one of the songs that Hillary Clinton submitted to her supporters to be her official campaign song), "Higher and Higher" by Jackie Wilson, "Think" by Aretha Franklin, and "The Rising" by Bruce Springsteen (a song also used periodically by Hillary Clinton[52]). Each of these songs did one of two things. First, some of these songs keep with the Motown tradition that "Signed, Sealed, Delivered, I'm Yours" does. An explanation for this may be that Obama wanted to emphasize songs by African American artists to draw attention to his race and the fact that, if successful, he would be breaking the ultimate "color barrier" in being elected the first African American president in U.S. history. Second, all of these songs associate the campaign with a singer who is a prominent supporter of the Democrat Party or its values. For instance, Aretha Franklin had previously performed her music at a free concert that kicked off the Democratic National Convention in 1996, and she also sang the national anthem at the convention; when interviewed at that event, Franklin admitted that she is a Democrat.[53] Her support for Obama and the Democratic Party was also demonstrated when she sang "My Country 'Tis of Thee" at President Obama's inauguration on January 20, 2009.[54] For another example, one can look to Bruce Springsteen. After refusing to be a part of Ronald Reagan's reelection effort in 1984, Springsteen remained neutral over multiple presidential elections. In 2004, Springsteen threw his support behind John Kerry's presidential bid, and "the Boss" gave an eleven state "Vote for Change" concert tour on Kerry's behalf.[55] In April 2008, Springsteen gave his celebrity endorsement to Obama while the candidate was still embroiled in a tough primary fight with Hillary Clinton.[56]

Obama's expanded use of musical selections included another U2 song that was used in John Kerry's 2004 campaign, "Beautiful Day." Obama unveiled the song in his first joint appearance with Hillary Clinton in 2008. After a hard-fought Democratic primary season that pitted the two senators against each other for over one year, Clinton finally conceded the nomination to Obama on June 7, 2008.[57] Clinton first appeared with Obama in the symbolically named New Hampshire city, Unity, on June 27, 2008.[58] At the nationally televised rally, the two former rivals made their way to the stage to U2's "Beautiful Day."[59]

Notwithstanding the music Obama used earlier in his campaign, at the 2008 Democratic National Convention he decided to use a song that had been strongly associated with George W. Bush just four years earlier. Indeed, the Obama campaign closed out the convention with "Only in America" by Brooks and Dunn.[60] Although Brooks and Dunn are very much supporters of the Republican Party,[61] it was quite apt that their song would be used to speak the message that "Only in America" can a black man rise from a relatively modest beginning and build his life to become president of the nation (indeed, Obama was the first black person elected head of government in any Western, predominantly white country). This was also likely part of Obama's general election strategy to lure in independent moderate voters. While many artists with political leanings that differ from a candidate will decry the use of their music, Kix Brooks commented on Obama's use of the song positively: "Seems ironic that the same song Bush used at the Republican Convention last election would be used by Obama and the Democrats now. . . . Very flattering to know our song crossed parties and potentially inspires all Americans."[62] Thus, even in the opinion of the conservative artists, the use of the song was fitting for the campaign, and, moreover, it was uplifting for his supporters and people of color across the country who may have believed a day such as this would never come to pass.

Obama expressed his musical tastes and tried to connect to the electorate by also revealing his iPod playlist. The Apple iPod is a personal digital music player which, when first released in 2001, was hailed as having as big of an influence on personal audio entertainment as Sony's first pocket-sized transistor radio did in the 1950s and the Sony Walkman portable stereo tape player did in the 1980s.[63] By 2008, the iPod had become ubiquitous throughout the United States, and Barack Obama was no exception. That year, Obama became the first presidential candidate to reveal the song list on his iPod (although the song list on President Bush's iPod was revealed to the media by an aide in 2005[64]). In a high-profile interview with *Rolling Stone* in June of that year, Obama took the use of multiple campaign songs to the next level by announcing the songs he had on the mobile music device. Although he announced that Stevie Wonder was his "musical hero," the Obama interview also noted that he "grew up on" 1970s R&B and rock performers such as Earth, Wind and Fire, Elton John and the Rolling Stones.[65] Obama stated that his eclectic iPod list of artists included "everything from Howlin' Wolf to Yo-Yo Ma to Sheryl Crow," and that he "probably [had] 30 Dylan songs" on his iPod.[66] Obama also noted that he listened to jazz performers, including Miles Davis, John Coltrane and Charlie Parker.[67] The future president also avowed that his playlist included rappers Jay-Z and Ludacris, although he went on to note that even though he thought they were "great talents and great businessmen," he was "troubled sometimes by the misogyny and materialism of a lot of rap lyrics," and that "[i]t would be nice if I could have my daughters listen to their music without me worrying that they were getting bad images of themselves."[68]

Obama's decision to reveal his iPod song list was another example, like Hillary Clinton's song voting, of using relatively new technology and music to promote one's candidacy. When choosing one or a few campaign songs, it builds a connection and expresses a few ideas about the candidate. However, when a candidate's entire playlist is publicly revealed, there is essentially "something for everyone," in that most voters will be able to identify with at least a few artists on the playlist whose music they like. This is also a way for a candidate to get a musical message out cheaply. The candidate can state well-known artists and their songs without playing them, thus not needing to secure a costly sound system for a recording or a live appearance by the artist. And since the lines of the song are not uttered or played, there is no need for the campaign to obtain permission from the copyright holder of the song. The way Obama discussed his song choices, with additional commentary, allowed him to state that although he liked certain artists (such as Jay-Z and Ludacris), he also thought some parts of their music were inappropriate for younger listeners. Thus, Obama could, in one statement, appease those voters who like the music of these artists, while also appealing to those who find the music distasteful. Simply playing a song at a campaign rally would not have the same, more complex effect on the electorate.

Yet, Obama's musical tactic, like Hillary Clinton's new way of employing music, comes with its own set of potential drawbacks. Just as a long playlist will likely produce at least a few artists that any given voter likes, it will also likely display a few artists that any given voter dislikes. This double-edged sword is particularly bad for a candidate who leaves out entire genres of music. In Obama's case, it did not appear that any country artists were represented on his playlist, which perhaps explains why he supplemented his musical selections by playing "Only in America" at the Democratic National Convention. This point notwithstanding, Obama deployed music in a new way in 2008, and in many ways it was just as innovative as Bill Clinton's use of music in 1992. Furthermore, Obama integrated his musical strategy, as several artists on his iPod, including Bruce Springsteen, Bob Dylan, and Jay-Z, publicly endorsed him in 2008.[69]

The Obama campaign's diverse use of music extended to the release of an 18-song compact disc titled *Yes We Can: Voices of a Grassroots Movement.* The CD, the title of which was one of Obama's campaign slogans in 2008, featured numerous artists, including Kanye West, John Legend, Sheryl Crow, Stevie Wonder, who sang both new and previously released songs. Not only did having multiple artists on one CD help to associate Obama with enough artists that a typical listener might like at least a few of them. In addition, the CD, which was released in September 2008, was sold exclusively by the Obama campaign during the election. The revenue raised from CD sales (the campaign charged $24.99 for a digital download and $30 for a physical compact disc) funded the Obama campaign. This not only associated the campaign with what it saw as favorable songs and celebrities, it also helped pay for the campaign itself![70]

Of course, not all celebrity association with the Obama campaign was so positive. The McCain campaign tried to capitalize on what it saw as Obama's celebrity factor by trying to link his rise to fame with celebrities who had taken on a negative public image. In the television ad "Celeb," a narrator for the McCain campaign states about Obama that "He's the biggest celebrity in the world, but is he ready to lead?" The sound of a crowd chanting "Obama, Obama" can be heard in the background. The visuals of the advertisement include a shot of the crowd when Obama spoke at the Brandenburg Gate in Berlin, followed by shots of Paris Hilton and, more relevant for our purposes here, musician Britney Spears.[71] This attack on Obama's celebrity, and the attempt to put him in lot with other celebrities whose public images have recently suffered, brings us full circle from the celebrity phenomenon that began with radio. This attempted attack is not surprising, given Obama's relative inexperience in government compared to McCain, as well as the backlash against celebrity involvement in politics, as evidenced by the success of Laura Ingraham's 2003 book, *Shut Up and Sing: How Elites from Hollywood, Politics, and the UN Are Subverting America.* Regardless of this backlash and McCain's attempt to capitalize on it, Obama did have many celebrity endorsements in 2008, many of whom were musicians.

From POW to Republican Nominee:
"Johnny B. Good"

Like Barack Obama and several other candidates in 2008, John McCain's campaign also made use of multiple songs between the Republican primaries and the general election. McCain set off on the campaign trail initially with the song "Johnny B. Good" by Chuck Berry.[72] The song talks of a boy named Johnny who grows up in the backwoods who grows up to become a famous musician and bandleader because of his ability to play the guitar. In many respects the song is autobiographical of Chuck Berry's life (as many of his songs are). For the McCain campaign, the song not only delivered the quick message that John McCain was a good pick for the presidency, but it also contained the candidate's name, harkening back to the use of "I'm Just Wild About Harry" (for Harry Truman) and "I Like Ike" (for Dwight D. Eisenhower). This made the association between song and candidate even more evident and easy for the public to remember. The fact that the song is an American success story about a young man who is able to achieve his dream[73] also aids in its effectiveness for the campaign. The song is not perfect for use in a presidential campaign, however. The Johnny in the song was admittedly fairly illiterate, not exactly an image that most politicians aim to project.[74] That said, the song's hook was a call to arms, telling McCain repeatedly to go forward—a message that the campaign was likely trying to send to its supporters. The song itself is relatively well known for Chuck Berry's use of the guitar and was very popular when released, climbing to number eight on the *Billboard* pop chart in 1958 and having been covered by dozens of major artists in the interceding half century.[75] The song also experienced something of a renaissance when it was prominently featured in the *Back to the Future* franchise of films in the mid-1980s to the early 1990s, thus making it familiar to younger generations of voters. Therefore, it is no surprise that McCain chose this song, as it was likely to appeal to a large cross-section of voters while simultaneously reminding them of the candidate's name.

However, McCain, like Romney and Obama, chose to hedge his musical bets a bit and work with more than one campaign theme song. For instance, at the Republican National Convention, McCain unleashed a new song: "Raisin' McCain" by John Rich.[76] Like "Johnny Be Good," this song has a catch line that mentions the candidate's name, and it then attempts to spur his supporters to "raise" him to victory.

> Well we're all just raisin' McCain
> Everywhere across the USA
> You can get on the train or get out of the way
> We're all just raisin' McCain

Not only does this song have a well thought out catchphrase, but it goes back to the musical attempts of "Tippecanoe and Tyler Too." The song speaks in specifics of the life of John McCain and outlines why the artist believes that this candidate is the best for the job:

> Well he got shot down in a Vietnam town
> Fighting for the red, white and blue
> And they locked him up in the Hanoi Hilton
> Thinking they could break him in two
>
> He stayed strong, stayed extra-long
> 'Til they let all the other boys out
> Now we've got a real man with an American plan
> We're going to put him in the big White House
>
> "RAISIN' MCCAIN"
> Written by John Rich
> Published by Rich Entertainment Group
> Administered by Kobalt Music Publishing America, Inc.

This song is the perfect marriage of the new "catchphrase" combined with a song that speaks to the qualifications of the candidate if you chose to listen further.

Another song prevalent in John McCain's general election campaign was "McCain-Palin Tradition" by Hank Williams Jr.[77] This song was a remake of an already popular song of Williams Jr. entitled "Family Tradition."[78] (It is interesting to note that this is not the first time Hank Williams Jr. rewrote a song for use by a presidential candidate. During the 2000 elections, Williams Jr. rewrote "We Are Young and Country" to say "This is Bush-Cheney Country.")[79] Much like John Rich, Hank Williams Jr. offers a catchy one line phrase that mentions McCain's name, this time also including his running mate Sarah Palin. Also like the song of John Rich, Hank Williams wrote verses that applied to the presidential race. However, instead of just speaking to the strengths of McCain and Palin, the song also calls negative attention to the "liberal media" and also to perceived negative qualities of the Democratic Party as a whole:

> The left wing liberal media have
> Always been a real close knit family
> But, most of the American People
> Don't believe em anyway ya see
> Stop and think it over
> Before you make your decision
> If they smell something
> They're gonna come down strong
> It's a McCain-Palin tradition

and

John N Sarah tell ya
Just what they think
And they're not gonna blink
And they're gonna fix this country
Cause they're just like you N ole Hank
Yes John is a maverick
And Sarah fixed Alaska's broken condition
They're gonna go just fine
We're headed for better times
It's a McCain-Palin tradition

The songs of Rich and Williams used by McCain are significant in that they both not only create a great catch phrase for the general public, but they also use the names of the candidates. The two songs offered here in support of McCain speak in detail of the man and his accomplishments (Rich) and of some of the actual issues in which this candidate disagrees with his opponent and his opponent's party (Williams Jr.). In these ways, they harken back to the campaign songs of the nineteenth and early twentieth centuries, where speaking to the strengths of the candidates, weaknesses of the opponents, and promoting a candidate to the public in specific ways was a staple of the music offered to the electorate by campaigns.

Whether McCain's strategy will be the mold for campaign songs of the future remains yet to be seen. There is no doubt that his musical style, especially with the use of "Raisin' McCain" and "McCain-Palin Tradition," was innovative (or at least it was a return to American campaign music's roots). However, much like Hillary Clinton's innovation, McCain ran a substantial risk of choosing a song that would not be found appealing by the average listener. Indeed, by creating a new song or even writing new lyrics to an old one, a candidate puts forth an untested song or set of lyrics that has no track record of listener support or popularity. When looking at the songs the McCain campaign used in this medium, he was relatively safe with his base by choosing "Raisin' McCain" and "McCain-Palin Tradition." One was a remake of an already popular country song. Both, as country western songs that spoke to conservative themes, were likely to have strong appeal to moderate to conservative voters.[80] However, in more liberal and more urban areas, it is likely that the song received a less than positive reaction from the average voter, making the songs' impacts on those voters and in those geographical locations questionable.

Overall, however, there is substantial evidence based on these cases that U.S. presidential election candidates choose campaign theme songs that have proven popularity with the voting public, especially the target audience they are attempting to connect with. Furthermore, a candidate often chooses a song that contains a catchy one-liner which can easily express his or her campaign message. Although the McCain campaign used some musical tactics that have been rare since the beginning of the pop music era, it does not change the fact that the use of prepackaged pop songs remained the norm in 2008. Indeed, most candidates only made use of pop songs, and even McCain made use of the existing lyrics and music from "Johnny B. Good." His running mate, Alaska Governor Sarah Palin, even had her own pop theme song during the campaign. Her competitiveness as a high school basketball player earned her the nickname "Sarah Barracuda," which stuck with her later in life. After being selected as the vice presidential nominee in 2008, the McCain campaign played the rock band Heart's 1977 hit, "Barracuda," at the Republican National Convention.[81] Ann and Nancy Wilson, two of Heart's members, objected to Palin's use of the song because, in their words, "Sarah Palin's views and values in NO WAY represent us as American women. . . . While Heart did not and would not authorize the use of their song at the RNC, there's irony in Republican strategists' choice to make use of it there."[82] The McCain campaign ignored these objections, however, and continued to play the song on Palin's behalf, as the campaign had properly obtained rights and paid fees with the American Society of Composers, Authors and Publishers (ASCAP), allowing them to publicly play the song.[83] Regardless of the legality of Sarah Palin's use of "Barracuda," the pop song was used to introduce her at numerous times during the general election, and it is one more example of the McCain campaign subscribing to the general trend of the last few decades of using pop songs, lyric-for-lyric, note-for-note.

Musical Misrepresentation: Being "Thunderstruck" with "A Little Less Conversation"

The use of the "one-line wonder" hook in a pop song is a great way for a political candidate to associate his or her name with that line in the song's hook. It can also be seen as an implied celebrity endorsement. Yet, this practice can lead to its own set of unique problems. The candidates, as well as their managers and advisors, are concerned with finding that song or songs that are both: a) popular and catchy enough to be remembered positively by the voters, and b) contain a one-line catchphrase that encompasses some specific aspect of what they wish the public to know about their campaign. However, they sometimes neglect to look at the song as a whole and understand what message they may be sending to the general public outside of this catchphrase. This is an issue for any candidate who may choose to take a song from the already established "popular" musical repertoire as opposed to having something written to suite them and their message. The candidate may try to project an image of a song that has nothing whatsoever to do with the artist's intent, and the image projected by the candidate may even clash with the intent of the artist. This is an issue that has presented itself since campaigns began using songs in this way.

An example of this problem was noted in the preface with John McCain's use of the AC/DC song "Thunderstruck" in 2008. The opening lines and driving beats of the song may have been a good way to start a campaign rally, and at first glance it looks like a song with a message that will be appealing to many voters. However, digging deeper into the song reveals a series of messages from the band that few, if any, presidential candidates would ever want to publicly project, such as driving in excess of the speed limit, spending time with strippers, and having promiscuous sex.[84] Let us look at two more examples of this musical misrepresentation to make this point. First, in order to demonstrate that this phenomenon was not a new development in the 2008 election, we will look at a more historical example: Bill Clinton's selection of "Don't Stop (Thinking About Tomorrow)." Then, we will return to the 2008 election and consider in detail Mitt Romney's choice of "A Little Less Conversation."

As discussed in chapter five, when Bill Clinton chose the song "Don't Stop (Thinking About Tomorrow)" for the 1992 presidential campaign he was trying to put a catchphrase into the heads of the voting public. Effectively, Clinton's message was that voters needed to consider their future and who would be best to lead them. On the surface, the Fleetwood Mac song he chose did exactly that. "Don't stop thinking about tomorrow" is a line from the song that was easily remembered and thus easily associated with candidate Bill Clinton. However, when one looks at the context of the piece, one quickly realizes that Christine McVie was singing about the separation with her husband, John McVie, after eight years of marriage.[85] That point notwithstanding, many of the lyrics of the song can be twisted and contorted to fit the context of the presidential message, such as:

> If you wake up and don't want to smile,
> If it takes just a little while,
> Open your eyes and look at the day,
> You'll sing a different way,

And

> Why not think about times to come,
> And not about the things that you've done,
> If your life was bad to you,
> Just think what tomorrow will do.

However, to go along with the above lines that would work toward his message, are lines that do not necessarily fit with the message Clinton was attempting to convey to the voters:

> All I want is to see you smile,
> If it takes just a little while,
> I know you don't believe that it's true,
> I never meant any harm to you.

The message of lines like this is not necessarily what you would want to convey to people whose votes you are attempting to court. In addition, the context of the song itself is not necessarily one that you would like the public to recognize either. If one looks at the song on the whole, instead of the opening lines, one could argue that Bill Clinton was trying to say the following: "I'll break my vows to you, but try to keep looking forward because things will get better eventually." It is highly unlikely that this could ever be a strong message for a presidential candidate. That point notwithstanding, Bill Clinton will now forever be associated with the song. After using the song at the 1992 Democratic National Convention, Clinton also had it played quite often during the fall campaign, and he asked Fleetwood Mac to perform the song on his inauguration day.[86] When Clinton spoke at the 2000 Democratic National Convention and each subsequent Democratic National Convention, "Don't Stop" was played when he appeared on stage.[87]

While the song that Bill Clinton chose could create a bit of controversy if taken within its true context, there is no doubt that Mitt Romney was not thinking about the overarching meaning to his first campaign song during the 2008 campaign, "A Little Less Conversation." Out of context, the song delivers a powerful one-line message to the public of "we need to stop talking and we need to start doing." However, taken within its full and original context, it is clear that Elvis was singing about a young man who would like the sexual "action" to come quicker between him and a woman, without spending a great deal of time talking about it. And, unlike Bill Clinton's selection, here it is much more difficult to make a connection to the campaign message with lyrics such as:

> A little less conversation, a little more action please
> All this aggravation ain't satisfactioning me
> A little more bite and a little less bark
> A little less fight and a little more spark
> Close your mouth and open up your heart and baby satisfy me
> Satisfy me baby

This presents complications on two levels. First, politically it may not be prudent to relay a message of "be quiet, don't think, and get in the sack with me." When one examines this far into the song, it projects a much less popular message among the voters. In addition to the political issues that may be there, there are also religious issues that are present. Since Romney was attempting to court supporters from the political right during the 2008 Republican primaries, the target listeners of this song may not have thought that having a song about promiscuous sex between two young people was appropriate (indeed, the 2008 National Republican Party platform statement regarding sex education was, "abstinence until marriage [is] the responsible and expected standard of behavior").[88] Once again, we see an example of a campaign attempting to co-opt a song but also misrepresenting a major part of the song's original meaning in the process.

With these musical selections by John McCain, Bill Clinton, and Mitt Romney, the issue is not the intent but the undesired consequences if the public were to look further than the one-line message being conveyed. However, the question still remains; does the public actually look further than this single line of text? When played at rallies or in campaign advertisements, campaign staff members are often able to work out the timing to ensure that these later lines are not played. One might also conclude that with the number of advisors and marketing experts each campaign has, the research done says that the "line will be mightier than the whole." One other aspect that should be considered is that by choosing a song from a particular time period, a candidate focuses on a certain age group. This may be another one of those intended or unintended consequences of selecting particular one line messages.

These are just a few of the cases where musical misrepresentation can be seen. Others of note would be Obama's use of "Signed, Sealed, Delivered," which is in actuality about a cheating lover attempting to plead his way back into the heart of his girl; Obama's use of "Think," which is a call to a stray lover to think about what they are doing; both Al Gore's (and Mitt Romney's) use of the song "You Ain't Seen Nothing Yet," which describes a young man's encounter with a devil woman and the "love" she gives to him; G.H.W. Bush's use of "This Land Is Your Land" which speaks more of socialism than the pro-capitalist views of the Republican Party; and McCain's use of "Johnny B. Good," a song about an uneducated guitar player.

Location, Location, Location!

In addition to the official campaign song that candidates tend to play at every campaign stop, all modern presidential candidates have song playlists for their rallies that they use to warm up their audience.[89] Unlike their "official" campaign song, however, this music will tend to change by geographical location. This is simply another example of candidates choosing songs that voters are likely to find appealing, as their musical tastes will differ from place to place.

Thus, a song played in one location may be very popular with the crowds, but in a different location the voters may be indifferent or even find the song to be unappealing, potentially spoiling the high spirits the campaign desires to create and maintain during the rally. This change of warm-up music from location to location goes a step farther than the use of multiple songs that candidates now use as theme songs. Indeed, in those cases noted above (including Romney and McCain), the given candidate made a permanent change in his respective campaign theme song. Those examples were temporal changes, made because of a change in the campaign, such as a primary victory or a nomination—and they were songs used in multiple locations or to a nationwide audience. In this section, however, we look at two examples of songs that were used to pump up two different crowds in two separate locations. These are songs that may have little to no value in a different location, because the average listener's tastes may be dramatically different in a different place. Thus, it makes perfect sense strategically for candidates to gear the music they are playing to the specific locations in which they are campaigning.

This concept can be demonstrated by examining the 2008 presidential campaign music of John McCain. The first example we see of this is with the use of the *Rocky* theme song, "Gonna Fly Now," by Bill Conti. This song was used in 2008 by other candidates, including Hillary Clinton[90] and Mike Huckabee.[91] It was also used by Walter Mondale in 1984. The song, however, is not usually used at various places around the country; instead, candidates primarily use it in one location. Indeed, candidates will often evoke the spirit of Rocky Balboa by playing this song at rallies in the state of Pennsylvania and more specifically in the city of Philadelphia. Given that the movie *Rocky* was filmed, and has become associated with, Philadelphia, it is no surprise that McCain played the song in Pennsylvania; this is a song and theme that people living in the area can relate to. Interestingly enough, though, one journalist pointed out that the song has become a bit of an overused cliché in Philadelphia, as well as out of place in the 2008 election by McCain because the movie *Rocky*, "involves a white boxer who went toe-to-toe but did not defeat the charismatic African-American champion with a funny name."[92]

During the campaign, McCain used this song frequently in and around the Philadelphia area. For instance, this song (among others) was used at a McCain rally in York, Pennsylvania, in August 2008,[93] and McCain again made use of this piece of music when holding a rally in the Philadelphia suburbs in October of 2008.[94] Now, to be fair, John McCain used the *Rocky* theme at several campaign rallies around the country, and late in the campaign he made it his official campaign song.[95] However, McCain did not use this song at every geographical location he visited during the campaign.

Indeed, when McCain visited Tennessee, the music he used was of a different variety. In this state he invoked not Rocky Balboa, but the song "Rocky Top Tennessee."[96] The song, which is one of eight state songs for Tennessee[97] and is an official fight song for the University of Tennessee Volunteers,[98] is a tribute to the state and its people. Assuredly, it was used by the McCain campaign as a way to positively identify a sense of place. At one rally in February 2008, McCain made use of "Rocky Top Tennessee" as well as John Mellencamp's "Our Country."[99] These songs were probably used there to appeal to the working-class values and sense of pride felt by those in the crowd at a McCain rally in Tennessee. Note, however, that the place of the song is very important and was chosen strategically based on the geographical location of the rally. If McCain had played "Rocky Top" in suburban Philadelphia and the *Rocky* theme in Tennessee, the resulting reactions from the crowd would likely have been very different. In fact, during the 2000 presidential campaign, Al Gore, a native son of Tennessee, made use of "Rocky Top" in a rally near Lansing, Iowa, to a noticeably flat crowd reaction.[100] McCain's strategic use of songs demonstrates an awareness by his campaign of the shifting listeners' preferences from location to location. It also shows that campaigns spend a significant amount of time thinking about music and how it might influence voters.

YouTube Strikes!!
The Unsolicited Campaign Song

In the 2008 elections, the website YouTube.com served as a source of many unsolicited campaign songs that were written by both the general public and professional musicians alike. One song that emerged on behalf of John McCain's campaign was "Lead the Way," which was written and performed by Judd Kessler. Kessler is a lawyer from Bethesda, Maryland, who also claims to be an amateur musician; he has qualified his performances with self-deprecating humor by saying "now as I do this, I want you to imagine someone with a real voice singing it."[101] The video he posted on YouTube was quite simple, consisting of him sitting at the piano in what can be assumed to be the living room or music room of his home. The song is a patriotic anthem that asked McCain to lead the country to be stronger and silence those who doubt what the United States has become. According to the lyrics:

Verse 1:
Some people say our nation
Once great and tried and true
Is now a house divided
Into states of Red and Blue

That the world that once looked to us
As the fount of liberty
Now questions if we know the way
To stay both safe and free

Chorus:
Lead the way, lead the way, John
To the way we want to be
Lead the way, lead the way, John
To strength and unity

Verse 2:
We know you fought and suffered
Not to have a hero's day
But because you love America
And cherish freedom's flame

An America that offers
Every woman, every man
The chance to stand in dignity
And be the best they can
(Chorus)

Verse 3:
Let's bind our nation's wounds, let's
show
The doubter's near and far
That we are still Americans
And we know who we are

We honor our commitments
We venerate the law
We love our privileged country
And we work to make its flaws

We strive to live with honor
And with generosity
To the poor within our country
And those oppressed beyond the sea

We don't have all the answers
And we seek no world domain
But we <u>do</u> know how to lead the fight
For a world that's safe and sane
(Chorus)

The song did not speak about John McCain in any specific manner other than to mention his service in Vietnam. While it also spoke of lofty ideals, such as striving "to live with honor, and with generosity" to help the poor and the oppressed, it also stated that "we don't have all the answers;" although this humble point is certainly true, it is not necessarily a message that a presidential campaign normally wishes to deliver. Regardless, this is one attempt by an average citizen who was not officially affiliated with a political campaign to affect change in the elections through the use of song. The tune had modest popularity showing a total of 6,560 views on YouTube[102] while also garnering a small amount of attention through public radio and television.[103]

Barack Obama had his share of unsolicited campaign songs on YouTube as well. One that garnered a great deal of attention was "I Got a Crush on Obama." The song, lip-synced by "Obama Girl" Amber Lee Ettinger, details the model/actress/singer's desires for the candidate.[104] The song was sung by Leah Kauffman, a 21-year-old student, who wrote the lyrics with a friend, 32-year-old advertising executive Ben Relles, and the music with her producer, Rick Friedrich.[105] In addition to lip-syncing, Ettinger appeared in the Internet viral music video that was produced by BarelyPolitical.com and which generated millions of hits when posted on YouTube.[106] Before the lyrics to the song begin, the video depicted Ettinger leaving a voice message for Obama, stating "Hey B, it's me. If you're there, pick up. I was just watching you on C-SPAN. Anyway, call me back."[107] Meant to be seductive, Ettinger appeared in revealing clothing while the following lyrics were sung:

You seem to float onto the floor
Democratic Convention 2004
I never wanted anybody more
Than I want you

So I put down my Kerry sign
Knew I had to make you mine
Smart, black, and sexy, you're so fine
'Cause I've got a crush on Obama.

I cannot wait, 'til 2008
Baby you're the best candidate
I like it when you get hard
On Hillary in debate
Why don't you pick up your phone?
'Cause I've got a crush on Obama
I cannot wait, 'til 2008
Baby you're the best candidate
Of the new oval office
You'll get your head of state
I can't leave you alone
'Cause I've got a crush on Obama.

You're into border security
Let's break this border between you and me
Universal healthcare reform
It makes me warm
You tell the truth unlike the right
You can love but you can fight
You can Barack me tonight
I've got a crush on Obama.

I cannot wait, 'til 2008
Baby you're the best candidate
I like it when you get hard
On Hillary in debate
Why don't you pick up your phone?
'Cause I've got a crush on Obama
I cannot wait, 'til 2008
Baby you're the best candidate
Of the new oval office
You'll get your head of state
I can't leave you alone
'Cause I've got a crush on Obama

B to the A to the R-A-C-K-O-B-A-M-A (Barack Obama) [8 times]
'Cause I've got a crush on Obama.

The song was replete with sexual references, including "*I like it when you get hard* on Hillary in debate" and "*You'll get your head* of state" (emphasis added). The Obama campaign denied any involvement with the song,[108] and the candidate stated that it was "just one more example of the fertile imagination of the Internet."[109] That said, Ettinger's desire for Obama did not transfer to the voting booth, as she failed to vote for her favorite candidate in the 2008 Democratic primaries.[110] By 2010, Ettinger was apparently no longer enamored with the president, stating to the *New York Post*, "[i]n my opinion, I feel like he should be focusing a lot more on jobs and the economy," and "[h]e did create some jobs, but most of them were government jobs and that doesn't really help the middle class."[111]

Another well-known, unsolicited pro-Obama song in 2008 was "Yes We Can" by music artist will.i.am of the Black Eyed Peas. The song was a huge success on YouTube with 1,621,857 views and made its way into the mainstream of the campaign as well. The song took a speech that was delivered by Obama at the New Hampshire primary on January 8, 2008 (which emphasized one of his campaign slogans, "Yes We Can") and recited portion of it verbatim through both spoken and sung word with a simple guitar accompaniment. In addition to will.i.am, there were several Hollywood and sports celebrities who leant their voices and faces to the song in support of Obama's campaign, including Kareem Abdul-Jabbar, Scarlett Johansson, John Legend, and Herbie Hancock.[112] The song's composer and lead performer said of its creation, "I was captivated. . . Inspired. . . That speech made me think of Martin Luther King. . . Kennedy. . . and Lincoln. . . and all the others that have fought for what we have today. . . What America is 'supposed' to be."[113] The text taken from Obama's speech that was used in the context of the song says:

> It was a creed written into the founding documents that declared the destiny of a nation.
> Yes we can.
>
> It was whispered by slaves and abolitionists as they blazed a trail toward freedom.
> Yes we can. . . .
>
> It was sung by immigrants as they struck out from distant shores and pioneers who pushed westward against an unforgiving wilderness.
> Yes we can. . . .
>
> It was the call of workers who organized; women who reached for the ballots; a President who chose the moon as our new frontier; and a King who took us to the mountain-top and pointed the way to the Promised Land.
>
> Yes we can to justice and equality.
> (Yes we can. . .)
> Yes we can to opportunity and prosperity.
> Yes we can heal this nation.
> Yes we can repair this world.
> Yes we can.
> (Si Se Puede, Yes we can. . .)

We know the battle ahead will be long, but always remember that no matter what obstacles stand in our way, nothing can stand in the way of the power of millions of voices calling for change.

(We want change! . . .)

We have been told we cannot do this by a chorus of cynics who will only grow louder and more dissonant. We've been asked to pause for a reality check. We've been warned against offering the people of this nation false hope. But in the unlikely story that is America, there has never been anything false about hope. We want change!

(We want change! . . .)

The hopes of the little girl who goes to a crumbling school in Dillon are the same as the dreams of the boy who learns on the streets of LA; we will remember that there is something happening in America; that we are not as divided as our politics suggests; that we are one people; we are one nation; and together, we will begin the next great chapter in America's story with three words that will ring from coast to coast; from sea to shining sea - Yes. We. Can.

(Yes we can. . .)[114]

Although "Lead the Way" and "Yes We Can" were examples of positive songs that were not solicited by presidential campaigns, not all of unsolicited songs in 2008 were positive. In fact, will.i.am's "Yes We Can" was transformed into a negative song for John McCain entitled "john.he.is," which was also done by will.i.am. The song took portions of various McCain speeches and appearances at town hall events to piece together some of the more unpopular things he had said, sometimes taken out of context. The song was constructed in the same way as was the case with "Yes We Can." In fact, there were prominent celebrities who appeared in this video as well showing their opposition to the McCain campaign. The song's lyrics say:

The work that we face in our time is great
in a time of war
and the terrible sacrifices it entails
the promise of a better future is not always clear
there's gonna be other wars
I'm sorry to tell you there's gonna be other wars
there's gonna be a lot of combat wounds
and my friends it's gonna be tough
and we're gonna have a lot to do
That old Beach Boys song, Bomb Iran?
Bomb Bomb Bomb, Bomb...
I'm still convinced that withdrawal means chaos
and if you think that things are bad now
if we withdraw--you ain't seen nothing yet
was the war a good idea, worth the price in blood and treasure?
It was a good idea
President Bush talked about our staying in Iraq for 50 years

Maybe a hundred, that's fine with me
I don't think Americans are concerned if we're there for a hundred years, or a thousand years, or ten thousand years.[115]

On YouTube.com, the negative campaign song actually had far more views than the positive song will.i.am wrote for Obama. With 2,211,212 views, john.he.is had nearly 500,000 more views that its counterpart. This speaks to the effectiveness of negative campaigning and campaign ads as opposed to positive campaigning and campaign ads.[116]

Obama also had his fair share of negative songs coming from the YouTube world. Some of these include "The Audacity for Hope," the "Obama Song" (a parody of "Don't Worry Be Happy"), and "Joe the Plumber." One of the cleverer and potentially more effective of these was "The Lord Barack Obama" otherwise known as "All Hail the Messiah, Obama," or the "Obama Soviet Anthem," which used the Russian National Anthem in an attempt to pin Obama as a socialist.[117] The song, like those of will.i.am, was written in part with lines from speeches by both Barack and Michelle Obama during the campaign. Although the lines in the song were not always quoted verbatim, the concepts were clearly associated with Obama, and some were recognizable as "snafus" that had occurred on the campaign trail. The text of the song says:

All hail the messiah
Obama, Obama
The path to the new socialist motherland
Our savior, our savior
Obama, Obama
The leader more famous than Lindsay Lohan
Bow down and praise the one
Give him your money and your guns
Give us a country
That makes your wife proud
Lord Barry heal the bitter ones
White and Clinging to faith and to guns
Hope for the change of the hope of the change!

Copyright © 2008 by Glenn Beck
Used by permission of Mercury Radio Arts and Premiere Radio Networks

The song was most notably associated with, and was used by, political talk show host and Fox News contributor Glenn Beck.[118] However, the song was so popular that there are no less than six different videos that were put to this song on YouTube. The total of those top six videos, which all contain the identical song, was over 1,650,000 views.

In its own unique way, the use of YouTube has harkened back to the singing campaigns of the nineteenth century by giving these original songs a wide audience and, in some cases, widespread popularity. It has also given the average citizen a larger than average voice within political campaigns, allowing them to offer their own opinions, endorsements, or denunciations of particular candidates and the ideas they represent, which the average person has not had until recent times. Whether this increased participation by the electorate is a good thing or a bad thing remains to be seen but it is more than likely here to stay in one form or another on the Internet.

From YouTube to JibJab

The website JibJab.com has engaged in a significant amount of political satire in recent years. While some of the work done on JibJab is later posted on YouTube (whether by their permission or not), the website runs as an independent identity that allows individuals to insert themselves into a variety of ecards in parodies from *Madmen* to *Star Wars*. The website also writes original works that comment on everything from the news to the New Year to political elections. In fact, JibJab has written songs and made videos for both the 2004 and 2008 presidential campaigns. In 2004, the website did a parody of "This Land Is Your Land," featuring singers who mimicked the voices of George W. Bush and John Kerry.[119] The song was nonpartisan, with JibJab not endorsing any candidate. Instead, the website aired a laundry list of negative elements for each candidate, such as allegations that John Kerry was a "flip-flopper" and that George W. Bush could not pronounce the word "nuclear." The song achieved its comic portrayal of the candidates by having each cartoon "candidate" sing verses demeaning the other and pumping themselves up. The lyrics state:

Bush:
This land is your land, this land is my land
I'm a Texas tiger, you're a liberal wiener
I'm a great crusader, you're a Herman Munster
This land will surely vote for me

Kerry:
This land is your land, this land is my land
I'm an intellectual, you're a stupid dumbass
I'm a purple heart winner, and yes it's true, I won it thrice
This land will surely vote for me

Bush:
You have more waffles than a house of pancakes
You offer flip flops, I offer tax breaks
You're a U.N. pussy and yes it's true that I kick ass
This land will surely vote for me

Kerry:
You can't say nuclear, that really scares me
Sometimes a brain can... come in quite handy

But it's not gonna help you, because I won three purple hearts
This land will surely vote for me

Bush:
You're a liberal sissy

Kerry:
You're a right wing nut job

Bush:
You're a pink coat commie

Kerry:
You're as dumb as a doorknob

Bush:
(HEY) You got that Botox

Kerry:
But I still won three purple hearts

Both:
This land will surely vote for me

Native American: (talking)
This land was my land

People: (As Wal-Mart and several other chain stores appear in the background)
But now it's our land

Schwarzenegger:
From California

Bill Clinton: (Clinton, no pants, with a bikini girl in his arms—slapped by Hillary
To the New York Is. . . hey what'd I do??

Kerry:
From the liberal wieners

Bush:
To the right wing nut jobs

Kerry:
This land belongs

Bush:
This land belongs

Both:
This land belongs to you and me

Bush:
(YEAH) oh and Dick Cheney too!

In the 2008 election, JibJab included more than just the final two candidates who were running, having George W. Bush and Dick Cheney make a cameo appearance, as did Hillary and Bill Clinton. Based around the popular Bob Dylan song, "The Times They Are A-Changin," the JibJab team made a parody called "It's Time for Some Campaigning." The song offered a comic assessment of the major players in the 2008 election. It poked fun at the Bush presidency, depicted John McCain as a warmonger, showed Hillary Clinton as a sore loser intending to run again for the presidency in 2012, and it portrayed Barack Obama as a man whose head is in the clouds with his ideas of "Hope and Change." The text says:

Bush:
Come gather 'round, Dick, Condi, Scooter 'n Rove,
It's time to get packin; we must hit the road,
But there's war, and recession, and bad mortgage loans,

Cheney:
And our legacy needs savin'!

Bush:
So forget he's a jackass who's liberally prone,

People:
Oh, it's time for some campaignin'!

Clinton:
Old party friends, time to say au revoir,
We failed to extinguish Barack's rising star.

Bill: (Holding a cigar, sitting in boxers next to a girl in a bikini—hit by Hillary)
You were so close, my dear, but I guess no cig. . .

People: (Bill (bandaged) and Hillary together at Obama rally)
And now their tune is changin'.

Clinton:
I'll be back in four years. Heck, it ain't all that far.

People:
Oh, it's time for some campaignin'!

McCain:
Gather, conservatives, lend me a hand,
Unless you want this liberal wuss in command.
I spent years in a rat hole in North Vietnam,

Choir:
And the jihad needs containin'!

McCain:
So forget my skin cancer and swollen left gland, 'cause

People: (McCain, in hospital gown, falls over dead)
Oh, it's time for some campaignin'!

Obama: (In a Disneyesque nature scene riding a Unicorn)
Gosh, I'm so tired of divisive exchange,
And I've got one or two things to say about change.
Like the change we must change and the change we hold dear,
I really like change. Have I made myself clear?

Clinton and McCain:
So he'll talk about change 'til you're deaf in the ear,

Obama & McCain: (Obama pushes Clinton off the screen and takes her place)
Oh, it's time for some campaignin'!

People:
Citizens gather from both far and near,
For a ritual we practice every four years,
When we promise you anything you wanna hear,
To win the crown we're chasin'!

We spend billions of dollars to make our points clear,
To get you to step up and cast your vote here,
Then we spin you around and poke you in the rear,
Oh, it's time for some campaignin'!
Yes, it's time for some campaignin'!

As with the 2004 counterpart, the 2008 song was nonpartisan and allowed each candidate's caricature a chance to ridicule and poke fun at himself or herself. These songs from JibJab are the equivalent to some of those which were composed in the early twentieth century by the composers of Tin Pan Alley, such as 1912's "The Election in Jungle Town." They are nonpartisan in nature, but give a fairly representative view of the stereotypes that the public holds of each candidate, and they do so in a comical way. These songs do not lend themselves to any one candidate, but rather offer an overview of the issues at hand within a campaign in an entertaining way that will hit home with the public in the Internet age. Like some of McCain's campaign theme songs, the JibJab parodies are examples of old musical trends reemerging in 2008. (It is also important to note that the JibJab songs were designed to be used with visual media and are far more effective when viewed in their complete version on their website.)

In many ways the 2008 elections were just another step in the progressions that were started by the changes in technology of the early twentieth century. The Internet, much like radio and television before it, has led to new developments in how music is used by presidential campaigns. As we will explore in chapter eight, the Internet allows more people more opportunities to be involved in the creation and distribution of campaign music, making the World Wide Web a powerful force in campaign strategies and tactics. The question is, how will the advancement of the Internet and other new technologies change the course of campaign songs in the future? How will the technological inventions of the future affect the campaign song and the candidate's use of them on the campaign trail? Will the technologies of today lead back to the singing campaigns of the past or are they gone forever? We make our predictions in chapter eight.

Notes

1.   Christopher Willis and Beth Fouhy, "President Obama's Vice President: Announcement Expected This Week," *The Huffington Post*, August 19, 2008, accessed August 2, 2010, http://www.huffingtonpost.com/2008/08/19/barack-obamas-vicepresid_n_119783.html.

2.   Romualdo Pastor-Satorras and Alessandro Vespignani, *Evolution and Structure of the Internet: A Statistical Physics Approach* (New York: Cambridge University Press, 2004), 2-6; J.R. Okin, *The Internet Revolution: The Not-for-Dummies Guide to the History, Technology, and Use of the Internet* (Winter Harbor, ME: Ironbound Press, 2004), 53-64; Keith Sutherland, *Understanding the Internet: A Clear Guide to Internet Technologies* (Oxford: Butterworth-Heinemann, 2000), 1-2; Richard A. Spinello, *Cyberethics: Morality and Law in Cyberspace* (Sudbury, MA: Jones and Bartlett Publishers, 2006), 29-31; James Harry Green, *The Irwin Handbook of Telecommunications* (New York: McGraw-Hill, 2006), 14; Christopher Harper, *And That's the Way It Will Be: News and Information in a Digital World* (New York: New York University Press, 1998), 201.

3.   William H. Dutton, et al., "The Politics of Information and Communication Policy," in *Information and Communication Technologies: Visions and Realities*, ed. William H. Dutton (New York: Oxford University Press, 1996), 388; Herbert Kubicek and William H. Dutton, "The Social Shaping of Information Superhighways: An Introduction," in *The Social Shaping of information Superhighways: European and American Roads to the Information Society*, ed. Herbert Kubicek, William H. Dutton, and Robin Williams (New York: St. Martin's Press, 1997), 9-16; Eric C. Coll, *Telecom 101 : Telecommunications for Non-engineers* (Champlain, NY: Teracom Training Institute, 2004), 332; John Cassidy, *Dot.con: How America Lost Its Mind and Money in the Internet Era* (New York: HarperCollins, 2002), 37-39.

4. Kathleen Hall Jamieson and Paul Waldman, *The Press Effect: Politicians, Journalists, and the Stories that Shape the Political World* (New York: Oxford University Press, 2003), 48.

5. Jamieson and Waldman, *The Press Effect*, 49.

6. Jamieson and Waldman, *The Press Effect*, 49.

7. William L. Benoit, et al., *Campaign 2000: A Functional Analysis of Presidential Campaign Discourse* (Lanham, MD: Rowman & Littlefield, 2003), 190.

8. Benoit, et al., *Campaign 2000*, 191.

9. Clifford A. Jones, "Campaign Finance Reform and the Internet: Regulating Web Messages in the 2004 Election and Beyond," in *The Internet Election: Perspectives on the Web in Campaign 2004*, ed. Andrew Paul Williams and John C. Tedesco (Lanham, MD: Rowman & Littlefield, 2006), 5.

10. Jones, "Campaign Finance Reform and the Internet," 6.

11. "About," Facebook, accessed August 11, 2010, http://www.facebook.com/face book.

12. "About YouTube," YouTube, accessed August 2, 2010, http://www.youtube. com/t/about.

13. "About YouTube."

14. Jim Willis, *100 Media Moments That Changed America* (Santa Barbara, CA: Greenwood Press, 2010), 188.

15. Greg Jarboe, *YouTube and Video Marketing: An Hour a Day* (Indianapolis: Wiley, 2009), 62.

16. Jarboe, YouTube and Video Marketing, 64.

17. "2008 Presidential Candidates: Ron Paul on the Issues," On the Issues, accessed August 24, 2010, http://www.ontheissues.org/ron_paul.htm.

18. Z. Byron Wolf, "Revolution Revived! Ron Paul Survives Challenge: White House Contender Raised Millions, Sparked Debate, but Nearly Lost Day Job," *ABC News*, March 4, 2008, accessed August 24, 2010, http://abcnews.go.com/Politics/Vote 2008/story?id=4389616&page=1; Z. Byron Wolf, "Ron Paul to End Campaign, Launches New Effort: Supporters Plot Shadow Convention, More Revolution," *ABC News*, June 12, 2008, accessed August 24, 2010, http://abcnews.go.com/Politics/Vote2008/story?id= 5056019&page=1.

19. Cynthia Phillips, "Ron Paul's Rally for the Republic," Bella Online: The Voice of Women, accessed August 24, 2010, http://www.bellaonline.com/articles/art58458.asp.

20. Matt Hawes, "Freedom Celebration Videos," Campaign for Liberty, April 1, 2009, accessed August 24, 2010, http://www.campaignforliberty.com/blog.php?view= 14875.

21. Jack Doyle, "I Won't Back Down, 1989-2008," PopHistoryDig.com, March 7, 2009, accessed August 25, 2010, http://www.pophistorydig.com/?p=932.

22. John Mellencamp, *The Concert at Walter Reed* (Bloomington, IN: Author House, 2007), 13.

23. Mellencamp, *The Concert at Walter Reed*, 13.

24. John Edwards, Marion G. Crain, and Arne L. Kalleberg, ed., *Ending Poverty in America: How to Restore the American Dream* (New York: New Press, 2007).

25. Mark Curtis, *Age of Obama: A Reporter's Journey with Clinton, McCain and Obama in the Making of the President, 2008* (Ann Arbor, MI: Nimble Books, 2009), 7.

26. Nick Bunkley, "Aiming to Be the Truck of Patriots," *New York Times*, September 26, 2006, accessed August 22, 2010, http://www.nytimes.com/2006/09/26/business/ media/26adco.html?ex=1316923200&en=26bfe833a4db385f&ei=5088&partner=rssnyt& emc=rss.

27. Erin Robinson, "Star-Spangled Ads: Chevy Touts New Pickups as Distinctly American," *Autoweek*, October 5, 2006, accessed August 22, 2010, http://www.autoweek.com/apps/pbcs.dll/article?AID=/20061006/FREE/61005003/1041/rss01&rss feed=rss01.

28. Bunkley, "Aiming to Be the Truck of Patriots."

29. Brit Hume, "Some Democrats See Big Trouble Coming at the Party's Convention This Summer," *Fox News*, February 18, 2008, accessed August 22, 2010, http://www.foxnews.com/story/0,2933,331112,00.html.

30. Hume, "Some Democrats See Big Trouble."

31. Carrie Dann, "Huck: More Than a Feeling, a Surge?," *MSNBC*, October 27, 2007, accessed August 22, 2010, http://firstread.msnbc.msn.com/_news/2007/10/27/4433290-huck-more-than-a-feeling-a-surge.

32. Dann, "Huck: More Than a Feeling."

33. Dann, "Huck: More Than a Feeling."

34. Garrett M. Graff, *The First Campaign: Globalization, the Web, and the Race for the White House* (New York: Farrar, Straus, and Giroux, 2007), 251.

35. "U2 Songs on Shortlist for Hillary Clinton's Presidential Campaign," *Sawf News* (May 18, 2007), accessed February 10, 2009, http://news.sawf.org/Gossip/37329.aspx.

36. "Hillary's Song: I Won't Sing 'Unless I Win,'" Associated Press, on News-Max.com (May 17, 2007), accessed February 10, 2009, http://archive.newsmax.com/archives/ic/2007/5/17/82109.shtml.

37. Brian Cogan and Tony Kelso, *Encyclopedia of Politics, the Media, and Popular Culture* (Santa Barbara, CA: ABC-CLIO, 2009), 222-23.

38. Cogan and Kelso, *Encyclopedia of Politics*, 223.

39. Cogan and Kelso, *Encyclopedia of Politics*, 223.

40. Graff, *The First Campaign*, 251.

41. Graff, *The First Campaign*, 251.

42. "Artist Chart History—Celine Dion," *Billboard* (2008), accessed February 15, 2009, http://www.billboard.com/bbcom/retrieve_chart_history.do?model.vnuArtistId=4468&model.vnuAlbumId=1102007.

43. Rosa Brooks, "Hillary's Tone Deaf Campaign," *The Los Angeles Times* (June 22, 2007), accessed February 15, 2009, http://www.latimes.com/news/opinion/commentary/la-oe-brooks22jun22,0,667255.column?coll=la-news-comment-opinions.

44. "The Billboard Hot 100: A Little Less Conversation," *Billboard* (2008), accessed February 15, 2009, http://www.billboard.com/bbcom/esearch/chart_display.jsp?cfi=379&cfgn=Singles&cfn=The+Billboard+Hot+100&ci=3070493&cdi=8830864&cid=10%2F26%2F1968.

45. "The Billboard Hot 100: A Little Less Conversation, Elvis Presley vs JXL," *Billboard* (2008), accessed February 15, 2009, http://www.billboard.com/bbcom/esearch/chart_display.jsp?cfi=379&cfgn=Singles&cfn=The+Billboard+Hot+100&ci=3046427&cdi=7889714&cid=08%2F10%2F2002.

46. "Soundtrack Searcher: A Little Less Conversation," *The Internet Movie Database* (1990-2008), accessed February 15, 2009, http://www.imdb.com/SearchSongs?%22a%20little%20less%20conversation%22; "A Little Less Conversation," *Songfacts* (n.d.), accessed February 15, 2009, http://www.songfacts.com/detail.php?id=2001.

47. Andrea Stone, "Romney Views Maine Win as Sign of Things to Come," *USA Today* (February 4, 2008), accessed February 15, 2009, http://www.usatoday.com/news/politics/election2008/2008-02-03-romney_N.htm.

48.   "The Billboard Hot 100: You Ain't Seen Nothing Yet," *Billboard* (2008), accessed February 15, 2009, http://www.billboard.com/bbcom/esearch/chart_display.jsp?cfi=379&cfgn=Singles&cfn=The+Billboard+Hot+100&ci=3070812&cdi=8863322&cid=12%2F07%2F1974.

49.   Icon Group International Inc., Staff, *Harrying: Webster's Quotations, Facts and Phrases* (San Diego: Icon Group International, Inc., 2008), 340.

50.   Stevie Wonder, et al., "Signed, Sealed, Delivered" (Milwaukee, WI: Hal Leonard Publishing Co., 1970); Kevin Chappell, "Campaign Rhetoric Gets Rough, Racial as South Carolina Primary Nears," *Jet*, January 28, 2008, 8.

51.   Joel Whitburn, *The Billboard Book of Top 40 Hits* (New York: Billboard Books, 2004), 687.

52.   Paul Farhi, "Candidates' Tunes Hit a Few Sour Notes: Lyrics in Campaign Theme Songs Can Be Hilariously Off-Key," *The Washington Post*. January 17, 2008, accessed August 24, 2010, http://www.washingtonpost.com/wpdyn/content/article/2008/01/16/AR2008011604152.html; Martin Halliwell, "Contemporary American Culture," in *American Thought and Culture in the 21st Century*, ed.Martin Halliwell and Catherine Morley (Edinburgh, Scotland, UK: Edinburgh University Press, 2008), 226.

53.   "Highlights of Blacks at the Democratic National Convention," *Jet*, September 16, 1996, 16.

54.   Joan Potter, *African American Firsts: Famous Little-Known and Unsung Triumphs of Blacks* (New York: Dafina Books, 2009), 288.

55.   Douglas Craig, "Bruce Springsteen," in *Culture Wars: An Encyclopedia of Issues, Voices, and Viewpoints*, ed. Roger Chapman (Armonk, NY: M.E. Sharp, 2010), 532.

56.   Halliwell, "Contemporary American Culture," 226.

57.   Kate Snow and Eloise Harper, "Clinton Concedes Democratic Nomination; Obama Leads Party in Fall," *ABC News*, June 7, 2008, accessed August 23, 2010, http://abcnews.go.com/Politics/Vote2008/story?id=5020581&page=1.

58.   Jeff Zeleny, "Working Together, Obama and Clinton Try to Show Unity," *New York Times*, June 28, 2008, accessed August 23, 2010, http://www.nytimes.com/2008/06/28/us/politics/28unity.html.

59.   Kevin Chappell and Sylvester Monroe, "Obama and Clinton Unite for Victory in November," *Jet*, July 28, 2008, 8.

60.   Chris Willman, "'Only in America' Could Obama Borrow the GOP's Favorite Brooks and Dunn Song," *Entertainment Weekly*, accessed August 3, 2010, http://popwatch.ew.com/2008/08/29/only-in-america/.

61.   Chris Willman, *Rednecks &Bluenecks: The Politics of Country Music* (New York: Norton, 2005), 71.

62.   Mario Tarradell, "Country Duo Brooks & Dunn Respond to Barack Obama Using Their Song During Democratic Convention," *Dallas News*, accessed August 11, 2010, http://musicblog.dallasnews.com/archives/2008/08/country-duo-brooks-dunn-respon.html.

63.   Brent Schlender, "Apple's 21st-Century Walkman CEO Steve Jobs Thinks He Has Something Pretty Nifty," *Fortune*, November 12, 2001, accessed August 23, 2010, http://money.cnn.com/magazines/fortune/fortune_archive/2001/11/12/313342/index.htm.

64.   Peter Wilkinson, "Bush Bares Soul with 'iPod One,'" *CNN*, April 13, 2005, accessed August 23, 2010, http://www.cnn.com/2005/SHOWBIZ/Music/04/12/bush.ipod/.

65.   "Inside Barack Obama's iPod," *Rolling Stone*, June 25, 2008, accessed August 23, 2010, http://www.rollingstone.com/music/news/13511/73040.

66.   *Rolling Stone*, "Inside Barack Obama's iPod."

67.   Angela Balakrishnan, "Presidential Playlist: Obama Opens up His iPod," *The Guardian*, June 25, 2008, accessed August 23, 2010, http://www.guardian.co.uk/world/2008/jun/25/barackobama.uselections2008.

68.   Geoffrey Gardner, "Obama's iPod Playlist Revealed," *National Public Radio*, June 26, 2008, accessed August 23, 2010, http://www.npr.org/blogs/newsandviews/2008/06/obamas_ipod_secrets_revealed.html.

69.   *Rolling Stone*, "Inside Barack Obama's iPod."

70.   Nekesa Mumbi Moody, "Kanye Joins All-Star Lineup for Obama CD," *USA Today* (September 22, 2008), accessed May 26, 2011, http://www.usatoday.com/life/music/news/2008-09-19-obama-soundtrack_N.htm.

71.   "The Living Room Candidate: Presidential Campaign Commercials 1952-2008," Museum of the Moving Image, accessed August 23, 2010, http://www.livingroom candidate.org/.

72.   Isaac Mass, "Raisin' McCain: Music to My Ears," *The Boston Globe* (September 5, 2008), accessed February 15, 2009, http://www.boston.com/news/politics/mass voices/2008/09/raisin_mccain_music_to_my_ears.html.

73.   Chuck Berry, "Johnny B. Goode," in *Chuck Berry*, by Chuck Berry (Milwaukee, WI: Hal Leonard Corporation, 1986).

74.   Berry, "Johnny B Goode."

75.   Dave Marsh, *The Heart of Rock and Soul: The 1001 Greatest Singles Ever Made* (New York, Plume, 1989), 2-3.

76.   Mass, "Raisin' McCain: Music to My Ears."

77.   Robert Dougherty, "Hank Williams Jr. Sings of 'McCain-Palin Tradition' at Rally." *Associated Content* (October 14, 2008), accessed February 18, 2009, http://www.associatedcontent.com/article/1109933/hank_williams_jr_sings_of_mccainpalin.html.

78.   Dougherty, "Hank Williams Jr. Sings."

79.   Chet Flippo, "Nashville Skyline: Presidential Politics Call on Country," *CMT News* (April 26, 2007), accessed June 10, 2011, http://www.cmt.com/news/nashville-skyline/1558207/nashville-skyline-presidential-politics-call-on-country.jhtml.

80.   "The Conservative Evolution of Country Music," *All Things Considered* (February 18, 2007), accessed February 21, 2009, http://www.npr.org/templates/story/story.php?storyId=7484160.

81.   Dean Goodman, "Rock Group Heart Says 'Barracuda' Use Is Fishy," *Reuters*, September 5, 2008, accessed August 23, 2010, http://www.reuters.com/article/idUSN 0451966120080905?feedType=RSS&feedName=entertainmentNews.

82.   Jocelyn Vena, "McCain-Palin Campaign Continues Playing Heart's 'Barracuda,' Despite Band's Protest," *MTV*, September 9, 2008, accessed August 23, 2010, http://www.mtv.com/news/articles/1594443/mccain-palin-still-using-heartsbarracuda.jhtml.

83.   Goodman, "Rock Group Heart Says."

84.   Although, contrary to this theory, Canadian Prime Minister Stephen Harper has publicly claimed that AC/DC's "Thunderstruck" is his favorite song! *See* Allison Dunfield, "Lighter Side: C'est What?," *Globe and Mail* (June 25, 2004), accessed February 23, 2009, http://www.theglobeandmail.com/servlet/story/RTGAM.20040520.wcest whatele0518/BNStory/specialDecision2004/.

85.   Bob, Brunning, *Rumours and Lies: The Fleetwood Mac Story* (London: Omnibus Press, 2004), 106-115; Marty Adelson, trans., "Don't Stop," The Penguin Lyric Interpretations, accessed August 11, 2010, http://www.fleetwoodmac.net/penguin/interpretations/d/dontstop.htm.

86.   Brunning, *Rumours and Lies*, 207.

87.   *See* Benjamin R. Barber, *The Truth of Power: Intellectual Affairs in the Clinton White House* (New York: Columbia University Press, 2001), 55; Rachel L. Holloway, "Political Conventions of 2004: A Study in Character and Contrast," in *The 2004 Presidential Campaign: A Communication Perspective*, ed. Robert E. Denton Jr. (Lanham, MD: Roman & Littlefield, 2005), 34.

88.   *2008 Republican Platform* (n.d.), The Committee on Arrangements for the 2008 Republican National Convention, accessed February 27, 2009, http://platform.gop.com/
2008Platform.pdf: 45.

89.   Margaret Talev, "Attending Obama Rally? Study the Music," *The Charlotte Observer* (November 3, 2008), accessed March 5, 2009, http://www.charlotteobserver.com/breaking/story/296966.html.

90.   Alex Spillius, "Hillary Clinton Edges Lead Over Barack Obama as Pennsylvania Votes," *Telegraph* (April 22, 2008), accessed March 9, 2009, http://www.telegraph.co.uk/news/1897974/Hillary-Clinton-edges-lead-over-Barack-Obama-as-Pennsylvania-votes.html.

91.   Alex Daniels, "At Session, Huckabee Elephant in the Room Teachers-Union Talk First by a GOP Hopeful," *Arkansas Online* (July 6, 2007), accessed March 9, 2009, http://www2.arkansasonline.com/news/2007/jul/06/session-huckabee-elephant-room/.

92.   Dave Pidgeon, "LIVE: McCain visits Philadelphia," *The Intelligencer Journal* (June 11, 2008), accessed March 9, 2009, http://blogs.lancasteronline.com/birdseyeview/2008/06/11/live-mccain-visits-philadelphia/

93.   Robert Stacey McCain, "All American Maverick," *The American Spectator* (August 13, 2008), accessed March 3, 2009, http://spectator.org/archives/2008/08/13/all-american-maverick.

94.   Brad Segall, "Sen. John McCain Campaigns in Philadelphia Suburbs," *KYW Newsradio* (October 14, 2008), accessed March 3, 2009, http://www.kyw1060.com/pages/3135143.php?contentType=4&contentId=2896584.

95.   David Gardner, "'Rocky McCain' vows to fight back: 'I believe I'm going to win it'," *The Daily Mail* (October 27, 2008), accessed March 3, 2009, http://www.dailymail.
co.uk/news/worldnews/article-1080714/Rocky-McCain-vows-fight-I-believe-Im-going-win-it.html.

96.   Juliet Eilperin, "McCain Picks Up John Edwards's Song," *The Washington Post* (February 2, 2008), accessed March 4, 2009, http://voices.washingtonpost.com/44/2008/02/02/mccain_picks_up_john_edwardss.html.

97.   "State Songs," (n.d.), State of Tennessee, accessed March 4, 2009, http://www.tennesseeanytime.org/homework/songs.html.

98.   "Songs of Tennessee," (n.d.), University of Tennessee, accessed March 4, 2009, http://www.utk.edu/athletics/tn_songs.shtml.

99.   Eilperin, "McCain Picks Up John Edwards's Song."

100.   Mark Coatney, "Gore on the River: Sleepless in La Crosse," *Time* (August 20, 2000), accessed March 4, 2009, http://www.time.com/time/nation/article/0,8599,52930,00.html.

101.   Judd Kessler, "Lead the Way—A Song for John McCain," YouTube, accessed August 3, 2010, http://www.youtube.com/watch?v=U4fdRR8VjHw.

102.   Kessler. These viewership numbers reflect the views recorded by the authors in August 2010. However, it is reasonable to expect that these numbers are approximately what they would have been on election day 2008. The viewership numbers for all YouTube.com videos in this section were as of August 2010.

103.   Judd Kessler, correspondence with author, April 14, 2011.

104.   Jake Tapper, "Music Video Has a 'Crush on Obama': Risqué YouTube Song Takes Obama Campaign by Surprise," *ABC News*, June 13, 2007, accessed August 29, 2010, http://abcnews.go.com/Politics/Story?id=3275802&page=1.

105.   Tapper, "Music Video Has a 'Crush on Obama.'"

106.   "Best of Obama Girl: Crush on Obama," BarelyPolitical.com, YouTube (June 13, 2007), accessed August 29, 2010, http://www.youtube.com/watch?v=wKsoXHYICqU.

107.   "Best of Obama Girl: Crush on Obama."

108.   Kate Phillips, "2008: Obama Girl and More," *The New York Times*, June 13, 2007, accessed August 29, 2010, http://thecaucus.blogs.nytimes.com/2007/06/13/2008-obama-girl-and-more/.

109.   Neil McCormick, "Barack Obama's 'Yes We Can' video," *The Telegraph*, February 14, 2008, accessed August 29, 2010, http://www.telegraph.co.uk/culture/music/3671190/Barack-Obamas-Yes-We-Can-video.html.

110.   Jacob Soboroff, "Obama Girl Didn't Vote? No She Didn't!" *The Huffington Post*, April 17, 2008, accessed August 29, 2010, http://www.huffingtonpost.com/jacob-soboroff/obama-girl-didnt-vote-no_b_97208.html.

111.   Jennifer Fermino, "'Obama Girl' now falling out of love," *The New York Post*, January 27, 2010, accessed August 29, 2010, http://www.nypost.com/p/news/national/obama_girl_now_falling_out_of_love_20IY02jVpUMvC0IQBLXvEI.

112.   Will.i.am, "Yes We Can," YouTube, accessed August 4, 2010, http://www.youtube.com/watch?v=SsV2O4fCgjk.

113.   Will.i.am, "Why I Recorded *Yes We Can*," *The Huffington Post*, February 3, 2008, accessed August 4, 2010, http://www.huffingtonpost.com/william/why-i-recorded-yes-we-can_b_84655.html.

114.   Select portions from "Remarks of Senator Obama After New Hampshire Primary," RE:Obama.com—The Important Speeches of Barack Obama, accessed June 23, 2011, http://www.reobama.com/SpeechesJan0808.htm.

115.   "john.he.is," U.S Labor Against the War, accessed August 4, 2010, http://www.uslaboragainstwar.org/article.php?id=15378.

116.   Martin P. Wattenberg and Craig Leonard Brains, "Negative Campaign Advertising: Mobilizer or Demobilizer," eScholarship at the University of California, accessed August 11, 2010, http://escholarship.org/uc/item/7gf3q1w1#page-2.

117.   Glenn Beck, O' Hail the Messiah Lord Obama," YouTube, accessed August 4, 2010, http://www.youtube.com/watch?v=WEwRB_gOUDg&feature=related.

118.   Glenn Beck, "Glenn Beck: Obama Soviet Anthem," GlennBeck.com, accessed August 11, 2010, http://www.glennbeck.com/content/articles/article/198/14148/.

119.   Evan Spiridellis and Gregg Spiridellis, "This Land," JibJab Media Inc., accessed August 4, 2010, http://sendables.jibjab.com/originals/this_land.

~ 8 ~

Campaign Music of the Past, Present, and Future

Where We've Been. . .

We began this book with a simple premise: since music has prehistoric roots and has throughout history been shown to have a great effect on us, it should come as no surprise that political candidates attempt to use music as a way to influence the electorate. Indeed, the history of the world is filled with artists using music to express political messages. Governments have also frequently made use of music, which in modern times has manifested itself for patriotic purposes, such as in national anthems and support for war, as well as for more sinister reasons, such as promoting genocide. That governments around the globe have attempted to censor songs in many different contexts is only more evidence of music's influence on us and the perceived political power of song.

Our account of music as used in presidential campaigns began with George Washington's election in 1789. The earliest "campaign" songs were really tributes to the candidates. However, as political parties quickly developed in the 1790s and early 1800s, campaign theme songs also rapidly evolved. Although in the first few decades after the Constitution the lyrics in these songs were still more about promoting America than the candidates, these songs continued progressing, becoming more specific and referring more often to the candidates' names. Then, during the seminal campaign of 1840, "Tippecanoe and Tyler Too" became the most important early campaign song. It spoke specifically about the candidates, and it marked the beginning of a period when song use became much more extensive and important within political campaigns. These changes can be attributed to multiple factors. First among these was the abolition of property qualifications to vote, which expanded the franchise to all white men. Second, the King Caucus ended. This, in turn, led to candidates using mass campaign techniques. Third, the reemergence of the two-party system caused more competition for voters, making the use of easier-to-remember songs and the insertion of campaign slogans into songs all the more important. Having two viable parties also produced a recurrence of more negative campaigning, which also manifested itself in song. When voting rights were expanded to African American men via the Fifteenth Amendment, presidential candidates' campaign songs stopped using lyrics with racial epithets that had become common before, during, and shortly after the Civil War.

The middle of the nineteenth century saw many other changes with respect to campaign music. The rapid technological advancements in the printing press created a rise in the use of more readily available song books. By the end of the century, the problem of retrofitting new lyrics to old melodies was ameliorated by the composition of completely new campaign songs by Tin Pan Alley. Not only did these arrangements have a musical style that appealed to newer and younger voters, they also gave rise to a completely new type of campaign music—the nonpartisan campaign song.

Moving into the twentieth century, campaign music became even more technologically driven. Tin Pan Alley composers rose and fell in terms of influence before being eclipsed by the power of radio and, later, television. As campaigns began using the mass media more, they adopted more of a commercial advertising model of marketing candidates to voters. Along with this, campaigns began exploiting the newly created phenomenon of celebrity, which was exacerbated by radio and television. Wholesale political campaigns led to songs that mentioned candidates' names even more, as there was less and less of a personal connection to the voter when compared to the earlier nineteenth century's retail-oriented campaigns. As Tin Pan Alley's influence faded, campaign songs displayed fewer and fewer new lyrics, instead adopting more and more of the original lyrics of a "canned" song. At the same time, the ratification of the Nineteenth Amendment, which guaranteed women the right to vote, led to subtle changes in campaign song lyrics. Finally, music moved on to the medium of television in the 1950s. At first, this meant strong, newly written campaign songs such as "I Like Ike" and "I Love the Gov." Over time, however, music in television advertisements evolved into background music that was deemphasized in favor of a more overpowering narration.

During the middle to late twentieth century, music in presidential campaigns transitioned to pop songs, which were used, lyric-for-lyric and note-for-note by the candidates. Although this trend began slowly with "Happy Days Are Here Again" in the 1930s, it then lay dormant for decades until the 1970s and 1980s. Several factors caused this change. First, the voting age was lowered from 21 to 18, necessitating the use of music that would appeal to younger voters. Second, the proven power of 1960s civil rights and Vietnam War protest music demonstrated to politicians the political influence of music. As baby boomers, who grew up on this music, came of age politically, music that appealed to them began to be used more and more. Also, politicians chose music that would be found appealing to the New Deal coalition, a group that had become accustomed to the use of popular music by their idol, Franklin Roosevelt. Furthermore, popular music was already tested and found to be safe among the general public, making it a logical choice for politicians trying to win the most voters. Finally, the celebrity-induced trend of candidates trying to associate themselves with a popular artist or song was taken to new heights during this period.

As the twentieth century progressed toward its end, music in campaigns continued to evolve, often due to a multitude of outside factors. Economic changes in the music industry as well as the birth of MTV helped further the focus on celebrity in popular music. Reflecting this, candidates desired even more to use preexisting songs, and they chose them for their message-laden hook. Also, as attention spans seemed to be shortening, the trend of briefer sound bites found its way into campaign music, and short clips of songs, instead of entire songs, were frequently played for live audiences and television viewers. While this use of music was in line with greater media trends, it also put more pressure on campaigns to find pre-packaged songs that were comprehensive enough to be useful to a candidate's message.

During this era, Bill Clinton took the use of music to a new level. Not only in 1992 did he use "Don't Stop," a song with multigenerational appeal that also expressed themes central to his campaign; in addition, Clinton appeared on talk shows and played his saxophone, which made use of music in a new way by a presidential candidate. This same election also saw a complete flop in campaign music with Ross Perot's "Crazy," a song that was likely amusing to the candidate and his core supporters but probably drew him no new supporters. As the century closed, candidates tried to take pop music and celebrity to the next degree, often seeking out musicians of particular views, in order to use their music or receive an explicit or implied endorsement. Of course, the natural outgrowth of this was that some artists denied candidates the use of their music if they disagreed ideologically with the candidate.

By the year 2000, the proliferation of pop songs in presidential campaigns led politicians to make use of multiple official campaign songs. That year, George W. Bush and Al Gore each used multiple pop songs, something which was a rarity in the pop music era prior to that election. Different songs began to be used by each candidate in primaries as compared to only the general election; this was done, in part, to appeal to the different types of voters who show up in each of these two types of contests. By this time, on the other hand, while parodied songs still existed, they had taken a backseat to the popular songs that campaigns were using en masse.

The most recent presidential election in 2008 saw the rise of the Internet, the cell phone, and the iPod in musical campaigning. Many candidates in the primaries used multiple songs that had already proved effective and that were easy to play repeatedly via CD or online. Candidates such as John Edwards and Hillary Clinton used songs that had recently been employed in high-profile commercial advertisements. Clinton, like her husband 16 years earlier, blazed a new musical campaign trail; in Hillary's case, this was allowing her supporters to vote for her campaign song both online and by text message. Barack Obama revealed to the public his musical "allegiances" by describing the songs and artists on his iPod. John McCain, perhaps seeing the rise of songs with new lyrics online, brought back the old trend of candidates using preexisting songs where artists inserted new lyrics specific to the candidate.

The 2008 election also saw campaigns lose a bit of control. Independent users online produced their own music, which varied from positive to negative to nonpartisan. Websites such as YouTube.com allowed average citizens to take part in the political process in this way by providing a platform to distribute their original musical thoughts on each candidate to the general public. Websites like JibJab.com, on the other hand, offered the public a nonpartisan look at the candidates through satirical parodies based on commonly known songs presented with accompanying animation.

. . . And Where We're Going

As much as technology has been a driving force of music in past presidential campaigns, it will continue to do so in the future. For the foreseeable future, including 2012 and beyond, the Internet and cellular technologies will be the driving forces behind campaign music and candidates' use of musical celebrities. As more and more people get their news about candidates and elections from the Internet, campaigns will continue to use this medium to communicate their musical messages to the voters. This is especially true with the growth of smart phones, which allow the user to keep constantly connected to the World Wide Web. One can expect more innovative use of this interactive medium, as Hillary Clinton did with song voting in 2008. Expect other technologies to be incorporated too, as Barack Obama did by describing the musical contents of his iPod.

The Internet, as it currently stands, is a highly democratized medium. Indeed, with so many websites used by so many people, the Internet is a beast that remains largely untamed by any one candidate or any one government. It is true that some consolidation may be under way with more and more Internet traffic going through a select number of websites, such as Facebook.com, Twitter.com, and Wikipedia.com. However, the Internet as a whole remains free to grow and change as the wants of the people change. This fact is proven by simply looking at the three websites above and noting that five years before the writing of this book they either did not exist or were largely unknown. The birth and death of websites on the Internet is a testament to the medium's constantly changing nature in ways that are not true for either television or radio.

The authors expect the Internet to stay relatively wide open for the foreseeable future. This will mean more unsolicited campaign songs produced by independent sources that are uncontrolled by the candidates themselves. As Barack Obama noted about Obama Girl's "I Got a Crush on Obama," "more stuff like this will be popping up all the time."[1] The authors could not agree more. In some ways, this is unregulated free speech at its best; in another sense, it is unfortunate for the candidates themselves, who will find it more difficult to communicate their own musical message to the electorate. In addition, candidates will have more than the traditional media outlets scrutinizing their speeches and town hall meetings, taking advantage of misstatements as could be seen with works like will.i.am's "john.he.is" as well as Glenn Beck's "The Lord Barack Obama." This is not always a negative for a campaign, however, as some will chose to focus on the positive messages that come from these events as could be seen with will.i.am's "Yes We Can."

The use of the Internet in the spreading of these unsolicited campaign songs may also lead to a trend from the past coming to fruition again in the campaigns of the future. The idea of the public submitting songs to campaigns to be considered for use by the campaign as either warm-up music or one of the main songs is not out of the question. This could happen formally with campaigns setting up a location for interested constituents to submit their works or, perhaps campaign staffers may now be asked to comb through the hundreds of songs written and placed on YouTube and other such sites to determine which song(s) may be appropriate for such use. Furthermore, it could also lead to a new version of Hillary Clinton's concept of having the public vote on a song for the campaign. Only now instead of voting on commercial songs, a candidate may use songs solicited from the public or use selected unsolicited songs from the web and allow the public to vote on those songs, thus getting people involved in two ways in the song selection process.

Whether or not music online will eventually fade into the position it now resides on television remains to be seen. While the Internet of the next few election cycles appears to still allow music to flourish in the forefront, the day may come when campaign music online is relegated to the same background position that it now largely resides in on radio and television. If the Internet truly stays democratized, this suffocating trend is unlikely to progress on the medium in the same way it has on the radio and television, however. In fact, there may be a growth in music through a quasi-revival of the "singing" campaigns of the nineteenth century through this technology. If that happens, there will be an important difference, though—instead of people singing the music as they did years before, in the future they would share and see the music on sites like YouTube and then spread these songs to their friends and acquaintances through social networking sites like Facebook and MySpace.

The other aspect that cannot be overlooked is that eventually "the next big thing" in media development will come to pass. The only technological constant in the use of campaign music has been change, and that campaign music adapts and finds its place within each new medium as it develops. The authors cannot possibly predict what these new media will be, just as few could have predicted the Internet in the 1950s, the television in the 1910s, or the radio in the 1860s.

However, it is clear that new media will continue to develop, and when they do, campaign music will also evolve with them.

The nearly century-long trend of celebrity fetishism by our politicians will also likely continue. The anti-celebrity advertisement run by the McCain campaign about Obama notwithstanding, the appeal to celebrity will remain a part of our politics as long as celebrities are celebrated on all of our major media. Indeed, in the same campaign where McCain was decrying Obama's celebrity status and trying to associate Obama with the cult of celebrity, McCain himself heavily relied upon country music celebrities John Rich and Hank Williams, Jr. This was a smart choice by McCain, just as it has been by other politicians who have made use of musical celebrities.

Celebrities will also continue to fight back against candidates who would use their songs without permission in order to appeal to a segment of the population or to secure an explicit or implied endorsement. This occurred in 2011 in anticipation of the 2012 Republican primary elections when candidate Michele Bachmann used Tom Petty's "American Girl" and Katrina & the Wave's "Walking on Sunshine." Both artists quickly insisted that Bachmann stop using their music. While Tom Petty's management group simply sent Bachmann a cease-and-desist letter, [2] Katrina & the Waves went one step further by issuing a statement saying, "Katrina & the Waves would like it to be known that they do not endorse the use of 'Walking On Sunshine' by Michele Bachmann and have instructed their lawyers accordingly."[3] As long as candidates continue to use "canned" music in the form of popular music as their warm-up and campaign songs, artist will continue to fight to make sure their music is only used by those who share the same political beliefs.

American political development is another factor that has always affected campaign music. Over the centuries, changes in political party structure and in the number of people who could vote led to changes in musical selections. This is necessary, as any music that is used needs to be appealing to the voters if it is to be effective.

Expansion of the electorate into new areas is unlikely in the United States, as the country currently has nearly universal suffrage. Yet, if the franchise is further extended to felons (in many states one cannot vote if currently serving time for a felony or if on probation or parole for a felony), it may change what type of music is used. Likewise, if the voting age is ever lowered to, say, sixteen years of age, one would expect campaigns to use marketing information to seek out music that would appeal to those new voters granted the franchise. As these extensions of the vote are unlikely, we will not spend further time exploring them here.

What is inevitable, however, is a changing of voting demographics in the United States. As the population changes, so will the songs that candidates need to use. In the near future, there are two trends that are of interest. First, the average age of the American citizen will increase as the baby boomers move into retirement. As this happens, one can expect politicians to continue to choose music that will appeal to this generation, given how large of a segment of the population they are. Whether baby boomers' music preferences change as they age, or if they continue to have a nostalgic liking for classic rock and adult contemporary, you can bet that politicians will reflect these preferences in their musical choices.

Second, the growing Latino population in the United States will draw the attention of more candidates and their song selectors. This has already begun to occur in other forms of campaigning in 2004 and 2008, as major party candidates in these elections resorted to producing a small number of Spanish language advertisements. As the number of Latino voters continues to grow at relatively high rates, one can expect politicians to choose songs that they think will be appealing to this group of voters too. This may mean choosing more songs from Latino artists, making use of Spanish language songs, or both. If anything, changing demographics such as this will mean the use of more and more songs within each political campaign, as candidates attempt to appeal to the wide variety of voters and change music as they move from rally to rally to be in tune with these demographics. Thus, the proliferation of official campaign songs that has taken place since 2000 is likely to continue.

Besides celebrities, changing demographics, and technological changes, there is no question that the content of the music, both in terms of the instrumentation and the lyrics, will continue to matter. Music that has a strong beat with a quick, uplifting tempo, will be used at a higher rate than songs that are slower as these songs do far less to create excitement around the candidate and their campaign. This is why classic rock songs tend to work themselves into many modern campaigns, while sentimental love songs and songs of regret tend not to do so. "Don't Stop," "You Ain't Seen Nothin' Yet," and "A Little Less Conversation" exemplify music that makes the listener want to stand up and move. Patsy Cline's "Crazy" does much less to inspire one to action. Furthermore, songs that combine a catchy hook with lyrics containing the pivotal message will be sought after and used by campaigns as it makes the song easy to remember and, consequently, easy to associate with the candidate when heard at later times away from a rally (such as bill Clinton's use of "Don't Stop," which will forever have association with him and his campaign/presidency).

Besides the music, the lyrics of songs will continue to be a consideration. This is why country songs are frequently used, as they express a patriotic message. Other popular songs that express themes of thinking about the future or making things better are other obvious lyrical choices. However, it is unlikely that one will see campaigns using Green Day's "American Idiot" or Rage Against the Machine's "Killing in the Name" as candidate song choices. Even if the rhythm and musical medley of these songs might be catchy, their lyrics send messages that most presidential candidates would find offensive or at the very least would be open to great misinterpretation by listeners.

A final consideration in song choice will be the use of marketing technology. This ties back to the Internet as well as credit card purchases and polling. As data is collected on what people buy and which Internet websites they visit, campaigns will be increasingly likely to craft musical messages that appeal to different groups of voters. For instance, if data reveals that people with certain political ideologies or living in certain areas like a type of music, campaigns will use that information to play more appealing music to those groups of people. This is already done through anecdotal means, such as when candidates use country music to appeal to moderate to conservative voters, or when candidates use "Gonna Fly Now" when campaigning in Philadelphia. The use of music in this way will become ever more targeted. Marketing research, and the data generated by it on both individuals and aggregated groups, will help candidates make song choices because they will have a better idea not only of what the public as a whole likes, but also what people in certain areas or who possess certain demographic characteristics prefer. Further, it will not just be the music used in and by the campaign, but the musical tastes of the candidate that are put to the test as well. Indeed, candidates will continue to disclose the playlists of their iPods, or other musical devices, to attract voters from various areas of the political spectrum and prove they are eclectic yet mainstream in their tastes. Or they may publically profess their affinity for music by artists (some controversial) who are not normally associated with their political point of view, such as Republican Primary hopeful Tim Pawlenty who spoke of how he likes certain songs by Lady Gaga including "Bad Romance" and "Born This Way."[4] In fact, questions regarding 2012 Republican candidates' musical tastes have surfaced as early as a debate held in June of 2011.[5]

What impending elections truly hold cannot be seen. What seems to be true is that music will have a place in the world of presidential campaigning, as it will always find a way to adapt to the needs of candidates and their campaigns. Thus, if we are to adhere to the command that we "don't stop thinking about tomorrow," we will be thinking about campaign songs and campaigning musicians for some time to come.

Notes

1.   Neil McCormick, "Barack Obama's 'Yes We Can' video," *The Telegraph*, February 14, 2008, accessed August 29, 2010, http://www.telegraph.co.uk/culture/music/3671190/Barack-Obamas-Yes-We-Can-video.html.

2.   Andy Greene, "Tom Petty to Michele Bachmann: Quit Playing 'American Girl,'" *Rolling Stone*, June 28, 2011, accessed June 30, 2011, http://www.rollingstone.com/music/news/tom-petty-tells-michele-bachmann-to-stop-playing-american-girl-20110628.

3.   Andy Greene, "Katrina and the Waves Join Tom Petty's Fight Against Michele Bachmann," *Rolling Stone*, June 29, 2011, accessed June 30, 2011, http://www.rollingstone.com/politics/news/katrina-and-the-waves-join-tom-pettys-fight-against-michele-bachmann-20110629.

4.   Catalina Camia, "Tim Pawlenty Likes Lady Gaga," *USA Today*, July 7, 2011, accessed July 15, 2011, http://content.usatoday.com/communities/onpolitics/post/2011/07/lady-gaga-tim-pawlenty-music-born-this-way-/1?csp=34news.

5.   Emmanuel Parisse, "Tea Party Diva Bachmann Dazzles at US Debate," Yahoo! News, June 14, 2011, accessed June 30, 2011, http://old.news.yahoo.com/s/afp/2011061 4/ts_alt_afp/usvote2012republicansbachmann.

Bibliography

4President Corporation. "Dwight D. Eisenhower TV Ad I Like Ike: 60 1952." Accessed July 14, 2010. http://tv.4president.us/tv1952.htm.

Adegbite, Ademola. "The Concept of Sound in Traditional African Religious Music." *Journal of Black Studies* 22, No. 1 (September 1991): 45-54.

Adelson, Marty, trans. "Don't Stop." The Penguin Lyric Interpretations. Accessed August 11, 2010. http://www.fleetwoodmac.net/penguin/interpretations/d/dontstop.htm.

Allen Richard V. and Chuck Downs. "Concert without Strings." *New York Times*, October 28, 2007. Accessed June 22, 2010.http://www.nytimes.com/2007/10/28/opinion/28allen.html?scp=14&sq=music%20censorship%20north%20korea&st=cse.

Ankeny, Jason. "Rage Against the Machine Bio." Vh1.com. Accessed July 31, 2010. http://www.vh1.com/artists/az/rage_against_the_machine/bio.jhtml.

Anonymous. "Agree Radio Raises Plane of Politics: Senators Moses and Harrison in Debate Find an Issue on Which They Are in Accord." *The New York Times*, October 25, 1928.

———. *A Miniature of Martin Van Buren*. S.I.: s.n., 1840.

———. "The Billboard Hot 100 for the Week Ending September 27," *The Billboard*, September 21, 1959.

———. "Bullet Proof (The Hero Who Never Lost a Battle)." *Albany Argus*, May 18, 1840.

———. *Cleveland and Hendricks Campaign Songster*. Cincinnati, OH: John Church & Co., 1884.

———. *Democratic Campaign Songster No. 1*. Cincinnati, OH: American Publishing House, 1860.

———. "Empire Club Song." In *The Campaign Democrat*. Louisville, KY: John C. Noble, July 30, 1856.

———, "God Save Great Washington." *Philadelphia Continental Journal*, April 7, 1786.

———. "GOP Convention Entertainment Sets Stage." *USA Today*. Accessed August 1, 2010. http://www.usatoday.com/news/politicselections/nation/president/2004-08-23-gop-entertainment_x.htm?csp=34.

———. "Highlights of Blacks at the Democratic National Convention." *Jet*, September 16, 1996.

———. "Hillary's Song: I Won't Sing 'Unless I Win.'" Associated Press. On News-Max.com (May 17, 2007). Accessed February 10, 2009. http://archive.newsmax.com/archives/ic/2007/5/17/82109.shtml.

———. "Hot 100." Billboard, June 18, 1966.

———. "Hot 100." Billboard, April 1, 1967.

———. "Hot 100." Billboard, March 23, 1968.

———. "Inside Barack Obama's iPod." *Rolling Stone*, June 25, 2008. Accessed August 23, 2010. http://www.rollingstone.com/music/news/13511/73040.

———. "Landon Version of 'Oh, Susannah' Holds Constitution is "Good Enough for Me.'" New York Times, June 8, 1936.

———. "Little Wat Ye Wha's A-Comin'." *Cincinnati Gazette*, July 30, 1828.

———. "Teacher's Pet." *Cheers*, season 3, episode 16. Directed by James Burrows. Original air date January 31, 1985.

———. "The Billboard Hot 100: A Little Less Conversation." *Billboard* (2008). Accessed February 15, 2009. http://www.billboard.com/bbcom/esearch/chart_display.jsp?cfi=379&cfgn=Singles&cfn=The+Billboard+Hot+100&ci=3070493&cdi=8830864&cid=10%2F26%2F1968.

———."The Billboard Hot 100: A Little Less Conversation, Elvis Presley vs JXL." *Billboard* (2008). Accessed February 15, 2009. http://www.billboard.com/bbcom/esearch/chart_display.jsp?cfi=379&cfgn=Singles&cfn=The+Billboard+Hot+100&ci=3046427&cdi=7889714&cid=08%2F10%2F2002.

———."The Billboard Hot 100: You Ain't Seen Nothing Yet." *Billboard* (2008). Accessed February 15, 2009. http://www.billboard.com/bbcom/esearch/chart_display.jsp?cfi=379&cfgn=Singles&cfn=The+Billboard+Hot+100&ci=3070812&cdi=8863322&cid=12%2F07%2F1974.

———."The Conservative Evolution of Country Music." *All Things Considered* (February 18, 2007). Accessed February 21, 2009. http://www.npr.org/templates/story/story.php?storyId=7484160.

———. *The Greeley & Brown Campaign Songster*. New York: Fisher & Denison, 1872.

———. *The Republican Campaign Songster for the Campaign of 1864*. Cincinnati: J.R. Hawley& Co., 1864.

———. *The Wide-Awake Vocalist, or, Rail Splitters' Song Book: Words and Music for the Republican Campaign of 1860*. New York: E.A. Dagget, 1860.

———. "U2 Songs on Shortlist for Hillary Clinton's Presidential Campaign." *Sawf News* (May 18, 2007). Accessed February 10, 2009.http://news.sawf.org/Gossip/37329.aspx.

Arterton, Christopher F. "The Persuasive Art of Politics." In *Under the Watchful Eye*, edited by Mathew D. McCubbins. Washington, DC: CQ Press, 1992.

"Artist Chart History—Celine Dion." *Billboard* (2008). Accessed February 15, 2009. http://www.billboard.com/bbcom/retrieve_chart_history.do?model.vnuArtistId=4468&model.vnuAlbumId=1102007.

Assayas, Michka. *Bono: In Conversation with Michka Assayas*. New York, Penguin Group, 2006.

Averill, Gage. *Four Parts, No Waiting: A Social History of American Barbershop Harmony*. New York: Oxford University Press, 2003.

Axelrod, Steven Gould, Camille Roman, and Thomas Travisano, eds. *The New Anthology of American Poetry: Modernisms: 1900-1950*. Piscataway, NJ: Rutgers University Press, 2005..

Ayton, Mel. *The Forgotten Terrorist: Sirhan Sirhan and the Assassination of Robert F. Kennedy*. Dulles, VA: Potomac Books, 2007.

Babington, Charles. "Edwards Fires Anti-Corporate Bombast." *The Boston Globe*, January 3, 2008. Accessed February 10, 2009. http://www.boston.com/news/nation/articles/2008/01/03/edwards_fires_anti_corporate_bombast/.

Bailey, Thomas Andrew. *Voices of America: The Nation's Story in Slogans, Sayings, and Songs*. New York: The Free Press, 1976.

Baker, Frank W. *Political Campaigns and Political Advertising: A Media Literacy Guide*. Santa Barbara: ABC-CLIO, LLC, 2009.

Balakrishnan, Angela. "Presidential Playlist: Obama Opens up His iPod." *The Guardian*, June 25, 2008. Accessed August 23, 2010. http://www.guardian.co.uk/world/2008/jun/25/barackobama.uselections2008.

Banks, Jack. *Monopoly Television: MTV's Quest to Control the Music*. Boulder, CO: Westview Press, 1996.

Barber, Benjamin R. *The Truth of Power: Intellectual Affairs in the Clinton White House*. New York: Norton, 2001.

BarelyPolitical.com. "Best of Obama Girl: Crush on Obama." YouTube (June 13, 2007). Accessed August 29, 2010. http://www.youtube.com/watch?v=wKsoXHYICqU.

Barker, Andrew. "Setting the Tone: Austria's National Anthems from Haydn to Haider." *Austrian Studies* 17 (2009): 12-28.

Barnard, Eunice Fuller. "Radio Politics," *The New Republic* (March 1924): 91-93.

Baum, Matthew A. "Talking the Vote: Why Presidential Candidates Hit the Talk Show Circuit." *American Journal of Political Science* 49, no. 2 (April 2005): 213-234.

Beck, Glenn. "Glenn Beck: Obama Soviet Anthem." GlennBeck.com. Accessed August 11, 2010. http://www.glennbeck.com/content/articles/article/198/14148/.

———. "O' Hail the Messiah Lord Obama." YouTube. Accessed August 4, 2010. http://www.youtube.com/watch?v=WEwRB_gOUDg&feature=related.

Been, Michael. "Let the Day Begin." Beverly Hills, CA: Neeb Music & BMI Chrysalis, 1989.

Benoit, William L., et al. *Campaign 2000: A Functional Analysis of Presidential Campaign Discourse*. Lanham, MD: Rowman & Littlefield, 2003.

Berlin, Irving. "(Good Times with Hoover) Better Times with Al." New York: Irving Berlin Inc., Music Publishers, 1928.

———. "I Like Ike." New York: Irving Berlin Inc., Music Publishers, 1950, 1952.

Berry, Chuck. "Johnny B. Goode." In *Chuck Berry*, by Chuck Berry. Milwaukee, WI: Hal Leonard Corporation, 1986.

"Billboard Hot 100." *Billboard*, November 9, 1974.

Blaney David L. and Naeem Inayatullah. "The Westphalian Deferral." *International Studies Review* 2, no. 2 (Summer 2000): 29-64.

Blecha, Peter. *Taboo Tunes: A History of Banned Bands and Censored Songs*. San Francisco: Backbeat Books, 2004.

Blues Brothers. Directed by John Landis. (1980; Hollywood: Universal Pictures, 1981), DVD.

Boller Jr., Paul F. *Presidential Wives*. New York: Oxford University Press, 1988.

Bono and Michka Assayas. *Bono: In Conversation with Michka Assayas*. New York: Penguin Group, 2006.

Boorman, Stanly. "Petrucci, Ottaviano: Publications." In Oxford Music Online, Oxford University Press 2007-2011. Accessed August 31, 2010. http://www.oxford msiconline.com.floyd.lib.umn.edu/subscriber/article/grove/music/21484?q=petrucci &search=quick&pos=2&_start=1#firsthit.

Borgmeyer, John and Holly Lang. *Dr. Dre: A Biography*. Westport, CT: Greenwood Press, 2007.

Bosmajian, Haig. *Burning Books*. Jefferson, NC: McFarland, 2006.

Boucher, Geoff. "Songs in the Key of Presidency." *L.A. Times* October 11, 2000. Accessed July 25, 2010. http://cgi.cnn.com/2000/ALLPOLITICS/stories/10/11/latimes. campaign.songs/index.html.

Bovard, James. *The Bush Betrayal*. New York: Palgrave Macmillan, 2004.

Brader, Ted. "Striking a Responsive Chord: How Political Ads Motivate and Persuade Voters by Appealing to Emotions." *American Journal of Political Science* 49, no. 2 (April 2005): 388-405.

Brand, Oscar and Anthony Seeger. Liner notes from *Presidential Campaign Songs 1789-1996*. Oscar Brand. Smithsonian Folkways Recordings, 45052, released in 1999. Compact disc.

Brand, Oscar. Vocal performance of "If He's Good Enough for Lindy (He's Good Enough for Me." By an unknown composer. On *Presidential Campaign Songs 1789-1996*, Smithsonian Folkways Recordings, 45052, released in 1999. Compact disc.

Brinkley, Alan. "1968 and the Unraveling of Liberal America." In *1968: The World Transformed*, edited by Carole Fink, Philipp Gassert, and Detlef Junker. New York: Cambridge University Press, 1998.

Britan, Halbert Hains. "The Power of Music." *The Journal of Philosophy, Psychology, and Scientific Methods* 5, No. 13 (June 1908): 352-57.

Britton, Nan. *Honesty or Politics*. New York: Elizabeth Ann Guild, Inc., 1932.

Broder, John M. "Perot Winds Up Campaign with New Theme: 'Crazy.'" *The Los Angeles Times*. Accessed August 7, 2010. http://articles.latimes.com/1992-1103/news/ mn-1248_1_ross-perot.

Bronson, Fred. *The Billboard Book of Number 1 Hits: The Inside Story Behind Every Number One Single, on Billboard's Hot 100 from 1955 to the Present*. New York: Billboard Books, 2003).

Brooks, Rosa. "Hillary's Tone Deaf Campaign." *The Los Angeles Times* (June 22, 2007). Accessed February 15, 2009. http://www.latimes.com/news/opinion/commentary/la-oe-brooks22jun22,0,667255.column?coll=la-news-comment-opinions.

Brown, A. Seymour and Bert Grant. "The Election in Jungle Town." New York: Remick Music Corp., 1912.

Brown, Courtney. *Politics in Music: Music and Political Transformation from Beethoven to Hip-Hop*. Atlanta: Farsight Press, 2008).

Bruck, Philip H. "Turn the Rascals Out." S.I.: s.n., 1892.

Brunning, Bob. *The Fleetwood Mac Story: Rumours and Lies*. New York: Omnibus Press, 2004.

Bryer, David E. *The Harrison Campaign Songster, 1892*. Logansport, IN: The Home Music Company, 1892.

Bunkley, Nick. "Aiming to Be the Truck of Patriots." *New York Times*, September 26, 2006. Accessed August 22, 2010. http://www.nytimes.com/2006/09/

26/business/media/26adco.html?ex=1316923200&en=26bfe833a4db385f&ei=5088 &partner=rssnyt&emc=rss.

Burkholder, J. Peter, Donald Jay Grout, and Clause V. Palisca. *A History of Western Music*. New York: W.W. Norton & Company, 2006.

Burns, Eric. *Invasion of the Mind Snatchers: Television's Conquest of America in the Fifties*. Philadelphia: Temple University Press, 2010.

Burns, R.W. *Television, An International History of the Formative Years*. London: The Institution of Electrical Engineers, 1998.

Cahn, Sammy and James Van Heusen. "High Hopes." Burbank, CA: Maraville Music Corp., 1959.

———. "High Hopes (Campaign Edition)." Burbank, CA: Maraville Music Corp., 1959.

Camia, Catalina. "Tim Pawlenty Likes Lady Gaga." *USA Today*, July 7, 2011. Accessed July 15, 2011. http://content.usatoday.com/communities/onpolitics/post/2011/07/ lady-gaga-tim-pawlenty-music-born-this-way-/1?csp=34news.

Camp, John Henry. *The Freemen's Glee Book: A Collection of Songs, Odes, Glees and Ballads, with Music, Original and Selected, Harmonized and Arranged for Each*. New York: Central Freemont and Dayton Glee Club, 1856.

Campbell, Lisa D. *Michael Jackson: The King of Pop*. Boston: Branden Publishing Company, Inc., 1993.

Campbell, Michael and James Brody. *Rock and Roll: An Introduction, Second Edition*. United States: Thompson Schirmer, 2008.

Caporaso, James A. "Changes in the Westphalian Order: Territory, Public Authority, and Sovereignty." *International Studies Review* 2, no. 2 (Summer 2000): 1-28.

Caporuscio, Aldo and Jacques Duval. "You and I." New York: BMG Music and Songs of Peer, Ltd., 2009.

Carlin, Richard. *Country Music: A Biographical Dictionary*. New York, Routledge, 2003.

Carney, J.J. and P.B. Story. "John W. Davis (Remember the Teapot Dome)." New York: J.J. Carney, 1924.

Carpini, Michael X. Delli. "Radio's Political Past." In *Radio: The Forgotten Medium*, Edited by Edward C. Pease and Everette E. Dennis. New Brunswick, NJ: Transaction Publishers, 1995.

Carr, David. "Music, Meaning, and Emotion." *The Journal of Aesthetics and Art Criticism* 62, no. 3 (Summer 2004), 225-234.

Cassidy, John. *Dot.con: How America Lost Its Mind and Money in the Internet Era*. New York: HarperCollins, 2002.

Ceaser, James W. and Andrew Busch. *The Perfect Tie: The True Story of the 2000 Presidential Election*. Lanham, MD: Rowman & Littlefield, 2001.

Celizic, Mike. "'Thriller' Video Remains a Classic 25 Years Later: Jackson Changed the Music Industry the Way Elvis, Beatles Did Before Him." *The Today Show*. Accessed July 31, 2010. http://today.msnbc.msn.com/id/24282347.

Cerulo, Karen A. "Sociopolitical Control and the Structure of National Symbols: An Empirical Analysis of National Anthems." *Social Forces* 68, no. 1 (September 1989): 76-99.

Chappell, Kevin. "Campaign Rhetoric Gets Rough, Racial as South Carolina Primary Nears." *Jet*, January 28, 2008.

Chappell, Kevin and Sylvester Monroe. "Obama and Clinton Unite for Victory in November." *Jet*, July 28, 2008.

Charlesworth, Chris. *The Complete Guide to the Music of Paul Simon and Simon & Garfunkel*. London: Omnibus Press, 1997.

Charleton, Katherine. *Rock Music Styles: A History*. New York: McGraw-Hill, 2011.

Chase, James S. *Emergence of the Presidential Nominating Convention, 1789-1832.* Champaign: University of Illinois Press, 1973.

Checkoway, Laura. "The Arsenio Hall Show." *Vibe,* May 2006.

Cherny, Robert W. "Graft and Oil: How Teapot Dome Became the Greatest Political Scandal of Its Time." *History Now.* Gilder Lehrman Institute of American History. Accessed June 10, 2010. http://www.gilderlehrman.org/historynow/historian5.php.

Chester, Edward W. *Radio, Television and American Politics.* New York: Sheed and Ward, Inc., 1969.

Chin, Gabriel J. and Randy Wagner. "The Tyranny of the Minority: Jim Crow and the Counter-Majoritarian Difficulty." *Harvard Civil Rights-Civil Liberties Law Review* 65 (2008), 80-83.

Clark, David G. "Radio in Presidential Campaigns: The Early Years (1924-1932)." *The Journal of Broadcasting, Volume 6 Issue 3 (Spring 1962)*: 229-238.

Clarke, Thurston. *The Last Campaign: Robert F. Kennedy and 82 Days That Inspired America.* New York: Holt Paperbacks, 2008.

Clayton, Adam et al. "Beautiful Day." Santa Barbara, CA: Universal-Polygram International Publishing Inc., 2000.

Cloonan, Martin. "Musical Responses to September 11th: From Conservative Patriotism to Radicalism." In *9-11—The World's All out of Tune,* edited by Dietrich Helms and Thomas Phelps. Bielefeld: Transcript Verlag, 2004.

CMT. "Brooks & Dunn Awards." Accessed August 1, 2010. http://www.cmt.com/artists/az/brooks_and_dunn/awards.jhtml.

Coatney, Mark. "Gore on the River: Sleepless in La Crosse." *Time* (August 20, 2000). Accessed March 4, 2009. http://www.time.com/time/nation/article/0,8599,52930,00.html.

Coe, Lewis. *The Telegraph: A History of Morse's Invention and Its Predecessors in the United States.* Jefferson, NC: McFarland & Company, Inc., Publishers, 2003.

Cogan, Brian and Tony Kelso. *Encyclopedia of Politics, the Media, and Popular Culture.* Santa Barbara, CA: ABC-CLIO, 2009.

Cogan, Višnja. *U2: An Irish Phenomenon.* New York: Pegasus Books, 2007.

Cohen, Sara. "Sounding out the City: Music and the Sensuous Production of Place." *Transactions of the Institute of British Geographers* 20, no. 4 (1995): 434-446.

Cohen-Almagor, Raphael. *The Scope of Tolerance: Studies on the Costs of Free Expression and Freedom of the Press.* New York: Routledge, 2006.

Cole, F. "The Hickory Tree." New York: Elton Printer, 1828.

Coleman, Jacquelyn Michele. "The Effects of the Male and Female Singing and Speaking Voices on Selected Physiological and Behavioral Measures of Premature Infants in the Intensive Care Unit." *International Journal of Arts Medicine* 5 no. 2 (1997): 4-11.

Coll, Eric C. *Telecom 101: Telecommunications for Non-engineers.* Champlain, NY: Teracom Training Institute, 2004.

Comstock, George and Erica Scharrer. *The Psychology of Media and Politics.* Burlington, MA: Elsevier Academic Press, 2005.

Conti, Bill, Ayn Robbins, and Carol Connors. "Gonna Fly Now." Los Angeles: United Artists Corporation, 1976, 1977.

Conway, M. Margaret. *Political Participation in the United States.* Washington, D.C.: CQ Press, 1991.

Coombs, Karen Mueller. *Woodie Guthrie: America's Folksinger.* Minneapolis, MN: Carolrhoda Books, Inc., 2002.

Copeland, David A. *The Media's Role in Defining the Nation: The Active Voice*. New York: Peter Lang Publishing, 2010.

Corcoran, Paul E. "Presidential Endings: Conceding Defeat." In *Presidential Campaign Discourse: Strategic Communication Problems*, ed. Kathleen E. Kendall. Albany: State University of New York: 1995.

Costa, Robert. "Songs for Campaign Seasons Past and Present." *The Wall Street Journal Online*. Accessed August 1, 2010. http://online.wsj.com/article/SB122290103509 796055.html.

Coxx, Jim. *Sold on Radio: Advertisers in the Golden Age of Broadcasting*. Jefferson, NC: McFarland and Company, Inc. Publishers, 2008.

Craig, Douglas. "Bruce Springsteen." In *Culture Wars: An Encyclopedia of Issues, Voices, and Viewpoints*, ed. Roger Chapman. Armonk, NY: M.E. Sharp, 2010.

Cray, Ed. *Ramblin' Man: The Life and Times of Woody Guthrie*. New York: W.W. Norton & Company, Inc., 2004.

Crenshaw, Kimberley Williams. "Beyond Racism and Misogyny: Black Feminism and 2 Live Crew." In *Words that Wound: Critical Race Theory, Assaultive Speech, and the First Amendment*, edited by Mari J. Matsuda et al. Boulder, CO: Westview Press, 1993.

Crew, Danny O. *Presidential Sheet Music: An Illustrated Catalogue*. Jefferson, NC: McFarland & Company, Inc., Publishers, 2001.

———. *Suffragist Sheet Music: An Illustrated Catalog of Published Music Associated with the Women's Rights and Suffrage Movement in America, 1795-1921*. Jefferson, NC: MacFarland, 2002.

Cullen, Jim. *Born in the U.S.A.: Bruce Springsteen and the American Tradition*. Middletown, CT: Wesleyan University Press, 1997.

Curtis, Mark. *Age of Obama: A Reporter's Journey with Clinton, McCain and Obama in the Making of the President, 2008*. Ann Arbor, MI: Nimble Books, 2009.

Cyrus, Billy Ray. Vocal performance of "We the People," by Richard Belmont Powell, Jimmie Lee Sloas and Anna Wilson. On *Southern Rain*, Sony B00004ZDOL. Compact disc. Released October 17, 2000.

Dahl, Robert A. "Myth of the Presidential Mandate." In *Politicians and Party Politics*, edited by John Gray Geer. Baltimore: The Johns Hopkins University Press, 1998).

Damore, David F. "Candidate Strategy and the Decision to Go Negative." *Political Research Quarterly* 55, no. 3 (September 2002): 669-685.

Daniels, Alex. "At Session, Huckabee Elephant in the Room Teachers-Union Talk First by a GOP Hopeful." *Arkansas Online* (July 6, 2007). Accessed March 9, 2009. http://www2.arkansasonline.com/news/2007/jul/06/session-huckabee-elephant-room/.

Dann, Carrie. "Huck: More Than A Feeling, A Surge?." *MSNBC*, October 27, 2007. Accessed August 22, 2010. http://firstread.msnbc.msn.com/_news/2007/10/27/44332 90-huck-more-than-a-feeling-a-surge.

Davidson, Donald J., ed. *The Wisdom of Theodore Roosevelt*. New York: Kensington Publishing Company, 2003.

Davis, Barbara J. *The Teapot Dome Scandal: Corruption Rocks 1920s America*. Minneapolis, MN: Compass Point Books, 2008.

Davis, Richard and Diana Owen. *New Media and American Politics*. New York: Oxford University Press, 1998.

de la Rocha, Zack. "Take the Power Back." *Rage Against the Machine*. New York: Sony Music Entertainment, 1992.

Dempsey, Judy. "Return of a Soviet-Era Genre Lost to Perestroika." *New York Times*, October 21, 2009, Accessed June 22, 2010 http://www.nytimes.com/2009/10/22/arts/22iht-realism.html?_r=2&sq=music censorship soviet union&st=cse&adxnnl=1&scp=11&adxnnlx=1277809553-YINwrBMCN7Boqg+j1MV9BQ.

Dennis, David B. *Beethoven in German Politics, 1870-1989*. New Haven: Yale University Press, 1996.

Denisoff, R. Serge. *Inside MTV*. New Brunswick, NJ: Transaction Publishers, 1988.

———. "Protest Songs: Those on the Top Forty and Those of the Streets." *American Quarterly* 22, no. 4 (Winter 1970): 807-823.

DePastino, Todd. *Citizen Hobo: How a Century of Homelessness Shaped America*. Chicago: University of Chicago Press, 2003).

Dershowitz, Alan M. *Supreme Injustice: How the High Court Hijacked Election 2000*. New York: Oxford University Press, 2001.

Devenish, Colin. *Rage Against the Machine*. New York: St. Martin's Press, 2001.

Diamond, Neil. Vocal performance of "America," by Neil Diamond, recorded 1980, on *The Jazz Singer Soundtrack*. Capitol Records, compact disc.

Doak, Robin S. *Calvin Coolidge*. Minneapolis, MN: Compass Point Books, 2004.

Domke, David and Kevin Coe. *The God Strategy: How Religion Became a Political Weapon in America*. New York: Oxford University Press, 2010.

Dougherty, Robert. "Hank Williams Jr. Sings of 'McCain-Palin Tradition' at Rally." *Associated Content* (October 14, 2008). Accessed February 18, 2009. http://www.associatedcontent.com/article/1109933/hank_williams_jr_sings_of_mccainpalin.html.

Doyle, Jack. "I Won't Back Down, 1989-2008." PopHistoryDig.com, March 7, 2009. Accessed August 25, 2010. http://www.pophistorydig.com/?p=932.

Dresser, Paul. "Parker, Parker." New York: James H Curtin, 1904.

Drinkere, Frederick E. and Jay Henry Mowbray. *Theodore Roosevelt: His Life and Work* (Washington, D.C.: National Publishing Co., 1919.

D'Souza, Dinesh. *Ronald Reagan: How an Ordinary Man Became an Extraordinary Leader*. New York: Touchstone, 1997.

Dunaway, Wilma A. *Slavery in the American Mountain South*. New York: Cambridge University Press, 2003).

Dunfield, Allison. "Lighter Side: C'est What?." *Globe and Mail* (June 25, 2004). Accessed February 23, 2009. http://www.theglobeandmail.com/servlet/story/RTGAM.20040520.wcestwhatele0518/BNStory/specialDecision2004/.

Dutton, William H., et al. "The Politics of Information and Communication Policy." In *Information and Communication Technologies: Visions and Realities*, ed. William H. Dutton. New York: Oxford University Press, 1996.

Dylan, Bob. *Lyrics: 1962-2001*. London: Simon & Schuster UK, Ltd., 2006.

Edwards, John, Marion G. Crain, and Arne L. Kalleberg, ed. *Ending Poverty in America: How to Restore the American Dream*. New York: New Press, 2007.

Ehrman, John. *The Eighties: America in the Age of Reagan*. New Haven, CT: Yale University Press, 2005.

Eilperin, Juliet. "McCain Picks Up John Edwards's Song." *The Washington Post* (February 2, 2008). Accessed March 4, 2009. http://voices.washingtonpost.com/44/2008/02/02/mccain_picks_up_john_edwardss.html.

Elleström, Lars. *Divine Madness: On Interpreting Literature, Music, and the Visual Arts Ironically*. Cranbury, NJ: Associated University Presses, 2002.

Ellison, Curtis W. *Country Music Culture: From Hard Times to Heaven*. Jackson: University Press of Mississippi, 1995.

Epstein, Lawrence Jeffery. *Political Folk Music in America from Its Origins to Bob Dylan*. Jefferson, NC: McFarland & Company, Inc., Publishers, 2010.

Erlewine, Stephen Thomas. "Taking the Long Way." In *Contemporary Country*, ed. Chris Woodstra, John Bush, and Stephen Thomas Erlewine. New York: Backbeat Books, 2008.

Evans, Richard J. *The Third Reich in Power*. New York: Penguin, 2005.

Ewen, David. *All the Years of American Popular Music*. Englewood Cliffs, NJ: Prentice-Hall, 1977.

Facebook. "About." Accessed August 11, 2010. http://www.facebook.com/facebook.

Fairbanks, George E. "Taft and Sherman." In *Fairbanks' Republican Campaign Songs*. South Cornish, NH: George E. Fairbanks, 1912.

Farhi, Paul. "Candidates' Tunes Hit a Few Sour Notes: Lyrics in Campaign Theme Songs Can Be Hilariously Off-Key." *The Washington Post*. January 17, 2008. Accessed August 24, 2010, http://www.washingtonpost.com/wpdyn/content/article/2008/01/16/AR2008011604152.html

Ferling, John. *Adams vs. Jefferson: The Tumultuous Election of 1800*. New York: Oxford University Press, 2004.

Fermino, Jennifer. "'Obama Girl' now falling out of love." *The New York Post*, January 27, 2010. Accessed August 29, 2010. http://www.nypost.com/p/news/national/obama_girl_now_falling_out_of_love_20IY02jVpUMvC0IQBLXvEI.

Fesnic, Florin. "Election Types." In *Encyclopedia of U.S. Campaigns, Elections, and Electoral Behavior, Volume 2*, edited by Kenneth F. Warren. Thousand Oaks, CA: Sage Publications, 2008.

Fest, Joachim. *Hitler*. Orlando: Harcourt, 1974.

Finnegan, Ruth. *The Hidden Musicians: Music-Making in an English Town*, reprint edition. Middletown, CT: Wesleyan University Press, 2007.

Flanders, Helen Hartness. *The New Green Mountain Songster: Traditional Folk Songs of Vermont*. New Haven, CT: Yale University Press, 1939.

Flippo, Chet. "Nashville Skyline: Presidential Politics Call on Country." *CMT News* (April 26, 2007). Accessed June 10, 2011. http://www.cmt.com/news/nashville-skyline/1558207/nashville-skyline-presidential-politics-call-on-country.jhtml.

Flynn, Kathryn A. and Richard Polese. *The New Deal: A 75th Anniversary Celebration*. Layton, Utah: Gibbs Smith, 2008.

Fox News. "Boston Guitarist Wants to Pull the Plug on Huckabee for Using Hit Song." February 14, 2008. Accessed February 10, 2009. http://www.foxnews.com/politics/elections/2008/02/14/boston-guitarist-wants-to-pull-the-plug-on-huckabee-for-using-hit-song/.

———. "Hillary Clinton Picks Campaign Song She Hopes Is Pleasing to 'You and I.'" June 19, 2007. Accessed June 3, 2010. http://www.foxnews.com/story/0,2933,284432,00.html.

Fox, William S. and James D. Williams. "Political Orientation and Music Preferences Among College Students." *The Public Opinion Quarterly* 38, No. 3 (Autumn 1974): 352-371.

Frank, Beryl. *The Pictorial History of the Democratic Party*. Secaucus, NJ: Castle Books, 1980.

———. *The Pictorial History of the Republican Party*. Secaucus, NJ: Castle Books, 1980.

Frazier, George. "Irving Berlin." *Life*, April 5, 1943.

Freedman, Paul, Michael Franz, and Kenneth Goldstein. "Campaign Advertising and Democratic Citizenship." *American Journal of Political Science* 48, no. 4 (October 2004): 723-741.

French, Howard W. "The Sound, Not of Music, But of Control." *New York Times*, October 25, 2007. Accessed June 22, 2010. http://www.nytimes.com/2007/10/25/world/asia/25shanghai.html?scp=5&sq=music%20censorship%20china&st=cse.

Frucht, Richard. *Eastern Europe: An Introduction to the People, Lands, and Culture.* Santa Barbara, CA: ABC-CLIO, 2005.

Gale, George W. "Line Up for Bryan." Cincinnati, OH: The Gale and Mullane Music Company, 1908.

Gardner, David. "'Rocky McCain' vows to fight back: 'I believe I'm going to win it.'" *The Daily Mail* (October 27, 2008). Accessed March 3, 2009. http://www.dailymail.co.uk/news/worldnews/article-1080714/Rocky-McCain-vows-fight-I-believe-Im-going-win-it.html.

Gardner, Geoffrey. "Obama's iPod Playlist Revealed." *National Public Radio*, June 26, 2008. Accessed August 23, 2010. http://www.npr.org/blogs/newsandviews/2008/06/obamas_ipod_secrets_revealed.html.

Garofalo, Reebee. *Rockin' Out: Popular Music in the USA.* Upper Saddle River, NJ: Prentice-Hall, 2002.

Genova, Tom. "Television History—The First 75 Years." TV History. Accessed July 14, 2010. http://www.tvhistory.tv/index.html.

Goehr, Lydia. "Political Music and the Politics of Music." *The Journal of Aesthetics and Art Criticism* 52, no. 1 (Winter 1994): 99-112.

Goldstein, Ken and Paul Freedman. "Campaign Advertising and Voter Turnout: New Evidence for a Stimulation Effect." *The Journal of Politics* 64, no. 3 (August 2002): 721-740.

Goodman, Dean. "Rock Group Heart Says 'Barracuda' Use Is Fishy," *Reuters*, September 5, 2008. Accessed August 23, 2010. http://www.reuters.com/article/idUSN0451966120080905?feedType=RSS&feedName=entertainmentNews.

Goodwin, Ida Cheever and Bruce Harper. "Keep Cool and Keep Coolidge." Plymouth, VT: Published by Home Town Coolidge Club, 1924.

Goss, Jon. "The 'Magic of the Mall': An Analysis of Form, Function, and Meaning in the Contemporary Retail Built Environment." *Annals of the Association of American Geographers*, 83, no. 1 (March 1993): 18-47.

Gottschild, Brenda Dixon. *Waltzing in the Dark: African American Vaudeville and Race Politics in the Swing Era.* New York: Palgrave, 2000.

Graff, Garrett M. *The First Campaign: Globalization, the Web, and the Race for the White House.* New York: Farrar, Straus, Giroux, 2007.

Green, James Harry. *The Irwin Handbook of Telecommunications.* New York: McGraw-Hill, 2006.

Green, Stanley. *Encyclopedia of the Musical Theatre.* New York: Da Capo Press, 1976.

Greene, Andy. "Tom Petty to Michele Bachmann: Quit Playing 'American Girl.'" *Rolling Stone*, June 28, 2011. Accessed June 30, 2011. http://www.rollingstone.com/music/news/tom-petty-tells-michele-bachmann-to-stop-playing-american-girl-20110628.

———. "Katrina and the Waves Join Tom Petty's Fight Against Michele Bachmann." *Rolling Stone*, June 29, 2011. Accessed June 30, 2011. http://www.rollingstone.com/politics/news/katrina-and-the-waves-join-tom-pettys-fight-againstmichelebachmann-20110629.

————. "'More Than a Feeling' Writer Says Mike Huckabee Has Caused Him 'Damage.'" *Rollingstone.* Accessed February 20, 2008. http://www.rollingstone.com/music/news/13511/70354.

Greenwood, Lee. "God Bless the U.S.A." Santa Monica, CA: Songs of Universal, Inc., 1984.

Greenwood, Lee and Gwen McLin. *God Bless the U.S.A.: Biography of a Song.* Gretna, LA: Pelican Publishing, 1993.

Grosvenor Jr., Charles R. "Song Parodies-Authors-William Tong." *Am I Right: Making Fun of Music, One Song at a Time.* Accessed June 6, 2011. http://www.amiright.com/parody/authors/williamtong.shtml.

Grout Donald J. and Bertil Wikman. *A History of Western Music (Revised Edition).* New York: W.W. Norton & Co. Ltd.

Guthrie, Woody. "This Land Is Your Land." In *The American Reader: Words that Moved a Nation,* edited by Diane Ravitch. New York: HarperCollins, 2000.

Hagar, Sammy et al., "Right Now" in *Van Halen–Guitar Anthology: Authentic Guitar Tab* by Van Halen. Van Nuys, CA: Alfred Publishing Company, Inc., 1995.

Haggard, Merle. *Merle Haggard: Poet of the Common Man: The Lyrics.* Edited by Don Cusic. Milwaukee, WI: Hal Leonard.

Hagood, Wesley O. *Presidential Sex: From the Founding Fathers to Bill Clinton.* New York: Carol Publishing Group, 1998.

Hale, Jon F. "The Making of the New Democrats." *Political Science Quarterly* 110 (1995): 207-232.

Halliwell, Martin. "Contemporary American Culture." In *American Thought and Culture in the 21st Century,* ed. Martin Halliwell and Catherine Morley. Edinburgh, Scotland, UK: Edinburgh University Press, 2008.

Hansen, Harry. *The Civil War: A History.* New York: Penguin Putnam, 1961.

Haque, Amber. "Psychology from Islamic Perspective: Contributions of Early Muslim Scholars and Challenges to Contemporary Muslim Psychologists." *Journal of Religion and Health* 43, no. 4 (2004): 357-377.

Harper, Christopher. *And That's the Way It Will Be: News and Information in a Digital World.* New York: New York University Press, 1998.

Harris, John F. *The Survivor: Bill Clinton in the White House.* New York: Random House, 2006.

Hasse, John Edward. *Ragtime: Its History, Composers and Music.* New York: Palgrave Macmillan, 1986.

Hawes, Matt. "Freedom Celebration Videos." Campaign for Liberty, April 1, 2009. Accessed August 24, 2010. http://www.campaignforliberty.com/blog.php?view=14875.

Heale, M.J. *Franklin D. Roosevelt: The New Deal and War.* New York: Routledge, 1999.

Hell-Bent for Election, Part One. October 28, 2007. Accessed May 2, 2011. http://www.youtube.com/watch?v=xhykCuN_BpY.

Hell-Bent for Election, Part Two. October 28, 2007. Accessed May 2, 2011. http://www.youtube.com/watch?v=3U3A6DWQ0zY&feature=related.

Hemming, Roy and David Hajdu. *Discovering Great Singers of Classic Pop: A New Listeners Guide to 52 Top Crooners and Canaries with Extensive Discographies, Videographies and Recommendations for Collectors.* New York: New Market Press, 1991.

Herder, Ronald, ed., *500 Best-Loved Song Lyrics.* Mineola, NY: Dover Publications, 1998.

Herman, Jerry. "Hello Lyndon." New York: Edwin H. Morris & Co., 1963.

Hijiya, James A. *Lee De Forest and the Fatherhood of the Radio*. Cranbury, NJ: Associated University Press, 1992.

Hillygus, D. Sunshine and Todd G. Shields. "Moral Issues and Voter Decision Making in the 2004 Presidential Election." *PS: Political Science and Politics* 38, no. 2 (April 2005): 201-209.

Hitchcock, H. Wiley and Pauline Norton. "Cakewalk." In *Oxford Music Online*, Oxford University Press 2007-2011. Accessed June 9, 2011. http://www.oxfordmusiconline .com.ezp1.lib.umn.edu/subscriber/article/grove/music/04568.

Hohenberg, John. *Reelecting Bill Clinton: Why America Chose a "New" Democrat*. Syracuse: Syracuse University Press, 1997.

———. *The Bill Clinton Story: Winning the Presidency*. Syracuse: Syracuse University Press, 1994.

Holloway, Rachel L. "Political Conventions of 2004: A Study in Character and Contrast." In *The 2004 Presidential Campaign: A Communication Perspective*, ed. Robert E. Denton Jr. Lanham, MD: Roman & Littlefield, 2005.

Holt, Michael F. *Political Parties and American Political Development: From the Age of Jackson to the Age of Lincoln*. Baton Rouge: Louisiana State University Press, 1992.

Huey, Steve. "Brooks & Dunn Biography." Yahoo Music. Accessed August 1, 2010. http://new.music.yahoo.com/brooks-dunn/biography/.

Hume, Brit. "Some Democrats See Big Trouble Coming at the Party's Convention This Summer." *Fox News*, February 18, 2008. Accessed August 22, 2010. http://www.fox news.com/story/0,2933,331112,00.html.

Hung, Chang-Tai. "The Politics of Songs: Myths and Symbols in the Chinese Communist War Music, 1937-1949." *Modern Asian Studies* 30, no. 4 (October 1996): 901-29.

Huntley, Elliot J. *Mystical One: George Harrison After the Break-Up of the Beatles*. Toronto: Guernica Editions, 2004).

Hurst, Craig W. "Twentieth-Century American Folk Music and the Popularization of Protest." In *Homer Simpson Goes to Washington: American Politics through Popular Culture*, edited by Joseph J. Foy. Lexington: The University Press of Kentucky, 2008.

Huston, James L. *Stephen A. Douglas and the Dilemmas of Democratic Equality*. Lanham, MD: Rowman & Littlefield Publishers, Inc., 2007.

Hutchinson, John W., ed. *Hutchinson's Republican Songster for the Campaign of 1860*. New York: O. Hutchinson, 1860.

Icon Group International Inc., Staff. *Harrying: Webster's Quotations, Facts and Phrases*. San Diego: Icon Group International, Inc., 2008.

Jackson, George Stuyvesant. *Early Songs of Uncle Sam*. Boston: Bruce Humphries Publisher, 1933.

Jackson, Joyce Marie. "The Changing Nature of Gospel Music: A Southern Case Study." *African American Review* 29, No. 2 (Summer 1995): 185-200.

Jackson, Laura. *Bono: His Life, Music and Passions*. New York: Kensington Publishing Corp., 2001.

Jamieson, Kathleen Hall, Erika Falk, and Susan Sherr. "The Enthymeme Gap in the 1996 Presidential Campaign." *PS: Political Science and Politics* 32, no. 1 (March 1999): 12-16.

Jamieson, Kathleen Hall and Paul Waldman. *The Press Effect: Politicians, Journalists, and the Stories that Shape the Political World*. New York: Oxford University Press, 2003.

Jarboe, Greg. *YouTube and Video Marketing: An Hour a Day*. Indianapolis: Wiley, 2009.

Jensen, Richard. "Armies, Admen, and Crusaders: Types of Presidential Election Campaigns." *The History Teacher* 2, no. 2 (January 1969): 33-50.

Johannsen, Robert W. *The Frontier, The Union and Stephen A. Douglas.* Champaign: University of Illinois Press, 1989.

Johnson, Allen. *Stephen A. Douglas: A Study in American Politics.* Charlston, SC: Bibliobazaar, 2008.

Johnson, Helen Kendrick. "The Meaning of Song." In *The North American Review, Vol. CXXXVIII*, edited by Allen Thorndike Rice. New York: 1884.

Jolsen, Al. "Harding, You're the Man for Us." (New York: s.n., 1920.

Jones, Clifford A. "Campaign Finance Reform and the Internet: Regulating Web Messages in the 2004 Election and Beyond." In *The Internet Election: Perspectives on the Web in Campaign 2004*, ed. Andrew Paul Williams and John C. Tedesco. Lanham, MD: Rowman & Littlefield, 2006.

Jordan, Richard Tyler. *But Darling, I'm your Auntie Mame!: The Amazing History of the World's Favorite Madcap Aunt.* New York: Kensington Books, 2004.

Kahan, Jeffrey B. "Bach, Beethoven, and the (Home)Boys: Censoring Violent Rap Music in America." *Southern California Law Review* 66 (September 1993): 2583-2610.

Kaid, Lynda Lee and Anne Johnston. *Videostyle in Presidential Campaigns: Style and Content of Televised Political Advertising.* Westport, CT: Praeger, 2001.

Keller, Scott. *Marine Pride: A Salute to America's Elite Fighting Force.* New York: Citadel Press, 2004.

Kenski Henry C. and Kate M. Kenski. "Explaining the Vote in the Election of 2008: The Democratic Revivial." In *The 2008 Presidential Campaign: A Communication Perspective*, edited by Robert E. Denton, Jr. Lanham, MD: Rowman & Littlefield, 2009.

Kerr, Harry D. and Abe Holzmann. "Get On the Raft with Taft." New York: Leo Feist, Inc., 1908 and 1912.

Kessler, Judd. Correspondence with author, April 14, 2011.

———. "Lead the Way—A Song for John McCain." YouTube. Accessed August 3, 2010. http://www.youtube.com/watch?v=U4fdRR8VjHw.

Key, Francis Scott. "The Star-Spangled Banner." In *Our Nation's Archive: The History of the United States in Documents*, edited by Erik Bruun and Jay Crosby. New York: Black Dog and Leventhal Publishers, 1999).

Keyssar, Alexander. *The Right to Vote: The Contested History of Democracy in the United States.* New York: Basic Books, 2000.

Kimball, George. "Origan of the John Brown Song." *The New England Magazine*, December 1889, 317-377.

Klotman, Phyllis R. and Janet K. Cutler. *Struggles for Representation: African American Documentary Film and Video.* Bloomington: Indiana University Press, 1999.

Kluger, Richard. *Simple Justice: The History of Brown v. Board of Education and Black America's Struggle For Equality.* New York: Knopf, 1976.

Koch, Nadine S. "Entertainment and Politics." Review of *Entertainment and Politics: The Influence of Pop Culture on Young Adult Political Socialization,* by David J. Jackson. *Journal of Politics,* Vol. 66, No. 3 (Aug., 2004): 975-977.

Köhler, Joachim. *Wagner's Hitler: The Prophet and His Disciple.* Cambridge, UK: Polity Press, 2000.

Kooijman, Jaap. *Fabricating the Absolute Fake: America in Contemporary Pop Culture.* Amsterdam: Amsterdam University Press, 2008.

Kootnikoff, David. *U2: A Musical Biography.* Santa Barbara, CA: Glenwood Press, 2010.

Kubicek, Herbert and William H. Dutton. "The Social Shaping of Information Super-highways: An Introduction." In *The Social Shaping of information Superhighways: European and American Roads to the Information Society*, ed. Herbert Kubicek, William H. Dutton, and Robin Williams. New York: St. Martin's Press, 1997.

Kunkel, Vicki. *Instant Appeal: The 8 Primal Factors that Create Blockbuster Success*. New York: Amacon, 2009.

Kuntz, Tom, ed. *The Titanic Disaster Hearings: The Official Transcripts of the 1912 Senate Investigation*. New York: Pocket Books, 1998.

Kusinitz, Kevin. "Celebrity Endorsements." *Weekly Standard*, May 23, 2008. Accessed July 11, 2010. http://www.weeklystandard.com/Content/Public/Articles/000/000/015/127joosu.asp.

LaFeber, Walter, Richard Polenberg, and Nancy Woloch. *The American Century: A History of the United States Since 1941*. New York: M.E. Sharpe, 2008.

Lamb, Bill. "Top 40 Pop Songs: The Best of the Best, 20. U2—'Beautiful Day' (2000)." Accessed August 19, 2010. http://top40.about.com/od/top10lists/tp/top40essentialsongsalltime.02.htm.

Lamm, Robert, "Beginnings." New York: Primary Wave Lamm & Spirit Two Music, Inc., 1969.

Larkin, Colin. *The Encyclopedia of Popular Music*. Ann Arbor: University of Michigan Press, 1998.

Larson, Thomas E. *History of Rock and Roll*. Dubuque, IA: Kendall-Hunt, 2004.

Lawrence, Vera Brodsky. *Strong on Music: The New York Music Scene in the Days of George Templeton Strong, 1836-1975*. New York: Oxford University Press, 1988.

Leab, Daniel J. "The Blue Collar Ethnic in Bicentennial America: Rocky." In *Hollywood's America: Twentieth-Century America Through Film*, edited by Steven Mintz and Randy W. Roberts. Malden, MA: Blackwell Publishing, 2010.

Leip, David. "Atlas of U.S. Presidential Elections." Accessed May 14, 2011. http://uselectionatlas.org/.

Letkemann, Jessica. "Stump Thumping." *Spin*, September 1998.

Leutwyler, Kristin. "Exploring the Musical Brain." *Scientific American*, January 22, 2001. Accessed June 16, 2010. http://www.scientificamerican.com/article.cfm?id=exploring-the-musical-bra.

Library of Congress. "Music for Public Occasions." Accessed May 17, 2011. http://memory.loc.gov/ammem/smhtml/smessay2.html.

———. "The U.S. Works Projects Administration Federal Music Project." Washington, D.C.: Library of Congress, 1999.

Lichter, S. Robert and Richard Noyes. *Good Intentions Make Bad News: Why Americans Hate Campaign Journalism*. Lanham, MD: Rowman & Littlefield, 1996.

Long, Kim. *The Almanac of Political Corruption, Scandals and Dirty Politics*. New York: Delacorte Press, 2007.

MacArthur, John R. *The Selling of "Free Trade": NAFTA, Washington, and the Subversion of American Democracy*. Berkeley: University of California Press, 2000.

MacDonald, Ballard and George Walter Brown. "Wilson—That's All!" New York: Shapiro, Bernstein & Co., Inc., 1912.

Machin, David. *Analyzing Popular Music: Image, Sound and Text*. Thousand Oaks, CA: Sage Publications, 2010.

Magidson, Herb and Robert King. "Mr. Hoover and Mr. Smith." New York: Shapiro, Bernstein & Co., 1928 & 1955.

Maisel, L. Sandy and Mark D. Brewer. *Parties and Elections in America: The Electoral Process*. Lanham, MD: Rowman & Littlefield, 2008.

Makanowitsky, Barbara. "Music to Serve the State." *Russian Review* 24, no. 3 (July 1965): 266-77.

Mäkelä, Janna. *John Lennon Imagined: Cultural History of a Rock Star*. New York: Peter Lang Publishing, 2004.

Maraniss, David. *First in His Class: The Biography of Bill Clinton*. New York: Touchstone, 1995.

Marano, Richard Michael. *Vote Your Conscience: The Last Campaign of George McGovern*. Westport, CT: Praeger Publishers, 2003.

Marley, Bob. *Bob Marley: Songs of Freedom*. Milwaukee: Hal Leonard Corporation, 1992.

Marsden, Peter V., et al. "American Regional Cultures and Differences in Leisure Time Activities." *Social Forces*, 60, No. 4 (June 1982): 1023-1049.

Marsh, David. *The Heart of Rock & Soul: The 1001 Greatest Singles Ever Made*. New York: Da Capo, 1999.

Martin, Andrew E. and Brian E. Spang. "A Case Study of a Third Presidential Campaign Organization." In *Ross for Boss: The Perot Phenomenon and Beyond*, ed. Ted G. Jelen. Albany: State University of New York Press, 2001.

Martin, Henry and Keith Waters. *Essential Jazz: The First 100 Years*. Boston: Schirmer Cengage Learning, 2009.

Martis, Kenneth C., et al. *The Historical Atlas of Political Parties in the United States Congress, 1789-1989*. New York: MacMillan, 1989.

Mass, Isaac. "Raisin' McCain: Music to My Ears." *The Boston Globe*, September 5, 2008. Accessed February 15, 2009. http://www.boston.com/news/politics/massvoices/2008/09/raisin_mccain_music_to_my_ears.html.

Mayer, Jeremy D. and Clyde Wilcox. "Understanding Perot's Plummet." In *Ross for Boss: The Perot Phenomenon and Beyond*, ed. Ted G. Jelen. Albany: State University of New York Press, 2001.

Mayfield, Geoff. "Holiday Shifts Pace; New Realities of Dixie Chicks." *Billboard*, June 17, 2006.

McCain, Robert Stacey. "All American Maverick." *The American Spectator* (August 13, 2008). Accessed March 3, 2009. http://spectator.org/archives/2008/08/13/all-american-maverick.

McCarty, William. *Songs, Odes, and Other Poems on National Subjects: Military*. Philadelphia, William McCarty, 1842.

McCormick, Neil. "Barack Obama's 'Yes We Can' video." *The Telegraph*, February 14, 2008. accessed August 29, 2010. http://www.telegraph.co.uk/culture/music/3671190/Barack-Obamas-Yes-We-Can-video.html.

McVie, Christine. "Don't Stop" Santa Monica, CA: Universal Music – Careers, 1976.

Mellencamp, John. *The Concert at Walter Reed*. Bloomington, IN: Author House, 2007.

———. "Our Country." Nashville, TN: Belmont Mall Publishing, 2007.

Meyer, Michael. "The Nazi Musicologist as Myth Maker in the Third Reich." *Journal of Contemporary History* 10, no. 4 (October 1975):649-665.

Milbank, Dana and Mike Allen. "Bush Fortifies Conservative Base: Campaign Seeks Solid Support Before Wooing Swing Voters." *The Washington Post Online*. Accessed August 10, 2010. http://www.washingtonpost.com/wp-dyn/articles/A50296-2004Jul14.html.

Miles, William. *Songs, Odes, Glees and Ballads: A Bibliography of American Presidential Campaign Songsters*. New York: Greenwood Press, 1990.

Miller, Randy et al. *Harry the K: The Remarkable Life of Harry Kalas*. Philadelphia: Running Press Book Publishers, 2010.

Mithen, Steven. *The Singing Neanderthals: The Origins of Music, Language, Mind, and Body*. Cambridge, MA: Harvard University Press, 2006.

Monaco, Bob and James Riordan. *The Platinum Rainbow: How to Succeed in the Music Business Without Selling Your Soul*. Sherman Oaks, CA: Swordsman Press, 1980.

Monk, Noel E. and Jimmy Guterman. *12 Days on the Road: The Sex Pistols and America*. New York: Harper Entertainment, 1990.

Moody, Nekesa Mumbi. "Kanye Joins All-Star Lineup for Obama CD." *USA Today* (September 22, 2008). Accessed May 26, 2011. http://www.usatoday.com/life/music/news/2008-09-19-obama-soundtrack_N.htm.

Moore, Don. "The 1924 Radio Election." Accessed June 8, 2010. http://www.patepluma radio.com/genbroad/elec1924.html.

Morella, Joe and Patricia Barey. *Simon and Garfunkel: Old Friends*. Secaucus, NJ: Carol Publishing Group, 1991.

Morgan, Marcyliena. *Language, Discourse and Power in African American Culture*. New York: Cambridge University Press, 2002.

Morreale, Joanne. *A New Beginning: A Textual Frame Analysis of the Political Campaign Film*. Albany: SUNY Press, 1991.

Morris, Edmund. *Theodore Rex*. New York: Random House, 2002.

Morris, Kenneth E. *Jimmy Carter: American Moralist*. Athens: University of Georgia Press, 1996.

Morton, John Fass. *Backstory in Blue: Ellington at Newport '56*. Piscataway, NJ: Rutgers University Press, 2008.

Mosley, Leonard. *Lindbergh: A Biography*. Mineola, NY: Dover Publications, 1976.

Murrin, John M., et al. *Liberty, Equality and Power: A History of the American People, Fifth Edition*. Canada: Cengage Learning, 2008.

Museum of the Moving Image. "The Living Room Candidate: Presidential Campaign Commercials from 1952-2008." Accessed July 14, 2010. http://www.living roomcandidate.org.

Nash, Graham William. "Teach Your Children." Nashville, TN: Nash Notes, 1970.

Nesbit, W.D. and R.N. Lombard. "Teddy Come Back!" New York & Chicago: Music Publishing House, 1910.

Newman, Melinda. "Hayes Vetos Dole's 'Soul Man.'" *Billboard*, September 21, 1996.

———. "Presidential Musical Race Heats Up: Genesis Boxed Set Postponed One Year." *Billboard*, September 28, 1996.

Niedenthal Paula M. and Marc B. Setterlund, "Emotion Congruence in Perception." *Personality and Social Psychology Bulletin* 20, no. 4 (1994): 401-411.

Norton, A.B. *The Great Revolution of 1840: Reminiscences of the Log Cabin Hard Cider Campaign*. Mount Vernon, OH: A.B. Norton & Co., 1888.

———, ed. *Tippecanoe Song of the Log Cabin Boys and Girls of 1840*. Mount Vernon, OH: A.B. Norton & Co., 1888.

Nudelman, Franny. *John Brown's Body: Slavery, Violence & the Culture of War*. Chapel Hill: The University of North Carolina Press, 2004.

Nuzum, Eric. *Parental Advisory: Music Censorship in America*. New York: HarperCollins, 2001.

O'Brien, Mary-Elizabeth. *Nazi Cinema as Enchantment: The Politics of Entertainment in the Third Reich*. Rochester, NY: Camden House, 2004.

Office of the Federal Register. "Historical Election Results: Electoral College Box Scores, 1789-1996." Accessed June 25, 2010, http://www.archives.gov/federal-register/electoral-college/scores.html.

Ogg, Frederic Austin. *The Reign of Andrew Jackson: A Chronicle of the Frontier in Politics.* New Haven, CT: Yale University Press, 1919.

Okin, J.R. *The Internet Revolution: The Not-for-Dummies Guide to the History, Technology, and Use of the Internet.* Winter Harbor, ME: Ironbound Press, 2004.

Oldroyd, Osborn Hamiline. *Lincoln's Campaign or the Political Revolution of 1860.* Chicago: Laird & Lee, 1896.

On the Issues. "2008 Presidential Candidates: Ron Paul on the Issues." Accessed August 24, 2010. http://www.ontheissues.org/ron_paul.htm.

Osgerby, Bill. *Youth Media.* New York: Routledge, 2004.

Osiander, Andreas. "Sovereignty, International Relations, and the Westphalian Myth." *International Organization* 55, no. 2 (Spring 2001): 251-287.

Owen, Diana. "Entertainment and Politics." Review of *Entertainment and Politics: The Influence of Pop Culture on Young Adult Political Socialization,* by David J. Jackson. *Political Communication* July 2008, Vol. 25 Issue 3: 333-334.

Paine Jr., Robert Treat. *The Works, in Verse and Prose of the Late Robert Treat Paine, Jun Esq.* Boston: J. Belcher, 1812.

Paoletta, Michael. "MTV's 'Juice': Shaping Lifestyles and Attitudes Around the World." *Billboard,* September 2, 2006.

Parisse, Emmanuel. "Tea Party Diva Bachmann Dazzles at US Debate." Yahoo! News, June 14, 2011. Accessed June 30, 2011. http://old.news.yahoo.com/s/afp/20110614/ts_alt_afp/usvote2012republicansbachmann.

Pastor-Satorras, Romualdo and Alessandro Vespignani. *Evolution and Structure of the Internet: A Statistical Physics Approach.* New York: Cambridge University Press, 2004).

Pearlman, Jeff. "Gonna Fly Now." *Runner's World,* July 2008.

Pease, Edward C. and Everette E. Dennis, eds. *Radio: The Forgotten Medium.* New Brunswick, NJ: Transaction Publishers, 1995.

Perlstein, Rick. *Nixonland: The Rise of a President and the Fracturing of America.* New York: Scribner, 2008.

Perone, James. *Songs of the Vietnam Conflict.* Westport, CT: Greenwood Press, 2001.

Pettegree, Andrew. *Reformation and the Culture of Persuasion.* New York: Cambridge University Press, 2005.

"Petty to Bush: Don't Play My Song No More." Vh1. Accessed August 1, 2010, http://www.vh1.com/artists/news/1436934/20000920/petty_tom.jhtml.

Petty, Tom and Jeff Lynne. "I Won't Back Down." New York: Gone Gator Music & EMI April Music Inc., 1989.

Phillips, Cynthia. "Ron Paul's Rally for the Republic." Bella Online: The Voice of Women. Accessed August 24, 2010. http://www.bellaonline.com/articles/art58458.asp.

Phillips, Kate. "2008: Obama Girl and More." *The New York Times,* June 13, 2007. Accessed August 29, 2010. http://thecaucus.blogs.nytimes.com/2007/06/13/2008-obama-girl-and-more/.

Piazza, Jim and Gail Kinn. *The Academy Awards: The Complete Unofficial History.* New York: Black Dog & Leventhal Publishers, 2008.

Pidgeon, Dave. "LIVE: McCain Visits Philadelphia." *The Intelligencer Journal* (June 11, 2008). Accessed March 9, 2009. http://blogs.lancasteronline.com/birdseyeview/2008/06/11/live-mccain-visits-philadelphia/

Plato. *The Republic.* Translated by Alan Bloom. New York: Basic Books, 1968.

Platt, George Washington. *A History of the Republican Party.* Cincinnati, OH: Krehbiel, 1904.

Pockell, Leslie M., ed. *100 Essential American Poems*. New York: St. Martin's Press, 2009.

———, ed. *The 100 Best Poems of All Time*. New York: Warner Books, 2001.

Polsby, Nelson W. and Aaron B. Wildavsky. *Presidential Elections: Strategies and Structures of American Politics*. Lanham, MD: Roman & Littlefield, 2008.

Post, Jerrold M. "The Political Psychology of the Ross Perot Phenomenon." In *The Clinton Presidency: Campaigning, Governing, and the Psychology of Leadership*, ed. Stanley A. Renshon. Boulder, CO: Westview Press, 1995.

Potter, Joan. *African American Firsts: Famous Little-Known and Unsung Triumphs of Blacks*. New York: Dafina Books, 2009.

Potter, Pamela M. "Music in the Third Reich: The Complex Task of Germanization." In *The Arts in Nazi Germany: Continuity, Conformity, Change*, edited by Jonathan Huener and Francis R. Nicosia. New York: Berghahn Books, 2006.

Project Look Sharp. "Media Construction of Presidential Campaigns Teacher Guide 1828 Doc. #4: 'Little Wat Ye Wha's A-Comin' Song." Accessed May 14, 2011. http://www w.ithaca.edu/looksharp/mcpcweb/unit2_1828_1840/pdfs/1828/tguide1828doc4.pdf.

Pulera, Dominic J. *Sharing the Dream: White Males in Multicultural America*. New York: Continuum International, 2004.

Räisänen, Antti V. and Arto Leht., *Radio Engineering for Wireless Communication and Sensor Applications*. Norwood, MA: Artech House, Inc., 2003.

Randel, Don Michael. *The Harvard Concise Dictionary of Music and Musicians*. Cambridge: The Bellknap Press of Harvard University Press, 1999.

Rapoport, Ronald B. and Walter J. Stone. *Three's a Crowd: The Dynamic of Third Parties, Ross Perot, and Republican Resurgence*. Ann Arbor: University of Michigan Press, 2005.

Ravina, Mark. "Japanese State Making in Global Context." In *State Making in Asia*, edited by Richard Boyd and Tak-Wing Ngo. New York: Routledge, 2006.

Reagan, Ronald. *An American Life*. New York: Simon & Schuster, 1990.

Reeves, Keith. *Voting Hopes or Fears?: White Voters, Black Candidates & Racial Politics in America*. New York: Oxford University Press, 1997.

Reeves, Richard. *President Reagan: The Triumph of Imagination*. New York: Simon & Schuster, 2005.

Rich, John. "Raisin McCain." Nashville, TN: Kobalt Music Publishing, 2008.

Ringgold, Gene and Clifford McCarty. *The Films of Frank Sinatra*. New York: Citadel Press, 1989.

Roberts, Robert North and Scott John Hammond. *Encyclopedia of Presidential Campaigns, Slogans, Issues, and Platforms*. Westport, CT: Greenwood Press, 2004.

Robinson, Erin. "Star-Spangled Ads: Chevy Touts New Pickups as Distinctly American." *Autoweek*, October 5, 2006. Accessed August 22, 2010. http://www.autoweek.com/apps/pbcs.dll/article?AID=/20061006/FREE/61005003/1041/rss01&rssfeed=rss01.

Rock & Roll Hall of Fame. "Sam and Dave." Accessed August 7, 2010. http://rockhall.com/inductees/sam-and-dave.

Rodnitzky, Jerome L. "Popular Music in American Studies." *The History Teacher* 7, no. 4 (August 1974): 503-10.

Rodnitzky, Jerry "Popular Music." In *The American President in Popular Culture*, edited by John W. Matviko, 33-44. Westport, CT: Greenwood Press, 2005.

Rogers, Randall Jay, Don Cook and Kix Brooks. "Only in America." Nashville, TN: Sony/ATV Music Publishing LLC & Peer Music III, Ltd., 2001.

Roscigno, Vincent J. and William F. Danaher, "Media and Mobilization: The Case of Radio and Southern Textile Worker Insurgency, 1929 to 1934." *American Sociological Review* 66, no. 1 (February 2001): 21-48.

Rosenthal, A.M. "On My Mind: This Censored World." *New York Times*, May 27, 1988. Accessed June 22, 2010http://www.nytimes.com/1988/05/27/opinion/on-my-mind-this-censoredworld.html?scp=2&sq=music%20censorship%20north%20korea&st=cse.

Ross, Earle Dudley. *The Liberal Republican Movement*. New York: Holt, 1919.

Ross, Emily and Angus Holland. *100 Great Businesses and the Mind Behind Them*. Naperville, IL: Sourcebooks, Inc., 2006.

Ross, Michael E. "Campaign Jukebox, 2004 Model: Candidate's Choice in Songs Seeks to Bond with Wide Range of Voters." MSNBC. Accessed August 1, 2010. http://www.msnbc.msn.com/id/4366491

Rossman, Gabriel. "Elites, Masses, and Media Blacklists: The Dixie Chicks Controversy." *Social Forces*, 83, No. 1 (September 2004): 61-79.

Rudder, Randy. "In Whose Name: Country Artists Speak Out on Gulf War II." In *Country Music Goes to War*, edited by Charles K. Wolfe and James E. Akenson. Lexington: University Press of Kentucky, 2005.

Sacks, Oliver. *Musicophilia: Tales of Music and the Brain*. New York: Vintage Books, 2007.

Sadler, Roger L. *Electronic Media Law*. Thousand Oaks, CA: Sage Publications, 2005.

Safire, William. *Safire's Political Dictionary*. New York: Oxford University Press, 2008.

Saltveit, Mark. "H. Ross Perot's Skeleton Closet." *Real People for Real Change* (1999). Accessed February 8, 2009. http://www.realchange.org/perot.htm.

Sammis, Kathy. *The Era of World War II Through Contemporary Times: 1939-Present*. Portland, ME: J. Weston Walch, 2000.

Sanders, Paul D., ed. *Lyrics and Borrowed Tunes of the American Temperance Movement*. Columbia: University of Missouri Press, 2006.

Santelli, Robert. "Preface." In *Hard Travelin': The Life and Legacy of Woody Guthrie*, edited by Robert Santelli and Emily Davidson, xi – xvi. Hanover, NH: University Press of New England, 1999.

Sarafianos, Aris "Pain, Labor, and the Sublime: Medical Gymnastics and Burke's Aesthetics." *Representations*, no. 91 (Summer 2005): 58-83.

Savage, Sean J. *Roosevelt the Party Leader, 1932-1945*. Lexington: University Press of Kentucky, 1991.

Saxon, A.H. *P.T. Barnum: The Legend and the Man*. New York: Columbia University Press, 1989.

Schimler, Stuart. "Singing to the Oval Office: A Written History of the Political Campaign Song." Accessed June 10, 2010. http://www.presidentelect.org/art_schimler_singing.html.

Schlender, Brent. "Apple's 21st-Century Walkman CEO Steve Jobs Thinks He Has Something Pretty Nifty." *Fortune*, November 12, 2001, Accessed August 23, 2010. http://money.cnn.com/magazines/fortune/fortune_archive/2001/11/12/313342/index.htm.

Schultz, David A. "From Saxophones to Schwarzenegger: Entertainment Politics on Late-Night Television." In *Lights, Camera, Campaign!: Media, Politics, and Political Advertising*, ed. David A. Schultz. New York: Peter Lang Publishing, 2004.

Seager II, Robert ed. *The Papers of Henry Clay Volume 9: The Whig Leader January 1, 1837-December 31, 1843*. Lexington: University of Kentucky Press, 1988.

Segall, Brad. "Sen. John McCain Campaigns in Philadelphia Suburbs." *KYW Newsradio* (October 14, 2008). Accessed March 3, 2009. http://www.kyw1060.com/pages/ 3135143.php?contentType=4&contentId=2896584.

Seibert, Jakob. *National Anthems*. Mainz Germany: Schott, 2006.

Selak, Ron, and Jr. and Amanda Smith-Teutsch. "Thousands Rally for McCain." *Tribune Chronicle*, September 17, 2008.

Semonche, John E. *Censoring Sex: A Historical Journey through American Media*. Lanham, MD: Roman & Littlefield, 2007.

Serving History. "Robert Griffin." Accessed August 11, 2010. http://www.serving history.com/topics/Robert_Griffin_.

Shirer, William L. *The Rise and Fall of the Third Reich: A History of Nazi Germany*. New York: Fawcett Crest, 1960.

Shuler, Marjorie. "Out of Subjection into Freedom." In *The Woman Citizen* (September 4, 1920.

Shumway, David R. "Your Land: The Lost Legacy of Woody Guthrie." In *Hard Travelin': The Life and Legacy of Woody Guthrie*, ed. Robert Santelli and Emily Davidson, 128 – 137. Hanover, NH: University Press of New England, 1999.

Silber, Irwin. *Songs America Voted By: From George Washington to Richard Nixon—the Gutsy Story of Presidential Campaigning*. Harrisburg, PA: Stackpole Books, 1971.

———, ed. *Songs of the Civil War*. Mineola: Dover Publications, 1995.

———, ed. *Songs of the Great American West*. Mineola: Dover Publications, 1995.

Silverman, Jerry. *New York Sings: 400 Years of the Empire State in Song*. Albany: State University of New York Press, 2009.

Simon, Paul. *Lyrics 1964-2008*. New York: Simon & Schuster, 2008.

Simon, Ron. "The Ed Sullivan Show." The Museum of Broadcast Communications. Accessed August 22, 2010. http://www.museum.tv/eotvsection.php?entrycode= edsullivans.

Simonsen, Robert A., ed. *Marines Dodging Death: Sixty-Two Accounts of Close Calls in World War II, Korea, Vietnam, Lebanon, Iraq and Afghanistan*. Jefferson, NC: McFarland, 2009.

Sissle, Noble and Eubie Blake. "I'm Just Wild About Harry." Los Angeles: Warner Bros. Inc., 1921 (Renewed).

Sklar, Rachel. "The Boss Picks a Boss: Bruce Springsteen Endorses Obama." *The Huffington Post*, April 16, 2008. Accessed June 4, 2011. http://www.huffingtonpost.com /2008/04/16/bruce-springsteen-endorse_n_96933.html.

Sloan, William David and James D. Startt. *The Media in America: A History*. Scottsdale, AZ: Publishing Horizons, Inc., 1990.

Smith, Kathleen E. R. *God Bless America: Tin Pan Alley Goes to War*. Lexington: University Press of Kentucky, 2003.

Smith, Samuel Francis. "America," in *Poems of Home and Country: Also Sacred and Miscellaneous Verse*, ed. Henry B. Carrington. New York: Silver, Burdett and Co., 1895.

Snow, Kate and Eloise Harper. "Clinton Concedes Democratic Nomination; Obama Leads Party in Fall." *ABC News*, June 7, 2008. Accessed August 23, 2010. http://abcnews.go.com/Politics/Vote2008/story?id=5020581&page=1.

Soboroff, Jacob. "Obama Girl Didn't Vote? No She Didn't!" *The Huffington Post*, April 17, 2008. Accessed August 29, 2010. http://www.huffingtonpost.com/jacob-soboroff/obama-girl-didnt-vote-no_b_97208.html.

Songfacts. "A Little Less Conversation." Accessed February 15, 2009. http://www.song facts.com/detail.php?id=2001.

Sonn, William. *Paradigms Lost: The Life and Deaths of the Printed Word.* Lanham, MD: Scarecrow Press, 2006.

Spann, C. Edward and Michael E. Williams. Sr., *Presidential Praise: Our Presidents and Their Hymns.* Macon, GA: Mercer University Press, 2008.

Spencer, Charles. "You Ain't Seen Nothin Yet." Nashville, TN: Sony/ATV Music Publishing, LLC, 1974.

Spillius, Alex. "Hillary Clinton Edges Lead Over Barack Obama as Pennsylvania Votes." *Telegraph* (April 22, 2008). Accessed March 9, 2009. http://www.telegraph.co.uk/news/1897974/Hillary-Clinton-edges-lead-over-Barack-Obama-as-Pennsylvania-votes.html.

Spinello, Richard A. *Cyberethics: Morality and Law in Cyberspace.* Sudbury, MA: Jones and Bartlett Publishers, 2006.

Spiridellis, Evan and Gregg Spiridellis. "This Land." JibJab Media Inc. Accessed August 4, 2010. http://sendables.jibjab.com/originals/this_land.

———. "Time for Some Campaigning." JibJab Media Inc. Accessed August 4, 2010. http://sendables.jibjab.com/originals/time_for_some_ campaignin.

Sporborg, James Douglas. *Music in Every Classroom: A Resource Guide for Integrating Music across the Curriculum, Grades K-8.* Englewood, CA: Libraries Unlimited, 1998.

Springsteen, Bruce. "Born in the U.S.A." New York: Bruce Springsteen, 1984.

Stambler, Irwin and Grelun Landon. *Country Music: The Encyclopedia.* New York, St. Martin's, 1997.

Stanton, W.J. "The Independent Exchange at Prairie City, IA," *Telephony, Volume 17, No. 5* (January 30, 1909): 126.

Starr, Edwin. Vocal performance of "War." By Norman Whitfield and Barrett Strong. Recorded 1970, on *War and Peace.* Motown Records. 33 rpm.

State of Tennessee. "State Songs," (n.d.). Accessed March 4, 2009. http://www.tennesseeanytime.org/homework/songs.html.

Stathis, Stephen W. *Congressional Gold Medals, 1776-2002.* Hauppauge, NY: Novinka Books, 2003.

Steinweis, Alan E. "Anti-Semitism and the Arts in Nazi Ideology and Policy." In *The Arts in Nazi Germany: Continuity, Conformity, Change*, edited by Jonathan Huener and Francis R. Nicosia. New York: Berghahn Books, 2006.

———. *Art, Ideology, and Economics in Nazi Germany: The Reich Chambers of Music, Theater, and the Visual Arts.* Chapel Hill: University of North Carolina Press, 1993.

Sterling, Andrew B. and Robert A. Keiser. "Be Good to California, Mr. Wilson (California Was Good to You)." New York: Shapiro, Bernstein & Co., Inc., 1916.

Sting. *Lyrics.* New York: The Dial Press, 2007).

Stone, Andrea. "Romney Views Maine Win as Sign of Things to Come." *USA Today* (February 4, 2008). Accessed February 15, 2009. http://www.usatoday.com/news/politics/election2008/2008-02-03-romney_N.htm.

Strange, Billy and Scott Davis. "A Little Less Conversation." New York: Elvis Presley Music, 1968.

Straubhaar, Joseph, Robert LaRose, Lucinda Davenport. *Media Now: Understanding Media, Culture, and Technology.* Belmot, CA: Wadsworth, 2009).

Strauss, M. and P. Fox. "Taft the Leader." Cincinnati, OH: Willis Music Co., 1912.

Strong, Martin C. *The Great Rock Discography*. Edinburgh: Canongate Books, 2004).

Stork, George, Clarence Fuhrman and Olivia Hoffman. "Click with Dick." Bryn Mawr, PA: Elkan-Vogel, Inc., 1960.

Studwell William E and Drew E. VandeCreek. *"Forward! Forward! Is the Word": Republican Presidential Campaign Songs of 1856 and 1860*. S.I.: s.n., 2000.

Sutherland, Keith. *Understanding the Internet: A Clear Guide to Internet Technologies*. Oxford: Butterworth-Heinemann, 2000.

Swartz, Eric. "U.S. Presidential Campaign Slogans." (2011). Accessed May 2, 2011. http://www.taglineguru.com/campaignsloganlist.html.

Talev, Margaret. "Attending Obama Rally? Study the Music." *The Charlotte Observer* (November 3, 2008). Accessed March 5, 2009. http://www.charlotteobserver.com/breaking/story/296966.html.

Tapper, Jake. "Don't Do Me Like That." Salon.com. Accessed August 1, 2010. http://www.salon.com/news/politics/feature/2000/09/16/bush/index.html.

———, "Music Video Has a 'Crush on Obama': Risqué YouTube Song Takes Obama Campaign by Surprise." *ABC News*, June 13, 2007. Accessed August 29, 2010. http://abcnews.go.com/Politics/Story?id=3275802&page=1.

Tarradell, Mario. "Country Duo Brooks & Dunn Respond to Barack Obama Using Their Song During Democratic Convention." *Dallas News*. Accessed August 11, 2010. http://musicblog.dallasnews.com/archives/2008/08/country-duo-brooks-dunn-respon.html.

Taylor, John. "Politics: Winners and Sinners of 1992." *New York Magazine*, December 21-28, 1992.

Tick, Judith and Paul Beadoin, ed. *Music in the USA: A Documentary Companion*. New York: Oxford University Press, 2008.

The Clash. Vocal performance of "Know Your Rights," by John Mellor and Michael Jones. On *The Clash: The Singles*. Sony Music Entertainment 63886, compact disc. Original release April 23, 1982.

The Committee on Arrangements for the 2008 Republican National Convention. *2008 Republican Platform* (n.d.). Accessed February 27, 2009. http://platform.gop.com/2008Platform.pdf: 45.

RE:Obama.com—The Important Speeches of Barack Obama. Select portions from "Remarks of Senator Obama After New Hampshire Primary." Accessed June 23, 2011. http://www.reobama.com/SpeechesJan0808.htm.

The Internet Movie Database (1990-2008). "Soundtrack Searcher: A Little Less Conversation." Accessed February 15, 2009. http://www.imdb.com/SearchSongs?%22a%20little%20less%20conversation%22

The National Archives. *Our Documents: 100 Milestone Documents from the National Archives*. New York: Oxford University Press, 2003.

Tong, William. "Dole Man Lyrics: Sung to the Tune of 'Soul Man' by Sam & Dave." Rock & Roll Parody Song List. Accessed July 31, 2010, http://bootnewt.tripod.com/doleman.htm.

———. "Song Parodies—Dole Man." *Am I Right: Making Fun of Music, One Song at a Time*. Accessed June 6, 2011. http://www.amiright.com/parody/60s/samdave0.shtml.

Toobin, Jeffrey. *Too Close to Call: The Thirty-Six-Day Battle to Decide the 2000 Election*. New York: Random House, 2001.

Tramo, Mark Jude. "Music of the Hemispheres." *Science* (January 5, 2001), 54-56.

Tunstall, Jeremy. *The Media in Britain*. New York: Columbia University Press, 1983.

Turner, John Frayn. *Frank Sinatra*. Lanham, MD: Taylor Trade Publishing, 2004.

University of Tennessee. "Songs of Tennessee," (n.d.). Accessed March 4, 2009. http://www.utk.edu/athletics/tn_songs.shtml.

US Department of Treasury, Bureau of the Public Debt., "Historical Debt Outstanding 1950-1999." Accessed July 28, 2010. http://www.treasurydirect.gov/govt/reports/pd/histdebt/histdebt_histo4.htm.

U.S Labor Against the War. "john.he.is." Accessed August 4, 2010. http://www.uslabor againstwar.org/article.php?id=15378.

vanHorn, Teri. "Tom Betty, Jon Bon Jovi, John Popper Play for Gore: Private Concert Follows Shortly After Gore's Concession Speech." MTV. Accessed August 10, 2010. http://www.mtv.com/news/articles/1424581/20001215/petty_tom.jhtml.

Van Natta, Jr., Don. *First off the Tee: Presidential Hackers, Duffers and Cheaters from Taft to Bush*. Cambridge, MA: Public Affairs Books, 2003.

Varesi, Anthony. *The Bob Dylan Albums: A Critical Study*. Toronto: Guernica Editions, 2002.

Vena, Jocelyn. "McCain-Palin Campaign Continues Playing Heart's 'Barracuda,' Despite Band's Protest." *MTV*, September 9, 2008. Accessed August 23, 2010. http://www.mtv.com/news/articles/1594443/mccain-palin-still-usingheartsbarracuda.jhtml.

Wagner, Heather Lehr. *The History of the Republican Party*. New York: Chelsea House, 2007.

Wallenstein, Gene. *The Pleasure Instinct: Why We Crave Adventure, Chocolate, Phero-mones, and Music*. Hoboken, NJ: Wiley.

Waltz, Bob. "Remembering the Old Songs: Jefferson and Liberty." Accessed June 17, 2010. http://www.lizlyle.lofgrens.org/RmOlSngs/RTOS-JeffersonLiberty.html.

Walvin, James. *Black Ivory: Slavery in the British Empire*. Malden, MA: Blackwell Pub-lishers, 2001.

Ward, John William. *Andrew Jackson: Symbol for an Age*. New York: Oxford University Press, 1955.

Ward v. Rock against Racism. 491 U.S. 781, 790 (1989).

Wardell, Kenneth. "We Want a Man Like Roosevelt." Brooklyn, NY: Charles Coleman, 1932.

Washington, George. "The Address of General Washington to the People of the United States on his declining of the Presidency of the United States." *American Daily Ad-vertiser*, September 19, 1796.

Washington, Luther A. Huston. "The Voters Still Sing, Though Faintly." *The New York Times*, September 27, 1936.

Watson, Henry Clay. *Camp-Fires of the Revolution*. New York: James Miller, 1850.

Wattenberg, Martin P. and Craig Leonard Brains. "Negative Campaign Advertising: Mo-bilizer or Demobilizer." eScholarship at the University of California. Accessed Au-gust 11, 2010. http://escholarship.org/uc/item/7gf3q1w1#page-2.

Weisberg, Jacob. "The Third Man." *New York Magazine*, April 8, 1996.

Welch, Richard E. *The Presidencies of Grover Cleveland*. Lawrence: University Press of Kansas, 1988.

Whitburn, Joel. *Joel Whitburn Presents Billboard #1s, 1950-1991: A Week-by-Week Record of Billboard's #1 Hits*. Menomonee Falls, WI: Record Research, 1991.

———. *The Billboard Book of Top 40 Country Hits*. New York: Billboard Books, 2006.

———. *The Billboard Book of Top 40 Hits*. New York: Billboard Books, 2004.

Wilentz, Sean. *The Rise of American Democracy: Jefferson to Lincoln*. New York: Nor-ton, 2005.

Wilkinson, Peter. "Bush Bares Soul with 'iPod One.'" *CNN*, April 13, 2005. Accessed August 23, 2010. http://www.cnn.com/2005/SHOWBIZ/Music/04/12/bush.ipod/.

Will.i.am. "Why I Recorded *Yes We Can*." *The Huffington Post*, February 3, 2008. Accessed August 4, 2010. http://www.huffingtonpost.com/william/why-i-recorded-yes-we-can_b_84655.html.

———. "Yes We Can." YouTube. Accessed August 4, 2010. http://www.youtube.com/watch?v=SsV2O4fCgjk.

Williams Jr., Hank. "McCain-Palin Tradition." Nashville, TN: Bocephus Music Inc., 2008.

Willis, Christopher and Beth Fouhy. "President Obama's Vice President: Announcement Expected This Week." *The Huffington Post*, August 19, 2008. Accessed August 2, 2010. http://www.huffingtonpost.com/2008/08/19/barack-obamas-vice-presid_n_119783.html.

Willis, Jim. *100 Media Moments That Changed America*. Santa Barbara, CA: Greenwood Press, 2010.

Willman, Chris. "'Only in America' Could Obama Borrow the GOP's Favorite Brooks and Dunn Song." *Entertainment Weekly*. Accessed August 3, 2010. http://popwatch.ew.com/2008/08/29/only-in-america/.

———. *Rednecks & Bluenecks: The Politics of Country Music*. New York: Norton, 2005.

Wolf, Z. Byron. "Revolution Revived! Ron Paul Survives Challenge: White House Contender Raised Millions, Sparked Debate, but Nearly Lost Day Job." *ABC News*, March 4, 2008. Accessed August 24, 2010. http://abcnews.go.com/Politics/Vote2008/story?id=4389616&page=1.

———. "Ron Paul to End Campaign, Launches New Effort: Supporters Plot Shadow Convention, More Revolution." *ABC News*, June 12, 2008. Accessed August 24, 2010. http://abcnews.go.com/Politics/Vote2008/story?id=5056019&page=1.

Wonder, Stevie et al. "Signed, Sealed, Delivered." Milwaukee, WI: Hal Leonard Publishing Co., 1970.

Wright, Jordan M. *Campaigning for President: Memorabilia from the Nation's Finest Private Collection,* New York: HarperCollins, 2008.

Yamashita, Samuel Hideo. *Leaves from an Autumn of Emergencies: Selections from the Wartime Diaries of Ordinary Japanese*. Honolulu: University of Hawaii Press, 2005.

Yellen, Jack and Milton Ager. "Happy Days Are Here Again." New York: WB Music Corp., 1929.

Yin, Robert K. *Case Study Research: Design and Methods*. Thousand Oaks, CA: Sage Publications, 1994.

Young, Angus and Malcolm Young. *The Definitive AC/DC Songbook*, edited by Angus Young. New York: Amsco, 2003.

Young William H. and Nancy K. Young. *Music of the World War II Era*. Westport, CT: Greenwood Press, 2008.

YouTube. "About YouTube." Accessed August 2, 2010. http://www.youtube.com/t/about.

Zanes, Warren. "Interview with Tom Petty, October 23, 2008." Accessed August 10, 2010. http://media.thewho.com/non_secure/pdf/TomPetty_Zanes_Interview_Oct31.pdf.

Zeleny, Jeff. "Working Together, Obama and Clinton Try to Show Unity." *New York Times*, June 28, 2008. Accessed August 23, 2010. http://www.nytimes.com/2008/06/28/us/politics/28unity.html.

Index

About the Authors

Benjamin Schoening is Assistant Professor of Music at the University of Wisconsin-Barron Country and music director of the Red Cedar Choir in Rice Lake. He holds a BA in French Horn and Voice Performance from Luther College (Decorah, IA), a MM from the University of Illinois in Orchestral Conducting, and a DMA from the University of Minnesota in Voical Performance. Schoening has performed as a recitalist both nationally and internationally, specializing in American and British Art Song, and is also an avid opera singer.

Eric T. Kasper is Assistant Professor of Political Science at the University of Wisconsin-Barron County and the municipal judge in Rice Lake. In addition to holding a Ph.D. in political science and a J.D. from the University of Wisconsin-Madison, Kasper is a member of the Wisconsin Bar Association. His first book, *To Secure the Liberty of the People: James Madison's Bill of Rights and the Supreme Court's Interpretation*, was published in 2010.